ASTROLOGICAL ROOTS:

THE HELLENISTIC LEGACY

JOSEPH CRANE

THE WESSEX ASTROLOGER

Published in 2007 by
The Wessex Astrologer Ltd
4A Woodside Road
Bournemouth
BH5 2AZ
England

www.wessexastrologer.com

ISBN 1902405242

A catalogue record of this book is available at The British Library

Cover design by Creative Byte, Poole, Dorset.

CONTENTS

CHART DATA
(All data and ratings are from astrodatabank unless otherwise specified)

Ali, Muhammad January 17 1942, 6:35 PM CST Louisville, Kentucky 38N15/85W46
Source: birth certificate or record; AA Rodden rating

Allen, Woody December 1 1935, 10:55 PM EST Bronx, New York 40N51/73W54
Source: birth certificate; AA rating

Aquino, Corazon January 25 1933, 4:00 AM CCT Malate, Philippines 14N34/120E59
Source: biography; B rating

Bernadette of Lourdes January 7 1844, 2:00 PM LMT Lourdes, France 43N06/0W03
Source: birth certificate or record; AA rating

Blair, Tony May 6 1953, 6:10 AM GMD Edinburgh, Scotland 55N57/3W13
Source: birth certificate or record; AA rating

Blake, William November 28 1757, 7:45 PM LMT London, England 51N31/0W06
Source: from memory; A rating

Brando, Marlon April 3 1924, 11:00 PM CST Omaha, Nebraska 41N16/95W56
Source: Source: birth certificate or record; AA rating:

Browning, Elizabeth March 6 1806, 7:00 PM LMT Kelloe, England 56N20/02W18
Source: biography; B rating

Bush, George July 6 1946, 7:26 AM EDT New Haven, Connecticut 41N18/72W56
Source: birth certificate or record; AA rating

Charles, Prince November 14 1948, 9:14 PM GMT London, England 51N30/0W10
Source: news report; A rating

Churchill, Winston November 30 1874, 1:30 AM LMT Woodstock, England 51N52/1W21
Source: from memory; A rating
(In this work Churchill's birth time has been 'rectified' to 1:31 AM)

Clinton, Bill August 19 1946, 8:51 AM AHST Hope, Arkansas 33N40/93W35
Source: from memory; A rating

Clinton, Chelsea February 27 1980, 11:24 PM CST Little Rock, Arkansas 34N45/92W17
Source: news report; A rating

Curie, Marie November 7 1867, 10:36 AM GMT Warszawa, Poland 52N15/21E00
Source: birth certificate or record AA rating

Dalai Lama July 6 1935 4:38 AM LMT Tengster Village, Tibet 36N32/101E12
Source: from memory; A rating

De Sade, Marquis June 2 1740, 5:00 PM LMT Paris, France 48N52/2E20
Source: Source: birth certificate or record; AA rating

Diana, Princess July 1 1961, 7:45 PM GDT Sandringham, England 52N50/0E30
Source: from memory; A rating

Dickinson, Emily December 10 1830, 4:40 AM LMT Amherst, Massachusetts 42N22/72W31
Source: biography; B rating

Elizabeth II, Queen April 21 1926, 2:40 AM GDT London, England 51N30/0W08
Source: birth certificate or record; AA rating

Fisher, Amy August 21 1974, 9:26 PM EDT Oceanside, New York 40N38/73W38
Source: news report; A rating

Freud, Sigmund May 6 1856, 6:30 PM LMT Freiberg, Germany 49N38/18E09
Source: birth certificate or record; AA rating

Garcia, Jerry August 1 1942, 12:05 PM PWT San Francisco, California 37N47/122W25
Source: Source: birth certificate or record; AA rating:

Jefferson, Thomas April 13 1743, 7:06:48 AM GMT Shadwell, Virginia 38N00/78W23
Source: Io Edition database: http://timecycles.com/
(Conflicting times, according to astrodatabank.)

Pope Benedict. April 16 1927, 4:15 AM CET Marktl, Germany 48N15/12E51
Source: birth certificate; AA rating

Pope John Paul II. May 18 1920, 5:30 PM EET Wadowice, Poland 49N53/19E30
Source: from memory; A rating

Joyce, James February 2 1882, 6:24 AM GMT Dublin, Ireland 53N20/6W15
Source: news report; A rating

Jung, Carl July 26 1875, 7:32 PM LMT Kesswil, Switzerland 47N36/9E20
Source: from memory; A rating

Kennedy, John May 29 1917, 3:00 PM Brookline, Massachusetts 42N20/71W07
Source: from memory; A rating

Kerry, John December 11 1943, 7:10 AM MST John Fitzsimons US Army Base, Colorado 39N44/104W50
Source: originally from memory; A rating. (Now C rating: disputed)

Lewinsky, Monica July 23 1973, 12:21 PM PDT San Francisco, California 37N46/122W25
Source: birth certificate or record; AA rating

McCain, John August 29 1936, 9:00 AM EST Coco Solo Air Force Base, Panama 9N22/79W53
Source: from memory; A rating

Merton, Thomas January 30 1915, 9:00 AM GMT Prades, France 42N37/2E26
Source: birth certificate or record; AA rating

Monroe, Marilyn June 1 1926, 9:30 AMJ PST Los Angeles, California 34N04/118W15
Source: birth certificate or record; AA rating

Mother Teresa August 26 1919, 2:25 PM MET Skopje, Serbia 41N59/21E26
Source: DD conflicting birth times

Mozart, Wolfgang January 27 1756, 8:00 PM LMT Salzburg, Austria 47N48/13E02
Source: biography; B rating

Onassis, Jacqueline Kennedy July 28 1929, 2:30 PM EDT Southampton, New York 40N53/72W23
Source: from memory; A rating

Padre Pio May 25 1887, 4:10 PM LMT Pietrelcina, Italy 41N12/14E51
Source: birth certificate or record; AA rating

Peron, Eva May 7 1908, 5:14 AM LMT Buenos, Aires, Argentina 34S36/58W27
Source: biography; B rating
(Some other sources give her a birth year of 1919.)

Stewart, Martha August 3 1941, 1:33 PM EDT Jersey City, New Jersey 40N43/74W04
Source: birth certificate or record; AA rating

Swaggart, Jimmy March 15 1935, 1:35 AM CST Ferriday, Louisiana 31N38/91W33
Source: birth certificate or record; AA rating

Taylor, Elizabeth February 27 1932, 2:15 AM GMT London, England 51N30/0W10
Source: from memory; A rating

Thatcher, Margaret October 13 1925, 9:00 AM GMT Grantham, England 52N55/0W39
Source: from memory; A rating

Wilson, Bill November 26 1895, 3:00 AM EST East Dorset, Vermont 43N15/73W00
Source: biography; B rating

PREFACE

Astrology is one of the great adventures of human civilization and has contributed greatly to people's lives and to our culture over time. Astrology's purpose is to use the positions of the planets and stars in the sky to gather information on the individual and on humanity. Astrology is a system that enables us to understand the past, present and the future within a universe full of meaning.

This noble enterprise has spanned different cultures and historical periods and has had its times of flowering and being on the fringes, yet over time astrology has remained with us, always adapting to new conditions.

The basic fields of astrology have not changed for thousands of years. Astrologers today are less concerned than those in the past with the direct effects of the planets on this physical earth, but instead read the sky for how it can symbolize circumstances and events in our lives. Some astrologers today apply the symbols of astrology to the larger and smaller movements of history, politics, and culture: the field of "mundane astrology." Based upon the rising degrees and planetary configurations for the time of birth, astrologers can determine the qualities of an individual, and make predictions about likely events in the context of that person's life. This is called "natal astrology" and it is the focus of this book.

Over many centuries, individual life circumstances may change but our human concerns have changed very little. For centuries people have wanted to know about their marriages and business prospects, their family and community and their own physical and psychological condition. They have also been interested in applying astrology to their prospective lovers or marriage partners and to their children. They also want to know how these issues change over a lifetime. As in the past, people are still interested in how long they or others might live.

In my view, modern astrology has become weaker by deviating from its tradition, and so I need to begin with some criticisms of modern practice.

Influenced by the theosophical movement of the 1800s, some astrologers have become interested in the soul's progress through lifetimes and its ongoing spiritual education. Sometimes the astrologer has been able to greatly help the individual; there is, however, a temptation to use astrological symbolism to impose one's spiritual ideology upon the client. A client can neither affirm nor deny the astrologer's speculations about previous lifetimes, and the astrologer can miss the urgency of the client's present circumstances.

Following the theosophical tradition, some astrologers try to use astrological symbolism to assert that human consciousness as a whole is evolving. As attractive as this notion may seem to us, I do not see that we have become better or worse, any more or less ethical or spiritual, over the many centuries of human culture.

Influenced by the speculations of Jungian psychology and other psychoanalytic schools of the mid-twentieth century, some astrologers have been more interested in examining the unconscious than the real life and circumstances of the person. This can result in astrological interpretations that accent the extreme and the unknowable. Newer astrologers often fall victim to this tendency.

Astrology's symbols are often reduced to psychological factors only, to the detriment of the multi-level richness of astrology's symbolism.

These two approaches - the transcendent and the psychodynamic - may also set up the astrologer as some kind of high priest, something for which most astrologers are not qualified. Astrology can do better by serving its original and ongoing purpose: helping people with the worlds in which they live, with specific questions about their lives.

My concern about the scope of modern astrology is matched by an apprehension about its methods. As a practicing consulting astrologer who has been trained well in modern astrological principles and techniques, I have become concerned about the current state of astrological technique. Lately my concern has become urgent.

I am troubled that in some ways our craft has become too simple. The work of modern astrologers is vastly superior to what passes for astrology in your local newspaper. Nonetheless, astrologers often make broad pronouncements based on single units of information: a Lunar Node in Cancer means that you need to be more emotional or nurturing; Neptune in the Twelfth house means you're clairvoyant.

Paradoxically, astrology has in other ways become too complex. The result is that the astrologer becomes dizzy and his or her interpretation fuzzy.

The astrologer may become bombarded with too much information from the many different techniques that are now available on his or her computer. Today's astrologers tend to include too many planetary bodies within an astrological interpretation and to turn astronomy's recent discoveries into wild speculation. In natal astrology, it is also unclear what factors the astrologer might turn to in order to answer a question. If every chart factor can apply to every issue, the astrologer and then the client can become overwhelmed.

There is a more fundamental way in which modern astrology has become too complex. Many basic features of astrology - houses and house systems, aspects and planetary rulers, for example - would be more powerful if used in simpler and clearer ways. This unnecessary complexity, in addition to the lack of knowledge of the visible sky around us and its rhythmic movements, have resulted in astrologers and their teachers too often working with systems that they do not understand. This cannot help the astrologer provide meaningful and accurate information to help a client with his or her life.

I want to examine astrology's foundations and to propose rebuilding its frame. For this purpose, I will take us back to Hellenistic astrology: western astrology's first form.

Remember the legend of the Gordian knot? A prophecy had it that whoever untied this knot would be the ruler of all Asia. When Alexander the Great was confronted with this task he simply took out a sword and cut through the knot. Soon enough the prophecy was fulfilled.

Modern astrology abounds with Gordian knots. Studying and using the work of a previous era, early in astrology's development, may help us cut through some of these knots. The astrology I introduce here is refreshingly straightforward and its techniques are easy to apply.

My purpose is to get under astrology's hood, look at its different parts, and figure out how to make the engine work better. This book is not a scholarly account of ancient astrology nor am I indulging in antiquarianism. I will present an account of our ancient tradition relevant to modern astrology and addressing many of its needs.

There are some conditions: the ancient tradition itself is complex, varied, and not complete. There is material in the tradition I need to leave out, and there are specific choices I need to make when there are several viable alternatives. This is inevitable, given the nature of the tradition and my need to present a relatively clear picture to the modern reader.

If you are new to astrology, this is not the only astrology book you will ever need, nor is it the only way to learn astrology. I hardly mention the Lunar Nodes. More prominently, I discuss Uranus, Neptune, and Pluto only briefly and do not include them in natalexamples. This omission may shock many people who practice modern astrology. Although I use the modern planets abundantly in my own consulting practice, I have found that they are not necessary for my purposes here. It is wonderful to see how much meaning one can find in the natal chart using only the visible planets.

Astrology, in my mind, is a human enterprise. To that end I have provided the reader with charts of people from history and contemporary culture. Most readers will be familiar with them.

The traditional astrology of India, sometimes called "Vedic Astrology" or "Jyotish", is similar in many ways to the Hellenistic tradition. One historical difference is that, unlike the tradition in the Indian subcontinent, which has been in continuous operation, Hellenistic astrology, for all intents and purposes, ended - only to rise again in another form. Astrology disappeared in the west when the Roman Empire fell, and in the east with the rise of Islam and the gradual decline of the Byzantine Empire. When astrology did return to Europe it was in a different form that has continued to the present day. Can a broken tradition, such as Hellenistic astrology, be *completely* restored? I don't believe it can be. Can one learn from and use the culture of a different era? Absolutely: this is partly what in history we call a "renaissance."

Over the past twenty years astrologers have uncovered much of its past, applied it to modern astrology, and so have enriched astrology greatly. I have had great company in this enterprise.

Since 1985, beginning with the re-publication of William Lilly's masterwork *Christian Astrology*, our field has experienced a revitalization of scope and method. Astrologers have found Lilly's work a treasure for the practice of horary astrology. In this important branch of astrology, one casts an astrological chart for the moment one asks a significant question. In addition, studying the work of Lilly's contemporaries has allowed astrologers to practice more systematic natal and mundane astrology. Since the 1990's, many astrologers have learned and practiced astrology from the works of astrology's past. Robert Zoller and others have demonstrated the importance of medieval astrologer Guido Bonatti, and his predecessors and contemporaries. Lee Lehman has contributed to a greater understanding of William Lilly, his contemporaries and his sources. Their work has helped establish the discipline of "traditional astrology" or "classical astrology."

During the last decade, Project Hindsight translated many primary works of astrology's traditions. Robert Hand prepared Latin texts from the medieval era, including Bonatti, adding commentary and practical applications of Hellenistic and medieval astrological technique. He has shown that techniques from the ancient and medieval world can improve one's skill as an astrologer.

His current work, using the name Archive for the Retrieval of Historical Astrological Texts (ARHAT), continues to be a resource for today's astrologers.

Robert Schmidt has translated and commented upon many primary sources of the Hellenistic era and in fact has translated most of the astrological texts I use here. I have found his commentary useful in understanding the varieties of the Hellenistic tradition. He has demonstrated the intellectual profundity of Hellenistic astrology and its relevance to modern thinking, and by taking the ancient tradition seriously, he continues to show its many strengths.

In many large and small ways my work has benefited by my association with Robert Hand and Robert Schmidt, and, in different ways, both men have influenced what you read here.

I am also indebted to Dorian Greenbaum, who produced a fine translation of Paulus Alexandrinus, its scholia, and a commentary on Paulus by Olympiodorus. She has also been an ongoing source of information, ideas, and encouragement as this book has developed.

Different people have helped me at different stages of this project. Stephanie Clement encouraged me to begin this book, and Jill-laurie Crane helped with early versions. Nadine Harris reviewed every sentence, gave suggestions about content and also helped the writing become clearer and easier on the reader. Melanie Schlossberg went through everything once again, giving another set of helpful suggestions. Cindy Jordan patiently completed the graphis. Margaret Cahill of Wessex Astrologer helped transform an unwieldy manuscript into a final work of which I am proud.

Although my work here could not have happened without the contributions of the people cited above, I owe an even larger debt of gratitude to my clients and to students who have been with me over the years. Many people continued to work with me as their astrologer as my technique was moving from a modern to a traditional to a Hellenistic perspective. My students allowed me to continue to study and apply the concepts and techniques of Hellenistic astrology, and gave me the occasion to make public some of this fascinating and wonderful material. They are my visible and invisible readers and audience and an ongoing inspiration to me.

Now we begin. I first offer some perspective on the circumstances and goals of ancient astrology and compare them to our modern era.

INTRODUCTION:
ASTROLOGY THEN AND NOW

The Hellenistic Era

The origins of ancient western astrology - what we call "Hellenistic astrology" - are mostly lost to history. We do know a few things. We know that Mesopotamian culture used planetary positions to forecast the future for king and country and that they considered the visible planets as their access to divinity. The first examples of planetary positions used to assess the fortunes of an individual date from about 400 BCE in Babylon.

Seventy years later, Alexander of Macedon and his armies stormed out of Greece and conquered the Eastern cultures of Persia, Mesopotamia, and Egypt. Alexander's conquest put into place an international synthesis unified by Greek language and culture. This new culture included astrology. When Rome conquered Greece and took over much of Alexander's eastern empire, Hellenistic culture spread into Western Europe and Africa. Our history books tend to call this the "Roman" era, but its culture was prominently Hellenistic.

Until the time of the Northern invasions and the ascendancy of Christianity, approximately 400 CE, Hellenistic culture and Roman hegemony supported and propagated astrology. Most astrologers of this time wrote in Greek; a few important ones wrote in Latin. The use of astrology spanned a broad area from the Indian subcontinent to modern Spain. Although international in scope, the home base of ancient western astrology was probably Egypt and what we call the Middle East.

Here is a short list of the names of ancient western astrologers who left writings behind. I will be referring to their work, as they are our sources for our understanding Hellenistic astrology.

- The earliest astrologers we know by name are **Nechepso and Petosirus**, Egyptian king and priest, respectively. Later ancient astrologers cite them as *their* ancient astrological sages. Their work, now lost, was probably from the third or second century BCE, and comes to us only when cited and quoted by others.
- In the first century CE, are **Dorotheus of Sidon** and **Manilius**, who was Roman. Dorotheus comes down to us in an interesting but fragmented text, which shows many later additions. He is a major figure in the Hellenistic tradition. Manilius' Latin text is unevenly written and his techniques are often at odds with those of other astrologers. It is not clear whether Manilius actually practiced astrology.

- **Vettius Valens** of Antioch lived in the second century CE, travelled widely and learned much of the astrology of his era. His *Anthology* gives us many worked-out charts and allows us to look over the shoulder of a master astrologer at his craft. This makes Valens an indispensable source for this tradition and therefore I use his work extensively. Valens is our only authority for some of the predictive methods we examine later in this book.

- **Claudius Ptolemy** was a natural philosopher (what we might call a "scientist") and astronomer from Alexandria. He lived in the late second century CE. Ptolemy provided an earth-centered model that allowed later centuries to calculate planetary positions. Ptolemy also recast the basic principles of astrology, using the natural science of his time, and provided a system of guidelines to do both natal and predictive work. His *Tetrabiblos* ("Four Books") is the single most influential document in astrology's history. We will be looking at Ptolemy's contributions throughout this book.

- Later astrologers who combined approaches from Ptolemy and Valens were **Hephaistio of Thebes, Antiochus of Athens, Paulus Alexandrinus**, and the writer known only as **Anonymous of 379.**

- An important astrologer who wrote in Latin was **Firmicus Maternus**, a fourth century Roman from Italy. His astrological work *Mathesis* contains a wealth of delineation material and some charts. This work survived in the west and was read during the medieval era. Later in his life Firmicus dropped astrology and became a Christian.

- The Arab-era Persian astrologer **Abu Mashar** lived in the ninth century and practiced a late form of Hellenistic astrology. His work, which was translated into Greek, was used by astrologers of Byzantium, and shows an influence from India.

Astrology in the ancient era was not primitive or pre-scientific; it participated in the cosmology, medicine, natural science and spirituality of the time. Ancient western astrology was embedded in contemporary philosophical traditions - Platonic and neo-Platonic, Aristotelian, Stoic and Hermetic. Today there is no relationship between astrology and modern academic philosophy. Today's astrologers are left to rely on some modern styles of psychology, occasional speculations from the "new physics" and occultism for philosophical support.

Hellenistic culture and Roman hegemony had major problems even at the best of times: its society was more stratified than ours, subordinated women, and had an economy fuelled by slavery. This should not prevent us from seeing their astrological practice as relevant to today's concerns. Astrologers and their clients haven't changed so much over the years, and astrologers from other eras continue to have much to teach us. Centuries from now, another culture will - hopefully - look upon our era as unenlightened and crude.

Please remember that the ancient era of western astrology did not end because its methods didn't work and were replaced by better methods, but because their entire culture fell. (Ancient astrology survived for hundreds of years afterwards during the Byzantine era in the East.)

Objections to Astrology, Then and Now

Every astrologer and student of astrology should become familiar with some of the standard criticisms of astrology and know how to respond to them. Over the years, my thinking about these objections has evolved. The objections to astrology in the ancient era are not dissimilar to those of our own.[1]

"It doesn't work"

Now and in the past, specific predictions do not always come to pass. For our ancestors, the requirements for accuracy were stronger. Because of their great influence, an astrologer's predictions could bend important political decisions: whether to challenge a general, a governor, or even the emperor, who to favor in the imperial succession, or which child you will groom for which station in life. Ancient astrologers were more inclined than we are to judge a person's birth fortunate or not or to determine how long they might live. Astrologers were periodically exiled from Rome and sometimes were executed, so accuracy was of key importance. Although the stakes are smaller for modern astrologers, our clients do count on us for good advice and accurate predictions.

All astrologers have made mistakes, possibly at the same rate as a modern doctor misdiagnoses a patient's illness or a lawyer gives bad advice to a client. Astrologers, like modern doctors and lawyers, apply the principles of their art to specific situations, using intuition, imagination, precedent, and experience. These respectives are based on fundamental principles, interpretations and applications. Being only human, from time to time we all fall short.

Scientific Objections

This objection considers that it is impossible for planetary positions and zodiacal signs to cause discrete events and qualities here on Earth, as the causal mechanism is, by modern understanding, impossible. This supposes that astrologers are looking for one specific planetary effect - like a planetary vibration - to justify their work: few do. Yet many astrologers are intimidated by this pointless criticism.

Attempts to account for "astrological effects" through some kind of theory of planetary magnetism or physical influences fall short of explaining the depth and complexity of astrology's symbols and its interpretative method.

Some astrologers wait expectantly for a statistical validation of astrology, which, in my view, has not yet come. Astrology cannot speak the language of statistical analysis.

Astrology becomes "pseudo-science" if astrologers try to make it into a modern science. Astrology has an observable basis in the movements of the visible sky and a set of basic principles, yet it is an art of interpretation. Astrology, now and in the past, includes different approaches and styles, not unlike that of an art, psychotherapy, medicine, or law.

Astrology is a wonderfully useful tool that allows us to question the mechanistic-materialistic assumptions of our present age. I, for one, think this is a good thing.

---

1.   See Barton, Tamsyn (1994) Ch. 2.

Astrologers as Wishful Thinkers

St. Augustine of Hippo, contemporary with the final flourishing of Hellenistic astrology, wrote that astrologers, like our modern tabloid psychics, publicize their correct predictions and ignore the wrong ones. In this way the astrologer is always right.[2] This is a powerful criticism that astrologers should grapple with. The experienced professional astrologer gains a lot of information directly from clients - "anecdotal" information - and from an understanding of astrology itself. Without an equal willingness to examine judgments that do not come to pass, the astrologer can fall into selective observation and wishful thinking. Astrologers can approach Augustine's objection in different ways.

I suggest that the astrologer deal with this objection by being as intellectually honest as possible. Some of the most interesting presentations I have been to concern themselves with charts and predictions that *do not* work. Working with wrong interpretations and predictions allows us to continue learning from our craft and becoming better over time.

One defense that astrologers use is, again, to find statistically verifiable astrological effects that support the validity of their interpretations and predictions. This brings us back to the pseudo-scientific approach that I discussed above. If one does find such statistical validation, we do not have the theoretical means with which to account for that validation. Secondly, even if an astrologer finds evidence that a specific astrological configuration will have a predictable result 90% of the time, I guarantee that the astrologer's future clients will fall in the remaining 10%.

An alternate approach articulated by the contemporary astrologer Geoffrey Cornelius was that it is not the astrological information itself that validates astrology but *the astrologer* whose insights allow that person to make an accurate interpretation or prediction.[3] We wish to validate the work of astrologers, not to find scientifically preordained "astrological effects." This implies that some astrological information may speak to the astrologer - lend itself to an interpretation or prediction - and some may not. If it does not, perhaps it is because there is not a good match between information and astrologer.

Astrologers know from experience that at times natal charts carry their information clearly and at other times there is too much noise in the signal. Some situations lend themselves to astrological clarity and some do not. Astrologers also widely differ in their "reading" ability with specific astrological factors: some of us, like myself, are "Chiron-challenged," and others can read a multigenerational history of unconscious conflict from somebody's Moon placement.

If we think of the astrologer less as a scientist (or a pseudo-scientist) and more as of an expert at divination, we are onto something important. The astrologer of quality is someone who has cultivated the skill of reading astrological and human situations together.

Religious or Spiritual Objections

Then, as now, religious objections to astrology were aimed more at the astrologer than at the validity of astrology itself. Is the astrologer acting out of impiety or hubris, dispensing information that properly only belongs to God? Or put another way - can an astrologer have real access to another

---

2.   Augustine, Book IV, Ch. 3.
3.   Cornelius (2003) Ch. 4.

person's karma? Are not these determinations better made by somebody with true spiritual accomplishment? This objection should humble and sober every astrologer, regardless of religious persuasion or spiritual stripe. To this kind of objection I have no objection; it serves to give us perspective and keep us honest.

Of the many ways in which astrology blends with different spiritual and cultural approaches, only two approaches appear to exclude astrological thinking altogether. One is today's conventional mechanistic-materialistic approach to reality. The other one, from some of the darker views of humanity in Augustine and Calvin, stresses our essential depravity and spiritual ignorance. If this is so, all diviners are frauds. I fear that some of these objections to astrology, particularly from fundamentalists, proceed from this dark view of human nature.

The religious objection continues, but from another vantage point: why are astrologers concerned with a person's projected fame, money, or love when there are more pressing spiritual issues? This objection views astrology merely as a worldly art. My reply is that astrology, past and present, does provide information and guidance about the changing potentials for worldly accomplishment and happiness. For most of us, meeting the worldly requirements of life is a prerequisite for the more reflective or spiritual life. Most of us are not saints. Astrologers should not be shy about giving people what they want and need: practical insight and advice about the ordinary - and, occasionally, extraordinary - matters in life.

Astrology, in one form or another, has co-existed with almost every spiritual approach humans have developed or have had revealed to them. The pantheistic or polytheistic world is meaningful already - astrology only adds a cosmic dimension to it. Astrologers with faith in the monotheistic religions can see the handiwork of God in the symbols and judgments of astrology. Those of a more philosophical spirituality may see our world as a material reflection of the perfect sky that is in turn a reflection of the Absolute. Someone who identifies with the spiritual traditions from the Indian subcontinent will see in astrology a symbolic representation of this lifetime's karma. Any religious or philosophical belief in which we are at home in our universe is compatible with the work of astrology.

Mundane and Psychological Objections

I now wish to address objections that might be applied to Hellenistic or medieval astrology by modern astrologers. Among our astrological contemporaries, it is sometimes fashionable to think of Hellenistic and medieval astrology as if it were concerned solely with outer circumstances. Ancient western astrology seems a far cry from our modern concerns with psychological or reflective matters.

I'd like to begin by pointing out that much in ancient astrology also applies to character and individual choice. For example, later we will examine the Lot of Spirit and Ptolemy's delineation of the Quality of Soul. Secondly, modern consulting astrologers are always working with clients on "outer" matters: work, money, love, career, family, and health. It is likely that the *practice* of both the ancient and modern eras of astrology contains the same diverse mix of interest in outer and inner concerns.

Astrology, ancient or modern, questions our fixed concepts of "inner" and "outer" life, and instead depicts a person's life in its entirety. It is pointless to practice "outer" astrology without recourse to the personal resources of the individual. To promote astrology concerned exclusively with the "inner" life, however, robs astrology of its practical and its magical power. Dividing astrology into "inner" and "outer" perpetuates the same Cartesian gulf between self and world that many of us wish to overcome.

Fate and Free Will, Once Again

Then, as now, questions of fate and "free will" are important for astrologers. Modern critics of ancient astrology, like ancient critics, find its language deterministic and its judgments fatalistic. This is an important and complex issue, with many implications.

Although we all prefer free will to fatalism, it is not always clear what we mean by either term. We routinely think of our lives as conditioned by cultural, economic, genetic and developmental factors. We have our personal styles and temperaments, over which we do not have much control; at best, we can modify these at the edges. Fortunately we do learn from life. Astrologers, like good psychotherapists, may help make available to people the wisdom gained from their life's experiences. Additionally, the act of choosing, which is an expression of personal freedom, always takes place within the context of conditions around us which we cannot control or change.

When we see chart delineations from professional astrologers that depict unsavory characters, we tend to believe that person acted unknowingly and within a limited range of choices. (This can be observed also in depictions of various well-known malefactors by the media and pop psychologists.) But wise thinkers from all cultures throughout history have told us that true freedom is the ability to do what you want, in the context of living the good life, which is a life of virtue and altruism. Both ancient and modern astrology reflect this insight.

We know that as a person develops, he or she becomes less enslaved by the conditions of his or her immediate environment, and develops an inner freedom over the temporary conditions of life. Maturity brings with it a certain kind of freedom, although one is nonetheless constrained by age, circumstance, income, and more. And within these constraints, the good life and happy life is still possible.

If we think of "free will" as merely doing what we want, only people with enormous incomes have free will. But even they don't have it! People who routinely get what they want, due to birth or a life of privilege, are often very unhappy.

Is not freedom also an alignment with the intent of the universe? It is not a long jump from a meaningful to an intentional cosmos. The ability to divine this intent is clearly one of the attractive features in astrological work, ancient or modern. Although the word "fate" is close to the word "fatalism," we also call fate "destiny," "calling," and "providence."

We have an innate desire to fit into the order of the cosmos. This has continued to inspire astrologers up to the present day. For example, here's a statement by Epictetus, a second-century Stoic philosopher who was probably no friend to astrology: "From everything that happens in the universe it is easy for the man to find occasion to praise providence, if he has within himself these two qualities: the faculty of taking a comprehensive view of what has happened in each individual instance, and the sense of gratitude."[4] This sentence could adorn every modern astrologer's consulting room.

Astrology, past and present, is concerned with the dynamics of free choice within the given conditions of our lives. Astrology symbolically depicts those conditions, inner and outer, and points to resources, inner and outer, that we can use to our advantage.

Natal and Predictive Astrology, Then and Now

Most of this book is about working with the natal astrological chart. Modern astrologers tend to look for large-scale factors, like chart patterns or aspect configurations - features involving many planets - to understand the meaning of an entire natal chart. Modern astrologers also typically look at the general distribution of planets within categories such as elements and modalities. We may blend in Sun, Moon, and Ascendant signs to form the person's "astrological signature."

These modern methods would be foreign to any ancient or medieval astrologer. Traditionally, the astrologer would look at the chart *and ask specific questions of it*. By knowing the criteria for answering these questions, the astrologer fashions a judgment about the person or event. In modern times, this survives as the method of analyzing a chart by systematically going through issues in the order of the astrological houses - First house for body and temperament, Second house for wealth, etc. Training in horary astrology can also help the student learn to ask questions and receive answers from the astrological chart.

In this book we will look at the appearance of the sky and the structure of the tropical zodiac, the planets and how we use them, houses or places, aspects, phases of planets with the Sun, and the role of fixed stars. We will also determine how to depict a person's general happiness, prosperity, fame, career, love and marriage, family, and character from the birth chart. We will conclude with an overview of time and prediction in ancient Hellenistic astrology.

The experienced modern astrologer may find some of this material difficult to adapt to; the beginner may not. The un-learning process is sometimes difficult, but I invite you to join me in this adventure. This is a journey that has benefited me as an astrologer and as a person and I hope you will profit from it in the same way.

---

4.   Epictetus, Book I, Ch. 6.

1

ASTROLOGY'S BRICKS AND MORTAR

Appearance and Form in Astrology

The symbolism used in astrology arises from the changing appearances of the sky. Astrologers filter these changing appearances through astrology's formal structures, and they use this information to interpret a situation or answer a question. In this way, astrology's symbolic structures allow the appearances of the sky to speak to us clearly, to help give our lives a sense of meaning and purpose, and to give us specific information about matters of concern.

In Chapter One we will look at the observed reality and the formal principles of the zodiac, its twelve signs or *zoidia* and their relationships to each other, the angles, and the planets. These relationships produce much of the meaning of the astrological chart.

In our time most people are not well acquainted with the geocentric (earth-centered) sky, the sky that is part of our rhythms of life. It is this apparent sky upon which astrology has its foundation.

Experiencing Reality

The modern era has seen a remarkable increase in science's understanding of the world, but this understanding has come at a price. We have learned not to trust our immediate experience, or the appearances of things, to provide us with valid practical information, yet this understanding is indispensable to the astrologer. The foundations of astrology imply that we can have direct knowledge of our world and that the cosmos does depict rhyme and reason in our lives. Astrology derives from our experience of day and night, our experience of change in our internal and external patterns, and the tracking of the sky that appears to move around us.

We note some appearances of the sky quite easily - the rising and setting of the Sun and Moon, the shapes of the Moon, and the changing amounts of light during the course of a year. We tend not to go much further. As modern people, if we track the phases of the Moon in the sky for an entire month, we have accomplished something. Much more difficult for us is noticing the patterns of a planet's visibility and motion.

Experiencing the patterns that emerge in the sky over time makes us feel that we are at home in our world, that there is indeed a beauty, splendor, and meaning in our lives. Before the introduction of electric lights, this experience of the sky was a more prominent part of our lives. As astrologers and astrology students we need to cultivate again the direct relationship that we have mostly lost.

This is what we see, but it is not what we are taught about in school.

When we go to school, however, we learn *heliocentric* astronomy. We learn that the Earth spins on its axis and the planets revolve around the Sun. We learn some modern cosmology, that the Sun is somewhere on the outer arm of a galaxy, a galaxy among a zillion other galaxies. We discover that a beam of light that we see as a twinkling star finds us after millions of years of travel. And we learn that, at last reckoning, our universe is thirteen billion years old. One can be very inspired by the discoveries of modern astronomy and cosmology, by its quasars and black holes and the millions of galaxies. But in the process of learning the facts about the cosmos, we forget how our sky appears to us when we look up.

We don't yet know how to be at home in cosmology's unimaginably vast universe. The observed sky, and modern astrology, have become intellectual concepts rather than what we actually feel or experience. Yet this observed sky retains an enormous power over us. Astrology, like Numerology, Tarot and I Ching, is a form of divination. All of these symbolic systems interpret events and give guidance for life's many and varied issues. Because astrology uses the sky's appearance to give us clear information that directly accesses reasoning and intuition, we can make interpretations based on logical and orderly information.

The Basic Rhythms of Life: Sect, Qualities, and the Seasons
We begin with our experiences of **day and night** and with the **cycle of the seasons**. These basic rhythms of life have a profound influence on us and such seemingly external conditions affect how we interpret astrology's signs and planets.

Day and Night
We begin our examination of ancient western astrology with the most ordinary of distinctions: that of day and night. Even those whose lives primarily take place indoors notice changes of day and night.

Up to the modern era, a new day began at sunrise, and for most of us (who don't work a late shift), a new day begins around daybreak. During the day, but especially during the morning hours, we have good focus and a high level of productivity. It is during this time that performance and accomplishment are asked of us. We see things clearly and try to speak logically. Even when we become drowsy in the early afternoon we continue to try to be productive.

As night descends, a more reflective, playful, and emotional tone takes hold. There is less emphasis on doing and more on being. Night is a time of ingathering: we relax and drop into a more informal mode. We may enjoy watching television or drinking some alcohol at night, but we might be concerned to find ourselves doing these activities during the day. How does this distinction between day and night find itself expressed in ancient astrology?

Planetary Sects of Day and Night

The Greek word we translate into "sect", *hairesis*, can mean a school or a church - not the buildings, but a group of people brought together by an idea or set of beliefs. When people referred to the philosophical *schools* of the Aristotelian academy or the Stoa, they used the word *hairesis*. A *hairesis* may be a *church*, like the Church of Christ Scientist, or a *cult* like the ancient Mithradic devotees. Modern equivalents may also include some of the meaning of *tribe* or *party*. In today's United States we discuss the political division into *red states* and *blue states*. These are two sects that define American politics today.

There are two sects in astrology: the day sect and the night sect. The chart as a whole, and specific planets within the chart, have a sect or an affiliation. Also, other factors such as placement relative to the Sun and the nature of the zodiacal sign in which a planet is posited may tilt a planet more toward a diurnal (daytime) or nocturnal (night time) preference.

To evaluate an astrological chart, an ancient western astrologer would first consider whether that chart is of a moment during the day or night. By "day"(diurnal), I mean when the Sun is above the horizon, and by "night"(nocturnal), when the Sun is below the horizon. Below are diurnal and nocturnal charts.

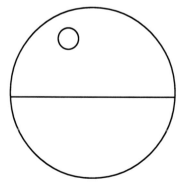

Diurnal: Sun above the horizon

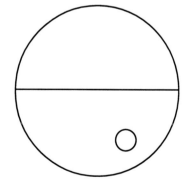

Nocturnal: Sun below the Horizon

According to this doctrine, some planets are by nature stronger in day charts and others are stronger in night charts:

- The planets of the **diurnal sect** are **Sun, Jupiter, and Saturn**. These planets are better or stronger in a chart in which the Sun above the horizon.

- The planets of the **nocturnal sect** are **Moon, Venus, and Mars**, and these are better or stronger in charts with the Sun below the horizon.

- **Mercury**, adaptable to both sects, is considered diurnal if it rises before the Sun and nocturnal if it sets after the Sun.

Notice one paradox. Saturn and Mars, the "malefics" or "evil-doers," are in sect when they appear to be opposed to their basic natures. Why is cold, dour Saturn in the day sect? Saturn, a planet of gravity, needs to be "warmed up," or "cheered up" to be more effective. And overheated hyperactive Mars: why is Mars a nocturnal planet? Mars needs to be "cooled down" or "watered down." The factors of day or night provide respective environments that can make these two immoderate planets more moderate, more reasonable. There are two conditions that bolster a planet's day or night sect quality:

- **Diurnal planets** are strengthened if on the same side of the horizon as the Sun. **Nocturnal planets** are strengthened if on the other side of the horizon from the Sun. *In either case these planets are above the horizon.*

- **Diurnal planets** are strengthened in the "masculine" signs **Aries, Gemini, Leo, Libra, Sagittarius, and Aquarius,** especially in a diurnal chart.

- **Nocturnal planets** are strengthened in the "feminine" signs **Taurus, Cancer, Virgo, Scorpio, Capricorn, and Pisces,** especially in a nocturnal chart.

Diurnal: Sun above the horizon   Nocturnal: Sun below the Horizon

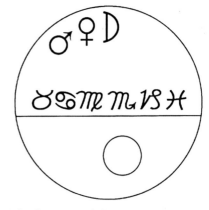

These planets are all very favorably placed according to the doctrines of planetary sect.

How might we *use* the doctrine of planetary sect? Let us compare a diurnal and a nocturnal chart. Because many of us are familiar with the personalities of Muhammed Ali and Jerry Garcia, we can use them as examples. We will examine their charts in greater detail in following chapters.

Muhammed Ali was born at night: we know this because the Sun is below the horizon. (The horizon is the horizontal line in the middle of the chart.) Being born at night favors his Moon, Venus, Mars, and Mercury (since Mercury sets after the Sun and is therefore considered nocturnal.) Of these four planets, Venus and Mars are on the other side of the horizon from the Sun, which enhances them further. Mars is even stronger because, in addition, it is in the "feminine" Taurus.

There are other factors that favor Venus and Mars, particularly that both are in angular houses - or what we will be calling "places" - the Seventh and Tenth respectively. Mars' condition is compromised because it is in the same sign - or what we will call "zoidion" - as is Saturn, a diurnal planet not as wellfavored in Ali's nocturnal chart. These considerations of planetary sect give us a good beginning in attempting to understand his chart.

Jerry Garcia, another icon of the late twentieth century, was a musician and leader of the rock band "The Grateful Dead." Because his is a diurnal chart, Sun, Jupiter and Saturn are better favored than Moon, Venus, and Mars. Because Mercury rises before the Sun, Mercury is also favored in this day chart. There are other favorable factors in this chart that we will work with in subsequent chapters: Saturn is not only in sect but also in its own triplicity. Jupiter is also in its exaltation in Cancer, and in the Tenth sign or "zoidion" from the Ascendant.

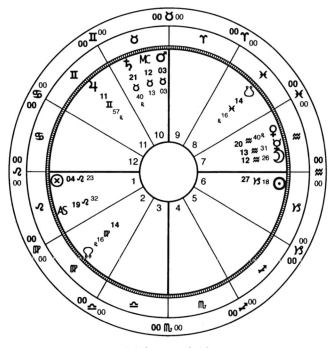

Muhammad Ali

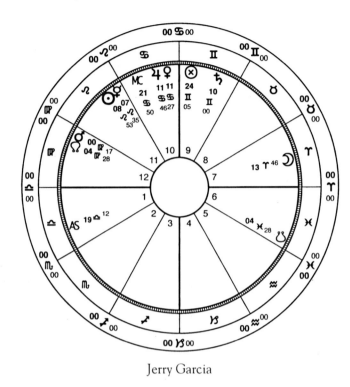

Jerry Garcia

(The modern astrologer may find the format of these two charts different from what he or she is used to. Here we use not a quadrant house system but one which uses whole signs. We will use this format throughout this book. I formally present and explain this system in Chapter Seven.)

The Cycle of the Seasons

We can now talk about the weather. Normally the adjectives we use for weather are that of hot, cold, wet, and dry. These four qualities pervade our understanding and language in many other areas of life. Claudius Ptolemy, living in Egypt in the Second century CE, translated our experiences of hot, cold, wet, and dry into astrological concepts. These four qualities depict the cycle of the seasons for the temperate latitudes of the Mediterranean area, and they can also be applied to the qualities of the signs of the zodiac, as the Sun's presence in these signs gives rise to the seasons. We can use the seasonal cycle to better understand the zodiacal signs that are familiar to us. Here is Ptolemy's cycle of the seasons:

*   The **winter solstice** represents the **coldest** time; from there wet begins to increase and cold wanes gradually. This is the ingress of the Sun into Capricorn.

*   **Wet** is at its maximum at the **spring equinox** when the Sun enters Aries. During springtime hot increases and wet decreases gradually.

How the signs of the zodiac were traditionally described

The zodiacal signs had a different significance in ancient and medieval astrology than they do in our modern practice. Similar to the animals depicted in the Chinese and Tibetan "zodiacs," modern signs are given discrete personal styles. This gave rise to the overemphasis of one's Sun sign in natal astrology. There is scant evidence of the signs or zoidia as personalities in ancient or medieval astrology. We will discuss many of these original attributes of the twelve signs - or "zoidia" - in the chapters that follow.

- Triplicity, what we call element: earth, air, fire, or water.
- Quadruplicity or Mode: cardinal, fixed, or mutable.
- Gender: masculine or feminine.
- Planetary rulership: domiciles (houses of the planets), exaltations and their opposites.
- Divisions of signs or zoidia into bounds, and decanic faces.
- The regions of the world governed by the signs or zoidia.
- The parts of the body governed by the signs or zoidia.
- Occupations and personal features.

- At the **summer solstice,** with the Sun in Cancer, the climate reaches maximum **hot,** and during the summer, dry increases.

- **Dry** reaches its maximum at the **autumn equinox** when the Sun enters Libra, and from there becomes colder until reaching the cold winter solstice, with Sun in Capricorn.

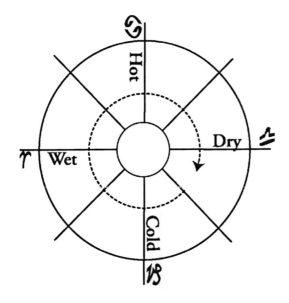

Modern astrologers tend to depict the zodiacal signs using psychological qualities for the elements of fire, earth, air, and water. No ancient astrologer did this. Astrologers did not emphasize the four elements when characterizing the zodiacal signs, and certainly not their psychological correlates. They did, however, use the four qualities as the constituents of the four kinds of temperament.[1] Ptolemy used the qualities of hot, cold, wet, and dry and combined them to give us a naturalistic view of astrology, connecting the zodiac with nature. For us, using the qualities of hot, cold, wet, and dry can greatly help us understand the dynamic of the twelve signs of the zodiac.

We will find the qualities of hot, cold, wet, and dry useful in discussing the twelve signs of the zodiac in a more modern and popular style. By factoring in the qualities of hot, cold, wet, and dry into our modern psychological style of depicting the signs, we add another layer of meaning.

The Twelve Signs or Zoidia and the Seasons

We begin with the zodiacal signs that signal the changing seasons: the cardinal signs. **Aries** is the sign of the spring equinox. We usually think of Aries within the fire triplicity, along with Leo and Sagittarius. Springtime is the season that is most **wet**. Wet has no form of its own but is contained in other forms. Wet brings things together, blurs distinctions, and forms puddles. Aries is *the wettest of the fire signs*; it is the most intuitive, creative, and least focused. Aries is also known for the messes it can leave behind.

Cancer is the sign that begins with the summer equinox, and the season is **hot**. Hot increases activity and can also go to **extremes** of expression. Cancer, however, is a water sign and we tend to think of signs in the **water** triplicity as sensitive, emotional, and imaginative. Cancer, more than Scorpio and Pisces, has hot qualities of dramatic emotionality. Cancer wears its heart on its sleeve, despite its desire to hide within its shell.

Libra, which begins with the autumn equinox, is in the **dry** season of the year. Dry separates and sees things as distinct. Unlike Gemini and Aquarius, the other signs in the air triplicity, Libra discriminates carefully between it and others, and defines itself by form and protocol.

Capricorn is an Earth Sign in the **cold** season. Cold is subdued and self-contained, sometimes brittle. Capricorn's reticence, sobriety and curmudgeonly qualities are legendary, especially in contrast to the restlessness of **Virgo** (in the hot and drying time of year) and the sensuality of **Taurus** (in the wet and warming time of year).

We can use the qualities of the northern hemisphere's seasons to explain some features of other signs. Beginning with the triplicity of water, **Scorpio** is a water sign but it is in a dry and chilling time of year, which helps explain Scorpio's pretense of aloofness. **Pisces**, however, a water sign near the wettest season, is thoroughly drenched.

In the air triplicity, **Gemini** is close to the hot place of the summer solstice and is more active and less focused than the other two air signs. **Aquarius** is a sign that has an emotional reserve, which is not a cover but true to its nature, since it is in the dominating cold of wintertime.

---

1.   For a lengthy discussion and application of temperament to modern astrology, see Greenbaum, Dorian (2005.)

The Triplicities

In the fire triplicity, **Leo** is both warm and becoming drier. Oddly, as with Virgo, Leo discriminates between itself and its environment - but with more focus on itself. **Sagittarius,** near the coldest time of year, is difficult to think of as cold. Its buoyancy, optimism, and love of freedom are not cold attributes, although its dogmatism and belief in its own rightness do seem colder.

The Planets and Their Visibility

In many cultures the month begins with the first visibility of the Moon, when the Moon's sliver appears over the western horizon. From there we can observe the phases of the Moon, or at least track them on our calendars. In many ancient cultures the first visibilities and disappearances of major fixed stars were dates of note and often began festivities honoring a deity linked to a particular star.

A pattern that has become lost to us in modern times is where and when planets appear in the night sky. The changes in the visibility conditions of the planets are more irregular and subtle than the fixed stars, yet these played an important role in the astrology of the ancient world. In our modern era, astrologers tend not to take into account the visibility of planets.

Ancient astrologers would note the following conditions:

- Whether a planet is **under the Sun's beams** and thus made invisible to observation by the Sun's light.

- Whether a planet is **heliacally rising**, that is, first emerging from the Sun. We will see later that such a planet can be quite prominent in an astrological chart.

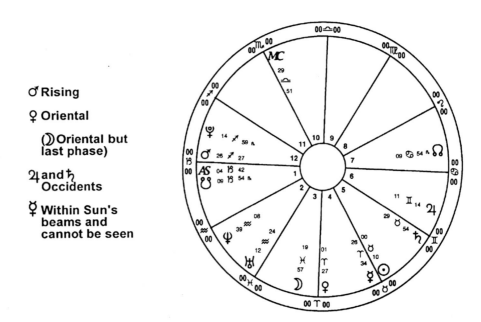

♂ **Rising**

♀ **Oriental**

☽ **Oriental but last phase)**

♃ and ♄ **Occidents**

☿ **Within Sun's beams and cannot be seen**

- Whether a planet is **heliacally setting**, that is, moving toward the Sun and about to lose visibility.

- Whether a planet rises before the Sun - **oriental** - or sets after the Sun - **occidental.** We will see later that most astrologers considered a visible planet stronger when oriental than occidental.

    The fact that these criteria have disappeared from our techniques of interpretation has diminished today's astrology.

In Which Direction does the Chart Go?

Every day each planet ascends, culminates, sets, and anti-culminates in the sky. In the astrological chart this daily cycle is depicted **clockwise. Counter-clockwise,** planets travel through the signs of the zodiac at their individual speeds. This ranges from twenty-seven days for the Moon to travel through the zodiac, to twenty-nine years for Saturn, to far longer for the modern planets Uranus, Neptune, and Pluto.

    It can be difficult to perceive that in the astrological chart, the planets move clockwise and counter-clockwise simultaneously. To better understand the two different motions of the planets, take an astrological chart and find the Sun, correlating its position with the time of day.

- Determine which planets are about to rise and which ones may be about to set. Trace the daily movement of the planets clockwise.

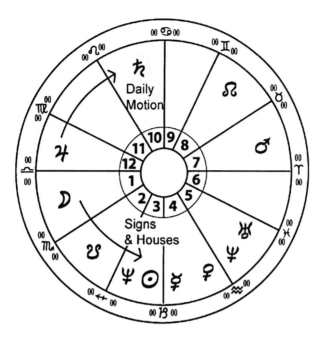

The daily motion from sunrise, etc., is clockwise.

The zodiacal signs and houses go counterclockwise

Signs or Zoidia?

Modern astrologers have traditionally referred to the twelve zoidia as the "signs" of the zodiac. If you think about this, the word "sign" tells us nothing about the zodiac or its twelve divisions. The word "sign" has an array of meanings: is a zodiacal sign different from a stop sign, a sign of the cross, or sign language? During the ancient period astrologers called these the twelve "*zoidia*," a word that has several interesting meanings. A *zoidion* is a living thing, also the seat of a god, also a picture or icon.[2]

Henceforth we will use *zoidion* to refer to a sign of the zodiac and the plural *zoidia* to refer to the twelve signs as a group.

---

2. See Translators Preface in Paulus Alexandrinus, *Introductory Matters*. Trans. R. Schmidt. Berkeley Springs, WV, Golden Hind Press.

- Then look at the planets' zodiacal positions, noting that the Sun spends a month in a sign or zoidion, whereas Jupiter takes twelve months. Trace the planets' counter-clockwise movement, perhaps comparing zodiacal positions a month and a year earlier and a month and a year later.

- Go back and forth from clockwise to counter-clockwise until you feel comfortable with the fact that the astrological chart depicts two simultaneous motions.

The Twelve *Zoidia* and their Inter-relationships

The zodiac, as you know, is divided into the familiar twelve sections we moderns call "signs," but which ancient astrologers called *zoidia*. Each zoidion has its own unique character but each also forms important relationships to others, which we call *aspects*. These structures of the zodiac do not follow any observed phenomena in the sky, but instead are based on relationships according to simple geometrical concepts. These are part of the formal principles of astrology.

Here are how the twelve zoidia relate to each other. *The zoidia divide into two types.* Every zoidion is either **masculine** or **feminine**:

Aries, Gemini, Leo, Libra, Sagittarius, and Aquarius are all masculine zoidia. The diurnal planets Sun, Saturn, and Jupiter do better in these zoidia, especially in diurnal charts.

Taurus, Cancer, Virgo, Scorpio, Capricorn, and Pisces are in feminine zoidia. The nocturnal planets Moon, Venus, and Mars are favored in these zoidia, especially in nocturnal charts.

The effect of these zoidia on the planets inhabiting them is to increase or decrease a kind of energy. To use an automotive metaphor: the masculine zoidia *shift to a higher gear* to make one's car go faster, as when one gets onto an interstate highway, and the feminine signs *shift to a lower gear*, to slow down the car as, for example, when going down a winding hill.

Planets in opposite zoidia - for example, Gemini and Sagittarius, Taurus and Scorpio, etc. - are both in either masculine or feminine zoidia. The zoidia also divide themselves into three **modes**:

The **cardinal** zoidia - those of the seasons' turnings - are Aries, Cancer, Libra, and Capricorn. They begin, respectively, the seasons of spring, summer, autumn, and winter. Modern astrologers say that these zoidia initiate action - they make things happen.

The **fixed** or solid zoidia, Taurus, Leo, Scorpio, and Aquarius, follow the cardinal zoidia. They all have stabilizing natures and slow down the pace of change.

The bicorporal or the **mutable** zoidia follow the fixed zoidia. These are Gemini, Virgo, Sagittarius, and Pisces. These zoidia are flexible, restless, and embody a changeable nature that may not be predictable or consistent.

The zoidia also divide into the four **triplicities**, which have come down to us as the four elements of fire, earth, air, and water. There is the fiery triplicity of Aries, Leo, and Sagittarius; the earthly triplicity is Taurus, Virgo, and Capricorn; the airy triplicity is Gemini, Libra, and Aquarius; the watery triplicity is Cancer, Scorpio, and Pisces. As stated above, ancient astrologers gave great importance to the triplicities but not to the elements themselves.

Every other zoidion, every third, and every fourth, constitute the basic geometrical structures in which the twelve zoidia relate to each other. These relationships are what we call aspects. Aspects are defined more as "looking" or "seeing" than "relating."

If two zoidia do not fall into any of these divisions, they do not relate to each other; they don't see each other. They are said to be in aversion or unconnected, the original meaning of the modern astrological term "inconjunct."

What do the twelve zoidia do?
Aside from measuring the planets along the ecliptic, the twelve zoidia structure the entire natal chart: each zoidion forms a **house** or **place**. All twelve are numbered counter-clockwise beginning with the zoidion of the Ascendant. These houses or places give information about different areas of life: body and temperament, money, family, relationships, career, troubles. These issues come to light as each zoidion relates to the zoidion of the Ascendant. In the ancient tradition, the first **house** or **place** was the *entire zoidion* into which the Ascendant would fall; the second was the entire zoidion following it; the third place was the entire third zoidion after that, and so on.

In the medieval tradition and later, astrologers generally used the four quadrants, begun by each of the four angles - the Ascendant, Imum Coeli, Descendant, and Midheaven - as the boundaries or cusps of the First, Fourth, Seventh, and Tenth. Since the angles are not necessarily at the beginning of the zoidia, and since the quadrants are uneven, this has the effect of splitting the zoidia from the houses or places.

The zodiac and the thirty degrees within each zoidion are where we place the **planets**. The planets are used by astrologers to describe and predict the pattern of change in the flow of events over time. Our word "planet" comes from Greek words meaning "wandering" or "wanderer." Planets are not tied to one position but move around; they speed up, slow down, and even go backwards - retrograde - in the zodiac. And, most importantly, we use one degree of the zodiac to mark an Ascendant, around which the entire chart develops.

Relating the Zoidia to the Houses or Places and the Planets
How, as systems, do the zoidia, houses or places, and the planets, relate to one another? In my view, modern astrologers have developed ways to relate these three systems that do not work well. They tend to bewilder the student and astrologer alike. We now look at these relationships from an ancient point of view.

Relating the Zoidia to Houses or Places
In the ancient tradition, the zoidia themselves defined the boundaries of the twelve houses or places, beginning with the zoidion of the Ascendant. There is a tendency among some modern astrologers to consider the First "archetypically" Aries, the Second, Taurus, the Third Gemini, and so on.

These are called the "natural houses," a name I find misleading. Sometimes there is a fit between a place and its corresponding zoidion but often there is not. For example, the Third house or place originally was called "the Place of the Moon Goddess," opposing the Ninth of the "Sun God," and both had important connections with religious practice. We find no trace of the Moon Goddess in our modern corresponding sign of Gemini or our modern understanding of the Third. Astrologers who use the "natural zodiac" consider Gemini to be of the same nature as the Third zoidion following the Ascendant. This distorts both Gemini and the Third.

Relating Zoidia to the Planets

The zoidia provide an environment for astrology's planets to manifest in different ways. We may feel as if we are always the same person, but we manifest differently, and feel differently in different environments. When we are in a nightclub, a museum, a sports stadium, at work, or at home, different features of who we are come to light. It is the same for the planets in their environments, defined partly by the zoidia they inhabit in the astrological chart.

The ancient doctrine of **planetary dignities and debilities** - domiciles or "houses of the planets," exaltations, detriments and falls - gives us a method to determine how comfortable or uncomfortable each planet is when placed in a particular zoidion. It has survived intact for the most part but has become simplified. I encourage astrologers to resist the temptation to fit the modern planets Uranus, Neptune, and Pluto into this system.

Mercury in Gemini and Mercury in Virgo are both in their own houses or domiciles, and Mercury is quite effective in both zoidia, but we may consider them as though they were two different Mercuries. The four other starry planets, Venus, Mars, Jupiter, and Saturn, also have two domiciles. The two luminaries, Sun and Moon, have one domicile each: Leo and Cancer.

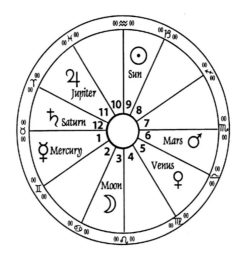

The Joys of the Planets

In addition to the more familiar **domicile** or **houses** of the planets and the **planetary exaltations** and **falls** or **depressions**, we will examine **triplicities** and **bounds** and **decanic faces**. Triplicities, for example, play a critical role in ancient and medieval astrology.

Relating Planets to Places or Houses

There is an ancient principle of "planetary joys," in which each of the seven visible planets has greater strength and happiness in a specific place from the Ascendant. These joys are a useful additional factor for assessing planetary strength. We will discuss them in detail later. They appear on the previous page.

The Ascendant, the Tropical Zodiac, and the Quadrants

We now return to the visible sky of astrology to discover how the astrological chart corresponds to important features of that sky. I will focus on some important features of the tropical zodiac, which measures changes in our visible sky throughout the year and throughout the day.

The **Ascendant** is the degree of the zodiac rising in the east. In the ancient language of astrology, the Ascendant was the *horoskopos*, the watcher or marker of the hour. It is from the Ascendant that one creates the astrological chart. Modern astrologers refer to the zoidion of the Ascendant as the "rising sign," and regard it as second in importance only to the placement of the Sun and Moon. In ancient and medieval astrology, it was the Ascendant that was the most significant single feature in the astrological chart.

The Ascendant marks where the ecliptic (the track of moving Sun and planets) and the plane of the earth's horizon come together to symbolize the specific moment that the astrologer wants to interpret: the birth of a person, a specific event, or a question. The Ascendant is always the point where the earth meets the sky along the ecliptic in the east. The Ascendant is how the astrological moment brings together heaven and earth. An astrologer who works with a chart with no time or an uncertain one can have no certain Ascendant, and cannot usually interpret such a chart with confidence. Without the Ascendant, the sky cannot relate to the specifics of a person's situation or the meaning of an event. The chart feels vague, a distant generality.

The Ascendant is therefore where the Sun rises in the east throughout the year, and where the ecliptic - the line in the middle of the band of the Zodiac - rises throughout the day. Throughout the year and throughout the day, the Ascendant is where the Sun goes from invisibility to visibility, from being hidden to appearing or emerging. The eastern horizon, including the Ascendant, is where planets and the stars go from invisibility to visibility.

After reading these next paragraphs you might want to go outside with a compass in hand. *If you are facing due east,* north of you is toward the left, south of you is toward the right. If you turn your head slightly right and left, you will see the approximate range of the Ascendant.

Pretend we have time-lapsed eyesight and can see where sunrise occurs throughout an entire year. The Sun does not rise at the same place throughout the year but has a fixed pattern of where in the east, northerly or southerly, it rises. Alternatively, you can use the time-step function of an astronomy program on your computer and set it for one step per five days, but also adjusting the

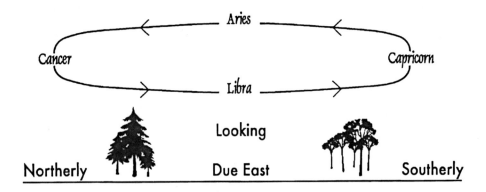

This depicts the Sun's movement on the eastern horizon during the year, and also the passage of the ecliptic across the eastern horizon every twenty-four hours.

time, as the Sun rises at different times during the year. Where the ecliptic line crosses the horizon line in the east would give you the range of the Sun on the Ascendant throughout the year. You will see that the Sun's rising has a movement that extends south and north of due east throughout the year.

If we examine the movement of the Ascendant throughout a day, we will observe that the Sun rising throughout the year and the Ascendant's movement throughout the day has exactly the same range.

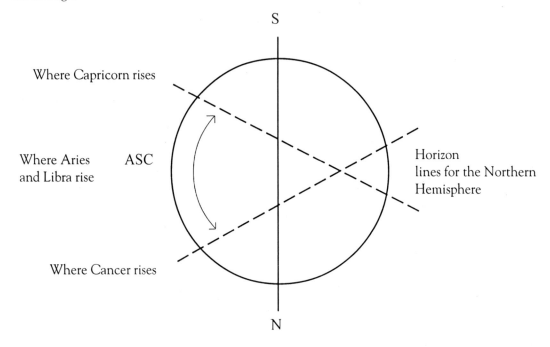

Tropical and Sidereal

Notice that we have said nothing thus far about the *constellations* of Aries, Taurus, Gemini, and so on. Most people who are not astrologers think of the zodiac as the band of the constellations, and at one time the constellations and the tropical signs did coincide. But they no longer do. In the **sidereal zodiac,** however, the twelve zoidia always coincide with the astrological constellations.

The **tropical zodiac** corresponds to the rhythm of the length of light during a year and the symmetry of the daily cycle that we have been examining. A sidereal zodiac does not have these rhythms and symmetries. Because of a slight wobble in the rotation of the Earth, from year to year the Sun's background of constellations moves very slightly backwards, so that at this time in history the tropical zoidion Aries corresponds to the front of the physical constellation Pisces, and eventually will move into the constellation Aquarius. At the spring equinox, when the Sun is at tropical 0 Aries, the background constellation of the Sun is the front part of the constellation Pisces. At the winter solstice, when the Sun is at tropical 0 Capricorn, the Sun's background constellation is the front of Sagittarius.

During the year, the Sun rises due east only at the spring equinox or autumn equinox. At other times, we have to look to the left and right of due east to locate the Ascendant. If the Sun rises in the north, left of due east, we are in spring or summer. If the Sun rises in the south, right of due east, we are in autumn or winter.

Facing east, we can mark out these sunrises during the year. The Sun rises in the east but it is most northeast in late June when it's at **0 Cancer,** to the left of due east. In the northern hemisphere this is the longest day. The Sun rises most southeast in late December when it's at **0 Capricorn,** to the right of due east. In the northern hemisphere this is the shortest day.

If you are living in the northern hemisphere, consider this: when you look at the Sun move on a winter day, the Sun appears distant, at a far angle; when you look at the Sun on a summer day, the Sun appears much closer to directly overhead. The Sun in the winter is above the horizon for a shorter time, and in the summer is above the horizon a longer time.

During the course of one full day, if we spend the day looking east, the path of the *ecliptic* extends north and south, left and right. The ecliptic rises and goes through the sky continuously. Where this path intersects the eastern horizon at any given moment is the Ascendant of that moment.

In one day, all twelve zoidia rise through the Ascendant and cross the sky, also culminating, setting, and moving below the earth. This occurs each and every day. During one day, the Ascendant's southernmost position is at the same place as when the Sun is at **0 Capricorn,** in late December.

The Ascendant's northernmost position during the day is at the same place as the Sun when it is at **0 Cancer,** in late June. These are the boundaries of the Ascendant. In the northern hemisphere, the parts of the ecliptic near 0 Cancer - the most northerly - spend **more time above the horizon,**

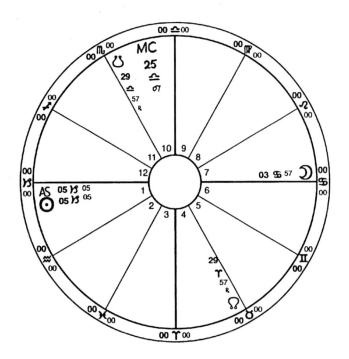

Charlotte Full Moon Sunrise
December 26, 2004
07.35 AM EST
35N14 80W51

Argentina Full Moon Sunrise
December 26, 2004
05.45 AM BZT
34S36 58W27

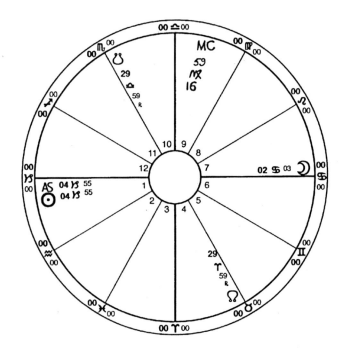

and the parts of the ecliptic near 0 Capricorn - the most southerly - spend **less time above the horizon**. When it is the first full Moon in the winter, when the Sun is in Capricorn and the Moon in Cancer, the Moon is much longer above the horizon than the Sun.

In the southern hemisphere, a planet in Capricorn spends the longest time above the horizon and a planet in Cancer the shortest.

On December 26 in Charlotte, North Carolina, the Sun spent nine hours above the horizon; in Buenos Aires on the same day, the Sun spent over fourteen hours above the horizon. This is because Buenos Aires is much further south than Charlotte. The southernmost zoidion, Capricorn, would be above the horizon for a shorter time in the northern hemisphere (e.g. Charlotte) and for a longer time in the southern hemisphere (e.g. Buenos Aires).

Since the Moon is in Cancer, the northernmost zoidion, her time of passage above the horizon is inverted from that of the Sun in Capricorn for each location. The Moon in Charlotte will be above the horizon longer than the Moon is Buenos Aires. Notice that in Charlotte there is much less distance between the Ascendant and Midheaven, because Capricorn has a smaller arc above the horizon in the Northern hemisphere. In Buenos Aires, in the southern hemisphere, Capricorn has a much larger arc and has a farther distance to travel from the Ascendant - rising - to the Midheaven - culminating.

Angles and Quadrants

Here is one more experiment, to find north and south in the sky: Facing east, if you stretch your arms out to the side, your left arm is pointing north and your right arm pointing south. The planets move south after they rise in the east and their "noon" positions are due south. At their "noon" positions, planets are on the **Midheaven** of an astrological chart. This pertains to the temperate zones of the northern hemisphere only. From the southern hemisphere, north (left) is where the planets rise toward their "noon" positions that are due north. Again, a computer astronomy or star program can be useful to help visualize this.

The **meridian** is a line, perpendicular to the horizon, which goes **due north and south**, crossing the north and south poles, circling directly over and under you. The meridian does not change its position during the course of a day, but if you move slightly, the meridian moves with you. Where the circle of the Sun - the ecliptic - crosses the meridian, is the **Midheaven**, which is always due south (in the northern hemisphere) or due north (in the southern hemisphere). The Midheaven degree was an important place in ancient astrology and has become even more important for modern astrologers.

The crossing lines of the horizon and the meridian form the **four quadrants** in the two-dimensional astrological chart. The standard presentation of the astrological chart emphasizes the four quadrants of the chart. Because the horizontal and meridian axes are rarely ninety degrees from each other (perfect only when 0 Aries or 0 Libra are rising), the quadrants are most often uneven in size. Unfortunately, the way that modern charts depict the quadrants can give rise to misperceptions. In "proportional" or "American" charts, the quadrants show up as equal in size, although most often they are not. In "non-proportional" or "European" charts, the meridian seems to incline at an angle

---

Using Paranatella

In *The Psychology of Astro*Carto*Graphy* , Jim Lewis and Kenneth Irving astrologically depict a map of the earth or part of the earth for any given time of an event or birth. Rather than using the astrological chart from one location, this technique uses a map of a location, a region, or the entire world for a particular time, upon which the lines for planets' rising, culminating, setting, and anti-culminating are plotted. For a given time, at some place in the world, each planet is upon one of these four angles. When two planets are at different angles, they form paranatella, which, in Astro*Carto*Graphy, form "latitude crossings." Planets in such a position with each other affect the entire degree of latitude on the Earth in which the co-risings occur.

      In her work with fixed stars, Bernadette Brady emphasizes the *parans* for planets and important stars. According to Brady and one of her ancient sources (Anonymous of 379), the angle of the star position indicates the period of life in which a particular star may be active. Paranatella or parans describe two or more planets **bodily** at angles. This is not necessarily by zodiacal degree, since a planet (but not the Sun) may be north or south from the line of the ecliptic, the line of the Sun's motion, and come to an angle at a slightly different time than its zodiacal degree will. We will explore these issues in greater detail when we discuss the fixed stars and how astrologers use them.

---

but the Ascendant-descendant line appears straight left to right as if always due east and west. In reality, it is the Ascendant-Descendant line that goes back and forth and the meridian that is always in the same position. They are only perpendicular to one another when 0 Aries or 0 Libra rise.

Why are quadrants important for astrology?

- The astrologically sophisticated reader is perhaps saying, "Because they make up the houses, and the horizon and meridian axes (the 'angles') form the cusps of the angular houses." This is a conventional view among astrologers. As we will see, however, the houses or places - the areas of life - are arranged not by the quadrants, but by the zoidia.

- The ancients drew an interesting parallel between the sequence of a day, depicted by the quadrants and angles, and a person's age in life.[3] This has a natural and wonderful simplicity.

    Ascending is the beginning of life; youth extends to *culminating* or the Midheaven degree, which represents the prime of life.

    Setting is like retiring, as one withdraws from visibility.

---

[3]   Paulus, Ch.7.

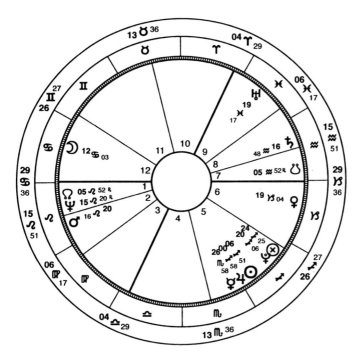

William Blake - European Style
Chart or Non-proportional
Houses

These charts are in the quadrant format familiar to modern astrologers

William Blake -
American Style Chart
or Proportional Houses

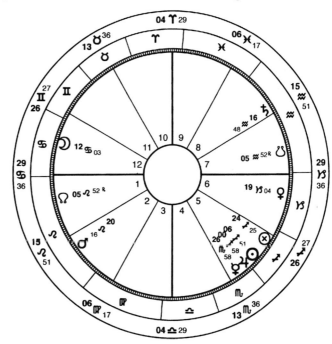

The *anti-culminating* place (Imum Coeli) is about death and its aftermath, including one's legacy. (The modern astrologer may have encountered this analogy in the horary astrology of the seventeenth century.)

- In modern astrology a planet near one of these angular degrees, especially on the Ascendant or the Midheaven, is quite powerful. When a planet is near rising, culminating, setting, and anticulminating degrees, that planet carries additional emphasis. It is as if it were written with an exclamation point.

- Angles are also important for **paranatella,** which means "co-rising," and is usually shortened to "paran." When a planet or star is on one angle and another planet or star is at the same or a different angle, they are said to "co-rise." This brings together the two celestial bodies interpretatively.

- **Primary directions** were a very important ancient predictive method that endured up to the early modern era. Significant positions in a chart, like the Sun and Moon, were directed by primary or diurnal motion. An astrologer might predict a crisis or major event when, for example, a planet below the horizon rose by direction, or a rising planet culminated. Later we will explore Valens' use of "ascensions" - how many degrees go over the Midheaven in the time it takes a zoidion to completely rise. In the final chapter I will introduce some of the complexities of Ptolemy's use of directions.

We have now finished a tour of astrology's foundations. We are ready to investigate its symbolic and interpretative applications, beginning with the planets. With planets, astrology shows us its human dimension. The planets are not lumps of rock and slushy gas, not ciphers for psychological states, but full-fledged characters - like actors on a stage - who go far beyond simple descriptions. As the characters of the astrological chart, they bring it to life. They are the animating principle or "soul" of the astrological chart.

2

ASTROLOGY'S PLANETS

From astrology's point of view, the movements of the planets create the patterns we must recognize in order to make sense of our lives in an ever-changing world. Planets depict general factors and specific situations in our lives; they have basic meanings that we can apply to ourselves in many ways. When we use astrology to inform ourselves about the features of our minds and bodies, or about areas of our lives such as occupation, parents, love and marriage etc., we often refer to planets.

The astrologer blends the intrinsic meanings of the planets with the areas of life that they govern: when considering a chart for indications of love and relationship, or how women are represented in a man's life, Venus is prominent as a significator. The descending zoidion - the "Seventh Place" - is also an important indicator. Someone, for example, with Gemini rising will have Sagittarius as the zoidion of the Seventh place from the Ascendant. Both Venus and Jupiter - the lord of Sagittarius - will have something to say about the native and his or her relationships.

About Planetary Meanings
In modern astrology, there's a tendency to think of planets mostly in psychological terms. For example, Mars is "anger" and "aggression" or Moon is "nurturing", yet the psychological features are only one part of the spectrum of the planets' applications. What comes to mind is the well-worn image of several blind people trying to understand the concept of an elephant. Each person can perceive only one part of its body - is an elephant the trunk, the legs, the roundness of the torso? Astrologers are the blind people and the basic meanings of the planets are the parts of the elephant. At the same time, the planets are the easiest of all astrological symbols to understand - they have an innate, tangible, even visceral reality in our lives, yet our understanding is always incomplete.

When presenting planetary symbolism, my preference is to use vignettes or narratives based on our experience. In this chapter, we'll begin with vignettes, and then look at various categories of experience that correspond to each planet.

Ancient and medieval astrologers used *aphorisms* to describe the planets' effects. An aphorism is a snapshot of how an astrological indicator can manifest, often bringing many different factors together. Here is an example from Antiochus of Athens: "If Kronos (Saturn) should be found to be the ruler of the Lot of Marriage and should happen to be in the setting place (Seventh place from the Ascendant), such a woman will be corrupted by an old man."[1] There is no one sense to the logic

---

1.   Antiochus of Athens, Part 1, Ch. 48.

of this statement. Saturn may represent either old men or corruption; the Seventh place is the place of marriage but, as the Setting Place, it also symbolizes old age. Antiochus does not spell out the logic of this aphorism: he leaves that to his student and reader.

The purpose of an aphoristic style is, I feel, to help the student think symbolically, learning how to combine symbols into depictions of situations. *They are not meant as ironclad principles of astrological determinism.* Astrological aphorisms are a learning device, although its depictions can be extreme.

Here we will focus on the five visible starry planets: Saturn, Jupiter, Mars, Venus, and Mercury. The Sun and Moon are more general indicators, although they do have some specific applications. Since the modern planets Uranus, Neptune, and Pluto are invisible to the eye and have looser connections to the astrological signs or zoidia, they will be discussed separately and in less detail. Hellenistic astrologers got on quite well without them.

When discussing the planets we will approach them in different ways: as doers of good (benefics) or evildoers (malefics), to indicate career, as qualities of body and soul, and as indicators of the stages of life. In Chapter Three will see how the different *familiarities* of the planets with the zodiac begin to tell us how they may be applied within in the natal chart.

Malefics and Benefics

Natal astrology, past and present, is mainly concerned with the components of worldly happiness. The basic descriptions of the planets reflect a concern with the vicissitudes of life, which are affected by the so-called malefics, **Saturn** and **Mars**, and the so-called benefics, **Jupiter** and **Venus**. We will discover, however, that like most seemingly good and bad things in life, the planetary benefics and malefics are more complicated and interesting than they may first appear.

The malefics Saturn and Mars, are on the whole, more difficult when placed out of sect - Saturn in a nocturnal chart, Mars in a diurnal chart. Although there are many other factors to consider, the out-of-sect malefic may be more malefic than the one that is in sect.

Saturn is that gray, dull, slowly moving light that is the most distant of the visible planets. Think of Saturn in human situations and you think of heaviness, gravity, restriction, oppression and depression - being weighed down. Saturn is an isolated and austere planet, one pleasing to only the most dedicated spiritual hermit. For the rest of us, Saturn indicates how we manage the depressing and repressive circumstances that occur in our lives. If we romanticize our growth experiences, we will tend to do so only after the difficult time has passed; at the time we tend to complain bitterly. Often, during these times, we lean upon those old-fashioned virtues and attitudes: discipline, hard work, humility and verbal restraint, lowering expectations and learning to be content with less. Maybe we can click into the virtues mentioned above, but sometimes that occurs at the end, not at the beginning, of the process.

Otherwise, we find ways to cut corners; we engage in finger pointing, backstabbing, accusations, and slanders, with a spiritual look on our faces and with the self-proclaimed best of motives. Our personal lives take a hit as well: perhaps our appearance and environment become degraded and we begin to feel rather seedy. While feeling sorry for ourselves, we become inert, or eat or drink too much, and we become a squalid, diminished version of ourselves. One sense of Saturn that has departed from modern astrology is its association with corruption and depravity. We see it here. If unchecked, we develop a jaded, cynical, untrusting attitude towards others and towards life. We drain the life from others, as our lives have been drained from ourselves. Like the nature of the planet Saturn, we become dry and very cold. All of us have Saturn in our chart, and as the greater malefic it represents our vulnerabilities and problems with life.

We continue with the fiery red planet **Mars**, the planet of anger, the god of war. Mars also reflects troubled and difficult circumstances, but the nature of those circumstances is different and thus so are our responses to them. The calamities of Saturn are often slow and inexorable; the difficulties brought by Mars are sudden and more immediately destructive. If Saturn is like finding that your house sits on a toxic waste dump and it will be impossible ever to sell, Mars is like coming home to find that vandals and thieves have paid a visit. If Saturn is oppressive, Mars is aggressive. If Saturn is cold and dry, Mars is hot and dry; Mars scorches, and it brings situations where you react by wanting to fight or retaliate. On your way to work in the morning, your fellow driver cuts you off and makes an obscene hand gesture. Later, when you have to wait in traffic because of a VIP motorcade escorting an unwelcome politician, you may want to respond in a Mars-like fashion. You finally get to work and you find out your erstwhile friend has just landed the project you had wanted - by casting doubts on your competence to your boss. At lunchtime the waitress is surly and the food is ill-flavored. Then your partner calls you while he or she is paying off the credit card bill, and is mad at some of your recent expenditures, although you feel you are generally the more frugal. To make your day complete, when you get home telemarketers are on the phone and religious missionaries are at your door. These are all situations where one is frustrated, where some kind of movement has been interrupted, and your response can range from annoyance to irritation to rage. The humor of the situation usually doesn't strike you until the next day.

Situations relating to Saturn may box us in; with Mars we can do something but often it is the wrong thing. With Mars we want to fight, to give somebody the "what for." At the very least we want to stomp our feet or give somebody a withering stare. Although we will later forget what made us so angry, at the time our hostile or angry response consumes our thinking and emotions. Sometimes we act like we're insane; think of the dual meaning of the word "mad."

Certainly there are occasions when fighting is necessary and helpful. Like our experiences with Saturn, the world of Mars is also unfair. Unlike with Saturn, Mars allows us to force a correction. This can be helpful to us and to others, but sometimes it becomes counterproductive. Mars' virtues are those of heroism and bravery, of fighting the good fight. Too often, however, we cause unnecessary harm, and this is why Mars is a malefic.

Jupiter and **Venus** are the benefics - the doers of good. Jupiter is the diurnal planet and Venus is the nocturnal planet. A person will have one of the two in sect, depending on whether that person is born during the day or at night. Although there are other factors to consider, the planet that is in sect tends to be more benefic.

Jupiter is a glowing planet, especially when he is on the other side of the zodiac from the Sun. Jupiter's movement through the zodiac is stately and dignified, and he stands in strong contrast to Saturn. Where Saturnine life-situations are about consequences and repercussions, Jupiter-ian (or Jovial) situations concern themselves with rewards and gifts. Jupiter brings possibility, prosperity and abundance; indeed Jupiter, not Venus, is the planet of wealth. Venus, as we'll see, concerns itself with beautiful objects; Jupiter is concerned with generosity and magnificence. A person with the nature of Jupiter is a benefactor: a teacher, a wealthy patron, or a mentor.

Jupiter is also an attitude - that there are more resources at hand than one might expect, that when there's trouble others can help you out. Think of the final scenes of Capra's *It's A Wonderful Life*. Much of the movie is purely Saturnine: not only is it a narrative of successive life disappointments, but Mr. Potter, the ugly old man - a character redolent of Saturn - stands ready to ruin our hero, George Bailey, a good man who feels unfulfilled. At a moment of pure Saturn - George Bailey is about to throw himself off a bridge - Clarence the Angel, surely a Jupiter figure, comes to him. Clarence shows what George Bailey's world would have been like if he had never been born, to see how diminished the lives of those he loves would have been without him. Upon returning to his real life, George finds that many friends have banded together to pay him back for his previous acts of generosity, and Mr. Potter will have to wait for another day to ruin our hero. Thus the movie comes to a wonderfully happy ending.

Jupiter's community spirit stands in strong contrast to Saturn's tendency to isolate. Like George Bailey, ordinarily we tend not to notice that people are often kind and helpful to us, and it sometimes takes a personal or community disaster for us to see it. Our lives are connected with the love and kindness of many others. Jupiter also depicts justice as a community ideal where all contribute to a common good and where all members of a community partake of a common wealth.

Jupiter is concerned with religion as a vehicle for shared outlook, as a social expression of spirituality. Since Jupiter is concerned with a wider perspective, and does not get bogged down with what is temporary and insignificant, it is well suited to deal with much of the content of religion.

Just as the malefics have their virtues, the benefics have their drawbacks. Modern astrologers sometimes stress that Jupiter overdoes things - being generous to the point of profligacy, optimistic to the point of fantasy, grand to the point of grandiosity. Traditional astrologers, thinking differently, stress that a poorly placed Jupiter is weakened, which may cause a person to be pettier, narrower, and less generous. My sense is that Jupiter inherently suffers from **naiveté**. Perhaps this is not, after all, the best of all possible worlds. Nevertheless, Jupiter is the Great Benefic, and brings favorable situations to our lives.

Jupiter is happily diurnal. In contrast to the coldness of Saturn, Jupiter has warmth, and in contrast to the dryness of Saturn and Mars, Jupiter is moist. Both warmth and moistness are life giving and life sustaining and are qualities of fertility.

Venus, that quick and radiant planet that appears before sunrise or after sunset, makes life bearable even at the worst of times. If Jupiter is social happiness, Venus is personal happiness. Venus is pleasure, love and the arts of all kinds. When we think of pleasure, we think of the fleeting daily pleasures that enrich our lives: enjoying a fine sunny day or a lovely landscape, consuming a fine meal and a rich dessert, listening to good music, noticing an attractive person. Venus covers the life-fulfilling enterprises of love and beauty, and the full range of romantic love, from the sentimental to the sexy. Love that is Venus marginally includes situations of sexual exploitation or depravity, as well as those of marriage as status climbing or obtaining a trophy lover. (Traditionally these show Venus in combination with Saturn.) Even in crueler or more cynical manifestations, the goodness of Venus is there, somewhere.

Venus also denotes beauty, hence art and adornment. From the perspective of survival or evolution, there is no reason for art and beauty to exist - they are the enrichment that makes us the best of human. Much art, like religion, can be a Jupiter expression of the ideals of community and shared experience, but there is more to art. Venus art tends to be for its own sake, spanning all dimensions of human attempts at beauty - visual art, music, dance, and entertainment, from the highbrow to the lowbrow. As we know from modern music, modern art, and some genres of film, the horrifying and the ugly can also be presented in a Venus manner.

Environmental beauty and personal adornment are huge industries in the economically developed world. From landscape architecture, interior design, clothing, perfume, jewelry, fad diets and workout routines, to plastic surgery and sports gear, we value having our clothes and our bodies as attractive as they can be. Venus beauty extends from the refined and elegant to the erotic, although from culture to culture and from generation to generation, our standards change. All these styles, however, are inherently in the nature of Venus.

What fault does Venus have? I call it **shallowness.** We can become distracted by temporary comfort; we may lose our perspective by seeking momentary pleasure, and fail to acknowledge deeper dimensions to beauty than what is immediate and obvious.

Venus, like Jupiter, has the qualities of warmth and moisture. This is an indication of Venus's moderating nature. As a nocturnal planet, Venus functions to cool down hot nocturnal Mars. Consider the painting of Venus and Mars by the fifteenth-century Florentine artist Botticelli: having made love, Venus soberly looks out into the distance while Mars is asleep, exhausted.

In most circumstances, Venus does less well when she has too much energy. Venus is however a warm planet. Don't our encounters with love and beauty warm us up? (Calling an attractive person "hot" implies sexual attraction, perhaps with an ingredient of Mars arousal.) It is of the nature of moisture to bring things together - and this is clearly an agenda of Venus. The later medieval and Arab astrological tradition regarded Venus as cool and moist, but to the Hellenistic tradition, the Goddess of Love was definitely warm!

Now we visit another dimension of life, one that tends to dictate what most of us do for too much of our time - our occupation. We're going to put aside the experiential dimension of planets and instead look for them to give us specific information about this important part of daily life.

Occupation: What You Do

Having discussed four planets in a general manner, we can begin to apply them and others to specific issues. The same planets in a chart can be used for different interpretative purposes. Our source is Ptolemy's *Tetrabiblos* Book IV, Chapter 4. By looking at each planet within different fields of inquiry, we can avoid being the blind person describing the elephant through one perspective only.

By "occupation" or "profession," we are less concerned with what God wants you to do (that's vocation, which means "calling") and more with what you actually do, what occupies you. We are less concerned here about whether a planet is s malefic or benefic; instead we focus on each planet as an indicator of different occupational possibilities. It is through the placements of Mars, Venus, and Mercury that we can learn the most about our profession. (We learn less from Saturn, Jupiter, Sun and Moon.) The strength of the position of the signifying planet may indicate *how well* one might do in an occupation.

Jupiter and Saturn do have *some* influence which we can discuss quickly: either may cause someone to become a "public servant," an administrator or a magistrate - what we might call a bureaucrat. Jupiter is traditionally cited more in this context. Leadership itself, however, is reserved for the Sun, as the Sun is an indicator of prominence or dominance. In addition, Saturn produces the gravedigger, the farmer, and the dockworker. When in a very good place, especially in a diurnal chart, Saturn can bring about the philosopher or priest. Valens tells us that Saturn produces tax and customs collectors.[2] I would include law enforcement, if combined with a dose of Mars.

However, when in aspect to the swifter Mars, Venus, or Mercury, Saturn and Jupiter become more important indicators for occupation. In the following paragraphs, I will try to bring the planetary lists of occupations from the ancient world up to date. There are relatively few lion-tamers, slave traders, and temple priestesses in our culture, but we do have computer programmers, pundits, and interior decorators.

Mars indicates people who fight or exert themselves physically for a living, from soldiers to bricklayers - although there's an argument for also using Saturn for bricklayers - to athletes. This includes people who use iron - for example, cooks and surgeons. I would expand this to include manufacturers or machine workers and repair people: people who *use tools* to put things together, move them, or take them apart. If Saturn assists by aspect, a person may work on underground tunnels (like Boston's "Big Dig"), or become embalmers or gravediggers. Jupiter may dispose one to being in the military, a ferryman (or subway, taxi or bus driver), or to working in restaurants or hotels.

The occupations of **Venus** follow our previous discussion. For a man, and when well disposed in the birthchart, Venus may indicate material fortune from a woman. Venus occupations range from clothing designers and those who model clothing or themselves, to artists, jewelers, musicians, actors, people who work in the beauty industry, and, of course, all manner of courtesans and escorts. Ptolemy says that Saturn would contribute to using these activities for commercial gain, yet *all* occupations are motivated for monetary gain. Jupiter indicates one who is particularly successful and rewarded, whose work is popular and worthy of honor, or who gains advancement (Jupiter) through women (Venus).

Mercury presents some surprises. Mercury occupations include accountants and scribes (including people who work with computers in our culture), salespeople (perhaps with a dose of Mars) and teachers. Philosophers - which today would include scientists and inventors - are mercurial, as are diviners of all kinds. *Mercury, not Uranus, is the planet of astrology.* Writers are obviously

---

2.   Valens, Book I, Ch. 1.

indicated by Mercury; with Venus one is inclined to be a musician or a poet. Jupiter may indicate judges; lawyers - those who construct arguments advocating a particular perspective - are mercurial. If Saturn assists, one might become the manager of the household of others (like Jeeves in the Wodehouse series), or dream interpreters (psychotherapists, maybe). If Jupiter assists, we get drafters of laws (legislators) orators (politicians or pundits), teachers of rhetoric or practitioners of persuasion (people in advertising), and those who spend time with superior persons (talk show hosts).

With Mercury and Mars working together, Ptolemy tells us, people can fashion statues, create models of animals, or be physicians - or adulterers. (I did not know the last one was an occupation.) If Saturn supports Mercury and Mars, the outcome is rather bleak - you may be a murderer, a highwayman, or a burglar.

How does one find the planet or planets of occupation in a natal chart? Almost all ancient astrologers look at houses or places from the Ascendant, as this indicates the prominence and productivity of a planet. Everybody mentions the angular places, especially the First (within the zoidion of the Ascendant) and the Tenth. The Fourth and Seventh are not as strongly emphasized. The Sixth and Second zoidia from the Ascendant - since they make trines to the Tenth - are also used to determine vocation, especially if there are no planets in the First or Tenth. To these, Ptolemy adds the planet that rises visibly just before the Sun ("oriental"), especially if the Moon is applying to it by aspect.

Let's try this out with the natal chart of **Jacqueline Kennedy Onassis** (see over the page.) She is the closest America has come to royalty. She wouldn't have an occupation, in an ordinary sense, until later in her life. After her second husband Aristotle Onassis died, Jackie moved back to New York City and became an editor and publisher. Which planet indicates this? It would be Mercury, of course. Mercury is in the all-important Tenth place from the Ascendant, and has priority over other planets, although Mercury is hidden by the beams of a very powerful Leo Sun. It was only after she was out of the public limelight, that she was able to have a conventional occupation and excel at it.

The next chart is **William Blake**, an eighteenth century artist and engraver who is better known to us as one of the great poets of the English language. Which planets could signify Blake's occupation? Venus in the Seventh house is the only angular planet that qualifies, and it is also the next planet that Moon aspects. Although Blake comes down to us today primarily as a poet, he made his living as an artist and engraver. That he was also a poet is indicated by the assistance Venus gets from Mercury in Scorpio, two zoidia away, in the productive Fifth.

The chart above is that of **Muhammad Ali**, who was a championship boxer in the 1960s and 1970s. His career was interrupted by the consequences of his refusal to serve in the Vietnam War. Later in life, although incapacitated by Parkinson's disease, he has become one of the heroes of contemporary American life.

Ali's chart has many different possibilities, since five of the seven visible planets are in the angular Tenth and Seventh houses. For issues of occupation, the Tenth house is more significant than the Seventh. This points to Mars and Saturn as the more relevant planets. Since Mars is also in sect, and Saturn is not, Ali would probably flourish more in a Mars-governed career than one

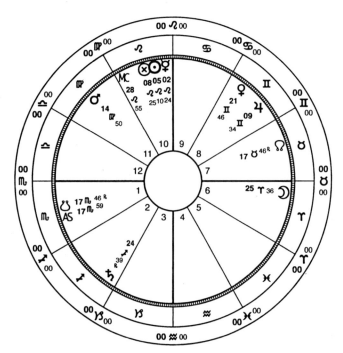

Jacqueline K Onassis

William Blake

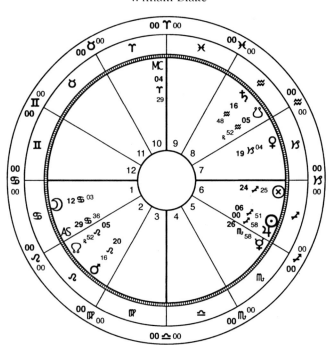

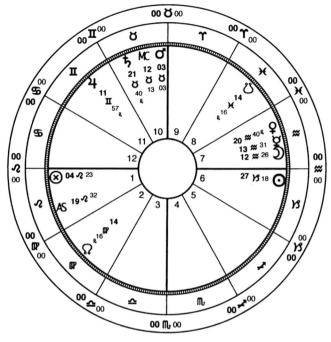

Muhammad Ali

governed by Saturn. We could call this Mars accompanied by Saturn. These planets together in the Tenth place is a clear marker for being in a socially sanctioned but violent profession - boxing. Ali has been far more than simply a boxer: this is indicated by the placements of Moon, Mercury, and Venus in the Seventh. We will follow up with this later.

We continue our discussion of the meanings of the planets by discussing planetary depictions of body and soul. For this we rely, once again, on Ptolemy.

Planets Governing Body

As Ptolemy does in the third book of the *Tetrabiblos*, we begin with body.[3] What are the influences of the planets on one's body type and the physical ailments that may befall us? Ptolemy's presentation contains foundations of traditional medical astrology, and has a strongly medieval feel to it. This is not because Ptolemy was a medieval astrologer but rather that the medieval tradition of medical astrology was strongly influenced by his work.

To determine what planet or planets may indicate a person's body, look at the Ascendant and Moon, planets aspecting these positions and planets in charge of these position. We find the planet or planets that show prominence.

---

3.   Ptolemy, *Tetrabiblos Book III*, Ch. 12 and Ch. 13.

Ptolemy and the Planets

You may have noticed that Ptolemy's name is mentioned quite often in this chapter. His emphasis on the planets, as opposed to, for example, lots, is one of the factors that distinguish him from other ancient astrologers. Ptolemy emphasized planets because they were more central to his rationale for astrology. According to Ptolemy, the planets, through their natures and their qualities (hot, cold, wet, and dry), influence the cosmic environment around us, which influences our personal and collective lives. His science may seem a bit odd to us today, but it formed the basis for his planetary symbolism, which has greatly influenced astrology ever since.

Each of the visible planets, and especially the five starry planets - Saturn, Jupiter, Mars, Venus, and Mercury - are related to specific attributes of the human body and its ailments. In addition to other factors signifying planetary strength or weakness, such as dignity, sect, and placement relative to the Ascendant, Ptolemy also considers whether the planet is rising ahead of the Sun - oriental - or whether the planet sets after the Sun - occidental. He clearly feels that an oriental signifying planet gives more positive attributes than an occidental one.

Body type can be signified by the planet or planets aspecting or responsible for the positions of Ascendant and Moon. This responsible planet is the "dispositor." Diseases of the body are indicated in part by malefics in the Seventh place, opposite the Ascendant or contacting planets there, and the Sixth place, which does not behold the Ascendant. Planets influence the body in accordance with their own natures:

- **Saturn,** a dark planet, tends to give dark hair and a dark complexion. Saturn gives better results when oriental: a more robust frame and moderate stature. When Saturn is occidental, the body has more distinctly Saturn-like features: it's weaker, dark-eyed, smaller and thinner. Saturn's qualities - cold and dry - tend to less flesh and more coldness to the touch.

   The ailments of Saturn include a cold stomach, which would create indigestion: digestion is a hot activity. Since Saturn cools the body down, the planet compromises the body's functioning in many ways. A person can become weak and emaciated. Ptolemy also mentions coughing and colic: this may be due to Saturn's obstructive nature. Saturn governs the right ear, whereas Mars governs the left ear. Saturn also governs the bladder, phlegm, and the bones; the bladder is a container, phlegm is often an obstructive factor in illness, and bones are the hard and dry materials of the body.

- **Jupiter** gives lightness of skin and hair, in contrast to Saturn's darkness. When oriental, Jupiter gives a body that is tall, of good color, and impressive; when occidental, the height is moderate and the light hair may be thinner and, in a man, tending toward baldness. Ptolemy says that Jupiter governs the lungs, arteries, and semen. Lungs and arteries are affiliated with air, as is the blood, hence circulation. Semen corresponds to a fertile generative principle that is associated to Jupiter. Just as Saturn and Mars have to do with hearing, Jupiter is affiliated with the sense of touch.

- **Mars,** as you might imagine, gives redness to the complexion. When oriental, red is mixed with whiteness; when occidental it's simply red. When oriental, Mars gives a tall body, but less so when occidental. When oriental, Mars gives somewhat curly hair; when occidental, the hair is straight and yellow. Ptolemy would not consider such hair blond and attractive but rather dry and pale. Mars governs the left ear, as stated above, and the kidneys, veins, and genitals. The ailments of Mars are many and predictable: spitting blood, itching or hot sores on the body, blemishes, tumors, or corrosive diseases. Mars is also responsible for miscarriages. These mishaps show qualities of hotness or the color red.

- According to Ptolemy, the **Venus** body type is much like Jupiter, except somewhat better looking in a feminine way. These people are more shapely, plump, and delicate, with soft features. Ailments happen when Venus is associated with malefic factors. With Saturn and Mars, Venus may indicate miscarriages for women. Placed in the wrong zoidia, with a waning moon and the testimony of malefics, men may be castrated or have their genitals injured, and women may be sterile. Venus is associated with the liver, the flesh in general, and the sense of smell.

- **Mercury,** when oriental, gives a yellowish complexion and moderate height. When occidental, Mercury gives a body that is smaller and leaner and ruddy. Mercury participates in ailments when it is configured with the malefics. He helps Saturn prolong illness and gather obstructing fluids in the throat, chest, and stomach. With Mars, Mercury produces greater dryness, as in sore eyes, skin eruptions, and the "sacred disease" - probably epilepsy. Mercury is associated with the tongue, bile, buttocks, and the faculties of speech and reason.

- **Sun** contributes to other planets by providing greater robustness and impressiveness. Sun is the faculty of sight, and its body parts include the brain and heart.

- **Moon** contributes to a body of better proportion and greater slenderness: this seems at odds with our usual understanding of Moon as the wet planet. Moon is associated with the stomach and womb, and governs the faculty of taste. In a general way, Sun governs right-handed parts and the Moon the left-handed parts.

When discussing ailments, Ptolemy mentions blindness. Later we will note star positions that can cause blindness. Ptolemy also felt that planets contribute to blindness:

- **Mars** can cause blindness from a blow, from iron or burning.

- **Mercury** can cause blindness from accidents in assemblies and gymnasiums and from attack by malevolent people.

- **Saturn** can cause blindness from cataracts, chills, and glaucoma, which are different kinds of obstructions.

Ptolemy also mentions conditions that help in the course of illness. If planets can overcome factors responsible for an illness, the illness can be moderate and treatable.

- **Jupiter** may bring the help of a wealthy or honorable person. In modern times this may indicate one's insurance coverage.

- With **Mercury**, treatment is possible through effective drugs or good physicians.

- **Venus** moderates an illness by divine healing - from oracles and gods.

- **Saturn** offers cure through the exposition and confession of the disease. This suggests to me modern group therapy or support groups, or counseling.

- **Mercury** offers the possibilities of being able to gain financially from the illness itself. We might publish a book about our illness or go on radio talk shows.

Character and Quality of Soul

Once again we rely on Ptolemy; he gives us the first systematic "psychological" astrology[4]. We'll deal with this material extensively in Chapter Five. Ptolemy is less concerned about the unconscious or introspective nature but rather behavior: how a person is disposed toward others, how someone acts. You could say that Ptolemy depicts character as *others* might appraise it - more from an objective than from a subjective viewpoint.

Ptolemy's description of the quality of soul follows the two chapters on the body that we have already discussed. His technique for determining the quality of the body is to examine the Ascendant and Moon, their position, their positions and dignities of their planetary lords, and what planets come into contact with them. For soul, it is to examine Moon and Mercury and their lords, in the same way. A full interpretation of the person would include body and soul together. Ptolemy believes that the soul can be described as objectively as the body. Different planets give different descriptions of character and behavior. Much depends, however, on the fortune or ill fortune of a planet's placement. We are seeing the planets from a different viewpoint than before. This is not because the planets have changed but because we are asking different questions.

Saturn, when fortunate, gives *gravitas* - an austere person, one with strong opinions, single-minded or very focused, a worthy friend and a reliable guide. Even when fortunate, however, a Saturn person is vulnerable to envy, greediness and miserliness, and may suffer from being too harsh (Ptolemy says "quick to punish.")

When unfortunate, Saturn is much worse: withdrawn, cowardly, possibly treacherous to others, and lacking in affection. Using words I would never use with my clients, Ptolemy calls these people "sordid" and "shameless." From our previous discussion we know that Saturn can incline us toward activities we might be ashamed of.

Jupiter, assisting Saturn, smoothes over Saturn's rougher edges, bringing out more warmth and nobility; Mars assisting brings out more harshness and vulgarity. With Venus, malevolent Saturn

---

4.   Ptolemy, *Tetrabiblos, Book III*. Ch. 14.

occupies itself with interpersonal matters - disliking women, being rigid, unpleasant, or unsociable. Interestingly, Ptolemy also contends that Saturn with Venus can make one blasphemous and impious - perhaps bringing together Saturn's cynicism and Venus's worldliness.

Jupiter, as indicator of quality of soul, is much pleasanter, to say the least. Jupiter's natural generosity, magnificence, and high-mindedness pervade one's character. This is more clearly the case when Jupiter is well placed. If it is not so well placed, Jupiter gives a tendency to not follow through on what one promises; one may lack the good perspective and honor that Jupiter in better condition may give.

Assisted by Venus, Jupiter gains a more affectionate nature, but if Venus is poorly placed, a person may be more frivolous and superficial. Mercury, when well placed, gives a more intellectual and skillful quality to Jupiter, but if not well placed, Mercury can make the Jupiter person babbling and dull-witted.

The **Mars** personality is active, ready to attack - I think of the hockey player throwing down his gloves, or the "hooligan" soccer fan in the stands. Mars people are also inventive and industrious, but can be treacherous and harsh. Venus helps this person's manners and elegance, and gives greater affection, but if Venus is poorly placed, he or she may be a coarse ogler and a seducer.

The **Venus** personality is far more pleasing and easy to get on with. Such a person, when Venus is well placed, is elegant and charming, cultured and tasteful. If Venus is not well placed, this person may become more careless, timid, and indiscriminate. Mercury assisting, when fortunate, brings out more artistry and eloquence; when unfortunate, Mercury inclines the Venus person to phoniness, ulterior motives and flattery.

Mercury inclines one to shrewdness, thoughtfulness, and quick thinking. Under less favorable conditions, Mercury people can be impulsive, forgetful, uncertain in intellect and frequently wrong.

Here are a couple of examples of planets that signify one's character. Both men have Mars as principal significator of quality of soul. Let's return to **William Blake**. Which planet is most capable of signifying the nature of Blake's character and behavior? We will learn how to determine such a dispositor in a later chapter. For now, trust that **Mars** has the most factors of disposition over the places of the Moon and Mercury, and also has affinity with the zoidion of the Ascendant. Mars is the planet that governs Blake's soul. How can Blake's behavior be one of Mars? Although he was not a soldier but a poet, a strident and polemical character is apparent in his poetry. Consider the last stanza of his best-known poem:

> I will not cease from mental fight,
> Nor shall my sword sleep in my hands,
> Until we have built Jerusalem
> In England's green and pleasant land.

With this verse in mind, note the strong aspect between Mars in the Second and Mercury in the Fifth. Mercury, clearly a planetary muse of poetry, is strongly influenced by Mars. How might

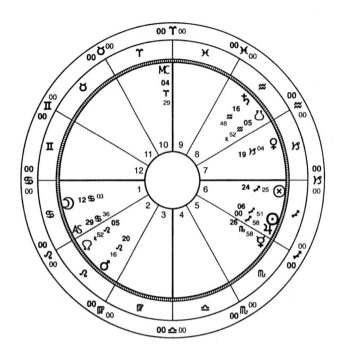

William Blake

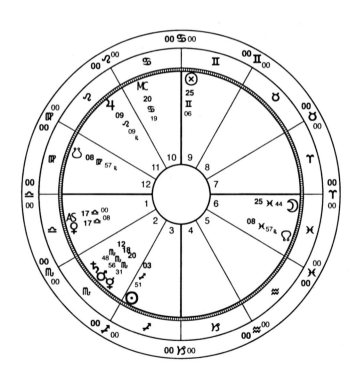

Bill Wilson

you also know that Blake suffered from depression? Notice the opposition from Saturn to Mars. Saturn is in its own "house" in Aquarius, but it is also in a difficult place (the Eighth) and is out of sect.

Here's another chart with **Mars** as the signifier of the quality of the soul: **Bill Wilson.** Who was Bill Wilson? He was the co-founder of Alcoholics Anonymous, and thus one of the great architects of personal change of the past century. Wilson's chart is very expressive on the subject of character and behavior, and shows how several planets can become involved.

Mars is the main dispositor for Moon and Mercury and governs the quality of Wilson's soul. In Scorpio, his own house, Mars is strongly dignified, and Mars is also present with Mercury and Saturn in Scorpio. Mercury helps us understand Wilson's role as a writer and communicator of ideas, a person with ingenuity and strong verbal skills. Mars is also in the company of Saturn. When young, Saturn may have accounted for his life as an active alcoholic, as Saturn may tend toward the degraded. Well into personal sobriety and public fame, Wilson continued to be haunted by depression: as with Blake, this is another manifestation of Saturn in contact with Mars, the planet signifying one's character.

One other planet is a major factor in Wilson's chart: **Venus.** She is in strong dignity, being in her own house in Libra, and she was rising when Wilson was born. The Ascendant often stands for body and sometimes the appearance of the native. Wilson was well known for his good looks and personal charm.

Sun and Moon

In a later chapter we will examine extensively the Lots of Fortune and Spirit, derived from the Sun and Moon. The Sun and Moon do have specific meanings, but Hellenistic astrologers describe them in less detail than the five starry planets. Sun and Moon are more general significators of the entire chart and its prospects. They give indications about the overall health of a person and can be used to determine length of life. They also have a philosophical or esoteric dimension.

Sun is a king or ruler, the father, or a leader in general. Sun is also the leader of the diurnal sect. Sun is likened to gold and has affinity to the heart, and also bestows practical wisdom. Sun is warm and dry, but neither quality is present to the extremes they would manifest in Mars. In ancient astrological prediction, Sun would indicate changes in reputation, honor, and leadership.

Moon signifies females, especially mother, but also women relatives, nurses, landladies, and a woman cohabiting with or married to you. The emphasis seems to be on domestic partners rather than romantic partners. As we will see later, Ptolemy sees Moon as the non-rational quality of the Soul, since it is the most body-like of the planets. In general, Moon gives indications about vitality and the health of the body.

Seven Ages of Person

We meet the planets again in yet one more context, that of human development. Notice, too, that the planets have *numbers* that are part of their nature. We will encounter some of these numbers again when we discuss planets as lords or *Chronocrators* of time in different predictive systems.

The first *four* years of a person's life are governed by **Moon** - the Moon is moist by nature, grows quickly, and changes continually, just like people of that age.

Mercury governs the following *ten* years. During this time we are increasingly able to talk and reason, and to develop our mind. At this time a child goes off to school. This takes us to age fourteen.

For the following *eight* years, **Venus** is in charge. This is the time of sexual maturation and raging hormones. Venus governs this age until twenty-two.

The fourth age is governed by **Sun**: for *nineteen* years. At this stage we are in the prime of life, which is the most public of times. We throw away our childish concerns; we embark on a career and the pursuit of distinction and honor. This takes us to forty-one.

Mars follows, unfortunately. For the following *fifteen* years, we are beset by struggles and problems. This corresponds to a rather long midlife crisis.

Beginning at age fifty-six, **Jupiter** dominates for the next *twelve* years. The hard work is over, and we gain wisdom and perspective: we become an elder.

Old age begins at sixty-nine and is of the nature of **Saturn**. Old age accords well with Saturn's dry and cold nature. Our mind begins to fail, our senses flatten, and we are less able to enjoy life. This period lasts until death.

Conclusion: Valens' Summary of The Planets

At the very beginning of his encyclopedic *Anthology*[5], Vettius Valens provides some interesting sound bytes for the planets. Three should be obvious: **Jupiter** is opinion, reputation and public esteem. **Mars** is action and difficulty. **Venus** is love, desire, and beauty. **Mercury** is law, custom, and fidelity (I'm not sure about this last one).

For **Saturn** Valens suggests "ignorance, necessity." The word "necessity" here is *ananke*, which is in part our being stuck with the results of our past ignorant activity. We all know how intractable our habitual neurotic patterns can be. (This is in contrast with *heimarmene*, which is what is allotted to us, such as the length of our lives.)

Valens, who calls the **Sun** the "eye of intellect" (*nous*), also likens Sun to light. Sun is the light of intellect, or consciousness, perhaps the unchanging awareness that attends to our perception of phenomena, and the means whereby we gain in understanding, wisdom, and contemplation of being.

The **Moon** Valens likens to "forethought" or *pronoia*, which is also intentional activity directed toward a goal. If we want to get into law school, we have to take the law boards, and we had better get a study guide - *pronoia* is an awareness that propels us into the future. For some time I had been baffled by this attribution of forethought to the Moon. I now think of this using more of our modern concepts of Moon: she symbolizes our ability to keep in tune with the rhythms of life, and, when aiming for a higher purpose, in tune with the harmony of the cosmos. A Stoic principle that informed

5.   Valens, Book I, Ch. 1.

How Should we Include the Modern Planets?

The invisible planets **Uranus**, **Neptune**, and **Pluto** were not discovered until modern times. They all move far more slowly than Saturn, the slowest visible planet, and must be looked at differently from the ones we've discussed so far. In this book I do not use these planets, since my focus is on the visible planets. In my own astrological practice, however, I continue to find the modern planets important for good interpretation - in their own place.

Using Uranus, Neptune, or Pluto to govern or be affiliated to specific zoidia has always struck me as a bad idea. Like the 800-pound gorilla in the well-known joke, the modern planets sit where they want: they tend to dominate the zoidion where they're placed. For this reason it makes no sense that Pluto, for example, would be weaker in Taurus or neutral in Sagittarius or more itself in Scorpio. One cannot say that an outer planet is better placed in one zoidion than another. These planets also move too slowly for their presence in a zoidion to mean much to an individual. In my own astrological practice, I confine their use to instances when they are conjunct an angle of a chart or are strongly conjunct or in aspect to one of the seven visible planets. Modern planets can add much to our understanding of how the visible planets functions in a person's chart. For that reason I mention them here. Although Uranus, Neptune, and Pluto are not "higher octaves" of anything, they do have resemblances to specific visible planets.

Uranus is an extreme version of **Mercury**. Uranus adds a note of upheaval and unpredictability as well as genius. Uranus mirrors Mercury's quickness and elusiveness, and requires freedom and spontaneity to function well.

Neptune adds a fluid, mysterious, and often illusory quality. Neptune suggests an otherworldly, ineffable dimension, which can wreck a person's sense of certainty and stability. In some ways, Neptune mirrors **Venus'** sense of longing, without its ability to be satisfied.

Pluto, like **Mars**, relates to power and power-struggles, although Pluto has a much more subtle and hidden dimension. Named for the Olympian God of the underworld, Pluto is the only planet of the three whose meaning corresponds to the God after which it was named.

ancient astrology proposed that our purpose is to act according to the conscious intention of the universe. Sun may help us do that through the use of intellect; Moon helps us adapt creatively to the vicissitudes of life.

In the next chapter, we'll add to our understanding of the planets by describing their affinity to signs of the zodiac. The affinity between planets and signs is a fittingly complex and relevant feature of ancient astrology that needs to be looked at thoroughly.

3

KINSHIP OF PLANETS AND THE ZODIAC

We begin with a simple question: "What is the relationship between the planets and the zodiac?" They relate in a number of ways, but most basic is that of kinship or affiliation. These relationships help us better understand the planets and the zodiac when we see how they work together. The word we translate as "affiliation," is from a Greek word suggesting kinship, which is from a root word meaning "home." Different planets are at home in different ways in different zoidia, and each planet is likewise not at all at home in some zoidia.

Whether being in a particular zoidion helps or hinders a planet brings us to the concepts of **dignity and debility**. There are many categories of dignity to be considered: the two kinds of dignity that have survived into modern astrology are the "sign rulers" for the planets or the houses of the planets, and their exaltations. A planet in *its own zoidion* is clearly at home, and placed in the opposite zoidion - *its detriment* - a planet is uncomfortable and weakened. (Detriment was a more important factor in medieval and modern astrology than in the Hellenistic tradition.) Each planet has a zodiac sign in which it is *exalted*; when placed in its opposite, it is *fallen or depressed*.

Hellenistic astrology gave us other systems of dignity that were carried forward into modern times but are not widely used today. These are the systems of *triplicities*, which differentiate diurnal and nocturnal charts, *bounds*, which divide each zoidion into unequal segments, and *decanic faces*, which divide each zoidion into equal segments of ten degrees each. This means that the planet is also dignified if in the zoidion in which it is the triplicity lord, or the portions of a zoidion where the planet is bound lord or decanic face lord. There are no debilities in these additional systems. A *dodekatamorion*, or harmonic placement of a planet, is in some way another system of dignity, and we will conclude with this factor. (Because of all these qualities of familiarity, a planet - or more than one planet - can act on behalf of the sign or zoidion. This is the concept of **dispositorship**, which we will take up in the following chapters.) We now tour the various categories of dignity and debility.

Exaltations and Houses

The system of exaltations, which is Babylonian in origin, is probably the oldest system of planetary dignities. Originally, each planet had a specific degree of one zoidion in which it was exalted. When we discuss Lots, we will use these degrees of exaltation for Sun and Moon. Using the specific degrees of exaltation also survives in Indian astrology or Jyotish.

In order to assess planetary strength or weakness, the Hellenistic tradition treated the entire zoidion as a planet's exaltation or depression. Like its Indian cousin, Jyotish, Hellenistic astrology greatly emphasizes this system of familiarity.

Firmicus tells us that the placement of a planet in its exaltation strengthens the natural force of that planet, and when positioned opposite its exaltation, in its depression or fall - the planet loses much of that force.[1] Later tradition referred to a planet placed in its exaltation as an "honored guest". When you are an honored guest, you are treated very well. In return, you tend to act graciously and with dignity: being such a guest brings out the best in you. Being in exaltation may bring out many of a planet's good qualities.

But what happens, then, if you are a guest and you think your host actively dislikes you? This is the condition of a planet being depressed, or in "fall." Its good qualities become muted, and it may act in a distorted or weakened manner. Here are the planets' exaltations and depressions or falls:

Planet	Exaltation	Depression or Fall (opposing sign)
♄	♎	♈
♃	♋	♑
♂	♑	♋
☉	♈	♎
♀	♓	♍
☿	♍	♓
☽	♉	♏

Using the language of modern astrology, I will delineate the planets in the zoidia of their respective exaltations and depressions. The reader should not become too impressed simply by planets being exalted or depressed. There are other factors to consider when assessing a planet.

- **Saturn is exalted in Libra**. Saturn's penchant for organization is useful for Libra's a sense of proportion; Saturn in Libra can embody fairness and objectivity. Libra's airiness lightens Saturn's tendency toward dourness and Libra's idealism relieves some of Saturn's cynicism. In Aries, where Saturn is fallen, Saturn loses its focus and its sense of priorities: Saturn becomes more impulsive and less careful.

- **Jupiter is exalted in Cancer.** Cancer gives additional warmth and emotional resonance to Jupiter's generosity and benevolence. In feminine Cancer, Jupiter's activity may be less grandiose but more personal and truly helpful. In Capricorn, its depression or fall, uplifted Jupiter is confined to a restrictive cold and dry place and for that reason Jupiter underachieves there.

---

1.   Firmicus, pp. 32-34.

- **Mars is exalted in Capricorn**. In Capricorn, Mars' impulsiveness is muted and the planet instead performs with greater intention, practical resourcefulness, and perseverance. In Cancer, however, Mars becomes overly sensitive.

- **Sun is exalted in Aries**. Aries brings out the Sun's fieriness and creativity. Since Sun is at tropical Aries at the beginning of spring, when life begins to flow abundantly, Sun's positive inspiration has many outlets for activity. Sun is depressed in Libra; at this time of the year, nature's life force begins to recede. In modern terms, Libra is relational and outer-focused and its attention to others may disperse the Sun's creative activity.

- **Venus is exalted in Pisces**. Since Venus is a planet about pleasure and desire, Pisces brings out Venus' sympathetic and sensitive nature. In Virgo, Venus has refinement but is drier, less affable, and generally thinks too much.

- **Mercury is exalted in Virgo**, a zoidion that Mercury also governs as its own house. Virgo brings out Mercury's precision and dry analytical abilities. Placed here, Mercury is less likely to indulge in its own cleverness or try to work the system for short-term gain. Mercury's ability to solve problems is enhanced when placed in Virgo. In moist Pisces, Mercury is surely depressed and fallen. Since Pisces is a zoidion of gathering together and emotional resonance (a feminine zoidion during a wet season), Mercury's ability to think clearly and objectively is compromised.

- **Moon is exalted in Taurus**. Moon's responsiveness takes on practicality and steadiness when in Taurus. Here I am reminded of Valens' attribute of forethought or pronoia to Moon. The fertility of Taurus' springtime stands in contrast to the darkening skies of later autumn, the skies of Scorpio. In Taurus, Moon's responses are less impulsive and more moderate, and she can act in a more harmonious manner. Contrast this to Moon in Scorpio. This feminine house of Mars is more extreme in its adaptations and is less trusting of life. There is too much effort, too much angst.

Antiochus of Athens, a late ancient astrologer, wrote about the polarities set up by planets in their exaltations and falls or depressions[2]:

- *Aries opposes Libra.* Sun is exalted in Aries and *Saturn* depressed. In Libra, Saturn is exalted and Sun depressed. This sets up an opposition between Sun, the planet of warmth and light, and Saturn, the planet of coldness and darkness.

- *Cancer opposes Capricorn. Jupiter* is exalted in Cancer, and *Mars* is depressed. In Capricorn, Mars is exalted and Jupiter depressed. Jupiter is about life and abundance, and Mars is about vexation and death.

---

2. Antiochus, Ch. 7.

- *Pisces opposes Virgo.* Venus is exalted in Pisces and *Mercury* is depressed. In Virgo Mercury is exalted and Venus depressed. Venus, the planet of desire, opposes Mercury, the planet of the intellectual faculty, since Pisces opposes Virgo. Antiochus appears to set up a "heart vs. head" polarity.

- *Taurus opposes Scorpio.* Moon is exalted in Taurus and depressed in Scorpio. Since nothing is exalted in Scorpio and fallen in Taurus, Moon is opposed by nothing. Antiochus tells us this: when fortune is high, nobody can depress it, and when fortune is low, nobody can exalt it. We will see later that the Lot of Fortune is the Lot of the Moon, that the Moon is concerned with the changing tides of fortune.

Here is a chart with several planets in exaltation and depression or fall. Saturn, Venus, and Moon are exalted; Mercury and Jupiter are depressed. How might they have affected her? Here is some biographical information that may be of help to you.

Elizabeth Barrett Browning was a well-known English poet from the Victorian era. Sickly and living with a dominating father, she met Robert Browning, another poet, ran off with him to Italy, and was subsequently disowned by her father. She spent the rest of her days living abroad as an expatriate, continuing to write and to be involved in social and political causes. Her most often quoted and parodied lines begin with: "How do I love thee? Let me count the ways."

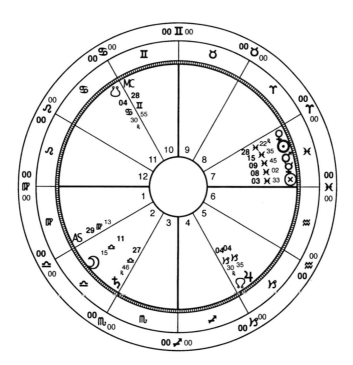

Elizabeth Barrett Browning

Saturn is exalted in Libra, in the same zoidion where one finds her Moon. This may indicate her powerful but difficult father, or may also signify her perseverance under adversity.

Venus is exalted in Pisces. Today she is best known for her love poetry.

Jupiter is fallen in Capricorn. In Italy with her new husband, she devoted herself to political causes and was known as a strong opponent of slavery. In terms of her character, however, I would hesitate to think of her as a generous, gregarious, buoyant person.

Mercury is fallen or depressed in Pisces. This placement does not diminish her intellect or intelligence but may render it more subjective and possibly prone to wishful thinking. Her love poetry, which many modern readers consider too sentimental, displays the Piscean exaltation of Venus and depression of Mercury.

The Houses of the Planets

The houses of the planets are familiar to even to those just starting out in astrology, although they're often referred to as "the signs that the planets rule." A planet in its own house is like you in your own house - you're at home there. Your favorite prints are on your walls; your favorite books are on your bed stand; you know what food is in the refrigerator and you may remember how long it has been there. The planet has much in common with the zoidion that is its house: it may be itself there, but, unlike an exalted planet, it may not be at its best. We will discover this to be the case with Saturn and Mars.

<hr>

The word "house," in Latin and in Greek

Astrologers currently use the word "house" to depict the zodiac, beginning with the Ascendant forming twelve segments of the "mundane sphere," bounded by the Ascendant and Midheaven axes and the intermediate cusps.

English astrologers in the past, translating the Latin word *domus*, used "house" for a different purpose: to depict planets where they are most at home, e.g., Aries is the "house" of Mars, Taurus the house of Venus, and so on.

Astrologers translated the Latin *domus* from the Greek *oikos*, which is a place where one lives or an area that is inhabited. ("Economy" is literally "law of the house.") A vacant house is not an "oikos," because nobody lives there: your *oikos* would not be your investment real estate but where you live. You would be comfortable, "at home," in your own house, and a planet in its own house has the same quality.

Those people who live in your house with you are your familiars, whether family or intimates or house mates. If you live with complete strangers, it is because you are in some kind of institution or shelter, not your own house. If you are not comfortable in your own house, you are in a difficult life situation.

From the Greek root *oikos* comes *oikeiosis*, which means familiarity. Both words are important astrological terms. The Stoic philosophers of antiquity used *oikeiosis* to describe how we learn to live in the best way.[3] One first develops ties of familiarity with oneself, then with those who are close, eventually with strangers and ultimately with the entire world, the *oikomenikon*. (This is where the word "ecumenical" comes from.)

The "houses" of planets is only one of the categories of familiarity among many. There is a natural fit between the planet and the sign or zoidion.

Below is a diagram that shows the pattern of the houses of the planets. The attribution of the planets to their zoidia follows a symmetry that was lost when astrologers began to include Uranus, Neptune, and Pluto. We will find that this pattern appears later when we discuss aspects.

Here many astrologers will recognize something similar to the symmetries from the 0 Cancer/ 0 Capricorn axis - the antiscia, or from the 0 Aries/0 Libra axis - the contra-antiscia. One needs to look at this diagram slightly differently, however. Think of this circle not by positions being symmetrical to one degree, as are antiscia and contra-antiscia, but constituting two almost identical but distinct halves. One half proceeds forward from Leo and the Sun, the other half proceeds backwards from Cancer and the Moon. You will notice that the governing planets proceed from the Sun and Moon in the order of the speed of their orbits, beginning with Mercury and ending with Saturn, the lord of Aquarius and Capricorn and opposite the zoidia of the luminaries Leo and Cancer.

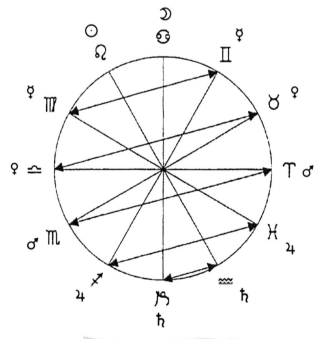

The Houses of the Planets

---

3.   Annas, Julia (1993) pp. 262-276.

Sun and Moon. Sun's house is Leo, the fixed summertime masculine zoidion that also is affiliated with kingship and the heart. Moon's house is Cancer, which is cardinal and feminine. Possibly this system began at a time during which Cancer and Leo were the zoidia of the most light during the northern hemisphere year. (Today the zoidia with the most light are Gemini and Cancer.)

Each starry planet has two houses. Each starry planet is at home in two zoidia, one a masculine and the other a feminine zoidion. People with two residences are at home in both places, and so are these planets. However, of the two houses, one is more the primary residence. Hephaistio, quoting Dorotheus, indicates that each planet prefers one of the two residences.

Backward from Cancer house is *Gemini*; forward from Leo is *Virgo*. These are the two houses of *Mercury*: the masculine Gemini and the feminine Virgo. Mercury in masculine Gemini is outgoing and talkative. Mercury in Gemini is the kind or person you want to have at a party or a brainstorming session. Feminine Virgo - also Mercury's sign of exaltation - is more responsible, thorough, and dependable. This is the person who helps organize and clean up after your party, and the favored person in an implementation session at work. Hephaistio, quoting Dorotheus, tells us that Mercury prefers Virgo to Gemini.[4]

Backward three zoidia from Cancer is *Taurus*[5], and forward three zoidia from Leo is *Libra*. These are the two houses of *Venus*: the feminine Taurus and the masculine Libra. Fixed feminine Taurus is more sensual and more straightforwardly in pursuit of its own pleasure. Libra, the masculine and cardinal sign, is more elegant and harmonizing. Nocturnal Venus prefers Taurus to Libra. The astrological aspect that is three zoidia away is the *sextile*, and the sextile is the nature of Venus.

Backward four zoidia from Cancer is *Aries*, and forward four zoidia from Leo is *Scorpio*. Both Aries and Scorpio are the houses of *Mars*. Aries is masculine and cardinal: here Mars can be as if on steroids. Nocturnal Mars prefers the Scorpio to Aries, since the fixed feminine zoidion tones down Mars' recklessness and bravado, and gives opportunities for meaningful - not pointless - conflict. Four zoidia away gives us the potent but stressful aspect of the *square*, and the square is the nature of Mars.

Going backward five zoidia from Cancer, you arrive at *Pisces*; going forward five zoidia from Leo brings you to *Sagittarius*. Feminine Pisces and masculine Sagittarius are the houses of *Jupiter*. Placed in Sagittarius, Jupiter has buoyancy and a tendency to expand. In feminine Pisces, Jupiter has greater faith and compassion. Diurnal Jupiter prefers Sagittarius. Five zoidia away gives us the aspect of the *trine*, a positive aspect that is the nature of Jupiter.

Opposing Cancer, six zoidia away, is *Capricorn*; opposing Leo is *Aquarius*. Feminine Capricorn and Masculine Aquarius are the houses of *Saturn*. Similar to their zoidia of exaltation and depression, there's a natural opposition between Sun and Moon and the planet of darkness - Saturn. This cold and dry planet is quite at home in cold and dry Capricorn. Saturn here maintains a consistent humorlessness and negative attitude. In masculine Aquarius, Saturn is capable of greater flexibility than in Capricorn. Diurnal Saturn prefers Aquarius to Capricorn. The aspect of the *opposition* is of the nature of Saturn.

---

4.   Hephaistio, Book I, Ch, 7.
5.   Counting the beginning zoidion as "one."

Is a planet undignified when in zoidia opposite its own house? What is the status of Venus in Aries or Mercury in Sagittarius? Later tradition, as mentioned before, considers planets are in these places to be in *detriment*. There is almost no mention of planets opposite their houses in Hellenistic astrology. In fact, in many of Vettius Valens' chart examples, planets are in zoidia that we would consider their detriments, yet Valens does not attend to this. Instead, a planet in depression or fall - opposite its exaltation - is a major consideration for Valens.

In one passage, however, Antiochus of Athens describes planetary polarities based upon the houses of the planets[6]: This is similar to his depiction of planetary polarities based on exaltation and depression that we examined above.

The houses of *Saturn* (Aquarius and Capricorn) oppose the houses of the *Sun* (Leo) and *Moon* (Cancer), since light is opposed by darkness.

The houses of *Jupiter* (Sagittarius and Pisces) oppose the houses of *Mercury* (Gemini and Virgo), since Jupiter desire's for abundance and possessions contradicts the intellectual quality of Mercury.

The houses of *Venus* (Taurus and Libra) oppose the houses of *Mars* (Scorpio and Aries), since delight and pleasure oppose fear and war.

Here is a natal chart with many planets in their own houses or opposite their own houses. We can use these planetary placements to understand her natal chart further.

In the late 1980s, **Corazon Aquino** became the leader of a popular rebellion against the Philippine dictator Marcos, and, when Marcos went into exile, she became president of the Philippines. Associates of Marcos had killed her husband a few years previously. Mrs. Aquino combined a restrained and humble personal style with quiet determination.

You will find these qualities in Aquino's natal chart by looking at planets in or opposite their own houses. *In context*, planets opposite the signs of their own houses (in detriment) can contribute to a person's success. Aquino's Sun and Jupiter are opposite their own houses. Yet Sun is with a dignified Saturn, and Jupiter is in the powerful Tenth place from the Ascendant. Aquino allowed herself to be carried forward by circumstance and provided a gentler and more humane alternative to the flamboyant dictator Ferdinand Marcos.

What is the effect of a debilitated planet upon the planet and the native? Recall from Chapter Two that Ptolemy used beneficial or difficult placements of planets to distinguish between the positive and negative characters of people. A planet placed well - in its own exaltation or house - appears to act more faithfully to its nature and more appropriately to the occasion; placed poorly, that planet's activity may be defective or excessive.

In a famous example from *Nicomachean Ethics*,[7] Aristotle discusses the virtue of courage as a positive response to fear; cowardice and recklessness are deficiencies of courage because they are extreme responses to conditions of danger. In the same way, a debilitated Mars can limit or overdo its activity, and thus lose its courage, giving way to being cowardly or reckless. This also may be the

---

6. Antiochus, Ch. 8
7. Aristtotle, Book II, Ch. 2.

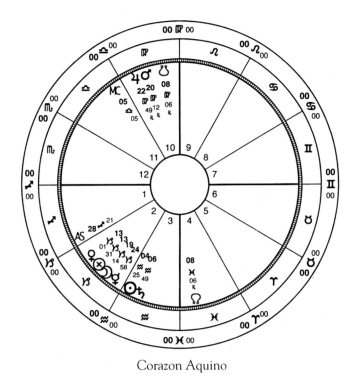

Corazon Aquino

case with other planets, based upon their dignity or debility. Venus can limit or exaggerate love and sensuality; Mercury can do the same with cleverness, Jupiter with abundance and optimism, and Saturn with discipline and resolve. This weakness can be compensated for by the creative activity of the native, and often this is the case.

The malefics, Mars and Saturn, demonstrate a paradox: Mars may be in its own house in Aries but can be reckless there; Saturn is at home in Capricorn, but this is a gloomy Saturn. A charged Mars or burdened Saturn may not be better for the native by being in its own house. This is due to that fact that a malefic tends toward extremes.

Aries is closer to Mars' qualities of heat and dryness; Capricorn is closer to Saturn's qualities of coldness and dryness. These intrinsic qualities need to be moderated. Venus and Jupiter may help do this when in aspect to a malefic.

Triplicities, Bounds, Decanic Faces

Three additional categories of dignity were lost to astrology from 1700 until late in the twentieth century, when they reappeared as astrologers rediscovered the work of William Lilly. The Hellenistic era used these dignities differently from the seventeenth century in England.

Triplicities

A planet in its own triplicity has dignity in that zoidion, even if that planet is in debility by house or exaltation. We return to the zoidia in trine to each other. This gives us four groups of three zoidia each, which correspond to the elements fire, air, earth, and water. Fire and air triplicities form the six masculine zoidia, earth and water triplicities form the feminine zoidia. Below is the diagram we first encountered in Chapter One, showing the zoidia that are in trine relationship to one another. Here we show the different zoidia that share the same triplicity lords.

I have chosen to use the Dorothean, rather than the Ptolemaic, sequence of triplicity lords. There are three lords for each triplicity: by day, by night, and a common or participating lord. For purposes of a planet being in dignity, we are concerned only with the triplicity lord that is in sect. For the purposes of a planet's dispositor, which is the topic of the next chapter, we will use the other two.

Triplicities synthesize planetary sect, the planetary houses discussed above, and the elements assigned to signs or zoidia.

	Day	**Night**	**Participating**
Aries, Leo, Sagittarius	Sun	Jupiter	Saturn
Gemini, Libra, Aquarius	Saturn	Mercury	Jupiter
Taurus, Virgo, Capricorn	Venus	Moon	Mars
Cancer, Scorpio, Pisces.	Venus	Mars	Moon

Aries, Leo, and *Sagittarius* are the zoidia of the fiery triplicity. Their triplicity lords are *Sun by day, Jupiter by night, and Saturn as participating lord.* Sun, the leader of the diurnal sect, is in its exaltation in Aries and its own house in Leo. Jupiter's house is Sagittarius. Saturn is the participating lord as he is the remaining diurnal planet.

The airy triplicity is *Gemini, Libra,* and *Aquarius.* Their triplicity lords are *Saturn by day, Mercury by night, and Jupiter as participating lord.* Saturn is the exaltation of Libra and has Aquarius as one of its houses. Mercury is the lord of Gemini. Jupiter remains as a diurnal planet and is participating lord. (Sun is in fall in Libra and opposite its house in Aquarius.) You may notice that the lords for the fiery triplicity are more diurnal than those of the airy triplicity.

The earthy triplicity is *Taurus, Virgo,* and *Capricorn.* Its triplicity lords are *Moon by night, Venus by day, and Mars as participating lord.* Moon is the exaltation of Taurus and the leader of the nocturnal sect. The triplicity lord by day is Venus, the lord of the house of Taurus. The participating ruler, Mars, is exalted in Capricorn.

The watery triplicity is *Cancer, Scorpio,* and *Pisces.* Its triplicity lords are *Mars by night, Venus by day, and Moon as participating ruler.* Scorpio is the house of Mars. Venus is exalted in Pisces. (Ptolemy uses Mars for day and night charts.). The participating lord is Moon, lord of the house in Cancer.

A planet can be in its own triplicity and yet be otherwise debilitated. Moon in Scorpio or Mars in Cancer in a night chart are in depression but in their own triplicities, which mitigates the

The Triplicities

factor of their being in fall. Venus in Virgo and Saturn in Leo in a day chart are weakened by depression (Venus) or detriment (Saturn), yet all are in their own triplicities.

Following the idea that the triplicities have an element in common, a planet in its triplicity has something in common with the zoidion of its triplicity. How might this work?

I offer an analogy to explain this. If you are an artist or astrologer, you might find yourself uncomfortable in a gathering of corporate climbers or skeptics. Nobody looks or acts like you do, but soon you find people who are like you in some important way - who may be Syrian, hockey fans, or gay - or all three. You are more comfortable now - you're more "in your element" - but still you're not completely at home with these people.

A planet its own triplicity can be a strong planet. If you have a nocturnal chart, Mercury in Gemini, Libra, or Aquarius is in his own triplicity. In a nocturnal chart, Moon in Capricorn or Virgo is in its own triplicity. A planet already dignified is enhanced if in its own triplicity. Moon in Taurus is both exalted and, in a night chart, is in her own triplicity; Saturn in Libra exalted and, in a day chart, is in his own triplicity.

Dividing the Zoidia into Bounds

"Bounds" divide each zoidion into five unequal parts, each administered by one of the five starry planets: Saturn, Jupiter, Mars, Venus, or Mercury. At first glance the planetary attributions seem arbitrary, but there are some patterns. The planet early in a zoidion's degrees usually has dignity by house, exaltation, or triplicity. Either Mars or Saturn - the one not in dignity in that zoidion - is bound lord for the last degrees of the zoidion.

There are different sets of bounds in the tradition, but all have one feature in common: the total number of degrees given to each planet are identical - Saturn has 57, Jupiter 79, Mars 66, Venus 82, and Mercury 76. These numbers correspond to different units of time that ancient astrologers have used when calculating the length of a person's life. Finding a powerful placement - planet or angle - in the chart and proceeding from its bound lord is often used for these calculations.

"Bounds" or "Terms"?

From William Lilly and others, traditional astrologers have presented this division to be the "terms" of the planets. The Greek word is *horia*, which are boundaries. In modern English, the first dictionary definition of "term" is some kind of denotation, e.g., "scientific terms." The second definition, which is relevant to us, is a limit: "terms of surrender." Often the limit is one of temporality: a "term of office" or a pregnancy coming to "full term." Because the bounds of a planet are related to determining life expectancy, the more temporal "terms" does fit.

Recent writers on ancient astrology have used "bounds" for this division. This is another word for boundary, used in the phrases "the bounds of sense" or "out of bounds," which implies boundaries of space and time. "Bounds" may indeed be slightly closer to "horia," and be less complex in its ordinary use than "terms." It was by contemplating the word "boundless" that I settled on calling them "bounds."

There are two major sets of bounds. The traditional "Egyptian" bounds are used pervasively in Hellenistic astrology. Ptolemy presents these traditional bounds, but then proposes a different set of bounds he had uncovered that he says seem more logical to him.[8] What follows are the Egyptian list and Ptolemy's revision of it. You may notice important differences in Leo, Libra, and Aquarius.

These boxes have three columns after each zoidion. After each planet, the next column lists how many degrees in that bound, and the third lists at what degree the bound *ends*. The five starry planets are distributed in their bounds, and arranged into rows. In Libra, the first six degrees are the bounds of Saturn. Those of Mercury proceed from six degrees for eight additional degrees until just before fourteen degrees Libra. Jupiter is the lord of the following bound of seven degrees.

The Egyptian system is the oldest extant version of the bounds. Ptolemy's list came to be preferred later due to the enormous influence Ptolemy had on later Hellenistic astrology. Firmicus, writing in the fourth century, used the Egyptian system. Others undoubtedly did also. Ptolemy's system was used during the Middle Ages in Europe, was used by William Lilly in the seventeenth century, and thus became the default system of modern traditional astrologers.

I tend to favor the Egyptian system for no other reason than, as Robert Zoller has repeatedly said, "the old ways are the good ways." For the most part I will use the Egyptian system. When using Ptolemy's techniques for determining the nature and quality of the native's soul, however, I'll use

---

8.   *Tebrabiblos*, Book I, Chap. 21 .

Aries			Taurus			Gemini			Cancer			Leo			Virgo		
♃	6	6	♀	8	8	☿	6	6	♂	7	7	♃	6	6	☿	7	7
♀	6	12	☿	6	14	♃	6	12	♀	6	13	♀	5	11	♀	10	17
☿	8	20	♃	8	22	♀	5	17	☿	6	19	♄	7	18	♃	4	21
♂	5	25	♄	5	27	♂	7	24	♃	7	26	☿	6	24	♂	7	28
♄	5	30	♂	3	30	♄	6	30	♄	4	30	♂	6	30	♄	2	30
Libra			Scorpo			Sagit.			Capri.			Aquarius			Pisces		
♄	6	6	♂	7	7	♃	12	12	☿	7	7	☿	7	7	♀	12	12
☿	8	14	♀	4	11	♀	5	17	♃	7	14	♀	6	13	♃	4	16
♃	7	21	☿	8	19	☿	4	21	♀	8	22	♃	7	20	☿	3	19
♀	7	28	♃	5	24	♄	5	26	♄	4	26	♂	5	25	♂	9	28
♂	2	30	♄	6	30	♂	4	30	♂	4	30	♄	5	30	♄	2	30

Egyptian Bounds

Bounds according to
Ptolemy

Aries			Taurus			Gemini			Cancer			Leo			Virgo		
♃	6	6	♀	8	8	☿	7	7	♂	6	6	♄	6	6	☿	7	7
♀	8	14	☿	7	15	♃	6	13	♃	7	13	☿	7	13	♀	6	13
☿	7	21	♃	7	22	♀	7	20	☿	7	20	♀	6	19	♃	5	18
♂	5	26	♄	4	26	♂	6	24	♀	7	27	♃	6	25	♄	6	24
♄	4	30	♂	4	30	♄	4	30	♄	3	30	♂	5	30	♂	6	30
Libra			Scorpo			Sagit.			Capri.			Aquarius			Pisces		
♄	6	6	♂	6	6	♃	8	8	♀	6	6	♄	6	6	♀	8	8
♀	5	11	♃	8	14	♀	6	14	☿	6	12	☿	6	12	♃	6	14
♃	8	19	♀	7	21	☿	5	19	♃	7	19	♀	8	20	☿	6	20
☿	5	24	☿	6	27	♄	6	25	♂	6	25	♃	5	25	♂	6	26
♂	6	30	♄	3	30	♂	5	30	♄	5	30	♂	5	30	♄	4	30

Ptolemy's bounds and note where the Egyptian system differs. We must now ask: how does one use bounds?

A bound lord is one more planet who can handle the affairs of a sign or zoidion: a dispositor. We will see in Chapter Five, when we discuss the *oikodespotes* or almuten, that a bound lord has a voice equal to any other category; the bound lord helps determine which planet may govern a particular place. Antiochus tells us that a planet is helped when in the bounds of a benefic, hindered in the bounds of a malefic.[9] A planet in its own bounds has dignity there - yet is unclear to me exactly how. Paulus tells us that a planet in its own bounds rejoices as if it were in its own house or exaltation.[10]

Decanic Faces

A system of decans divides the zodiac into thirty-six equal segments. Each zoidion is portioned into segments of ten degrees each - hence "decans," meaning ten.

Some modern astrologers use another decan system that was imported from the Indian tradition during the medieval era.[11] According to that system, the lords of the three decans are the lords of the zoidia of the triplicity of that zoidion. Capricorn, of the earth triplicity, has Saturn as the first planetary ruler for the first ten degrees, then Venus (for Taurus) the second portion of ten degrees, and Mercury (for Virgo) governs the third. In Aquarius, of the air triplicity, Saturn governs the first ten degrees, Mercury (for Gemini) governs the second, and Venus (for Libra) governs the third.

The Hellenistic tradition gives us a different system. In this system we divide the zodiac into the same thirty-six segments, with each zoidion having three decanic faces. Here Mars governs the first decan or face of Aries. Sun governs the second decan of Aries, and Venus governs the third decan. Mercury is the decan lord of the first face of Taurus, Moon of the second and so on. Repeating throughout is the order of the descending spheres of the seven visible planets: Saturn, Jupiter, Mars, Sun, Venus, Mercury, and Moon. The complete table follows.

One cannot present the sequence of decans without noting how the planetary days of the week follow them. I illustrate with the first four zoidia. Remember that Tuesday is the day of Mars, Wednesday the day of Mercury, Thursday the day of Jupiter, and Friday the day of Venus.

Day of Week	0 - 10	10 - 20	20 -30	Zoidion
Tuesday	♂	☉	♀	♈
Wednesday	☿	☽	♄	♉
Thursday	♃	♂	☉	♊
Friday	♀	☿	☽	♋

---

9.   Antiochus, Part I, Ch. 12.
10. Paulus, Ch. 3.
11. March & McEvers (1977) Lesson 12.

♈ Aries		♉ Taurus		♊ Gemini		♋ Cancer		♌ Leo		♍ Virgo	
Face	Dg	Face	Dg	Face	Dg	Face	Dg	Face	Dg	Face	Dg
Mars	10	Mercury	10	Jupiter	10	Venus	10	Saturn	10	Sun	10
Sun	20	Moon	20	Mars	20	Mercury	20	Jupiter	20	Venus	20
Venus	30	Saturn	30	Sun	30	Moon	30	Mars	30	Mercury	30
♎ Libra		♏ Scorpio		♐ Sagit.		♑ Capri.		♒ Aquar.		♓ Pisces	
Face	Dg	Face	Dg	Face	Dg	Face	Dg	Face	Dg	Face	Dg
Moon	10	Mars	10	Mercury	10	Jupiter	10	Venus	10	Saturn	10
Saturn	20	Sun	20	Moon	20	Mars	20	Mercury	20	Jupiter	20
Jupiter	30	Venus	30	Saturn	30	Sun	30	Moon	30	Mars	30

The Faces of the Zoidia

This system probably originated with the Egyptians, who, for the purposes of calculating time, divided the visible sky into thirty-six groupings of stars, and used them to determine the time of night or the week of the year. Decans later became groups of images, or "faces," and the face of the Ascendant would give determinations about your appearance and your body. (This survives well into the medieval tradition.[12]) It was possibly later in the ancient tradition that these segments were given planetary lords.

Much of the lore of the *decanic images* has been lost. The *Liber Hermetis*, an anthology of ancient astrology texts that comes down to us in Latin, renders them into specific images but supplies no sense of how to use them. Later writers give delineations for the decanic faces, but these delineations don't always match the nature of the planetary lords, nor do they correspond with each other.

Antiochus lists decans which "cause licentiousness."[13] In this context, he mentions Sun, Moon, or Ascendant in the third decan of Aries, ruled by Venus. (Nobody seems to like the third slice of Aries.) Other attributions escape my understanding.

Paulus tells us that a planet in its own decan may be treated as if the planet were in it's own house.[14] Using decan placement to calculate a planet's dignity survived into medieval astrology, but it was a very small dignity.

---

12.   See Ibn Ezra, Ch. 2.
13.   Antiochus, Book II, Ch. 6.
14.   Paulus, Ch. 4.

Antiochus and Paulus valued decanic faces, although Ptolemy and others did not use this system to determine a planet's dignity or a zoidion's dispositor. Nor do we have worked-out examples from people who did use them.

The *dodekatamoria*

Here we consider an "advanced" astrological technique: harmonic placements. Similar to bounds and decans a planet's placement in a division of a particular zoidion could make that planet stronger. The criteria for interpretation also return us to our previous discussion of benefics and malefics. In brief, harmonic placements recalculate astrological positions based on multiplying that position by a predetermined number.

Using harmonic placements in astrology has a long and interesting history. Many people are familiar with the *varga* charts of Indian astrology or Jyotish. The best-known varga chart is the *navamsa* or ninth harmonic chart. These charts recast natal placements to give an additional chart that the astrologer also interprets. Contemporary astrologers, following the pioneering work of John Addey, use harmonic placements to look at charts from the viewpoint of different "aspect families." In this way, planetary combinations appear that one would otherwise not see.[15]
I will explain how these are calculated through an example:

A *twelfth* harmonic divides the entire zodiac of the "radical" birth chart into *twelve* equal divisions, *each of which will be cast as an entire zodiac*. In that way, each zoidion of the entire zodiac divides into twelve segments of two and a half degrees each. Each of these two and a half degree segments becomes one zoidion of the harmonic chart. (For the sake of clarity I will italicize the zoidia of the reconstituted harmonic positions.)

In this way first segment (two and a half degrees) of each zoidion is *Aries*, the second *Taurus* up to five degrees. The last two-and-a-half degree segment, the twelfth, is *Pisces*. The resulting planetary positions are all brought together into a new twelfth harmonic chart; any two planets in the original chart that are in close degrees *of any zoidion* will appear to be conjunct in a modern twelfth harmonic.

I supply **Mozart's** chart to illustrate modern twelfth harmonic positions. Mars and Saturn are in early degrees of Cancer and Aquarius: they will both appear in *Aries* in a twelfth harmonic chart. Sun would appear in *Gemini* and Mercury in *Cancer*: although they are close to one another: Sun and Mercury are in different two and a half degree segments (the boundary being seven and a half degrees). Venus, in the last degree of Aquarius, will appear in *Pisces* in a twelfth harmonic chart.

The Indian twelfth harmonic, the dwadasama, does this. The first two and a half degree segment is not *Aries but that zoidion itself*. For the position of 2 Taurus, then, beginning with Taurus, its dwadasama will not be in *Aries* but late within the first segment of *Taurus*, as this is such an early degree. The last segment would not be *Pisces* but the twelfth zoidion from Taurus, which gives us *Aries*. This version has also made its way into modern astrology.[16]

---

15. See Harvey and Harding, *Working with Astrology*.
16. See March & McEvers (1977) Lesson 12.

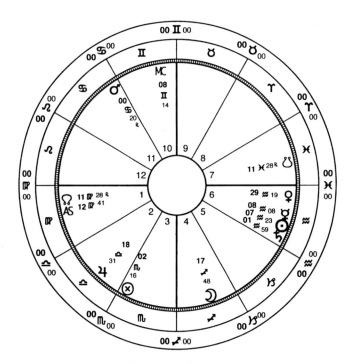

Wolfgang Amadeus Mozart

The Hellenistic variant of the Indian twelfth harmonic is the *dodekatamorion*, which means "twelfth-part." Here, however, the arithmetic is a bit different: one multiplies the natal position not by twelve *but by thirteen*[17].

The number thirteen itself has some interesting properties. Thirteen degrees is close to the average daily motion of the Moon. Thirteen also relates to how the Sun and Moon can move together: if Sun and Moon are in the same early degree of a particular zoidion, they are likely to continue together in the same zoidion each month, and after thirteen "months" of Sun-Moon conjunctions, both return to the same positions.

Why then, do ancient astrologers call the thirteenth harmonic the "twelfth part"? Here one calculates not from 0 Aries but from the position itself, and then goes twelve times. This gives the position times 12 times the original position, which yields a harmonic of 13.

Multiplying by thirteen allows one to begin at the beginning of a zoidion and mathematically arrive at the beginning of the same zoidion: 2 Scorpio continues to be within the zoidion Scorpio. The last degrees of a zoidion will also return to that zoidion Scorpio. A thirteenth harmonic divides each zoidion into segments of 2°18' 28" each.

---

17.   See Robert Hand's discussion of the *dodekatamoria* in the editor's introduction to Valens *Anthology* Book I

One could multiply any position by thirteen and reduce by multiples of 360 to a number below 360 degrees to arrive at the harmonic position. Far easier, however, is to use the division of *every* zoidion into thirteen segments to determine the dodekatamorion of any position in the natal chart. Simply remember that the first division is the zoidion itself, the second the following one, and so on. In this way, one can note dodekatamoria positions simply by noting the natal positions and referring to this table.

First	0° to 2°18' 28"
Second	2°18' 28" to 4°35' 56"
Third	4°35' 56" to 6°55' 24"
Fourth	6°55' 24" to 9°13' 52"
Fifth	9°13' 52" to 11°32' 30"
Sixth	11°32' 30" to 13°50' 58"
Seventh	13°50' 58" to 16°09' 26"
Eighth	16°09' 26" to 18°27' 52"
Ninth	18°27' 52" to 20°46' 20"
Tenth	20°46' 20" to 23°04' 48"
Eleventh	23°04' 48" to 25°23' 16"
Twelfth	25°23' 16" to 27°41' 44"
Thirteenth	27°41' 44" to 30°

Returning to Mozart's chart, recalculated Mars and Saturn, early in Cancer and Aquarius respectively, would remain in *Cancer* and *Aquarius*. Sun at 7 Aquarius 23 and Mercury at 8 Aquarius 08 would be in the fourth division and appear in *Taurus*. Venus in the last degree of Aquarius would appear in *Aquarius*.

According to the Hellenistic tradition as we currently understand it, one is interested in the zoidion, not the degrees, of a dodekatamorion. This is the same as the *varga* charts in Jyotish.

Calculating One Harmonic Position

To illustrate harmonics, I calculate a harmonic placement for one position. First, multiply its degrees and minutes (Aries is 0, Taurus is 30, etc) by the number of the harmonic. Often one will get a number greater than 360. If so, subtract 360 or multiples of 360 until the number becomes less than 360. Converting that number to signs or zoidion and degrees, one arrives at the harmonic placement. Here is an example:

For a twelfth harmonic position for the Sun at 2 degrees Taurus, multiply 32 (two degrees of Taurus from 0 Aries is 30 plus 2) by 12, the number of the harmonic. 32 times 12 gives 384.

Subtracting 384 from 360 gives 24, which corresponds to 24 degrees of *Aries*.

Since 2 Taurus is within the first two and a half degree segment of Taurus, it is clear that its harmonic placement would be in *Aries*.

How could one use these harmonic placements? It is tempting to use the dodekatamoria in a way similar to the Indian navamsa, calculating all positions into an independent chart. One would pay attention to whether the recalculated planets now align with malefics or benefics, note other features of the harmonic chart itself, and note whether the harmonic placements fall in the same zoidia as in the original natal chart. However, there is no evidence for this treatment in Hellenistic astrology.

According to Firmicus, it is bad if the dodekatamorion of the full Moon by day is in the bounds of Mars or Saturn.[18] However, his text abruptly breaks off into another topic, which is usually evidence of that text being corrupt. (Firmicus also uses twelfth harmonic, not thirteenth harmonic, positions.)

According to Paulus, whose text is much clearer and probably closer to the mainstream Hellenistic tradition, dodekatamoria can enhance the goodness or badness of benefics or malefics.[19] This is especially so if a benefic's or malefic's dodekatamoria are in the birthchart in zoidion that are angular or in important places like the zoidion of Sun, Moon, or the Lot of Fortune.

Olympiadorous, commenting on Paulus, adds that one can also calculate the dodekatamoria of important positions and see if they fall in the zoidia of the benefics or malefics. He reverses Paulus' procedure.

Here are three brief illustrations of charts according to Paulus' and Olympaodorous' treatment of dodekatamorion placements. We also note when the dodekatamoria for the luminaries, Ascendant, Midheaven, and the Lot of Fortune fall in each other's zoidia. Since the dodekatamoria of every planet or position does not have these features, I will only mention the ones that do.

Jackie Onassis

The dodekatamorion of the Ascendant is Gemini; of the Midheaven is Leo; and of Lot of Fortune is Scorpio. The dodekatamorion for Onassis' Ascendant falls in Gemini, the same zoidion as her Venus and Jupiter. This enhances their positive qualities and the importance of these two planets, compensating somewhat for their placements in the weak Eighth place from the Ascendant. The Tenth place of Leo in Onassis' natal chart also contains dodekatamoria for Sun, Mercury, and Part of Fortune. The fact that the recalcualted Lot of Fortune falls in the zoidion of the powerful Tenth gives further indication of her material prosperity.

George Bush

The dodekatamorion for Jupiter, Venus, and Moon all fall in Taurus. The dodekatamorion for Ascendant falls in Scorpio. Bush gives us a situation the opposite from that of Jackie Onassis. The dodekatamoria of Moon, Venus and Jupiter all fall in the zoidion of his Midheaven and his Lot of Spirit. In brief, this augurs very well for activities that come from Bush's initiative.

---

18.   Firmicus, pp. 42-43.
19.   Paulus, Ch. 22.

Emily Dickinson

The dodekatamorion of Jupiter falls in Virgo, as does Saturn, the Midheaven, and the Lot of Spirit. What interests us here is that the dodekatamorion of Dickinson's Jupiter, the great benefic, keeps company with some important but problematic positions. In Chapter Six, we will discuss the connection between Dickinson's Saturn and Lot of Spirit, a combination that gives her a great deal of reserve and also perseverance. Jupiter's dodekatamorion adds to this configuration. This contributes greatly to Dickenson's independent and distinctive voice.

We are ready to move into our next area of inquiry. We have taken a tour of how a planet may be dignified or debilitated based upon its placement in a zoidion; now we discover different ways in which a planet can be a dispositor.

4

TRIPLICITIES

This chapter begins the exploration of *disposition*. This determines which planet or planets manage the affairs of a particular zoidion - or a part of a zoidion - by virtue of having familiarity with it. To dispose means to arrange or set to order, to distribute. (Don't confuse "dispose" with "dispose of", meaning to get rid of.)

Being a dispositor does not mean that the planet "rules" a zoidion, which implies that the planet is in charge of the zoidion. Planets, the wanderers of the sky, are in no position to rule over the unchanging zodiac. The planet disposing for the zoidion is like a sports or theatrical agent, building manager, or estate executor. Just as there are competent and incompetent agents, managers, or executors, a disposing planet can do a good job or poor job for its client.

There are different ways in which a planet or planets can be the dispositor of a zoidion. This chapter discusses using triplicity lords as dispositors - that's one possibility.

In the next chapter, our interest is in determining the quality of the soul for the native. For this we will determine the *oikodespotes*: the planet or planets that have the greatest affiliation with the places of Moon and Mercury. The *oikodespotes* is the origin of the later doctrine of *almutens*. Planets other than the house lord (or "sign ruler") can qualify as a dispositor, depending on other categories of dignity. For example, a position in Capricorn may have Mars, not Saturn, as almuten - Mars is the exaltation lord for all of Capricorn; for several degrees of Capricorn, Mars is also the bound lord. In that way Mars may govern an important degree in the natal chart.

Sometimes, however, the matter is quite simple. The *only* candidate for dispositor of the lots is the appropriate house lord. (Lots, which have come down to modern astrology as "Arabic parts," project the distance between two planets from a third point, usually the Ascendant. We will discuss the Lots extensively in Chapters Six and Ten.) We first should review how the astrologer gains information from the chart.

Stages in Astrological Interpretation
How does the astrologer interpret a natal chart? Any good astrologer goes through these stages quickly and even unconsciously.

The astrologer begins by *asking some question* of the chart. What do you want to find out about: general happiness, material prosperity, character, parents, career, or religion? Modern astrologers sometimes miss this step completely; traditional astrologers, more accustomed to specific methods to answer different questions, do not.

One then *determines the factor or factors in the chart most appropriate to answer the question.* Sometimes this is a *planet*: Venus is useful for answering questions about love, Sun in a diurnal chart or Moon in a nocturnal chart for general happiness, Sun for father, Moon and Mercury for character. Often the Ascendant can supply information about the native's vitality or body type; the Ascendant and Moon together can answer questions concerning body and health. We will see in Chapter Six how *lots* can help us understand other things about the individual. We will see in Chapter Seven that *houses or places* can supply information about career (Tenth), illness (Sixth and Seventh), family (Fourth), and religion (Ninth and Third).

After determining which feature of the chart is useful for answering a specific question, the astrologer *assesses the condition of a plane of significance*: its sect, house or place, condition of dignity or debility, whether it is oriental or occidental, and the planets that aspect it. The astrologer may also assess whether the planet is in a cardinal, fixed, or mutable zoidion, what quadrant of the chart it resides in, or its phase with the Sun. This would depend on what criteria were being used to answer the question.

Another planet or placement may give further information, especially if it is with a placement - planet or position - we have already designated. For example, Mercury may be close to the Ascendant, or Saturn may be with the Lot of Spirit in the same zoidion. The astrologer's assessment of an issue changes greatly if an accompanying planet is a benefic or malefic, is in or out of sect, in exaltation or in depression.

The next step is finding *what planet or planets govern the place in question. Here* the dispositor comes in.

The last step is *evaluating the condition of the disposing planet or planets* - is it angular, in a sign of familiarity to it, having aspects by benefics or malefics? Do they rise ahead of the Sun in the morning or set behind the Sun in the evening? Are there important fixed stars configured with them? This may give a final judgment of that area of life for the native.

Triplicity Lords as Dispositors

The use of triplicity lords was prevalent in ancient western astrology but not in the astrology of Ptolemy. From Dorotheus of Sidon: "I tell you that everything which is decided or indicated is from the lords of the triplicities, and as for everything of afflictions and distress which reaches the people of the world and the totality of men, the lords of the triplicity decide it." [1] Although astrology stopped relying on triplicity lords after the Renaissance, let's look at them again and see what they can add to astrological interpretation.

Here, again, is the list of triplicity lords. Previously, in our discussion of planetary dignity, we were only interested in the lord in sect in a day or night chart. Here we are interested in all three lords.

---

1.   Dorotheus (tr Pingree), p 132.

	Day	Night	Participating
Aries, Leo, Sagittarius	Sun	Jupiter	Saturn
Gemini, Libra, Aquarius	Saturn	Mercury	Jupiter
Taurus, Virgo, Capricorn	Venus	Moon	Mars
Cancer, Scorpio, Pisces	Venus	Mars	Moon

To examine an area of life, look at the relevant triplicity lords, giving precedence to the one that is in sect in a diurnal or nocturnal chart. One question is a most basic one for the astrologer and client: is this a good or hard life for the native? How, then, can the person make his or her life happier and more meaningful? To answer these questions we note the "luminary of time" - the Sun in a diurnal chart and the Moon in a nocturnal chart.

For an examination of love, you might look at the triplicity lords for the place of Venus: if Venus is in Virgo in a day chart, for example, also consider the respective conditions of Moon and Mars, which are the other two triplicity lords for planets in Virgo.

To see how these conditions may change throughout a life, use the triplicity lord in sect for the first part of life, the one out of sect for the second part, and the common or participating lord for the third.

Therefore, our interest is less in the condition or qualities of the Sun or Moon but the condition and qualities of the triplicity lords themselves. We will look at all three lords, from the planet in sect to the one not in sect to the participating lord. This will help us with a general understanding of the trajectory of the native's lifetime. We begin with an example from Vettius Valens, from Book II of his *Anthology*[2].

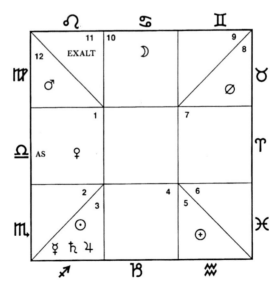

---

2.   Valens, Book II, Ch. 22.

Because this is a nocturnal chart, with the Sun below the horizon, the luminary of sect is *Moon*, which is in its own house in Cancer in the powerful Tenth. We now evaluate the condition of Moon's triplicity lords.

Since Moon is in the water triplicity by night, we begin with *Mars* in Virgo in the Twelfth, then *Venus* in Libra in the First, and then *Moon* is the participating lord. Because Mars is in the difficult Twelfth place, the first period of this person's life could be difficult. The native's life would be more happy and prosperous later, because the other two triplicity lords are angular and in their own houses.

Although we could stop here, Valens does not. Valens notes that the *Lot of Exaltation* - the relationship between the luminary of sect and the degree of that planet's exaltation degree - is in Leo. Sun, in the Second place, is therefore the lord of the Lot of Exaltation. Valens notes that the Lot of Fortune is in the Sixth. However, the lord of Exaltation in Leo (Sun) is in the Tenth zoidion *from the Lot of Fortune*. Because Sun, the planet of social prominence, creates a connection between the Lots of Exaltation and Fortune, the native will not only attain greater happiness but also high rank later in life. Valens counts the zoidia not just from the Ascendant but also from important positions like the Lot of Fortune. The Sun is in a mediocre place in the Second, but Sun becomes more powerful by virtue of being in the Tenth place from the Lot of Fortune. Note also that the Lot of Fortune in the Sixth becomes more favorable due to its lord, Saturn, also being in the Tenth zoidion from the Lot of Fortune. This analysis has important implications for our later discussions of lots, places, and planetary aspects.

Returning to our topic of triplicity lords, we now apply them to three famous British Prime Ministers. Also known as the "Iron Lady," **Margaret Thatcher** was Prime Minister of the United Kingdom from 1979 to 1990, during which time she dismantled much of its state welfare system. She was unyielding toward political opponents, Argentina and Irish nationalists. Thatcher was adored for her toughness but criticized for being politically dictatorial and personally cold. Any modern astrologer would note Saturn rising in Scorpio in Thatcher's natal chart. (I would add that Saturn is in sect in her diurnal chart.)

Thatcher's Sun is in the Twelfth place and, in Libra, is in fall. This might cause one to expect her to be much meeker and milder than she actually was. To understand this we need to examine the Sun's triplicity lords.

The diurnal triplicity lord is *Saturn*. Angular and with a sextile from Jupiter, Saturn is very powerful in her chart. Since the Lot of Spirit is in Capricorn, Saturn's own house, Saturn becomes even more important. Margaret Thatcher is very self-directed, but in a Saturnine way. The Lot of Spirit, as we'll soon discover, is a place of initiative, of doing things according to your own will.

Mercury is the nocturnal triplicity lord and therefore is second in importance in Thatcher's diurnal chart. Mercury is in its own bounds but in the Twelfth place from the Ascendant and within the Sun's beams. Mercury receives aspects from both Venus and Jupiter, and is conjunct Spica, a very fortunate fixed star. Looking carefully at Mercury shows its many advantages.

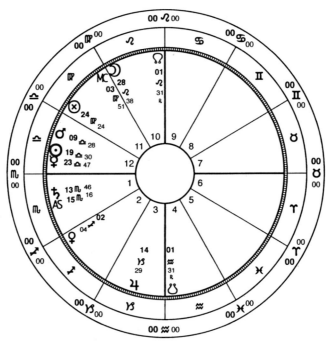

Margaret Thatcher

With the Sun, Mercury is also in the Tenth zoidion from the Lot of Spirit. Both Sun and Mercury become more important through its affiliation with the Lot of Spirit. She acts from her own point of view, her own vision, even when this has seemed inexpedient.

Jupiter, the participating lord of the airy triplicity, is with the Lot of Spirit. Jupiter is in fall or depression in Capricorn but in his own bounds. This gives Jupiter a measure of dignity in spite of being opposite his exaltation. Being in Capricorn and in sextile from its lord, Saturn, this is a Jupiter that is short on idealism, waxes cynical, but can be strong in dealing with the mechanics of implementation.

Margaret Thatcher was a unique politician, totally confident and self-reliant. Her opponents would say that she listened to nobody except herself. During most of her tenure as Prime Minister, she enjoyed great popularity, which her Tenth house Moon in Leo helps to explain.

Next is an exceptionally well-known British Prime Minister: **Winston Churchill**. After a full life in and out of public office, Churchill returned to power at the beginning of the Second World War to lead the UK in its war against Hitler. He also helped shape the world after the Second World War, and won a Nobel Prize for Literature. Churchill was more idealistic and grandiose than Thatcher, but equally fierce.

Since Churchill was born at night, the luminary of sect is *Moon*, in the Eleventh place in Leo. As Moon is in the fire triplicity, the triplicity lords are respectively *Jupiter, Sun*, and then *Saturn*. Although all are out of sect in Churchill's nocturnal chart, they are all placed fortunately.

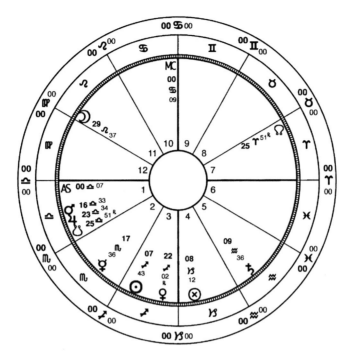

Winston Churchill [3]

Jupiter is angular, in its own bounds, and, as Valens would say, "culminates with respect to the Lot," i.e., Jupiter is in the Tenth place from the Lot of Fortune. Jupiter is with Mars, that is in sect, but, in Libra, is opposite its own house. Jupiter is also conjunct Spica, the very fortunate fixed star also prominent in Thatcher's chart. Jupiter and Mars in the First indicate Churchill's messianic zeal but also, to his critics, an arrogant self-righteousness.

Sun, which is the second triplicity lord for Moon, is in the Third place from the Ascendant, which is cadent but not terrible. Sun has a fine sextile relationship with the house lord of Sagittarius, Jupiter. Churchill's Sun is also conjunct the Mars-like fixed star Antares. Although Churchill continued to be aggressive and abrasive throughout his life, his middle years were actually the most difficult for him. He was out of power and, in the 1930s, one of a minority who warned the English people about Hitler's intentions.

Churchill's third triplicity ruler is *Saturn*, which covers his role in the Second World War and his two stints as Prime Minister. The status of Saturn, out of sect, but in a fortunate place (the Fifth) and in its own house in Aquarius, but also occidental - setting after the Sun - is mixed. A quick look at Churchill's speeches during this time shows Saturn themes of steadfastness, endurance,

---

3. Time given for Winston Churchill is 1:30pm GMT. This gives him an Ascendant of 29Virgo 56. *I have cast this chart for one minute later*, which gives this Ascendant just into Libra. This "rectification" brings Mars and Jupiter into the zoidion of his Ascendant and is in conformity with the major events of his life, as we will see in Chapter 12 and 14.

and sacrifice for a higher purpose. There is another side to Churchill and Saturn. Like Abe Lincoln during the American Civil War, Churchill experienced great personal difficulties during this conflict. When out of office, he was also subject to depression.

After being voted out of office just months after the end of the Second World War, Churchill came back and won again. He became the archetypal elder statesman on the world scene and when he died he was acknowledged to be one of the twentieth century's towering political figures.

Now let's look at **Tony Blair**. Three years after assuming leadership of the Labour Party in 1994, Blair became Prime Minister, just before his forty-fourth birthday. He took office in a landslide victory and so far his party has been returned to power twice but he stepped down in 2007. Blair is known to be domestically liberal and internationally assertive. Lately his star has dimmed greatly due to his backing of and contribution to George Bush's invasion and occupation of Iraq. Judging from Blair's natal chart and his life, he is a scrappy politician with great resilience.

It is hard not to notice that Blair was born with Mars rising in Gemini. Mars is out of sect in his chart, but may be assisted by Mercury, its dispositor by house, and by Venus, which is with Mercury and in the Eleventh place. This suggests Blair's cleverness and charm, which accompany his love of a good fight.

Since Blair was born during the day his luminary of sect is Sun. With his Sun in Taurus, we look at *Venus*, then *Moon*, then *Mars*.

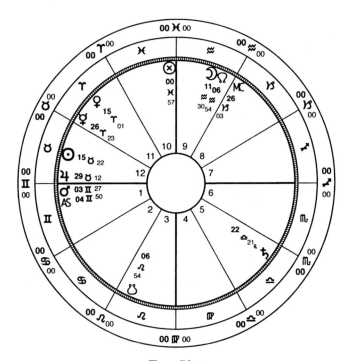

Tony Blair

Venus is in Aries, opposite her own house, but is favorably placed in the Eleventh. He gets off to a good start.

Moon is in the Ninth place, which is cadent but also in trine to the Ascendant. Moon is made stronger by is its dispositor by house, Saturn, who is in sect, exalted in Libra, and is in the favorable Fifth place, also in trine to the Ascendant. Blair's middle years conform to this placement, and would include the present time in his life. Any competent politician mixes lunar adaptability with Saturnine consistency and endurance. Blair appears to be one of them.

For a general indication of the last third of Blair's life, we judge the third triplicity lord, *Mars* in Gemini. Mars is out of sect but strongly placed in with the Ascendant. Because Mercury is in Aries and Mars in Gemini, there is an exchange of houses (a mutual reception, in modern terms) between these two planets that also have a sextile relationship. Since Mars governs the last third of Blair's life, he may continue to soldier on well past the end of his time as Prime Minister. All indications are against his retiring to write memoirs and be overpaid on the lecture circuit.

Now we examine the triplicity lords of some people in other walks of life. We have looked at **Muhammad Ali** for his career as a boxer; what about his happiness, prosperity, and fulfillment in his lifetime? Born at night, Ali's *Moon* in Aquarius has *Mercury, Saturn,* and *Jupiter* for her triplicity lords.

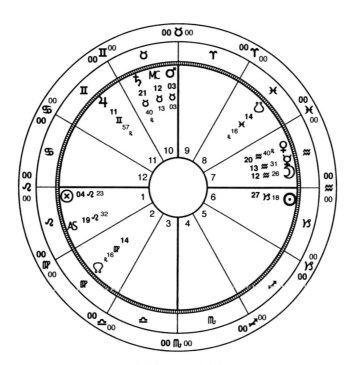

Muhammad Ali

Mercury is also in Aquarius, and is angular in the Seventh place. Although Mercury is with Venus, Mercury is also witnessed (aspected) by both malefics in the Tenth, with Jupiter helping by a trine aspect. Mercury may point to Ali's precociousness, Venus accompanying Mercury to his charm. Testimony from the malefics in the Tenth symbolizes his early ability to gather critics and enemies; that Mercury squares them from their Tenth place - called predomination - may have given him the upper hand over his detractors. This early period governs his time of being an Olympic and professional heavyweight champion.

Saturn, Ali's second triplicity lord, is out of sect, but is in the Tenth house and with Mars. Mars, as we have noted in an earlier chapter, is a rather appropriate planet to describe Ali's profession as a boxer. Saturn's position here doesn't doom Ali, but did create obstacles and hardships for him. As boxing champion, Ali continued to be extremely controversial, especially after he became a Black Muslim. He was stripped of his championship title and his right to compete in the ring for refusing the Vietnam War draft. In mid-career, Ali re-established himself as boxing champion and gained in public reputation, although he continued to be controversial.

Jupiter, the third triplicity lord, well placed in Ali's chart and depicts his becoming cast as heroic during these later years of his life. (The reader may recall, for example, that Ali lit the flame to begin the 1996 Olympics in Atlanta, GA.) This prompts us to ask what is so good about Jupiter, as it is in detriment (opposite his own zoidion in Gemini), and out of sect. Ali's Jupiter has many other fine qualities: Jupiter is in his own terms, is in his joy in the Eleventh place from the Ascendant and is not in any aspect to those nasty malefics.

We now visit another part of the world, Argentina, and the natal chart of **Eva Peron**. The year of her birth is popularly considered 1919. This is open to question: she had her birth records destroyed and an alternate year of 1908 is not only plausible but is far more likely than 1919. (Her birth *time* is more secure.) By the time of her death in 1952, Eva Peron had become one of the world's most powerful women. An actress and owner of an Argentine radio company, she met and married Juan Peron and helped him become President of Argentina. She used her popularity with the lower economic classes to champion their causes and to become an international celebrity.

Although Eva Peron was born near sunrise, she has a nocturnal chart. We thus look to the Moon in Leo, and her triplicity lords are *Jupiter, Sun, and Saturn.*

Jupiter in the fourth has some interesting features. Jupiter is well dignified, being in its own triplicity and bounds. The Fourth place from the Ascendant is angular and Jupiter is therefore prominent. (The Fourth concerns itself with family and one's origins.) More troubling, however are the aspects to Jupiter from Mars and Saturn, without a compensating aspect from Venus: the testimony of the malefics would degrade her early life.

In fact, she was an illegitimate child and grew up in poverty. Eventually she made her way to Buenos Aires and moved up slowly. The major reason Peron had her birth records destroyed was that they would reveal her birth as illegitimate - and possibly reveal her true age. It seems that, from an astrological point of view, the malefics are contributing to her difficulties.

Jupiter's dignity also tells us that Peron could benefit from her background. Although she was wealthy by the time she entered public life, Peron cited her impoverished background to portray herself a woman of the people, and fashioned this as a major part of her public image. Here we see the impact of the angular and dignified Jupiter: she gained much from her early life.

Peron's second triplicity lord is *Sun*, which is fortunately located in the First. Here we are taken to Peron's public success. Although her initial access to prominence was by being married to Juan Peron, much of her success was from her own exertion: the Sun as her triplicity lord in the First indicates this. One can make a strong case that Eva was a major reason for Juan Peron's becoming President.

The third triplicity lord is *Saturn*, indicating much greater difficulty. Saturn is in the difficult Twelfth place from the Ascendant and, in Aries, Saturn is in fall. This part of her life is taken up by political opposition and disappointment and becoming physically ill.

There are two indications that Peron would be revered in death and afterwards: the aspects from the benefics to Saturn, the third triplicity lord, and the placement of Jupiter in the Fourth from the Ascendant, which tells us about death and its aftermath.

There is more to say about Eva Peron's chart, and we will continue our exploration in Chapter Six when we discuss the Hellenistic lots.

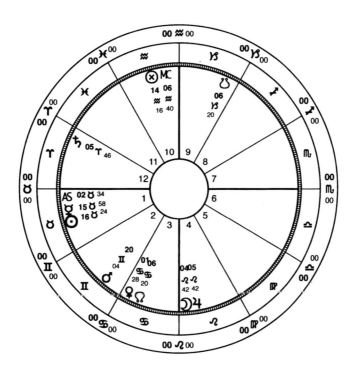

Eva Peron

Triplicities and Love

One can use the triplicity lords for other areas of life. Dorotheus recommends using the triplicity lords for Venus for matters of love and marriage. I give some examples here. (We will look further at matters of love and marriage in later chapters.) I begin with an example of triplicity lords of Venus that is astonishingly straightforward: **Amy Fisher.**

In 1992, Fisher, then sixteen years old, was arrested for shooting the wife of her boyfriend, who had the inauspicious name of Joey Buttafuoco. Fisher's trial and subsequent jail sentence became tabloid fodder for much of the early 1990s, and she was referred to at that time as the "Long Island Lolita." After serving six years in prison, Fisher resumed her life. She is currently a columnist for a Long Island newspaper. She married a man she met from an online dating service and has one child.

Can we find Fisher's teenage romance in her birth chart? Venus is in Leo, and the triplicity lords in her nocturnal chart are *Jupiter, Sun,* and *Saturn.*

Joey Buttofuoco clearly corresponds to Fisher's natal *Jupiter*. Jupiter is dignified in Pisces but is otherwise in difficult condition: it in the Twelfth place from the Ascendant, is retrograde, and has an opposition from Mars. Mr. Buttofuoco owned an auto-body shop and had a large car with tinted windows: from Fisher's point of view, he was a great benefic. That Jupiter was otherwise in poor condition indicates that his dignity was far less than she imagined. Jupiter's placement in the Twelfth may correspond to the clandestine nature of their relationship.

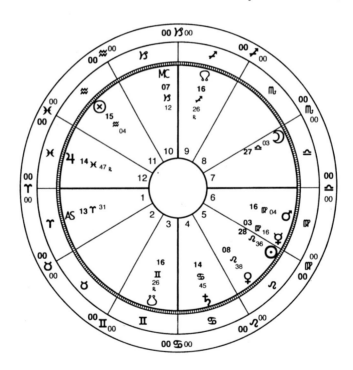

Amy Fisher

We meet Fisher's current husband with the second triplicity lord, the *Sun in Leo*. This second planet is in far better condition, being in dignity by house and in the more prominent Fifth place from the Ascendant. Sun is with Venus; otherwise, no planets aspect this position. This placement appears to account for Fisher's happier current life.

Saturn is angular, in the Fourth, and is opposite his own house. This will yield a more mixed result for Amy Fisher. Saturn may indicate settling down into a normal life with a stable if not interesting marriage. In the context of the first part of Fisher's life, this result would not be a great loss for her.

Here is the natal chart of **Woody Allen**. The triplicity lords for Venus correspond to three distinct phases of Allen's life.

Woody Allen's *Venus* placement appears luckier than it has turned out to be for him. In fact, he has had several long-term relationships, which, up until recently, have all ended badly. Venus is in her own zoidion in Libra, and her triplicity lords are *Saturn, Mercury, and Jupiter.* All are angular: relationships have been quite eventful and productive for Woody Allen.

Mercury, Venus' first triplicity lord, in Sagittarius, is opposite its own house. Mercury is also with a very dignified Jupiter (in its own house, triplicity and bounds), but Mercury is under the Sun's beams and receives an aspect from Saturn. Mercury shows promise but it is insecure where it is: Jupiter, with Mercury, may provide enough positive force to retrieve the situation somewhat: he

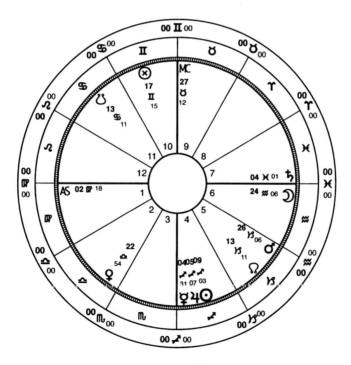

Woody Allen

can write movies about his insecurity. Many years ago, during his first years of being famous, I watched an interview with Woody Allen on the television program *Sixty Minutes*. When the interviewer asked Allen about the effects of his new fame, he replied, "Now I strike out with a higher class of women."

Saturn, the second triplicity lord for Venus, positioned in the Seventh, may depict Allen's long relationship with Mia Farrow. Saturn indicates responsibilities and perhaps confinement within relationships. Sun, Mercury, and particularly Saturn's house lord, Jupiter, are all in a Tenth place "predominating" square to Saturn. This suggests to me Mia Farrow's strong character and good reputation.

Jupiter, the third triplicity lord for Venus, may describe Allen's current relationship with Soon-Yi Previn, whom he married in 1997. Jupiter, like Mercury, is under the Sun's beams - perhaps indicating the secretive beginning of his relationship - but is in its own zoidion and is angular. It may well be that this current relationship is the best one of the three for Allen. Jupiter's square from Saturn, angular and out of sect, reminds me of the very difficult time he had in court and in public esteem, beginning in 1992 when his relationship with Soon-Yi Previn was revealed. It seems that the public has not yet forgiven him for this relationship.

We continue by working with the triplicity lords of Venus for two men of historical interest. **Thomas Jefferson's** love life has been of note recently as DNA testing has confirmed that he did have descendants from a long-term relationship with Sally Hemmings, who was one of his slaves.[4]

In Jefferson's case, like Woody Allen's, the sequence of Venus' triplicity lords align with discrete periods in his life.

In Jefferson's chart, we see that Venus has much strength: she is in sect, in her own house in Taurus, is angular in the Fourth, and has an aspect from Jupiter, although Jupiter is not placed well. Venus's difficulty is her square from *Saturn* and *Mars*. Saturn poses the greater difficulty, since Saturn is out of sect and, in Leo, is opposite his own house. Jefferson, for all his many fine qualities, was spectacularly unhappy and unlucky in love. He seemed unlucky in three distinct ways, represented by the three triplicity lords. For Venus in earthly Taurus in a nocturnal chart, her triplicity lords are *Moon*, *Venus*, and *Mars*.

Moon is in sect and in the strong Eleventh place from the Ascendant. Moon, however, has no relationship to the benefics Venus and Jupiter, and the aspects from the malefics Saturn and Mars pose another difficulty. The fact that both malefics contact Moon - any contact - causes difficulties, especially from the planet out of sect - Saturn. Jefferson married young but his wife died when he was thirty-nine.

For the middle years of Jefferson's life *Venus* is her own triplicity lord. This middle period would give Jefferson his best chance at romantic happiness. A few years after his wife died, and he was in Europe, Jefferson met Maria Cosway, a well-known artist who was married. (That Venus is dignified in Taurus corresponds to Cosway's high social status.) Evidently Cosway was ready to

---

4.   There are different times for Jefferson. This one, from the Time Cycles data base, is one I have worked with in the past, and has much to offer for our investigations here.

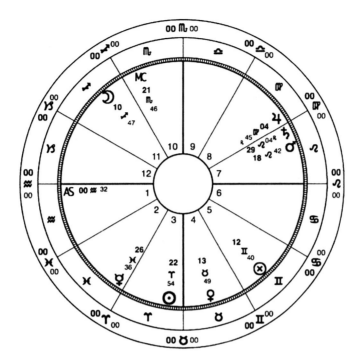

Thomas Jefferson

leave her husband to be with Jefferson, but Jefferson decided not to pursue the relationship. These are some of the difficulties brought on by the aspects from Saturn and Mars.

Mars represents the later years. Mars in Leo is in sect and in aspect - by trine - to Sun, its house lord. Saturn, with Mars in Leo, hinders Mars by its co-presence in Leo. Saturn is a planet of consistency and longevity but also one that can tend toward degradation. Both features describe his relationship with Sally Hemmings. Although Jefferson denied the relationship, it was cause for bad press during the latter years of his life. (It is interesting that Jefferson's Lot of Accusation, which features Mars and Saturn, is close to the Ascendant and opposite the two malefics. This would be the case for anybody with Saturn and Mars conjunct in the natal chart.) When we discuss the Lots as they relate to love and marriage, we will take up Jefferson again.

The next historical figure was contemporary with Jefferson but embodied a rather different style.[5] The **Marquis De Sade** might not have been so well remembered if he were not such a good writer. Note that Moon in Virgo and Mercury in Taurus have a "mutual reception" or an exchange of dignities: Moon is in Mercury's house and exaltation and Mercury is in Moon's exaltation.

The reader is probably familiar with De Sade's reputation. His sexual tastes included violence, perhaps mutilation, coupled with a tendency toward self-proclamation. By the standards of any era, he would be thought of as extreme.

---

5.   As with Jefferson, the birth data is plausible but not completely certain.

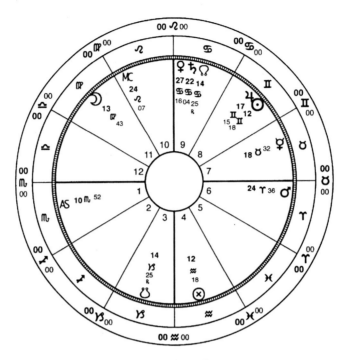

Marquis de Sade

De Sade's chart gives us some indications of his proclivities, although many people whose charts have similar features have not expressed them as did De Sade. Venus with Saturn can indicate marrying somebody older or beneath one's station or, at an extreme, sexual exploitation or depravity. The square from Mars in Aries to Venus adds vigor and a possibility of violence, if carried to an extreme. Mercury's aspect to Venus may add some inventiveness in the area of sexuality, and indicates his ability to write about it.

The triplicity lords for Venus in Cancer are *Venus* (as De Sade was born during the day) *Mars*, and *Moon*.

At the age of twenty-three he married the daughter of a government official and had three daughters. This was the most dignified arrangement he would have. Venus has dignity, being in her own triplicity. The presence of Saturn and the aspect of Mars compromised - and, in his case, corrupted – the value of his Venus placement. Without doubt his strange activity began in his marriage.

Mars is out of sect, and in its own house in Aries, in a strong square to Venus and Saturn. This combination articulates the part of his life for which he is best known. It includes exploitation (Venus with Saturn), violence linked with sexuality (both malefics configured with Venus), having to flee the country, and being thrown into jail (more Saturn).

Moon has more to do with his writing career, as Moon is strongly configured with Mercury. We note that Venus and Saturn both testify to Moon, indicating the content of his writing.

In Chapter Six we introduce Lots, and in Chapter Ten we look at three lots concerned with love and marriage. The planets governing two of them lots take us back to this configuration of Venus with Saturn, aspected by Mars. The third lot, which describes love as a downfall, is happily situated with Jupiter and Sun.

We continue our investigation of dispositors. We see how a planet or planets govern one or several positions in the natal chart that together relate to a one important issue. We will examine the determination of soul and its characteristics.

5

PLANETARY LORDS AND DETERMINATION OF SOUL

In this chapter we extend our discussion of dispositorship to show how one planet or many planets can have hegemony over positions in the natal chart. A dispositor, again, is a planet in charge of another planet or position in the natal chart. In modern astrology we would call it a planetary "ruler." In the last section we looked at the triplicity lords as dispositors for the luminary of sect and for Venus. In this chapter we explore how Hellenistic astrologers determined which planet or planets are most important for a specific issue.

Many ancient astrologers developed criteria to determine a chart's most important planet. Usually this was done to help answer the question of how long a person will live. Here we will look at a different issue: how to determine the planet or planets reflecting a person's "soul." Once again, our source is Ptolemy [1]

For our purposes, "soul" does not pertain to an immortal essence. The moving bodies of the sky cannot represent such a timeless entity. In astrology, if the psyche, or soul, is to be represented by planets, it must have a changeable nature and be subject to modification over time.

Is the word "soul" like Aristotle's principle of aliveness? [2] According to Aristotle, the soul is the "form of the body," that which differentiates something alive from something that is not. However, this is not the meaning Ptolemy intends for "soul." In the chapters of *Tetrabiblos* preceding his discussion of soul, he discusses the attributes and ailments of the body. This appears to encompass Aristotle's principle of aliveness.

Today, we might substitute modern concepts of *mind* for Ptolemy's use of "soul." I would add, however, that this "mind" is one that manifests through patterns of behavior and interaction with the world. We concern ourselves with the part of a person's character that is apparent to others. Yet this is not a reductive behaviorism: a planet's symbolism can range from internal disposition to patterns of overt behavior. First we'll discuss how a planet becomes a planetary lord.

What is an Oikodespotes?

The *oikodespotes* is the planet that wins over other planets, like a lawyer who beats out the other lawyers to work a celebrity court case. The *oikodespotes* does not *rule* over the sign or planet or position, but has more muscle there than other planets do.

---

1.   *Tetrabiblos*, Book III, Ch. 14.
2.   Aristotle, *On the Soul* Book II, Ch. 1.

Oikodespotes brings us back to our previous discussion of *oikos* as a dwelling. "*Despotes*" recalls the word "despot," and means a master or lord - a ruler. Think of the word "lord" more as the manager of a set of apartment buildings or as the general manager of a sports team, rather than as its owner. This is the planet that takes responsibility for the natal position.

How does one choose which planet or planets have governance over other planets or positions (e.g. Ascendant, Part of Fortune) in a natal chart? The answer turns out to be more complex and interesting than the modern practice, which is to use the house lord alone. We return to the categories of planetary dignity outlined in Chapter Three, now to look at these as categories of disposition.

We begin with the **house lord**. Ancient western astrologers considered the house lord of the zoidion of the lot to be the planet governing the lot. If one's Lot of Fortune is in Virgo, Mercury is the lord of that lot.

It appears that ancient astrologers did not solely use **exaltations** as dispositors. We have seen that a planet being in exaltation is a strong factor - perhaps the strongest - for planetary dignity, but may not be the critical factor in disposition. For example, the dispositor for a Saturn in a degree of Pisces would never be Venus if Venus were only Pisces' exaltation lord.

In the previous chapter we saw that ancient astrologers used **triplicity lords** to indicate different general periods of one's life. In this chapter we will see the triplicity lord that is in sect being used as a dispositor. Valens and others used **bounds** as sole dispositors but only for determining physical viability and one's length of life. **Decanic face** generally does not appear to be used as a sole dispositor except for the Ascendant.[3]

For disposition over a number of natal positions, Ptolemy suggests that you seek the planet that has the greatest number of affiliations, all considered as equal, for a particular zoidion or degree of that zoidion. He uses five affiliations to determine which planet has the most muscle at any given degree. Consider the chart of Marie Curie on the following page, a simple example of one position: her Moon is at the seventeenth degree of Pisces.

- The house lord for Pisces is *Jupiter*.

- *Venus* is exalted in Pisces.

- The triplicity lord for a day chart in Pisces is *Venus* in Dorotheus' system of triplicities. (If we use Ptolemy's, it would be *Mars*.)

- *Mercury* is the bound lord for the seventeenth degree of Pisces, using either the Egyptian or Ptolemy's system of bounds.

- The fifth category that Ptolemy uses is *not* the decanic faces but is called **phase or configuration**. According to Robert Schmidt, from reading further in Ptolemy, phase or

---

3.   For the use of decans as sole dispositors, see Teucer of Bablyon, excerpted in *The Astrological Record of the Early Greek Sages*. (1995).

configuration gives us the one planet that is visible, i.e. not within Sun's beams, and that most closely aspects the planet in question.[4] In Curie's chart, the planet aspecting Moon most closely is *Sun*, which is at fourteen Scorpio and makes a trine to Moon.

For Marie Curie the oikodespotes for Moon is *Venus*, as Venus is the exaltation of Moon and also Moon's triplicity. Curie's Venus is conjunct Saturn in the Twelfth place from the Ascendant, so that Venus is in a painful and difficult position. The planetary lord or oikodespotes is the manager; for the enterprise to work out well, the manager should be competent and effective: here the planetary lord for Moon may be rigid, depressed, or degraded in some way. Venus' difficulties make for difficulties for the Moon.

Ptolemy's oikodespotes differs from the medieval doctrine of *almuten* in two important ways. The later doctrine calculates the almuten using a *weighted* point system. For Marie Curie's Moon, Jupiter would get five points as the house lord; Venus would get four points for exaltation; Venus would receive an additional three as Moon's triplicity lord; and Mercury would get two points for being bound lord.

You may recall, from Chapter Three, a category of dignity called decans, whereby each zoidion was divided into three segments of ten degrees each, with each decan governed by a different planet.

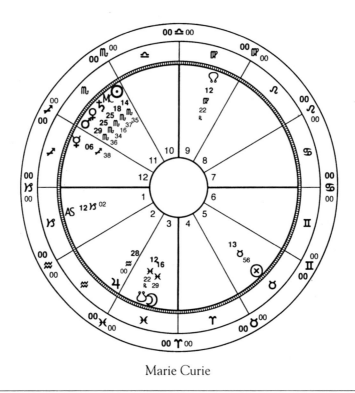

Marie Curie

4.   Schmidt, R. Translator's Preface. Ptolemy, *Tetrobiblos Book IV*. (1998) He refers to Ptolemy, Book II, Ch. 7.

The later doctrine of the almuten used the decan lords as a very minor dignity - but one point - instead of Ptolemy's "phase or configuration" described above.

Why is the oikodespotes or almuten important in natal astrology? Although modern astrologers often think of a planet's house lord as its dispositor, the almuten - the planet with more governing credentials - may be another planet altogether. Here are some examples:

- Sun in Taurus in a nighttime chart has Venus governing as house lord, but Moon is lord of both exaltation and triplicity. Moon would be the oikodespotes or almuten for Taurus, not Venus.

- An Ascendant in early Libra in a daytime chart has Venus as lord of the house, but Saturn is the lord of exaltation, triplicity, and bound. Once again, it would not be Venus, but rather it is Saturn who is the oikodespotes or almutens.

One can have one oikodespotes for **many places** in an astrological chart. Here are some examples of using an oikodespotes for multiple positions. To find the "giver of life" in the natal chart, a factor to help determine how long one would live, Ptolemy would derive an oikodespotes from many places, if the appropriate luminary were weak. Here is the sequence:

- For a day chart, Ptolemy would use Sun, if the Sun is in an effective place, i.e. angular, in sextile or trine to the Ascendant, and above the horizon.

- If it is not, consider Moon, if Moon is effective according to the same criteria.

- If Moon is not in an effective place, use the planet with the most categories of disposition over Sun, prenatal new Moon, and Ascendant.

- If you cannot find a governing planet that is in an effective place, simply use the Ascendant.

- For a night chart, first look at Moon, then Sun, then, if neither is in an effective place, find the planet with the most categories of dignity over Moon, Moon's position in the full Moon prior to birth, and the Lot of Fortune. Here is another oikodespotes taken from a multiple position. If this fails to provide a planet in an effective place, use the Ascendant, if the Moon is waxing; or one would use the Lot of Fortune, if the Moon is waning.

Previously, we discussed Ptolemy's planetary signifiers for body type. To find the oikodespotes for body type, seek the planet with the most categories of disposition over Ascendant and Moon. This planet's features will help describe the body, using the descriptions we discussed in Chapter Two. Now we determine an oikodespotes for a person's soul or character.

Finding Soul in the Chart

Since the soul's impulses are many and various, Ptolemy says, one should be careful to use many factors when delineating the qualities of soul in a natal chart. He gives us a system with more nuance and flexibility than the modern practice of relying on signs and elements alone, yet Ptolemy's system is not so complex that an astrologer would find it unusable.

On the surface, Ptolemy's formula for soul (*psyche*) appears quite simple. He looks at the place of natal Mercury, symbolizing reason; this he combines with Moon, "the most body-like of the lights," which governs our non-rational faculties. He then notes whether Mercury and Moon are in cardinal, fixed, or mutable zoidia, what planets aspect each of them, and their phase relationships with the Sun.

He then assesses the condition of the planetary lord or oikodespotes over Mercury *and* Moon. Ptolemy tells us that Mercury is *logikon kai noeron*, logical and reasonable. Mercury represents more what today we might call "mind", especially in its capacity to use language and make judgments. Moon, on the other hand, is more sensory and *alogikon* - that is, Moon symbolizes more what we feel and sense and less what we say to others and to ourselves. As "*logikos*" is a word implying the use of language, we can think of Mercury as that part of us that uses language, perhaps that which rationalizes. This distinction does not indicate that Moon is somehow inferior to Mercury. Moon and Mercury are the quickest of the planets. Our Mercurial mind moves quickly, but our lunar responses and emotions move much more quickly. When we are emotionally charged, we usually find ourselves *in the middle* of a visceral or emotional response because it has come upon us so quickly. This is reflected astrologically in the fact that that Moon moves a *minimum* of six times more quickly than Mercury. Ptolemy does not set up a polarity between Mercury and Moon, between *logikos* and *alogikos*. He does not evaluate these two planets separately, but instead regards them as functioning cooperatively to manifest a person's "soul." It appears that Ptolemy regards these functions as continuous, not separate from each other.

As Ptolemy precedes his discussion of the soul with two chapters on the body and its ailments, one may surmise that his principle of life for human beings must reflect a continuum of body, emotion and sensation, as well as language and thought.

The medieval astrologer Antonio de Montulmo was strongly influenced by Ptolemy's analysis, but gives us a wholly Aristotelian perspective. Although there is some overlap, he casts the Ascendant primarily as the body or the most basic nutritive soul, Moon as the sensitive soul, and Mercury as the intellectual soul. He would compare and contrast these positions and their dispositors to obtain information about the conditions of each of these three souls.[5] Ptolemy is more holistic. Let's look at his criteria for examining the positions of Moon and Mercury.

- Note the condition of Moon and Mercury - are they in sect or in some dignity? Are they in profitable places?

- What planets aspect Moon and Mercury? Are these planets malefics or benefics? Remember that malefics and benefics can give bad or good testimony, and can diminish or enhance a planet's status.

- In what modes (cardinal, fixed, mutable) are the zoidia of the Moon and Mercury?
    If **cardinal**, a person is more outgoing, purposeful, inquisitive and inventive, and perhaps interested in astrology and divination.

---

5.   Montulmo, Ch. 9.

If **fixed**, a person is constant, firm, patient, steady, perhaps argumentative and overachieving.

If **mutable**, a person is variable and versatile and unsteady, inclined toward love, music, and bending the truth.

• What are the phase relationships between Sun and the oikodespotes? We will discuss this final condition in detail in Chapter Nine, when we examine phases of planets to the Sun. These phases form the conditions of a planet's appearance and speed.

• What is the governing planet or planets for Mercury and Moon? Again, to determine this you look at the following categories:

  • The house lords of the zoidia of Mercury and Moon.

  • The planets exalted in the zoidia of Mercury and Moon.

  • Their triplicity lords by day or night.

  • Their bound lords.

  • Planets aspecting each one but which are not under the Sun's beams (within fifteen degrees of the Sun).

Giving equal weight to each planet appearing in each category, one counts them all up. Is there a clear winner or are two or more planets vying for governance? Of those planets, is one problematic and the other well-positioned? Is the oikodespotes in a cardinal, fixed, or mutable sign? Now that we have the oikodespotes, is it dignified, in favorable places - angular, trine or sextile the Ascendant but not cadent - and is it witnessed - aspected - by benefics or malefics? Ptolemy gives us an illustration of how different planets can affect a planetary lord by being in aspect to it.

If the malefics Saturn and Mars aspect the oikodespotes, a person may become wicked and have an impulse to do bad things. Will he or she get away with it? Note the strength of the malefics; if they are overcome by benefics Jupiter and Venus, he or she will be unable to act on his or her wicked intentions or be easily caught and punished. (This is a good thing.) The testimony of the benefics prevents one from doing bad things, even if this is not the purpose of the perpetrator.

On the other hand, if the benefics are in aspect to the oikodespotes, this can make for a person with very good intentions. If these benefics are well placed, this person will be known for his or her goodness. Remember that benefics give good testimony, in aspect with a significant planet. If, however, Jupiter and Venus are overcome by malefics, that person's acts of kindness or generosity may backfire: he or she may well find out that no good deed gone wrong goes unpunished. This would be considered bad testimony.

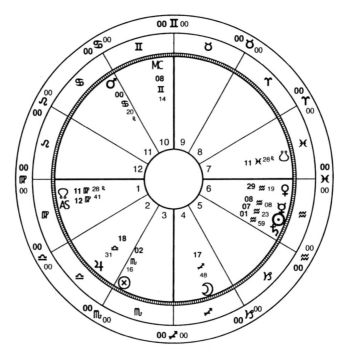

Wolfgang Mozart

Notable Souls

I begin with somebody with a very complex soul: **Wolfgang Mozart**. Here we have two strong candidates for the job of oikodespotes of the soul, yet one of them does a better job for him than the other.

First we find the signifying planets. Moon is in Sagittarius, a double-bodied or mutable sign. Mercury is in Aquarius, near Sun. With Virgo rising, Mercury is also lord of the Ascendant. First we examine Mozart's Mercury; it is in fixed Aquarius, giving resolve and stubbornness.

Mercury is also in its own triplicity in a night chart in the airy triplicity - Mercury has some dignity. Being in the cadent (or "falling") Sixth place, and within the Sun's beams, and with Saturn, Mercury is hindered in its effectiveness.

Moon is angular although waning, and next forms an aspect to Jupiter, her house lord. A mutable Moon can display fickleness and affinity for love or music(!).

Although Mozart was an immense musical genius whose reputation has grown with time, the quality of his soul was more ordinary. Unlike some other major composers, however, most of us would feel comfortable having a meal or a beer with him. We will now find the planet with the most authority over the positions of Moon and Mercury.

- Mercury is in the house of *Saturn*, the exaltation of nobody, the triplicity of *Mercury*, the bounds of *Mercury* (Venus by the Egyptian table). The closest aspect is with is *Moon*. (According to the Hellenistic tradition, conjunctions are not aspects in a strict sense.)

- Moon is in the house and triplicity of *Jupiter*, the bounds of *Mercury*, and is applying to *Jupiter*.

Using the Egyptian table of bounds, Jupiter gets three counts and Mercury two, with Moon and Saturn receiving one each. Using Ptolemy's table, it's a tie between Jupiter and Mercury. Even if you give Jupiter the most categories of dignity, I would look at Mercury as well, since Mercury is also lord of the Ascendant.

If Mozart was consulting with you, what analysis and what advice would you give him? Mercury would indicate Mozart's verbal cleverness, playfulness, and love of puzzles. Mercury's difficult position in Mozart's chart may also point to immaturity.

Jupiter, the oikodespotes for his character, is in a better position - although receiving the testimony of the malefics - and indicates his well-intentioned generous, humane and socially engaging nature.

Since Mercury is also the house lord of Virgo, his Ascendant may point to personal features that were more visible to those who encountered him. The testimony of malefics to Jupiter, as Saturn trines Mozart's Libra Jupiter and Mars squares it, may indicate the controversy that surrounded his character during his lifetime and afterwards, that perhaps people's "testimony" was too harsh. Nonetheless, I would stress the potential of Jupiter, especially since Jupiter is Moon's house lord and at the same time receives an application from Moon. With a longer life and greater maturity, and perhaps with more financial success, Jupiter might have given Mozart greater happiness in life. However, due to the influence of the malefics, he may have always had hindrances.

The Lunar Nodes

Modern astrologers emphasize the lunar nodes far more than do ancient astrologers. In fact, ancient astrologers hardly use the lunar nodes at all. The nodes do not appear prominently until the medieval era, when they were imported from Jyotish or Vedic astrology. Today many western astrologers depict the North Node as embodying one's path of growth in life and the South Node as the overlay of past patterns.

What are the lunar nodes? In fact, they are artificial positions used to predict eclipses. During an eclipse, Sun and Moon are lined up in the zodiac (by longitude) and also up and down (by latitude). The lunar nodes are convenient markers to show where Moon crosses the path of Sun by latitude. Where Moon would cross the ecliptic is the location of a lunar node. When the Moon is furthest in latitude from the Sun, Moon is seen to square the nodes.

- During an eclipse, the Sun, Moon, and North or South Node all line up together. At that time the Moon is close to the Sun's degree by conjunction or opposition both in latitude and longitude. Ordinarily, twice a month, when the Moon is close to the South or North Node, the Moon crosses the latitude of the Sun, which is on the ecliptic.

> - When Moon is furthest away from the lunar nodes, she is in a close square to both nodes, and is furthest up or down from the Sun, in greatest northern or southern latitude. In *Tetrabiblos* Book Three Chapter Fourteen, Ptolemy refers to these conditions as Moon being at the "bendings." This also occurs twice a month. The Nodes of the Moon, Ptolemy says, can contribute to the determination of the soul or character of the person:
>
> - When Moon is at the nodes, the native experiences greater activity and excitability.
>
> - When Moon is at the bendings, in a square aspect to the nodes, the native is more versatile and has a greater capacity for change.
>
> On both occasions, whether conjunct a node or square them, there is an increase in activity: at the node the activity appears more restless, and at the bendings, this activity appears to be more deliberate.
>
> Marie Curie has Moon five degrees away from the South Node; Tony Blair's Moon in Aquarius is four degrees away from the North Node. Mozart's Moon in Sagittarius is square the nodes at eleven Virgo and Pisces and is at the bendings. According to Ptolemy, Curie and Blair would have a tendency toward excitability and Mozart would tend to more deliberate activity. So far I am unconvinced by these examples; further investigation awaits me.

Now we look at the founder of psychoanalysis, **Sigmund Freud**. Mercury and Moon give us a lot of information about Freud. Mercury is angular and fast of motion. Mercury is fixed, attesting to Freud's firmness and steadiness of thought - some considered him inflexible. Mercury is applying to a dignified Jupiter and the malefics do not contact. His was a confident and far-reaching intellect.

Moon gives us a different picture: like Mozart's it is in a mutable zoidion. Moon, however, is also with Saturn and in the difficult Eighth place from the Ascendant. This adds a problematic quality, perhaps a tendency to be overly in control. Both malefics and benefics cast aspect to the Moon, but especially Jupiter, which casts a predominating Tenth place square to Moon from Pisces. Here is an indication of Freud plumbing the rich depths of the life of the emotions, perhaps to uncover some of their riches.

It is not easy to figure out which planet is the oikodespotes of the places of Mercury and Moon. It is Venus: she is the house and triplicity lord of Mercury in Taurus and also the bound lord of Moon. It is difficult to imagine Freud as magnetic, shallow, and people pleasing, as might be the nature of Venus having governance over one's soul. At close range, Freud was in fact an affable but careful and controlled person. Among other possibilities one would be hard-pressed to think of his character being Venus. We now need to take a closer look at Freud's Venus in Aries, analyzing her position and then go on to her significance.

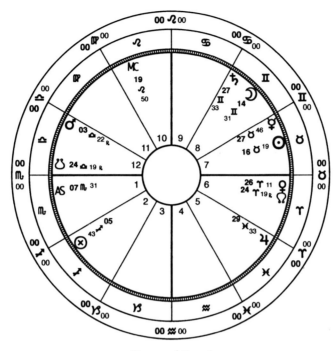

Sigmund Freud

- In Aries, Venus is opposite her own house, and is in the difficult Sixth place. Freud's is a daytime chart and Venus is also out of sect. Venus is not terribly comfortable.

- Looking at aspects from other planets, Jupiter in Pisces is not helpful, as he does not aspect Venus. There is a sextile from Saturn to Venus and Mars opposes Venus. There is plenty of testimony from the malefics.

- Mars is out of sect, opposite its own house, retrograde, and in the Twelfth. This is a less than positive influence.

- Saturn is in sect and is dignified in his own triplicity and bound. Being in the Eighth zoidion from the Ascendant does weaken Saturn. It is these aspecting planets that tell us much.

It was in the content of his work, more than his personal style, that Venus' influence shows up. For somebody as committed to his calling as was Freud, his work was his means of behaving in the world, and thereby expressing his Venus as oikodespotes for his soul.

One may recall from Chapter Two that Venus with an assist from Saturn could depict a person earning a living from love, e.g., as a prostitute or a romance novelist. There is also an implication of lewdness. Freud manifested these possibilities, but in an utterly unique way. You can probably credit Saturn with his restrained and sublimated manifestation of Venus.

After trying hypnosis, cocaine, and then abreaction, Freud discovered that if a client solves his or her relationship with the therapist, this helps the client solve his or her psychological difficulty at its root. It was Freud who pioneered relationship therapy.

Another of Freud's positions was that repressed sexuality, usually in the normal course of growing up, is the foundation for much personal and social neurosis. More than any major figure since the Marquis De Sade (who also has Venus placed with malefics), Freud was tuned into the polymorphous nature of sexuality. Because Venus is the oikodespotes for Freud's soul and character, this whole matter was close to the nature of who he was.

This leaves us with two ways to look at Saturn's role with Freud's Venus: his emphasis on what we might consider moral depravity, and his stubborn adherence to a controversial theory in the face of great opposition.

When I first read Freud in my twenties, I admired him for taking a problem further and further until he was satisfied that he had answered it sufficiently. His exposition of dreams, depression, violence and war, and the origin of culture, all show a stubbornly penetrating and inquiring mind. I see not only the influence of Saturn on Venus, but also the application of Mercury to a dignified Jupiter in Pisces.

We now look at the chart of a very outspoken and influential American politician, Arizona senator **John McCain**, who at the time of writing is making another attempt to be elected president. His natal chart is rather transparent, and his public reputation reflects well the features of his soul.

McCain has Mercury and Moon, both angular, in the First and Fourth places respectively. Both are in cardinal signs. McCain certainly comes across as decisive.

A quick look through the planetary dignities tables shows that the oikodespotes for this man's soul is Saturn.

• Mercury in Libra has Saturn as its exaltation, triplicity, and bound lord.

• Moon is in Capricorn, Saturn's house. Mars does come in a close second, since Mars is the exaltation and bound lord for Moon in Capricorn and is Mercury's closest aspecting planet.

McCain's chart indicates how a malefic can be a positive feature of a natal chart. In the Sixth place, Saturn is cadent - unconnected with the Ascendant - perhaps, though, there is some affiliation: Libra and Pisces are antiscia or in zoidia of *equal power*. (We will discuss this feature in our upcoming discussion of aspects.) I wouldn't put much on that, however.

Saturn is in sect, and has aspects from both Venus and Jupiter. Venus' aspect is hardly worthy of mention, as Venus is in fall and in the Twelfth, in the same zoidion as the Lot of Fortune. The aspect from Jupiter, however, is powerful and favorable. Jupiter in Sagittarius, in sect, and in his own house, is also a major dispositor for Saturn in Pisces. Jupiter, testifying to Saturn, has allowed McCain to have a positive outlook in spite of his many difficulties. Ptolemy would remind us that McCain would be a failure if his intention were to do wrong: this is the influence of a benefic on a malefic lord. Some years ago he was involved in an attempt to pressure a governmental agency on

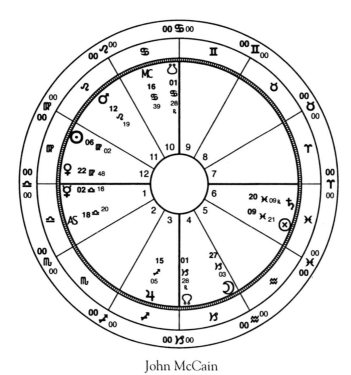

John McCain

behalf of a campaign contributor, and the experience converted him to the cause of campaign finance reform in the United States.

How is McCain Saturnine? One first thinks of his long-term residence at the "Hanoi Hilton" as a POW during the Vietnam War. Since then he has been a politician with a conservative social agenda, an advocate of fiscal responsibility, and has been a leader for the cause of campaign finance reform. His persistence through many setbacks has helped make him a major American politician. McCain's critics see him as a steady and sincere person with an edge of sanctimony and humorless intensity. These two sets of opinions both have the flavor of Saturn with an assist from Jupiter.

There is more to say about McCain's chart. Mercury close to the Ascendant in Libra reflects this politician's tendency to be quoted often; as he is most often seen with a camera or microphone in front of him. Saturn, the major dispositor for Mercury, indicates that his knack for communication is not spontaneous but calculated. McCain's Mars placement is so interesting that I will reserve it for the chapter on phases of planets with the Sun.

What if the oikodespotes is debilitated?
Let us now discuss somebody who is a bit more complicated and far less transparent than John McCain: the nineteenth century American poet **Emily Dickinson.**

Emily Dickinson is currently on everybody's very short list of the greatest American poets. This is ironic, since during her lifetime she had but seven poems published - anonymously. She lived a very quiet life, almost in seclusion, and never married. At the same time her poetry shows a wide range of interest: her work ranged from the birds and insects in her backyard to contemplations on love, fame, and death. Today most people who are familiar with her know her poems about death.

Dickinson's Mercury is in Sagittarius in the Second; Moon is in Libra in the Twelfth. Mercury and Moon are in sextile to one another within two degrees, yet neither carries an aspect to the Ascendant.

Which planet prevails as the oikodespotes? Governing her soul is *Jupiter*, the house and triplicity lord for Mercury, and the closest aspect to the Moon.

• Jupiter is in fall in Capricorn and is in the cadent Third place from the Ascendant. This diminishes Jupiter's range. What planets are in aspect to Jupiter?

• Mars casts a square, and Mars has strength in her chart. Saturn, out of sect and in square to Dickinson's Sun, Mercury, and Venus, is in trine to Jupiter. Saturn, in the Eleventh and with her Lot of Spirit, occupies a more decisive position for Dickinson. In the next chapter we will take up the strong involvement by the Lot of Spirit in her chart. Since Saturn is the dispositor for Jupiter, this aspect to Jupiter would take priority.

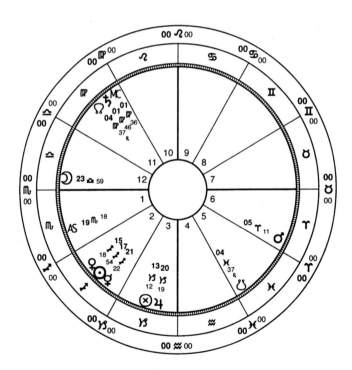

Emily Dickinson

When met with disappointing news from a would-be publisher, she did not become angry and look for another one, as many people would do. She gave up, wrote poetry about the evanescence of fame, and became the best back yard poet ever. Her poetry packed great profundity into few lines, and she was doubtless also the author of a great many daily kindnesses. This is all Jupiter governed by a prominent Saturn.

We will revisit her chart several times, in our discussions about the lots, parental units, and in the chapter about the fixed stars. These discussions will add much to the information we have about her.

What if there's no clear winner?

Let's look back upon the American presidential election of 2004, and here compare its two competitors, George W. Bush and John Kerry. We begin with the winner of that election: **George W. Bush.**

Mercury, in the First, about to rise above the Ascendant, is in Leo with Venus. Mercury is fixed, which manifests clearly in his firmness of opinion. (As we will discover in Chapter Seven, Mercury in the First is in his joy.) Moon is in the cadent Third but is conjunct Jupiter, so one finds generosity and confidence in his emotional life. Being in cardinal Libra can only strengthen this quality. (Moon is also in her joy, being in the Third.)

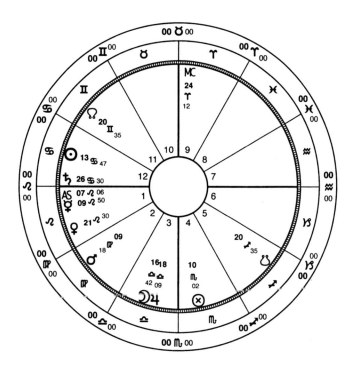

George W. Bush

Which planet is in charge of Bush's soul? What we have is a close race between *Sun* (house and triplicity lord for Mercury), *Saturn* (exaltation and triplicity lord for Moon), *Venus* (house of Moon, and bound lord of Mercury), and *Jupiter* (bound lord for Moon and her closest aspect). What do we do? We compare all these positions, to see what they say about the native.

- *Sun* is in the Twelfth with Saturn: this is a difficult placement. In spite of some of his policies, Bush does not do well as a member of an elite, symbolized by Sun; indeed a personal strength is his common touch. Mars, testifying from Virgo and out of sect, is no help. Bush would not do well playing monarch.

- *Saturn* does not seem to work well for him either. Although Saturn in the Twelfth is in its joy and is in sect, it is also opposite its own zoidion, occidental and inside the Sun's beams. This latter factor may point to discipline and objectivity (Saturn) being overcome by subjective bias (Sun). The Saturn part of Bush's character tends not to emerge except when in crisis. At that time we may see Mars, in sextile to Saturn from the Second, coming to his rescue. We know that the assistance of Mars is not an unmixed blessing.

- *Venus*, being in the same zoidion as the Ascendant, is a happier planet for Bush. This position makes Venus more accessible for Bush, and with Venus we see his congeniality and charm, as well as his tendency toward shallowness. In the same zoidion as Mercury, Venus allows that even in his formal addresses Bush is able to talk directly to the listener. Venus and Mercury together in the First give Bush an interpersonal poise and cleverness.

- *Jupiter* in Libra is less favorably positioned than Venus, although Jupiter is in its own bounds. Since Jupiter also receives a sextile from Venus, the lord of Libra, Bush's character has a high-minded and visionary quality. As I'll discuss later, Jupiter's placement in the Third may point to his well-publicized religious connection.

How might we compare these differing planets and interpretations of soul? Sun and Saturn could represent the futility of many of his early years. The desire to be important (Sun) was thwarted by an insecure and self-conscious Saturn. He later developed more of the interpersonal skill we see with Venus in the First with Mercury, witnessed by Jupiter.

There's a wide chasm dividing American public opinion about Bush's character. Some see the kind-hearted and comforting Venus and Jupiter person. Others see a more cynical and self-absorbed Sun and Saturn in the Twelfth, and feel that the Venus/Jupiter qualities are just a carefully crafted veneer.

Now let's evaluate **John Kerry**, who lost the 2004 Presidential election and may re-emerge for 2008. Here there *is* a clear winner for which planet becomes the oikodespotes.

Kerry's Moon is mutable, Mercury cardinal. The Moon keeps company with the two malefics. Mercury's only aspect is a sextile from Venus, which isn't terribly helpful, as Venus is in the Twelfth and opposite her own house. We need to proceed to the lord of both positions.

The oikodespotes for Mercury and Moon is *Mercury* himself, because the Moon is in Gemini and Mercury is in his own bounds (Egyptian system).

- Mercury is in sect in Kerry's (nocturnal) chart and only Venus gives testimony. Venus is not strongly positioned to be much help to Kerry.

- Mercury in Capricorn, however, has an important relationship to Saturn in Gemini: they are in each other's houses. This mutual reception strengthens both planets. Furthermore, Saturn and Mercury are symmetrically positioned equally from both sides to the Aries-Libra axis. This relates the planets to one another, as their ascensional times are the same. (We discuss this in detail in Chapter Eight.)

Kerry's character and soul is the nature of Mercury and Saturn. Kerry has great mental and verbal agility but a carefulness that undoubtedly frustrates his supporters and his loved ones. He is a thoughtful person, of the sort that Mercury and Saturn together can produce. This can create good judgment, but also a reserve that hinders any personal charm and an ability to present his views in a quick and compelling manner, i.e. he needs to loosen up. Especially with his Mercury being in Saturnine Capricorn, Mercury's charisma requires the active involvement of benefics, as Mr. Bush enjoys. Also, since Kerry has a nocturnal chart and Saturn is out of sect, this brings a greater heaviness to this planet than would otherwise be the case.

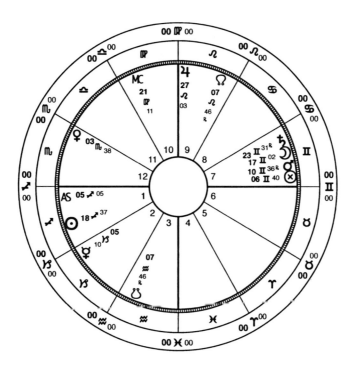

John Kerry

Note also that Kerry has Sun in Sagittarius conjunct the Ascendant, and the lord of this position is Jupiter in Leo, so that Sun and Jupiter also exchange signs, that is, participate in a mutual reception. Does this give a grandness of character? Those who are close supporters of Kerry believe he has Sun-Jupiter greatness of character; aside from simply being tall, he does seem to have an imposing presence. Kerry's detractors would think of this combination as confirming his reputed pomposity and self-absorption.

When the oikodespotes is the Sun or Moon

Ptolemy does not mention this as a possibility, but he does discuss the contributions of the luminaries to the determination of soul. The ancient tradition is loath to use Sun and Moon to signify particular issues, since the luminaries speak more generally about the native as a whole.

I conclude this discussion with the natal chart of a Sun-like person and a Moon-like person. The Sun-like person is not a politician or poet or deep thinker, but a rock star - **Jerry Garcia.**

Garcia, who died in 1995, was the central personality and musician of the rock band The Grateful Dead. They were well known for lengthy tours all over the world. Their adoring public, the Deadheads, in many ways the remnants of the hippie movement of the 1960s, followed them around from city to city and were almost tribal in their sense of affiliation to each other and to the band.

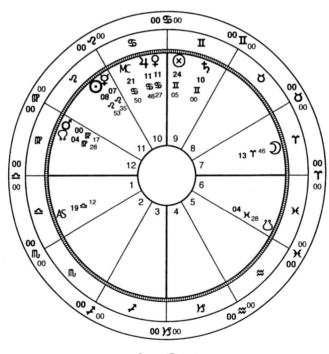

Jerry Garcia

Jerry Garcia was at the center of this tribal loyalty. Clearly Sun is oikodespotes for Garcia's soul and character:

• Mercury in Leo is in Sun's own house and triplicity, and Moon is in the Sun's exaltation and triplicity.

• The Sun is dignified in Leo, in its own house and triplicity, and is in the very favorable Eleventh place. The Sun is also familiar with Mercury (perhaps overwhelming it) and receives a trine from Moon.

Such a glorious Sun can give the native great reputation, honor, and success. (In a less wonderful a position, Sun cannot be completely himself and renders the native humbler, less conspicuous, and with less success.) Although not having an ostentatious personality, Garcia's presence magnetized people toward him. Garcia was like the Sun, not in his outward behavior but in the impact he had on others. What planets testify to Garcia's royal Sun? First of all, we note his Saturn placement. Saturn is in sect, in its own triplicity, and oriental, rising ahead of the Sun. Here we have a positive Saturn, which probably expresses itself in Garcia's discipline and steadiness, and exercised a restraining influence on his showiness. It is Saturn that helped Garcia's style become distinctive, one very different from his solar peer and contemporary, Mick Jagger of the Rolling Stones.

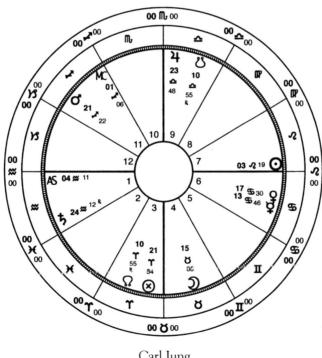

Carl Jung

Our lunar contribution is the natal chart of **Carl Jung**, the patron saint of many an astrologer. Jung's chart has two important influences from the modern planets: Neptune has an exact square to Jung's Sun, and Uranus squares his Moon. Using the methods I have outlined here, there is much to be gained examining Jung's chart without Uranus and Neptune. The modern planets in Jung's chart are interesting but, however, not required.

Jung has Aquarius rising and Saturn is present in that zoidion, in his own house and receiving a trine from Jupiter in Libra. Like Freud, Jung tended toward being reserved and careful at close range. Under Jupiter's aspect, Jung could influence others through his wisdom.

- Moon is the oikodespotes for Mercury and Moon. In Jung's nocturnal chart, Moon is the exaltation and triplicity lord for Moon, and the house and triplicity as well as the closest aspecting planet to Mercury.

- Moon's position is noteworthy and positive: she is angular and has an exchange of dignities with Venus, as they are in each other's houses. Saturn in the First has a predominating tenth place square to Moon: hence the self-control, the carefulness and reserve at close range - and the pipe.

If Moon represents the non-rational - the more emotional and instinctive - quality of soul, Jung had special access to this facet of who we are. Although Freud may have had the more incisive and far-reaching intellect, Jung's contribution was a personal understanding of the innermost recesses of mind - an understanding from the inside out. Moon also helps us understand Jung's interest in dreams and with psychic phenomena - one does not require Neptune for this.

The dominance of Moon and Venus also indicate Jung's ability to work with and understand the inner lives of women. It is no accident that many of the great Jungians - and Jungian astrologers - are women.

The next chapter departs from Ptolemy and discusses the Lots. They have come down to modern astrologers through the medieval tradition, and are often called "Arabic Parts." The Hellenistic tradition used lots as a major feature of natal delineation. I have found that using lots greatly enhances our understanding of the natal chart.

6

THE HELLENISTIC LOTS

Lots give additional astrological information about our lives. Every Hellenistic astrologer except Ptolemy used lots as a major feature of the natal chart, and those of us who have begun to use the Hellenistic lots as they used them can confirm their interpretative power. I can no longer work with an astrology chart unless I know the placements of the major lots.

Lots have survived into modern astrology as "Arabian Parts." Some astrologers use a list of lots from the medieval era. Even more modern astrologers use Ptolemy's version of the Lot of Fortune. We will consider this common formula for the Lot of Fortune and that of its reciprocal, the Lot of Spirit. Then we will discuss lots that use the Lots of Fortune and Spirit with one other planet. These are called the "Hermetic Lots": Necessity, Eros, Courage, Victory, and Nemesis. We will continue with the Lots of Exaltation, Accusation or "Being Away from Home", and Basis - the good, bad, and basic. In a later chapter we will work with lots specific to love, marriage and parents.

Lots are positions in a chart that synthesize three factors. The astrologer notes the number of degrees between two positions, and adds that number to a third position, usually the Ascendant. For example, if there are 63 degrees from one position to another, the corresponding lot is 63 degrees from to the Ascendant. If you reverse position and go from the second planet to the first, the distance from the Ascendant will be 297 degrees.

Why do we call them "Lots" and not "Parts?" Once again, it is a matter of using more accurate language. The Greek word *klaros* has the same range of meaning as the English "lot": a parcel of land, a game of chance ("drawing lots," "casting lots", "lottery"), and "lot in life." It is interesting that the words *klaros* and *morion* - the Greek word for degree - are both words for "fate." Our word "part" simply means a portion, and conveys no information relevant to the meaning of these positions.

We begin with the Lots of Fortune and Spirit. These are affiliated with the distance between Sun and Moon, and between Moon and Sun, which is added to the Ascendant. It is no accident that the most important lots involve these three general positions. The Lots of Fortune and Spirit concern two reciprocal issues in our lives: the turnings of the "wheel of fortune" and how we make our own choices and initiate activity. Here are the formulae for both lots, as I originally learned them. This formula appears in Ptolemy, but I will argue for a different procedure.

- For the Lot of Fortune, find the arc - the number of degrees - *from the Sun to the Moon*, and project that same number of degrees in zodiacal order from the Ascendant. The mathematical formula is AS + Moon – Sun (See the following panel.)

- For the Lot of Spirit, take the arc from the *Moon to the Sun*, and again project that number from the Ascendant. The formula is AS + Sun − Moon.

These lots are positioned symmetrically on either side of the Ascendant. If one lot is sixty-three degrees counterclockwise from the Ascendant, the other will be 297 degrees counterclockwise or 63 degrees the other way, which would be clockwise. One may also say that the Ascendant is the midpoint between the two lots. Any two other lots that use the same positions but reverse the order will have a symmetrical relationship to the Ascendant.

Hellenistic astrologers cast the Lots of Fortune and Spirit in a different way from Ptolemy. *This procedure above is correct for daytime charts only.* For nocturnal charts, we *reverse* the order of the planets used above: the Lot of Fortune instead uses the arc from the Moon to the Sun, and the Lot of Spirit uses the arc from the Sun to the Moon. This bears repeating. The traditional Hellenistic version of the Lots of Fortune and Spirit are:

- For daytime charts, the Lot of Fortune uses the distance from the Sun to the Moon, and for nighttime charts it uses the distance from the Moon to the Sun.

- For daytime charts, the Lot of Spirit uses the distance from the Moon to the Sun, and for nighttime charts it uses the distance from the Sun to the Moon.

Someone with a nocturnal chart whose Lots of Fortune and Spirit were calculated using Ptolemy's method will have these two lots reversed. With the information above, the reader should be able to glance at a chart and determine whether the placements of the Lots of Fortune and Spirit are correct.

Why these Lots reverse and why it is important

It is standard procedure to reverse the order of the planets involved in a lot, depending on whether the chart is diurnal or nocturnal.

To construct the lot, when finding the distance between two planets, *the planet you begin from* is the priority, and usually this is the planet more in sect for the chart. This is why for the Lot of Fortune in a diurnal chart you begin with the Sun, and in a nocturnal chart you begin with the Moon. In both cases one begins from the *luminary of sect*.

The placements and relative positions of the Lots of Fortune and Spirit will correspond to the phases of Sun and Moon in the natal chart. (We will discuss these phases in detail in Chapter Nine.)

A person born at a New Moon, with the Sun and Moon together, will find the Lots of Fortune and Spirit close together with the Ascendant. An example is Marlon Brando, the eminent and controversial American movie actor (see over for the chart). Brando's Lot of Fortune is conjunct his Ascendant, reflecting the fact that he was born at the New Moon. The Lot of Spirit is also conjunct the Ascendant on the other side of the Ascendant, at 02 degrees Sagittarius.

Someone who was one born at a Full Moon will have the Lots of Fortune and Spirit together but opposite the Ascendant. An example of this is John Kerry. Kerry's Lot of Fortune conjoins his

How to Find Lots by Numbers

The standard formula for a Lot can be also expressed mathematically as A + B – C:

- "C," The number subtracted, corresponds to the planet or position *one would begin from*
- "B" is the planet or position *one would go to.*
- "A" is the position *to which would add the distance from C to B*. This is almost always the Ascendant.

By night, the formula for the Lot of Fortune is AS + Sun – Moon: "A" is Ascendant, "B" is Sun, and "C" is "Moon." This is another way of saying that, by night, the distance from Moon to Sun is the same as the arc of the Ascendant to the Lot of Spirit. Let's calculate a Lot of Fortune using this formula:

Using simple addition and subtraction, you need to convert to "absolute longitude". For Moon in the first degree of Capricorn and Sun in the twenty-first degree of Scorpio, you would calculate:

Ascendant	187°55'	(07 Libra 55)
+ Sun	+230°00'	(20 Scorpio)
	417°55'	
– Moon	(270°50')	(0 Capricorn 50)
=	147°05'	which turns out to be 27 Leo

In your mind's eye, envision the distance from 00 Capricorn and 20 Scorpio. That would be eleven zoidia and 20 degrees. Move eleven zoidia and 20 from 07 Libra and that's about 27 Leo, which is very close to what we arrived at arithmetically. I have found it beneficial to practice locating a lot in this way.

Moon, opposing Sun, which is on the Ascendant. The Lot of Spirit is very close to the Lot of Fortune, since the arc from the Sun to the Moon is about the same distance, whether measured from one luminary or the other. Because John Kerry was born almost at the Full Moon, the arc from the Moon to the Sun, and from the Sun to the Moon, will both be close to 180 degrees, and both lots oppose the Ascendant. As the Sun was rising and the Moon was setting at his time of birth, his lots are also close to Moon. A person born at a Quarter Moon will find the two lots opposing each other, as with Kerry's 2004 opponent.

George Bush has the Lot of Spirit in *Taurus*. Because he has a diurnal chart, the Lot of Fortune proceeds from Sun to Moon. Take the distance and add it to the Ascendant. As Bush's Sun is 24 degrees from his Ascendant, the Lot of Fortune will be 24 degrees from his Libra Moon, and is located in Scorpio. Bush's Lot of Spirit traces the path from Moon to Sun. That places his Lot of Spirit in early Taurus. Because of the square between his Sun and Moon, his two lots are opposed to one another.

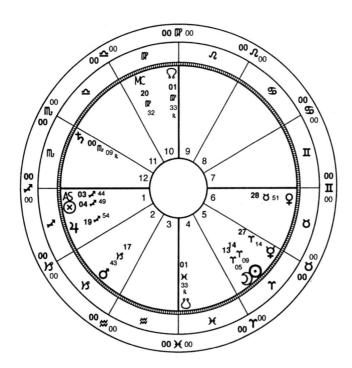

Marlon Brando
- Lot of Spirit 02 Sagittarius

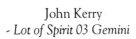

John Kerry
- Lot of Spirit 03 Gemini

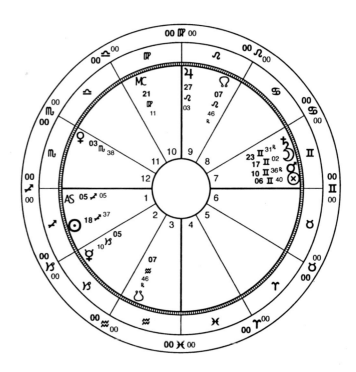

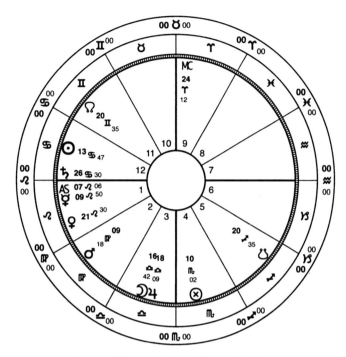

George W. Bush - *Lot of Spirit 04 Taurus*

Lots of Fortune and Spirit in Practice

The Lot of Fortune, "the Lot of the Moon", pertains to the natural flow of events in our lives. We are all subject to the alterations of larger economic, political, and cultural trends. We may have astrological indicators for great wealth or be endowed with talent for the electric guitar, but an economic depression or mass revival of the polka may hinder these outcomes. Our bodies themselves are subject to all kinds of events - regardless of how healthy our lifestyles are or how carefully we drive. Some people persistently draw Aces and Kings and others persistently draw Twos and Threes. The Lot of Fortune proceeds from the more empowered planet in sect to the planet not in sect. It describes the influence of the world on us, not of ourselves on our world.

You may recall, from Chapter Four, that Dorotheus and Vettius Valens used the triplicity lords of the Sun or Moon to interpret the overall happiness or misery of the native. The triplicity lords' position and angularity, as well as the placement of their respective house rulers, describe a native's overall opportunities for happiness and a good life over the course of a lifetime. We may also apply this procedure to the Lot of Fortune and its lord.

The Lot of Spirit, "the Lot of the Sun," describes change that occurs because of our intention. If the Lot of Fortune describes how much money we can make, the Lot of Spirit describes how we choose our vocation, how we answer our "calling." If the Lot of Fortune describes our overall health, the Lot of Spirit describes how we try to keep our bodies healthy. The Lot of Spirit is a place of will more than circumstance. Our intentions may go counter to the "natural" flow of things, as those of us who have dieted or adopted any new habit can attest: hence the Lot of Spirit goes in the direction from the planet not in sect to the one in sect.

Shifting the Places of Reference

We now encounter a critical way in which the Hellenistic tradition differs from common modern astrological practice. Although we think of the houses or places proceeding only from the Ascendant, there are other options available to us.

For the Lot of Fortune, we note the placement of planets - especially the dispositor of the Lot - *from the zoidion of the Lot of Fortune*. The Lot of Fortune becomes a First place for matters related to the Lot of Fortune. Depending on what kind of question the astrologer is answering, one may note the zoidia from other lots as well.

Instead, Ptolemy advocated using *planets' zoidia* to be a First place for issues specific to that planet. To answer questions about one's father, one proceeds from the Sun by day or Saturn by night and cast the other zoidia from that planet. For questions concerning one's mother, cast the twelve places from Venus by day and from Moon by night. For information about your siblings if they have had the same mother as you, go from the Tenth place from the planet of one's mother. This is not unique to the Hellenistic tradition.

For the charts of women, Indian astrology or Jyotish commonly works with the twelve places from the Moon the "Moon chart", to supplement the Ascendant chart.

The Hamburg School or Uranian system of modern astrology, pioneered by Alfred Witte, casts houses or places from the Sun, Moon, Lunar Nodes, and Midheaven, as well as from the Ascendant, to answer specific questions.[1] Here the Ascendant is one of many possibilities. I return to the Hellenistic tradition.

It often happens that a planet is in a difficult place from the zoidion of the Ascendant but is in a better place from the zoidion of the Lot of Fortune. In this case the planet's position related to the Lot of Fortune enhances the effectiveness of that planet, partly compensating for the weakness of its position from the Ascendant. If, however, a planet governing the Lot of Fortune is in good condition related to the Ascendant and poor condition related to the Lot of Fortune, that planet's effectiveness is weakened.

The Ascendant, more than the Lot of Fortune or any other lot, is a general indicator of the condition of the individual, and placements of the zoidia from the Ascendant are important considerations. We will discuss this in detail in Chapter Seven. To answer specific questions, however, we will work with other positions and cast the zoidia from those positions. I supply an example of the difference it makes casting places from lots.

Eva Peron has the Lot of Spirit in *Cancer*. The Lots of Exaltation and Accusation are in Aquarius. The Lot of Marriage (involving Venus and Saturn) is also in Aquarius.

---

1.   See Brummond & Rudolph (1992) pp. 51-58.

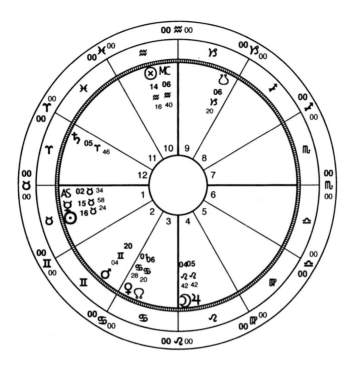

Eva Peron - *Lot of Spirit 20 Cancer*

When we surveyed her natal chart during our discussion of the triplicity lords, we noticed that Saturn is in a difficult position in the Twelfth from the Ascendant and in fall. When we work with Eva Peron's lots we must return to Saturn, as Saturn is the lord of the Lots of Fortune, Exaltation, and Accusation. (We will say more about the Lots of Exaltation and Accusation soon, and the Lots of Marriage in Chapter Ten.) Saturn's governance makes its position even more critical for Peron's prospects.

Our interest is heightened when we notice that *Saturn is in the Tenth place from the Lot of Spirit*, which is with Venus. Here we have found a key to Peron's success: the sweat of her own brow, the hard road. She used Venus as a means to find success - being an actress and marrying a politician - and these means were of her own devising (Lot of Spirit). Through Saturn, her Lot of Spirit connects with the Lots in Aquarius. Because of Saturn's difficult placement, her ambitions could have been thwarted, yet she found ways to become successful. This configuration is a perfect example of how to become a self-made person, and, perhaps, a tragic hero.

Examples of Lots of Fortune and Spirit

We begin with the natal charts of two extremely creative artists with more will (Lot of Spirit) than wallet (Lot of Fortune). Adding the Lot of Exaltation to the mix, we can see how one would interpret a natal chart using several lots at once.

In **Mozart's** chart, much hinges on Mars, because Mars is the lord of the Lot of Fortune and located in Cancer, it is with the Lot of Spirit.

Mozart's Lot of Fortune is in mixed condition. The Third place from the Ascendant is neither a wonderful place nor one of the worst. Both malefics Saturn and benefic Venus are angular to the Lot of Fortune from the cadent Sixth, resulting in a draw between them

The lord of the Lot of Fortune - Mars in Cancer - gives a sense of who is in charge. Mars is a powerful but unstable planet for Mozart. Mars is in the Eleventh from the Ascendant, a strong place, but the Ninth from the Lot of Fortune, which would be considered cadent. Mars is in sect and in his own triplicity, but is in fall and retrograde. Of the benefics and malefics, only Jupiter casts an aspect to Mars. Mozart's Mars sometimes comes to the rescue and other times veers wildly off the mark, like a valiant warrior who, on occasion, shows up drunk and out of control.

Does the placement of the Lot of Fortune indicate his financial difficulties? Granted, the payment given at that time to an independent composer in Vienna would not be adequate to his talent or his productivity. The more difficult problem was that Mozart spent money extravagantly and impulsively: the culprit here is Mars. At best, Mozart practiced involuntary frugality.

The Lot of Spirit, which is in Cancer in the Eleventh, occupies the same zoidion as Mars, who is lord of the Lot of Fortune. Moon in Sagittarius governs the Lot of Spirit.

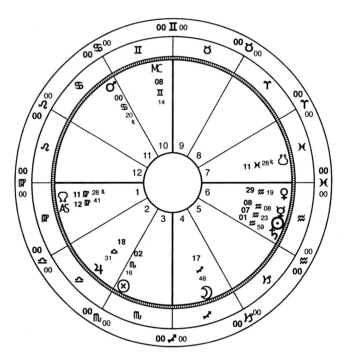

Wolfgang Mozart - *Lot of Spirit 23 Cancer*

We see Mozart here as a headstrong and willful person: someone who must get his own way. Although often his independent spirit resulted in extraordinary accomplishment, there were other times when he alienated people unnecessarily and created his own problems. When Mozart's independent spirit governed his music, he produced sublimities like *The Marriage of Figaro, Don Giovanni* and many other masterpieces; when his independent spirit governed him, he could be impulsive and reckless.

This interpretation is supported by the placement of Mozart's Lot of Exaltation in Capricorn. A cadent Saturn that is out of sect and under the Sun's beams governs the Lot of Exaltation. Mars also opposes this Lot. This factor, along with the Mars-like character of his Lot of Spirit, served to block Mozart from the greater fame and appreciation that should have flowed in his direction during his lifetime. However, because their lords, Moon and Saturn, are in sextile to one another, there are possibilities for improvement.

Although Mozart was often well thought of during his lifetime, especially by fellow musicians, it was after his early death that he became thought of as one of the great geniuses of Western culture. His chart gives some indication of posthumous glory. The Fourth zoidion from his Ascendant, Sagittarius, contains the Moon, which is in sect and governed by Jupiter in Libra. The lord of the Fourth, Jupiter, casts a fortunate sextile upon the Moon. The Fourth place governs one's death and its aftermath. Mozart's early death may have served to augment his reputation.

We now turn from the musical to the pictorial and poetic arts, in the person of **William Blake**. Here is another artistic genius with good spirit but little fortune. We have already examined William's Blake's natal chart for his vocation and his character. Now we will discuss his Lots of Fortune and Spirit.

The Lot of Fortune is in Sagittarius. Jupiter, governing the Lot, is in its own house with the Lot of Fortune. However, Jupiter is in the sixth zoidion from the Ascendant, a cadent house, and is under the Sun's rays. The Lot of Fortune and Jupiter receive aspects from the malefics Saturn and Mars, without a direct aspect from Venus that might compensate. Ordinarily, it seems fortunate to have the Lot of Fortune with Jupiter in Sagittarius, but in Blake's chart Jupiter has problems.

When we examine the position of Blake's Lot of Spirit in Pisces, we are again brought back to Jupiter. The house lord of Pisces, Jupiter, is in the tenth zoidion from the Lot of Spirit. The Lot of Spirit's position is better than that of the Lot of Fortune. The Lot of Spirit is in the ninth place from the Ascendant, which is more favorable than the Lot of Fortune in the sixth. Pisces, the zoidion of the Lot Spirit, receives aspects from Venus but not from either Mars or Saturn. This reverses the situation existing with the Lot of Fortune, which is aspected by malefics only. How might we interpret this? This indicates that Blake's life would contain reversals and difficult financial circumstances. Jupiter's position in its own house means that his external life was not totally bleak, although Jupiter offers more promises for success than Blake would actualize. Similar to Mozart, Blake's talent should have brought him greater worldly success.

The Lot of Spirit is more promising, especially the aspects to it by benefics. Blake was a fiercely independent man. His career path as an engraver and poet resulted from deliberate choice;

You want this Lot prominent in your chart

A Lot with a very positive outcome for the native is appropriately called "The Exaltation of the Nativity." I refer to it as **The Lot of Exaltation.** Recall that every planet's exaltation is not just a sign or zoidion but a degree contained within it. The Lot of Exaltation is the one place you might use the exaltation degrees. Here is how it is derived.

- By day, measure the arc starting from the Sun to its exaltation degree at 19 Aries.
- By night, measure the arc from the Moon to its exaltation degree at 2 Taurus.
- Add the result to the Ascendant.

To judge an especially propitious nativity, we would not rely on the placement of this Lot and its lord but would also ask: what is its relationship to the Lots of Fortune and Spirit? Are all their house lords in good condition and good places in the birth chart? Remember from Chapter Four that in the chart example from Valens the lord of the Lot of Exaltation, the Sun, was the Tenth zoidion from the Lot of Fortune. This increased the rank and fame of the person whose chart Valens was considering.

---

a different choice might have given him better chances for money and fame during his lifetime. His spiritual, artistic, and poetic inspiration was uncompromising and was well ahead of his time. (The modern astrologer may note that Uranus is also in Pisces, giving further fuel to Blake's independent and eccentric nature.) The weakness of Jupiter, together with Mars - the oikodespotes of his "soul" - receiving an opposition from Saturn, manifest in Blake's problems with depression.

As with William Blake, **Emily Dickinson** has Jupiter with her Lot of Fortune and Saturn with her Lot of Spirit. Resemblances end there, however. Governing her Lot of Fortune is Saturn in Virgo in the Eleventh, so that Saturn governs both Dickinson's Lot of Fortune and Jupiter. Jupiter is in fall and both Jupiter and Saturn are out of sect. This has a limited and grim feel to it. Dickinson lived in her father's house her entire life but had enough funds to get by. She neither had nor needed to spend much money. This strong Saturn influence may also explain her frail physical constitution.

As with Mozart, the lord of Dickinson's Lot of Fortune is with the Lot of Spirit, giving the same self-directed character. If Mozart's Lot of Spirit had a Mars-like nature, Dickinson's was Saturnine. Dickinson's limited lifestyle was entirely of her own making. She had some opportunities to marry and move on, and even to become a published poet. Instead she made herself the absolute dictator of her life: of her bedroom, where she wrote and collected her poetry, and of her back yard, to which so much of her best writing referred. If Mozart and Blake made the most of their willfulness and temper, Dickinson made the most of her confinement. And now we examine a rather different type of woman from Emily Dickinson.

Martha Stewart is one of today's most successful businesswoman. She has been able to transform upscale cooking and home advice into a billion-dollar media industry. Her recent legal difficulties

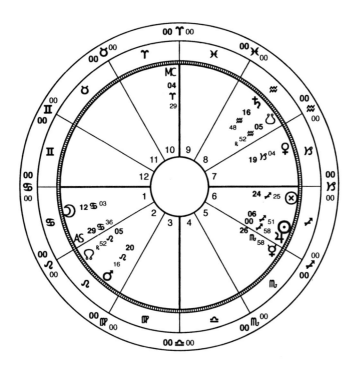

William Blake
- *Lot of Spirit 04 Pisces*

Emily Dickinson
- *Lot of Spirit 22 Virgo*

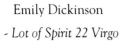

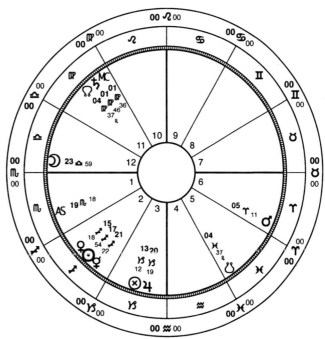

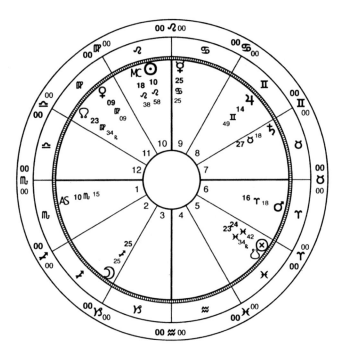

Martha Stewart - *Lot of Spirit 25 Gemini*

have served to make her even better known worldwide, and have solidified opinions for and against her.

Stewart's Lot of Fortune is in Pisces in the Fifth, governed by Jupiter. At first this looks terrible, as Jupiter is in the Eighth place from the Ascendant and opposite his own house - what we would call in detriment - in Gemini. Compensating for Jupiter's position in the Eighth place from her Ascendant is that he is oriental and in sect. Jupiter is stronger by being angular from the Lot itself, in the Fourth place from the Lot.

Saturn does not aspect Jupiter but Mars does and difficulties do arise from this over-exuberant out of sect Mars. Stewart has made many enemies on her way to greater power and wealth, which has created a bad press for her. Mars accounts for the financial impulse that was the source of her legal difficulty and the rash behavior that eventually led to her prison term. The Jupiter-Mars connection can provide an overconfidence bordering on arrogance: this has been a source of her success and her difficulty.

Stewart's Lot of Spirit is in Gemini and alongside Jupiter. As with Mozart and Dickinson, the lord of Fortune is in the same zoidion as the Lot of Spirit. With Mozart we saw alongside Spirit a feisty Mars; with Dickinson a restricting Saturn; with Stewart Jupiter gives an overconfidence bordering on arrogance - especially with the testimony of Mars. Stewart's Jupiter in Gemini is in detriment - opposite his own house in Sagittarius - but is oriental and in sect.

The Lord of the Lot of Spirit is Mercury, in Cancer in the Ninth. Ordinarily the lord being in the Second place from the lot would not be favorable, but Mercury is also oriental, outside the beams of the Sun and in sect. Mercury is also with the Lot of Exaltation and also receives a strong aspect from Mars. The Lot of Spirit and the Lot of Exaltation have created a keen business mind that has given her fame and mixed glory; the oppositions and contentions, once again, come from the testimony of Mars.

The bottom line of this analysis is the strength of Jupiter with both lots, in spite of its position in Gemini in the Eighth place. (The Hellenistic tradition was more concerned with the weakness of a planet opposite its exaltation - its fall or depression - than in its detriment, opposite its house.) During Stewart's business career she has repeatedly found creative and innovative ways to bring the domestic into the public sphere, becoming wealthy by bringing elegance and frugality to the general public.

The Hermetic Lots: Derived from Fortune and Spirit

We now expand our inquiry to include lots that we derive from Fortune or Spirit and one of the five starry planets: Mercury, Venus, Mars, Jupiter, and Saturn. Paulus tells us these lots are from the lost text *Panaratus* ("All-Virtuous"). Paulus attributes these lots to Hermes himself, which tells us two things about this list: he considers them to be very old, and he looks upon them with reverence. The first two lots are the Lots of Fortune and Spirit; the other five build from them. Two lots use the *benefics* and the *Lot of Spirit*:

- The **Lot of Eros** takes the distance from Spirit to Venus by day; by night it is measured from Venus to Spirit.
  By day the formula is AS + Venus – Spirit.
  By night it is AS + Spirit – Venus.

- The **Lot of Victory** takes the distance from Spirit to Jupiter by day; by night it is measured from Jupiter to Spirit.
  By day the formula is AS + Jupiter – Spirit.
  By night it is AS + Spirit – Jupiter.

There is a pattern that makes it easy to learn these formulae. The Lot of Spirit, the Lot of the Sun, is more diurnal than either benefic. (Remember that the computation of a lot usually begins with the planet in sect, the Lot of Spirit being the exception.) Because of this, day charts begin with the Lot of Spirit and night charts begin with the planet used in the lot.

Both the Lots of Eros and Victory describe fortunate circumstances. The Lot of Eros is not about erotic love, but voluntary association and friendship. The Lot of Victory sounds a lot like Jupiter itself: gratified expectations, enterprise, and success.

The other four lots involve the Lot of Fortune, and show us that the Lot of Fortune, the Lot of the Moon, is wholly nocturnal. Because of this, for day charts one begins with the planet and for night charts one begins with the lot.

- The **Lot of Courage** proceeds from Mars to Fortune by day, by night it is measured from Fortune to Mars.
  By day the formula is AS + Fortune – Mars
  By night it is AS + Mars – Fortune.

- **The Lot of Nemesis** starts from Saturn to Fortune by day; by night it is measured from Fortune to Saturn.
  By day the formula is AS + Fortune – Saturn
  By night it is AS + Saturn – Fortune.

The Lot of Courage relates to boldness and strength but also to plotting and evildoing: it has the same range as Mars itself. The Lot of Nemesis is Saturnine and thoroughly wretched: hidden negative factors, weakness ("impotence"), exile, loss, and death. The next lot is a bit surprising:

- The **Lot of Necessity** starts from Mercury to Fortune by day, and the reverse by night.
  By day the formula is AS + Fortune – Mercury.
  By night it is AS + Mercury – Fortune.

The Lot of Necessity relates to restrictive and difficult situations: imprisonment, subordination, battles, and adversarial relationships. What is surprising is that Mercury is not a malefic, yet this lot describes difficulties. Why? The Lot of Necessity shows the possibilities of adapting - and perhaps overcoming - difficult circumstances in life. The Lot of Necessity, involving Mercury, is the lot of *ananke,* which is necessity resulting from your ignorance, from making mistakes. The influence of Mercury allows one to use cleverness and even guile as a means to recover from difficulties.

It may be instructive to compare the Lot of Necessity involving Mercury to the Lot of Nemesis involving Saturn. Originally a *nemesis* was the occasion of divine wrath, the gods' retribution. Consequences from the gods may come as a result of one's pride, injustice, or impiety - or, perhaps, for example, from Hera - simply because Zeus took a liking to you. Like Oedipus, you may be totally innocent of intent but nonetheless guilty of the deed. You are, at any rate, toast; there is no higher court of appeal. Note that the descriptions of the Lot of Nemesis relate to situations that are more or less permanent, including death.

Both nemesis and necessity are situations that are difficult but necessity, involving Mercury, does not require that you be doomed. Because Mercury is crafty and changeable, like an action hero in trouble, you may come up with a plan.

An Intriguing Alternative

Our main source for the Hermetic Lots is Paulus Alexandrinus, who gives us the calculations for them that I have noted above. The Lots of Eros, Necessity, Courage, Victory, and Nemesis each involve one of the starry planets. There is another version, however, that merits consideration.[2]

According to Firmicus Maternis[3], the Lots of Eros and Necessity involve not Venus and Mercury but the Lot of Fortune and the Lot of Spirit *together*. (This duplicated the *Lots of Basis*, which we discuss below.) For the place of Eros, which Firmicus calls "sexual desire," he uses the distance from the Lot of Spirit to the Lot Fortune and projects the distance from the Ascendant. For the Lot of Necessity, he uses the distance from Fortune to Spirit and projects that distance from the Ascendant. Just like the Lots of Fortune and Spirit themselves, the Lots of Eros and Necessity will be symmetrically distant from the Ascendant.

Greek Horoscopes is an annotated collection of astrological charts and fragments of charts from the Hellenistic era. Two charts from this collection[4], both of which are nocturnal, appear to use the same formula as Firmicus but reverse the order of Fortune and Spirit for night charts.

According to this alternative formula, the Lots of Eros and Necessity are second in importance only to the Lots of Fortune and Spirit, and are more important in the astrological chart than the Lots of Courage, Victory, and Nemesis.

As this version of the Lot of Eros proceeds from the Lot of Spirit to the Lot of Fortune, priority is given to the Lot of Spirit. This emphasizes the *personal* nature of the Lot of Eros, which is usually depicted as determining matters of friendship and voluntary alliance. Firmicus, by considering this Lot to be that of sexual desire, emphasizes the willfulness of that response. (This is consonant with the meaning of the Lot of Spirit.) On the other hand, this version of the Lot of Necessity, by giving priority to the Lot of Fortune implies that necessity is primarily a creation of outer circumstance.

Matters pertaining to the Lot to Eros, although personal, are also conditioned by outer circumstance - represented by the Lot of Fortune as the minor player. We might call this appetite. Although the Lot of Necessity pertains primarily to external conditions, the use of the Lot of Spirit, as a minor player, reminds us that it is also our habitual personal responses to circumstance that limit our possibilities, that bring us a kind of self-made necessity.

Although this alternative for the Lot of Eros and Necessity is interesting and provocative, for our purposes here I will continue with Paulus' determination of these lots. I continue to use Venus for the Lot of Eros and Mercury for the Lot of Necessity. I invite the reader to try out this other version on his or her own.

---

2. Dorian Greenbaum, personal communication, October 2006.
3. Book VI, Chap, 32, sections 45-46.
4. #138, 338.

Once again we look at the birth chart of **Jacqueline Kennedy Onassis**. Previously, we saw that Mercury in the Tenth was overwhelmed by the Sun in its own house in Leo. The Midheaven degree is close to the royal star Regulus, a benefic star of the nature of Jupiter and Mars. We now look at the Lot of Fortune, at 8 degrees Leo, which is in the Tenth and also close to Sun. (A lot is never considered under the Sun's beams, since a lot is not a planet.) The Lot of Fortune is positioned well, ruled well, and well aspected in Onassis' chart.

Remember that the Lot of Fortune indicates what happens to you. What happened to Jacqueline Onassis brought her great fame and prominence. Although many of us might consider her very lucky, Onassis herself was ambivalent about what fate had brought her, although less ambivalent about the fortune.

The Lot of Exaltation is also in the Tenth and is also governed by a powerful Sun in Leo. Even the paparazzi that fed off her revered her.

Onassis' Lot of Spirit is in Aquarius, in the Fourth place from the Ascendant, closely opposing her Midheaven degree. For Onassis, personal initiative was expressed by her having a private life. Saturn, the dispositor for her Lot of Spirit, is in the Eleventh zoidion from the Lot of Spirit, forming a sextile. The governance of Saturn suggests that a private life of relative freedom might come to her later in life. Because Saturn is in sect and configured well with her Lot of Spirit, this eventually did come to pass.

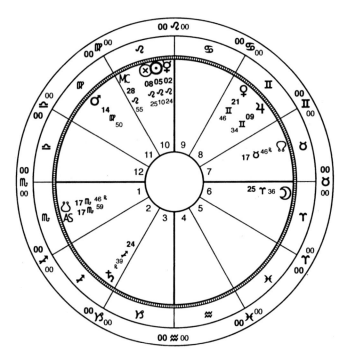

Jacqueline K Onassis - *Lot of Spirit 27 Aquarius*

Of course if she really wanted to be left alone, she could have married someone other than a charming senator with presidential ambitions. She might also have stayed away from elderly shipping billionaires.

The Lot of Necessity falls in Scorpio, the zoidion of her Ascendant. Since there are 6 degrees between Mercury and the Lot of Fortune, the Lot of Necessity is 6 degrees from her Ascendant degree. Since this in the First, her confinement came from who she was, not from one particular situation: one could say that her persona as a tasteful and refined celebrity confined her. The strong involvement of Mars indicates how she might deal with this. Because Mars governs her Lot of Necessity and her Ascendant, her response could be quite aggressive. This Mars may be behind the incident where she punched a photographer as well as her bitter court dispute over Aristotle Onassis' fortune after his death.

Her Lots of Eros and Victory are both located in Pisces. Because Venus and Jupiter are close to each other, these two lots are also close to one another. Jupiter is in an angular relationship to both Lots, but Mars opposes them. Jupiter, which governs both lots, also has its problems:

• Jupiter receives testimony from both Saturn (opposition) and, from Mars in Virgo, a difficult square.

• Jupiter is in the weak Eighth place, where, along with Venus, this planet cannot make many positive contributions.

• Jupiter is in detriment in Gemini: opposed to its own house (Once again, this is less of a factor in Hellenistic than in medieval or modern astrology.)

Jupiter, when poorly configured, raises hopes but disappoints. When involved with the Lot of Eros, it may indicate a life that is filled with people but lonely. When such a Jupiter is involved with the Lot of Victory, that life may have more surface glory than real fulfillment.

Since Jupiter is the Eighth place from her Ascendant, suggesting death, the freedom she eventually won came when the men she married both died. The Eighth place from the Ascendant in her chart is also the Eleventh from the Lot of Fortune: Valens' Place of Acquisition. This is a clear indicator that the source of her fortune was from inheritance.

The natal chart of **Bill Wilson**, a co-founder of Alcoholics Anonymous, displays a different destiny. The Lots of Necessity, Courage, and Nemesis are in a place of difficulty in the Sixth. Jupiter, the house lord for Pisces, brings some benefit: he is in his joy in the Eleventh. But there is no relationship between Pisces, the location of these lots and Leo, where Jupiter is. It would be much better if there was an aspect between the zoidion of these lots and their dispositor. Making matters more difficult, both Mars and Saturn behold these lots, and the more benevolent and strongly placed Venus does not. Between age eighteen and forty, Wilson's alcoholism had progressed from a minor personal flaw to a debilitating illness for which there was no hope of recovery. Looking at these problematic lots in Pisces, we find ample astrological symbolism for the mess that had become of his life.

Our outlook changes when we consider the Lot of Spirit and the Lot of Eros: they are exactly conjunct, to the degree, in Aquarius. (Since Eros involves Venus and the Lot of Spirit, they are

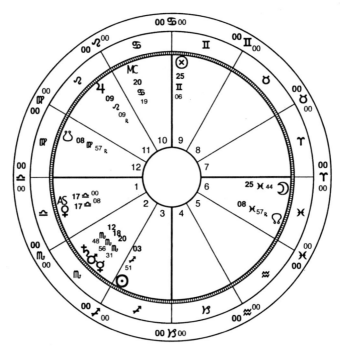

Bill Wilson - *Lot of Spirit 08 Aquarius*

close because Venus is conjunct the Ascendant.) The lord of Spirit and Eros is Saturn, who is strongly placed in relation to the Lots, ten zoidia away in Scorpio. Once again, the presence of Mars with Saturn does make matters difficult; one would not expect an easy time bringing forth the positive possibilities from these Lots. Jupiter from the Eleventh, in aspect to the Lots and their lord, is a positive influence upon them.

In light of Wilson's life, the combination of the Lots of Spirit and Eros is an auspicious configuration. Remember that the Lot of Eros is not about sexuality, but rather friendship and voluntary association, and that the Lot of Spirit is how we use our own initiative. Being the co-founder of Alcoholics Anonymous, the first of many Twelve Step programs, Wilson expanded the concept of friendship and support to form healing communities that currently operate all over the world. This shows that a difficult chart can have redemptive qualities. The Lots of Spirit and Eros give a good indication of how redemption took place in his life.

Now we discuss the natal chart of **Jerry Garcia**, the principal member of the Grateful Dead. This is a breathtakingly positive natal chart. Many planets are in dignity: Sun is in his own house, Jupiter in exaltation, and Venus and Saturn in their triplicities. Saturn, Jupiter, and Venus are all oriental to the Sun and in addition Jupiter and Venus are in the powerful Tenth place from the Ascendant. The Sun is also its own triplicity lord and is in its joy in the Eleventh. Sun's other triplicity lords are

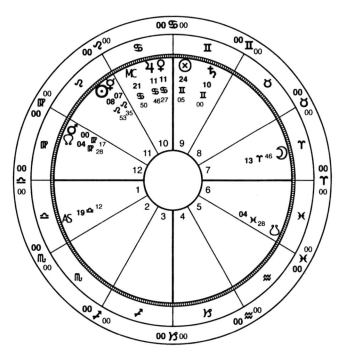

Jerry Garcia - *Lot of Spirit 14 Aquarius*

Jupiter, in exaltation in the Tenth, and *Saturn*, in triplicity in the Ninth. (Saturn's position tells that the last third of life would be a bit less fortunate for Garcia.)

The fact that there are so many planets in dignity means that their expression will be, for the most part, positive and appropriate. Being oriental gives them further strength and their location in fortunate places from the Ascendant gives them the potential for effectiveness and prominence.

As with Jacqueline Kennedy Onassis, Garcia's Lots of Eros and Victory are close to one another, reflecting the closeness of Venus and Jupiter in his natal chart. Onassis' lord for these two lots is in the Eighth from the Ascendant, but the Fourth from the lot. In Garcia's case, Jupiter, the lord of the Lots of Eros and Victory, is in the powerful Tenth place from the Ascendant but the Sixth from the lots. These two factors - the placement of the lord of a lot in relationship to the Ascendant and the lot itself - are both important, and give mixed results.

Although not resulting in the worldwide celebrity of a Jacqueline Onassis, Garcia's Lots of Eros and Victory are better placed than hers. The Tenth zoidion from the Ascendant argues for prominence and celebrity. Jupiter in Garcia's chart is more favorable than Jupiter in Onassis', as his Jupiter is also in exaltation and conjunct Venus that is in her own triplicity. The strength of Garcia's Jupiter more than compensates for the weakness of the placement of these lots in the Sixth zoidion from the Ascendant.

The fact that the Lot of Courage is in Leo, with the Sun, argues for its strength, but it can be also a source of difficulty. The Lot of Courage does involve Mars and ranges from being valiant to cruel. Jerry Garcia may have been willful but nobody would consider him aggressive or full of machismo. Other factors are involved.

One indication of his laid-back personal style can be found in his Lot of Spirit in Aquarius. This Lot is in the Fifth place from the Ascendant, and its lord, Saturn, is in the Fifth place from the Lot. The Lot of Exaltation is also with Saturn. This placement makes Saturn a very important planet for Garcia's personal creativity and good reputation. Saturn, although a malefic, is placed well in Garcia's chart: in sect, oriental, and in its own triplicity.

You may recall our discussion of the dodekatamoria from Chapter Three. Saturn is the dodekatamorion of the Ascendant and the dodekatamorion of Saturn falls with the Ascendant. Since Saturn is placed so well in Garcia's chart, its connection to the Ascendant by dodekatamorion makes Saturn a stronger, not a more difficult, planet. Garcia's Saturn works hard, and it has modesty, focus, and discipline. This Saturn was powerful enough to help him turn his life around after being arrested, being placed in a drug treatment facility, and almost dying from a diabetic coma.

Saturn and the Lot of Spirit also indicate some of Garcia's peculiar greatness. Although his Sun is powerful enough to magnetize people, he never suffered from a tendency to show off or act in a condescending way. Indeed, part of his enduring popularity is his undramatic style.

Including the Bad and the Basic

We close with a discussion of two more lots: one that uses both malefics and another that uses both the Lots of Fortune and Spirit. The lot using Mars and Saturn is called the "Lot of Accusation," or "The Place of Necessity."

• By day take the distance from Saturn to Mars, that is, from the planet in sect to the planet out of sect, and add that distance to the Ascendant.

• By night take the distance from Mars to Saturn, and again project that distance from the Ascendant.

Another name for this is the "Lot of Being Away from Home." Absence from home, in this case, does not mean having a second house in the country or being on vacation, it means exile: being without a place to live, even without gasoline in your car or credit cards and probably with nobody near you who speaks your language. In this context we now look at the chart of a voluntary exile, the celebrated writer **James Joyce**. He left Ireland as a young man and pursued his writing career in different places in Europe. However the locale for all his writings was his native Ireland.

The Lots of Fortune and Spirit are close to one another in the Seventh, reflecting Joyce's Sun-Moon opposition. Both are in difficult positions in Joyce's chart. What makes them difficult is the lord of the lots: Moon in the Eighth zoidion from the Ascendant and the Second from both lots. Since Moon is with the Lot of Necessity, which involves Mercury and the Lot of Fortune, it indicates Joyce's need to survive through his wits alone.

The Lot of Being Away from Home, involving Saturn and Mars, also has a peculiar position. Placed in Scorpio, it is governed by Mars in Gemini, which is cadent but in its own joy and is in the Eighth place from the lot itself. So far this also looks difficult.

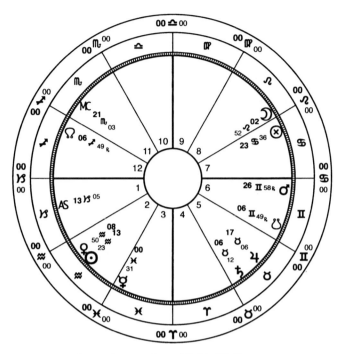

James Joyce - *Lot of Spirit 02 Cancer*

However, The Lot of Being Away from Home is fortunate to be in the Eleventh place from the Ascendant and to have so many other planets that are angular to it - Venus, Sun, Jupiter, Saturn, and Moon. Joyce's exile from his native Ireland was lonely and bitter (Moon is in square to Saturn), yet was also the springboard for much of his creative output (Sun, Venus, Jupiter).

Another name for the lot that involves the malefics is the Lot of Accusation. Venus and Saturn aspect the lot; in Aquarius and Taurus, Venus and Saturn are in each other's houses. The prominence of these two planets bring to mind that *Ulysses* was banned in the United States for several years on account of its sexual content. *Ulysses* was considered pornographic. Indeed, that he was a "dirty writer" is my memory from first hearing about Joyce. Helping to create a positive outcome are two other lots: the Lot of Victory and the Lot of Basis.

The Lot of Victory, involving Jupiter and the Lot of Spirit, is in the Second zoidion from the Ascendant, with Sun and Venus. Its lord, Saturn, is angular to the lot. The Lot of Victory brings many of Jupiter's benefits, such as confidence and connectedness, and it is helped by the exchange of dignities between Venus and Saturn.

The **Lot of Basis**, as its name implies, anchors the natal chart. It is derived in the same way for both diurnal and nocturnal charts: take the distance from the Lot of Fortune to the Lot of Spirit or from Spirit to Fortune, *whichever is shorter*, and add that distance to the Ascendant. For people born near a New Moon or a Full Moon, the Lot of Basis will be near the Ascendant, since in both cases, there is little distance between the Lots of Fortune and Spirit.

One may use the Lot of Basis to support an interpretation for the general happiness or prosperity of the native - if the lord of the Lot of Basis connects with the Lots of Fortune and Spirit and their lords. Here Basis is in Aquarius with Venus and Sun, its lord Saturn is angular to it, and Jupiter also testifies to it.

In Joyce's case, the Lot of Basis brings Sun and Venus qualities to the foundation of his natal chart. The lord of Basis, Saturn, gives discipline and tenacity. He spent seven years writing *Ulysses*. Joyce was nearly blind when he wrote his last and most difficult work, *Finnegan's Wake*. It took him seventeen years to write this book; he said that it should take his readers the same amount of time to read it.

We conclude our discussion of lots with another look at the 2004 US Presidential candidates. **Kerry's** Lots of Fortune and Spirit in Gemini are both with the malefics Mars and Saturn, and have Mercury as their dispositor. Mercury resides in the Second place from the Ascendant; Capricorn and Gemini are contra-antiscia - equally rising - zoidia, and they do have some connection. This recalls our discussion in the previous chapter.

When we look at Mercury, it is hard for us not to think of Saturn, since Saturn is the dispositor for Capricorn, and Mercury in Capricorn and Saturn in Gemini are in each other's houses. Saturn is also the planet with disposition over Moon and Mercury. Once again, when you think about John Kerry, think Saturn and Mercury.

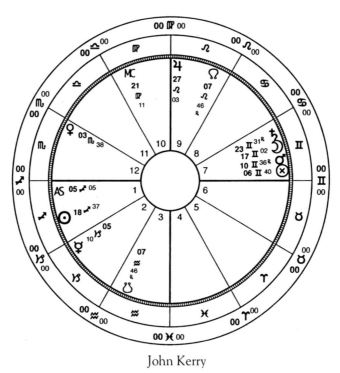

John Kerry

These planets show his reputed remoteness, his dryness of intellect, and his circumspection. Perhaps one can also detect a manipulating quality, since Mercury, the planet of politicians, governs both lots. Perhaps Saturn even brings a dose of cynicism. Mars, close to the Lot of Spirit and in sect, is in stronger condition than Kerry's Saturn. Many who have worked with or known Kerry would rather see his Mars than his Saturn: Mars makes him more passionate about his positions in general, and gives him a willingness to take a chance. Mars and Mercury also exchange dignities: Mars is in Mercury's house, and Mercury is in Mars' exaltation.

Because John Kerry was born at the Full Moon, and because his Lots of Fortune and Spirit are close together, his Lot of Basis is conjunct his Ascendant.

Ascendant, Sun, and Basis have one planet disposing them all: Jupiter in the Ninth in Leo. Jupiter exchanges dignities with the Sun - they are in one another's houses - and they are also in trine. This gives Kerry a strong personal presence, the look of a leader. Remember, however, that Jupiter is both out of sect and retrograde, and so it is less powerful than it could be. Kerry's rise to prominence has had its share of reversals and delays. As with Blake's Jupiter in the Sixth under the Sun's beams, this Jupiter does not deliver what it promises.

The Lot of Basis, like the Lots of Courage, Accusation, and Nemesis, are all in Sagittarius in the First. In this, we see another manifestation of Jupiter, the lord of these lots. His strength is his personal sense of purpose and his downfall is his grandiosity, arrogance, and relentless self-promotion. These are issues of the Ascendant run amok.

Kerry's Lot of Exaltation is in Libra, in Eleventh place, close to his Midheaven degree. This could be fortunate. Less helpful is its lord, Venus, in Scorpio and in the Twelfth place. Although by every account Kerry has been successful in life, detractors have continually dogged him.

Speaking of Kerry's nemesis and accusation, here is the 2004 Presidential victor. Another look at **George W. Bush's** chart will help us summarize how to use the different lots together.

Like Jacqueline Kennedy Onassis, Bush's Lots of Fortune and Spirit are angular. With Onassis they are in the Tenth and Fourth, respectively. Bush's is the reverse: his Lot of Spirit is in the Tenth place from the Ascendant and his Lot of Fortune is in the Fourth. The lord of the Lot of Fortune is Mars in Virgo, in the Eleventh place from the zoidion of the lot (The Eleventh from the Lot of Fortune is the Place of Acquisition, which is strictly about money.) The Lot of Fortune is strongly placed but its lord, in the relatively weak Second place from the Ascendant, is not. Although Bush got a big break from his wealthy and well-connected family, he never quite succeeded in his own business.

The planet governing Bush's Lot of Spirit in Taurus is more fortunate, since its lord is Venus. She is angular in the zoidion of the Ascendant and is placed very well there. The same Venus also governs his Lot of Exaltation, which is also in the Tenth in Taurus. Bush is at his best when pursuing his own agenda, his own vision. In spite of his pedigree and connections, a self-made quality has contributed to his success: it has been up to him to take advantage of his connections, making them reflect his own style.

Venus, governing the Lots of Spirit and Exaltation, is in the same zoidion as Mercury, the planet of politicians, and neither malefic - Saturn in Cancer or Mars in Virgo - give negative testimony

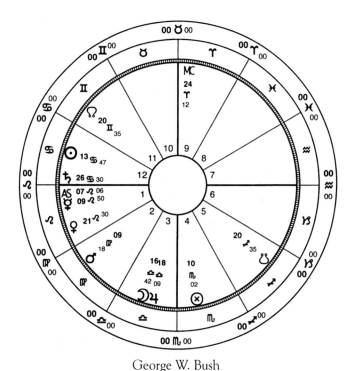

George W. Bush

on Venus or Mercury. On the other hand, Jupiter is in sextile to Venus and Mercury. Bush so far has proven quite capable of mastering his political adversaries, regardless of their strength and determination: possibly this is from his ability to connect with people personally.

The Lots of Eros, Necessity, and Nemesis all fall in Scorpio, with the Lot of Fortune, in the Fourth from the Ascendant. In general, the Fourth signifies father and family, and Eros there indicates the significance for Bush of his family connections. The placements of the Lots of Necessity and Nemesis show that, by his own action and the actions of those around him, family fortune is a source of his limitations and difficulties. To paraphrase Ann Richards, the Texas governor whom Bush defeated in the 1990s: if someone is born on third base, he might think he hit a triple. For readers who are not fans of baseball, this means that Bush was born to great advantage and acts as if he was its author.

Bush's Lot of Accusation is in Virgo, with Mars. This suggests his fighting campaign style and his slashing attitude toward his opponents, a short temper, and his action of taking his country into war regardless of the short-term and long-term consequences. These vulnerabilities are reflected in his Lot of Accusation, the place showing where he might be blamed.

I conclude with Bush's Lot of Basis. This lot is in Aquarius, in the Seventh zoidion from the Ascendant. Notice that Fortune, Spirit, Basis, and the lord of Spirit are all *angular* to the Ascendant and to one another. Depending on its rulers, this can be a powerful configuration, indicating a life of great activity and possibly great success. The Lot of Basis, however, is a concern. The lord of Basis is Saturn, in sect but in a difficult place, the Twelfth from the Ascendant and the Sixth from the Lot of Basis.

One wonders about hidden negativities, even a fate of self-undoing that may have already affected his life. (We have seen it with his problem drinking.) It is no wonder that many political opponents mistrust his motives and suspect hidden agendas. As Saturn is in sect and is in its joy in the Twelfth place, this has yet to cause him permanent harm. Saturn could also become triggered by a planetary period or transit, bringing difficulties into his life. His difficulties in the second half of 2005 are an example of this, which we will examine later.

The next three chapters concern themselves with the twelve places, with aspects, and with phases of the planets and their conditions of visibility. In the chart examples thus far we have already mentioned these factors, and we need to look at them more closely. These are features of the Hellenistic tradition that deserve our serious consideration. The modern astrologer will learn much about the original formulations of these important astrological features.

7

THE TWELVE PLACES

In this chapter we take up the matter of the twelve houses or places. Previously we have seen natal charts divided not by quadrants but by the twelve zoidia. We have also seen charts in which the twelve zoidia proceed not only from the Ascendant but also from other positions, notably the Lots of Fortune and Spirit. We have also called them not "houses" but "places."

What are the astrological houses or places for? As with dignity, astrologers have used a planet's placement within a house or place to assess the condition of a planet. We will also examine why planets in some places from the Ascendant are more effective than in others. There are good places and not so good places for a planet to reside.

Secondly, houses or places also provide information about specific areas of a person's life, e.g. money, relationships, partner, career, and personal appearance and style. We will explore some of the original meanings of the twelve places and conclude by looking at the Third and Ninth places for religious and spiritual matters.

Not "Houses" but "Places"

As we have seen in Chapter Three, "houses" are signs or zoidia in which particular planets are most at home. (This follows the Greek word *oikos* for the "house of the planets", as used in Hellenistic astrology.) In this way, Jupiter's houses are Sagittarius and Pisces; Mercury's houses are Virgo and Gemini. Dispositorship is often based on this factor: Jupiter can govern positions in Sagittarius and Pisces in the natal chart. Mercury governs positions in Virgo and Gemini.

Astrologers also used the word "houses" to refer to the twelve sections of the birth chart. They arise from the Ascendant degree being designated as the "cusp" or boundary of the First, and the Midheaven as the "cusp" of the Tenth. Adding their opposite positions we have the Seventh and Fourth. This gives us the four quadrants we have discussed earlier. One derives the remaining houses by trisecting the quadrants in different ways. Unfortunately, the word "house" in this context gives us no insight as to what these sections might mean or how to use them for interpretation. Using the word "houses" for these segments is as uninformative as using the word "signs" to refer to the twelve segments of the zodiac.

This was never a problem for ancient astrologers, because they had two different words for these two features of the natal chart. The "house of the planets" were their *oikoi*. The twelve houses from the Ascendant, however, were called *topoi*. The Greek *topos* has the same range of meanings as our English "place": a location, a position, a place or passage in a book, and, most important, a *topic* of study or consideration.

Ancient astrologers used *topos* or "place" to refer to an entire zoidion that contains an important chart factor, for example, the "place" of the Lots of Fortune or Spirit in a natal chart.

Our English word "place" refers to a specific location, as in "my place or yours?" "Place" is also a reference to a center of activity, like "knowing one's place" and "I'm not in a very good place today." Astrology's twelve sections are also *topics*, matters to consider or inquire into. All these are well within the range of the Greek *topos* and the English "place," and so I refer to them henceforth as the twelve places.

They are not "temples" either

Manilius lived in the first century BCE and wrote a very long poem called the *Astronomica* about astrology and the fixed stars. At the end of Book Two of this work Manilius uses the word "temples" to designate the twelve astrological places. This is intriguing, as a temple (Lat: *templum*) was originally a space marked out for observation and for augury. Another definition of *templum* is a broad space, or the "space or circuit of the heavens."

However, Manilius' use of the word "temples" to describe the twelve places is inconsistent and inconclusive. His first mention uses the word *pars*, which is the Latin translation for our "part" (hence the "Part of Fortune", etc). This makes sense when a lot (or "part") designates an entire zoidion. Manilius's second mention uses the Latin *locus*, which has the same range of meanings as the Greek *topos*, our word "place." When Manilius again uses *templum*, it is within a passage already thick with poetical construction. He uses *templum* later to summarize his material, almost as an afterthought. All of Manilius's words - *pars*, *locus*, and *templum* - are quite instructive, giving us a sense of what these twelve places actually are. *Templum* seems more a poetic construction than a literal one, however.[1]

Whole Sign and Quadrant Systems

The original ancient practice was to begin the astrological places with the entire zoidion of the Ascendant as the First, with the other eleven zoidia continuing in a counterclockwise direction. This is the "whole sign house system." This is commonly used in Jyotish or Indian Astrology, and some computer programs refer to it as the "Vedic" system. We first must work out what this system entails. I begin by supplying a chart that many would consider problematic.

Elizabeth Browning's natal chart is constructed using two different systems. The chart on top divides the twelve places using a quadrant system attributed to Porphyry, which was also used in the ancient era. Since 29 Virgo is the cusp of the First place, 29 Pisces becomes the cusp of the Seventh, placing all planets earlier in Pisces in the Sixth.

The chart below uses a "whole sign" system: the twelve zoidia as the twelve places. Because Browning's Ascendant is 29 Virgo, in a whole sign system *all* the preceding twenty-nine degrees are

---

1.   Dorian Greenbaum, personal communication, July, 2004.

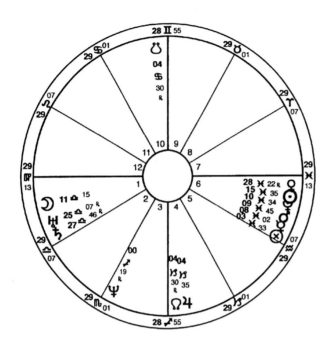

Elizabeth Barrett Browning

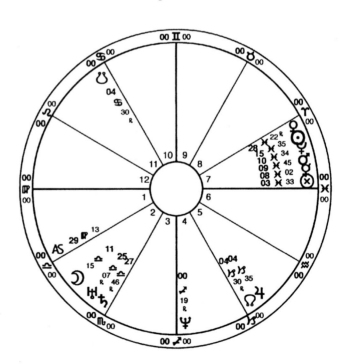

in the First place. Therefore *all* her planets in Pisces are in the Seventh, because the Seventh opposes the First and Pisces opposes Virgo. Since the information from these two charts is different, two astrologers using these different systems could interpret these two charts quite differently. If Browning were born only a few minutes later, Libra would rise, and, in a whole sign system, *all* planets would appear in different places. With Libra rising, all of Browning's planets in Pisces would be in the Sixth place, since Pisces is six places from Libra.

If we use whole signs or the zoidia as the twelve places, charts like those of Elizabeth Barrett Browning, William Blake, or Winston Churchill could change radically if the birth time changes only slightly. This may be a very good reason to get birth times that you are confident about. Alternately, you might want to "rectify" charts to be sure the time given is accurate. You could do this by noting major events in the person's life and comparing the timing of those events with the indications of astrology's predictive techniques. It may be that Browning's chart with Libra rising gives more accurate indications of life events and changes than her chart with Virgo rising. We will see later that this is the case with Winston Churchill.

It may also be necessary to tolerate an anxiety attack or two on the way to better astrological work. One advantage of using the twelve zoidia as places, instead of a quadrant system, is that the astrologer is forever freed from the burden of interpreting charts that contain "interceptions." This feature, common in quadrant charts, puts three zoidia together in the same place, so that two or three different planets may be responsible for the same place. I will illustrate this by using Tony

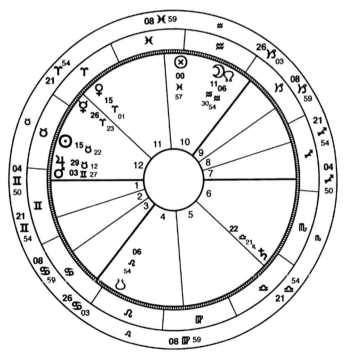

Tony Blair

Blair's chart rendered in quadrant style. He was born at far northern latitude in Edinburgh, Scotland, and the zoidion of his Ascendant is Gemini, a northernmost zoidion.

Note that Taurus and Scorpio are "intercepted" - within the Twelfth and Sixth places respectively. Also, Leo and Scorpio are within the Fourth and Tenth places. Gemini, Cancer, Sagittarius, and Capricorn all comprise two adjacent places. In this circumstance, how does one identify planetary lords that govern these places? In modern astrology these considerations usually have made for interpretative mud. In a whole sign system, no two zoidia inhabit the same place and all places are of equal length.

Another uncertainty that occurs in modern astrology is that there are different viewpoints about the boundary between one place and the next. Many modern astrologers use the lines between the places - the "cusps" - as the clear boundary between one place and the next. However, a planet on the right side of the Midheaven or slightly above the Ascendant is nonetheless considered a planet in the Tenth or First. For example, in Tony Blair's chart, is his Mars, which is conjunct the Ascendant but above the Ascendant degree, a First or a Twelfth place planet? Following Lilly, some astrologers include planets within five degrees of a cusp of *any* place in the previous one, so that Blair's Third would begin at 03 Cancer. Using the whole sign system, there are no such differences in approach.

Additionally, the astrologer is forever freed from having to choose from among the various quadrant systems and to explain their differences to clients and students. Some modern systems, like Koch and Placidus, are technically close to each other. Psychologically oriented modern astrologers often use the Placidus system; those who specialize in predictive astrology use Koch. Some modern astrologers use the Meridian system which casts houses from the Midheaven. People trained in seventeenth century horary astrology likely use Regiomontanus, because this was the "rational" system used by William Lilly. Dane Rudhyar, the great American astrologer of the last century, advocated using the Campanus system. Those who are inspired by medieval astrology may use the Alcabitius, and those who follow the seventeenth century French astrologer Morinus can use the system by that name. One's choice of system appears to be based on one's affiliations within the astrology world, and not upon the merits of any one system. There is an alternative: one could take Alexander of Macedon's sword and cut through the matter entirely and not use a quadrant system at all!

Using a whole sign system, places other than the Ascendant can easily mark the "First place" for an issue. We discussed this in the last chapter. For example, one can start with the place of the Lot of the Father in order to understand one's father's finances, home, or career, casting the zoidia from that lot. This is similar to the medieval and modern practice of derived houses, which was also used in Hellenistic astrology.[2] Manilius and Vettius Valens derived places from the Lot of Fortune. In the Hellenistic system, aspects that exist between places are also the aspects between the zoidia themselves, and so aspect relationships between the twelve places are clearer. The Tenth zoidion always squares the First, the Second and Sixth always trine the Tenth. We met this factor in Chapter

---

2.   *The Anthology*, Bk 9. This is yet untranslated. Personal communication, D. Greenbaum, March 2006.

Two when we discussed occupation. You will see more on this in Chapter Eight when we discuss aspects.

Some ancient astrologers did make use of one quadrant system: the Porphyry system. This system trisects the total degrees of the quadrants, from Ascendant to Midheaven degree, from Midheaven degree to setting degree, and upon the opposite sides. The system is used in the two previous examples to illustrate a quadrant system. However, divisions based on quadrants did not yield "places" - in the sense of topics - but instead were used to help assess the condition of a planet within the context of calculating the length of a person's life. This was a very specialized use for quadrants and rarely occurs in example charts given in texts. (We will see this in Chapter Fourteen.) Ancient astrologers used the twelve zoidia projected from the Ascendant or another marker to judge specific issues of a person's life.

We now consider a major objection to using the twelve zoidia as places: the Midheaven. Modern astrologers usually regard the degree of the Midheaven as the Tenth house cusp. The whole sign system, however, casts this convention a drift. The Midheaven is the degree where a planet culminates and begins its downward descent toward setting. According to modern understanding, a planet that is close to the degree of the Midheaven is very important and is appropriately displayed at the top of the natal chart.

- Using a whole sign system, if Sagittarius or Capricorn - a southernmost zoidion - rises, the Midheaven degree could be in Scorpio and be the eleventh zoidion from the Ascendant.

- If Gemini or Cancer - a northernmost zoidion - rises, the Midheaven degree is likely to be in Pisces and located in the Ninth place. You may have already noted this in the charts we have considered thus far. Note that Blair's Midheaven degree in Capricorn would be in the *eighth* zoidion from his Gemini Ascendant.

These relationships would be reversed in the southern hemisphere. A chart similar to Blair's but at the extreme latitudes of the southern hemisphere could place its Midheaven degree in the *twelfth* place. The astrologers' fascination with a planet at the degree of the Midheaven may be based upon its apparent prominence at the top of the conventional quadrant chart. Some considerations are in order about this:

1.   A planet conjunct the Midheaven degree is not necessarily bodily upon the Midheaven, but is instead close to that degree of the zodiac - at least closer than any other degree. Moon, with a range of six degrees of north or south latitude from the ecliptic, may bodily arrive at the meridian a few minutes before or after its closest zodiacal degree arrives. In our later discussion of the fixed stars, we will pursue this further.

2.   A planet on the Midheaven, either bodily or by degree, is not necessarily the most elevated planet: that planet with the highest altitude. (I should note that *altitude* - elevation on the horizon - is different from *declination*, which is the distance from the celestial equator. 0° degrees of altitude is on the horizon itself, whereas 90° is directly overhead. By contrast, 0° degrees of declination is on the equator and 90° on the North or South Pole.)

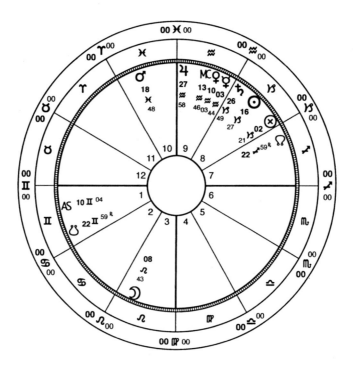

Bernadette of Lourdes

The planet with the greatest altitude or highest elevation may be that planet which most closely squares the Ascendant degree, depending on planet's latitude north and south of the ecliptic. The planet highest in altitude is likely to be ten zoidia from the Ascendant, rather than near the Midheaven degree itself. As an example, here is the natal chart of Bernadette of Lourdes, whom we will investigate later. I use the *Solar Fire* astrology computer program to give me the altitudes of her planets. Venus is close to the degree of the Midheaven, and Venus' altitude is 27°31 north of the horizon. Mars, which is much closer to a square with the Ascendant than it is near the Midheaven, has a higher altitude of 33°03 north of the horizon. Mars, not Venus, is the most elevated planet here. One should not think, however, that the degree of the Midheaven was not important to ancient astrologers. This degree, regardless of which zoidion it falls in, relative to the Ascendant, helps mark the four quadrants in the natal chart. These are used in the following ways:

1.   The journey of life proceeds counterclockwise from the Ascendant and the prime of life is at the Midheaven degree.

2.   The Midheaven degree, along with the other angular degrees, is important for determining paranatella. Literally "co-rising" paranatella may occur when two planets or a planet and star culminate together, or when one is present upon the Midheaven and a second one is at another angle. When culminating, this can be significant for what can manifest in the prime

of life. (We discussed this at the end of Chapter One and we will take it up again when we discuss the fixed stars.)

3.   In predictive work, ancient astrologers directed or advanced - "profected" - the Midheaven degree to predict matters of occupation and reputation. We will take this up in our chapters on ancient prediction.

Hellenistic astrologers used the Midheaven degree mostly for predictive purposes, and not as an important factor for natal delineation. In fact, of the charts given to us by Hellenistic astrologers, most of them do not mention the Midheaven degree at all! From the viewpoint of astrology's traditions, one would be on firm ground to omit the Midheaven degree for natal interpretation, as peculiar as that might be to many modern astrologers.

It was in the mid-1990s that I learned that the whole sign system could be a serious option to a modern astrologer. After working with it for a few years, I was not certain that this system worked significantly better than using quadrant systems.[3] Later, I quietly turned to whole signs with my clients and classes, even though what they had in front of them was the familiar quadrant chart. Today, after a decade of use, I am convinced of the superiority of a whole sign house system.

In the mid-1990s it was rare to see a whole sign system used by a conventional Western astrologer; today it is becoming more common. It is ultimately up to you. I guarantee that, like getting internet cable, or like when Augustine became a Christian or Reagan a Republican, if you begin to use whole sign system you will never go back to what you once used.

Effective and Ineffective Places

Whether a planet has usefulness in the natal chart - can achieve its function - depends in part on the planet's zoidion - its place - relative to the Ascendant. Most astrologers, present and past, agree on which places enhance and which ones diminish a planet's functioning. There are two criteria for judging how effectively each of the twelve places renders a planet located there.

•   Is the planet in a place that is angular, succedent, or cadent from the Ascendant?

•   How does the planet's zoidion aspect the zoidion of the Ascendant?

We begin with the first criterion. **Angular** places include, besides the First, the Tenth (or Midheaven place - not the degree of the Midheaven), the Seventh (or Setting Place), and the Fourth, (or Subterraneous Place). The Greek for what we call "angular" is "kentron," which is a sharp point and has also been translated, for astrological purposes, as "pivot," or place of turning.[4] This is close to a term from mechanical physics, *centrode*. A centrode is the center of density and gravity of a dynamic body, like a machine. The chart is such a dynamic body. It is hard to underestimate the importance ancient astrologers gave to a planet's position when in an angular place. A planet in an angular place may be loud and strong, but it may not always be an ally. In the

---

3.   Crane, Ch. 2.
4.   David Cappabianca, personal communication, March 2006.

Seventh, a planet may even cause the person difficulties, since the Seventh place always opposes the First.

Planets in **succedent** places are less powerful than angular ones. These places follow the angular ones: the Second, Fifth, Eighth, and Eleventh places. The least effective places, according to this model, are the **cadent** or "declining" places (*cadere* is the Latin "to fall"). These are the remaining places: the Third, Sixth, Ninth, and Twelfth.

Now we look at the second criterion: a zoidion's *aspect* to the zoidion of the Ascendant. The **Fifth** place of Good Fortune is in *trine* to the Ascendant zoidion, below the horizon. The **Eleventh** place of Good Spirit is in *sextile* to the Ascendant zoidion, above the horizon. Both are succedent.

The **Third** place of the Moon Goddess is in *sextile* to the Ascendant from below the horizon. The **Ninth** place of the Sun God is in *trine* to the Ascendant zoidion from above the horizon. Both are cadent, but sometimes are called the "good declines." The Third and the Ninth places are relevant to religious orientation.

Some places *square* the Ascendant's zoidion: these are powerful places. Two angular places do this. The **Tenth** place of the Midheaven (not the degree of the Midheaven) is always squared to the First and is the most effective place of the twelve, except for the First itself. As we know, the Tenth can tell us what one does. The **Fourth** is the Subterraneous Place; although not as potent as the Tenth, a planet in the Fourth can be effective. Usually the Fourth gives information about father and home.

The **Seventh** place, or Setting Place *opposes* the First. As we will see, there are major differences among ancient astrologers about the helpfulness of a planet there.

Some places *have no aspect* to the Ascendant: their zoidia are not connected to the zoidion of the Ascendant. This condition strongly diminishes the effectiveness of any planets found in these places. The **Second**, the Gate of Hades, diminishes the strength of a planet, but not completely. This is because the zoidion of the Second follows the First. The remaining places are more difficult: the **Sixth** (Bad Fortune), the **Eighth** (Idle), and the infamous **Twelfth** (Bad Spirit).

Putting together both criteria of angularity and aspects to the Ascendant, we get a clear sense of the relative strength of all twelve places. The only variation seems to be in some of the chart interpretations of Vettius Valens. For Valens, a planet or lot in the Third and Ninth places, otherwise known as the "good declines" mentioned above, would be in just as difficult a position as one placed in as the Sixth or the Twelfth.

A few years ago, one of my students asked me, "Why is the First such a strong place when it's below the horizon, and planets there are in the dark; and why is the Twelfth such a bad place when it's just above the horizon, where the Sun rises into?"

Using our knowledge that the strength of the places largely depends on their relationship to the First, we can answer his question. The First anchors the entire natal chart and any planet located there is prominent. The Twelfth has no aspect relationship with the First and is also cadent. The conditions of day or night or the visible horizon are irrelevant to this issue. It is the relationship between the zoidia of the First and Twelfth that is critical.

It is interesting that modern astrology continues to assess these places very much in the same way. This tradition has continued, but modern astrology has long ago lost its rationale.

Valens and "The Place of Acquisition"

As mentioned in the previous chapter, Vettius Valens saw the Eleventh place or zoidion from the Lot of Fortune as the "place of acquisition." The Eleventh zoidion from the Lot of Fortune is located two zoidia behind of the place of the Lot. As the Lot of Fortune is about the general happiness of the native, the Eleventh place from this Lot is specifically about money. Following are a few examples of using the Eleventh from the Lot of Fortune as the Place of Acquisition.

We begin with the chart of Jacqueline Kennedy Onassis. In her chart, there are some troublesome features of Jupiter and Venus in Gemini, since both are in the Eighth place from the Ascendant. We now note that these two planets are also in the Eleventh place from the Lot of Fortune, which is in Leo. To say that Onassis was financially comfortable is quite an understatement. This is also a further confirmation that the deaths of her two husbands (Eighth from the Ascendant) left her very well off financially.

One who had far less money than Jackie Onassis is **Bill Wilson**. The Eleventh zoidion from Lot of Fortune in Gemini is Aries, whose lord is Mars. Mars is in the Second place from the Ascendant and governs the Second.

No astrologer, ancient or modern, would be thrilled to see Saturn, Mars, and Mercury all in the Second. I could imagine Wilson vigorously (Mars in his own house in Scorpio) entering a life of

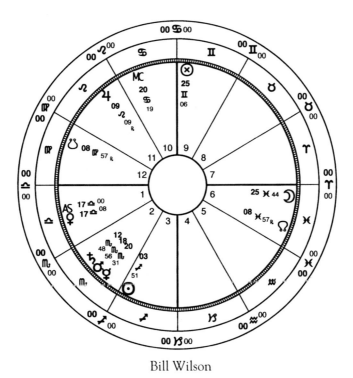

Bill Wilson

crime (Saturn), perhaps by being a swindler or con artist (Mercury). Other interpretations are possible.

Wilson's first career was as a researcher for a Wall Street investment firm. He has been credited with originating the concept to help investors make wise choices based on direct information. Here one feels the presence of Mercury. This promising career, however, was limited by his other occupation - that of the town drunk, where we encounter Saturn in its identity of corruptor and degrader.

Later Wilson's work was to spread the word about Alcoholics Anonymous. This was not, however, an abundant source of personal revenue. Beginning in the late 1930s he was able to receive a small stipend from John D. Rockefeller, and later he was able to derive a modest income from his AA writings. Wilson never had an income commensurate with his fame and cultural impact. Saturn continues to loom large, compromising an otherwise useful Mars in Scorpio.

George W. Bush. The Eleventh from the Lot of Fortune in Scorpio is Virgo, where Mars is located, the lord of the Lot of Fortune. (The Eleventh zoidion from the Lot is also the Second place from the Ascendant.) Since it is in Virgo, Mercury governs this Place of Acquisition, lord Mercury is well placed in the First. This indicates that Bush would make his fortune through his own initiative, and would be happier as an entrepreneur than as a corporate officer. This promise is compromised, however, by the presence of Mars in this place. Being out of sect, occidental, and witnessed only by Saturn, Mars does not create luck in the acquisition of money. Any business dealings based on impulsiveness, or wherever anger became a factor, would work out badly for him. What may come to his rescue is the strength of Venus, lord of the Lot of Spirit, who is with Mercury.

William Blake. The Lot of Fortune is in Sagittarius, and the Eleventh place, the Place of Acquisition, is in Libra. This favors his acquisition of money, since Libra is angular and Venus, governing this place, is also angular, in the Seventh. Just as the strength of the Lot of Spirit rescues Bush, so the difficulty of Blake's Lot of Fortune weakens its possibilities for him. Venus, the lord of the Place of Acquisition, indicates once again that he made his living from his engravings, his visual artistic creations.

Wolfgang Mozart. His Lot of Fortune is in Scorpio and therefore Virgo is the Eleventh zoidion from that Lot and is the Place of Acquisition. This is the place of the Ascendant, and Mozart was, for most of his adult life, an independent composer. When we look for Mercury, Virgo's lord, however, we are back in the Sixth, under the Sun's beams. The Sixth place is called "Bad Luck." The presence of Saturn in the Sixth, even in its own house in Aquarius, does not improve matters for Mozart. Much of Mozart's income, especially early in his career, depended on the good favor of those in positions of ecclesiastical or civil authority.

Eva Peron. The Lot of Fortune in Aquarius makes Sagittarius the Place of Acquisition. In the Eighth place from the Ascendant, Peron was dependent on others for funds. Yet she became

Manilius' Circle of Athla

Many people who have studied traditional astrology are familiar with Manilius's sequences of places from the Lot of Fortune, usually referred to as the Circle Of Athla. The Greek word *athlon* means a prize, such as is given to the winner of a contest. The concept of a prize is consistent with the meaning of the Lot of Fortune. Manilius gives no chart examples where he uses this technique. His descriptions of the places from the Lot of Fortune differ from other ancient astrological writers and from what has been handed down by tradition. Here is the rather unusual list of places from the Lot of Fortune.

1. Home
2. Warfare
3. Business
4. Law
5. Marriage
6. Means
7. Dangers
8. Class
9. Children
10. Character
11. Health
12. Success

financially successful on her own before marrying Juan Peron. When we look for the lord of Acquisition we find Jupiter, who is angular in the Fourth, conjunct Moon, and governed by Sun in the First. During her life she demonstrated adaptability (Moon) and initiative and creativity (Sun in the First) in her pursuit of material fortune.

Now that we have seen how places can proceed from locations other than from the Ascendant, we return to the twelve places from the Ascendant. What follows are the original descriptions of the twelve places.

In its depiction of the twelve places, Hellenistic astrology does not provide the same completeness and detail that we find in the medieval era. The ancient definitions of the twelve places are nonetheless important for us. In some cases they carry meanings that later astrology has built upon. In other cases, it may be useful to restore some of the meanings that have been lost over time.

My sources are Vettius Valens from the second century CE and Paulus Alexandrinus and Firmicus Maternus from the fourth. Paulus and Firmicus concern themselves with the effects of

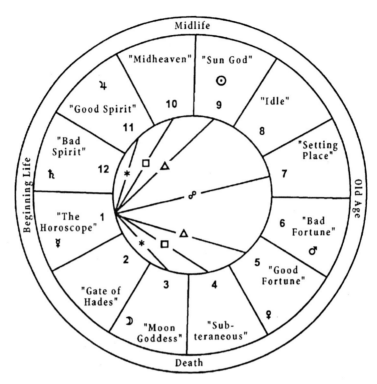

Topics of the Twelve Places

different planets in each of the twelve places. Valens describes the effects of planets when they govern these places.[5]

All three authors use the aphoristic method I described earlier. The reader encounters different planetary combinations as specific outcomes, and often these outcomes are cast in very positive or very negative terms. The aphoristic method, in my view, is meant to be instructive and not determinative. The teacher uses this method to train the student's eye or mind, not to decree that having planets in the Fifth mean you are blessed or that having planets in the Twelfth mean you are doomed.

First

The *Horoscope* is the foundation of the individual. (*Horoskopos* is another word for our Ascendant, is a watcher or a marker of the hour.) It is likened to a ship's rudder guiding our journey. This place is also called "life," because it pertains to the viability of the life force. (One's life may be endangered when the Ascendant degree arrives by direction to the degree of a malefic.) Firmicus tells us that any planet here is magnified in its effect, and that Jupiter cannot be much better placed when placed in the First. In particular, **Mercury** rejoices in the First.

---

5.   Firmicus, Bk. III; Paulus, Chap. 22; Valens Book III, Ch. 12, 15.

Second

This is the *Gate of Hades*, and, in Greek, the Second is called "life", *bios*. This is not the life force in general, for that is the First, but what materially *supports* our life: money and property. Because the Second place always makes a trine to the Tenth, a planet in the Second is useful for determining one's occupation. The Second can help determine whether the native will be prosperous, and Jupiter placed there promises much. If Saturn is present in the Second, it can ruin one's inheritance or financial legacy. This interpretation does not differ from modern practice.

Third

This is the place of the *Moon Goddess*, and **Moon** is in her joy here. Later astrologers claim that the Third concerns lower mind and one's neighborhood, but there is no evidence of this in the ancient tradition. Paulus and others mention the Third as the place for siblings. This idea is consistent with modern practice.

Valens and Firmicus regard the Third as a place of religion and of prophecy. According to Valens, Saturn in the Third can indicate that one is a blasphemer, and Jupiter here can indicate a prophet. Valens also says that if Moon or Mercury governs the Lot of Fortune or the Ascendant and is in the Third, a person can tell the future or participate in a god's mysteries. According to Firmicus, Mercury in the Third, especially with the Sun, tells us that a person is a priest, magician, healer, or an astrologer. We will meet the Third place again when we look at religion and spirituality in astrology.

Fourth

The *Subterraneous Place* is about legacies, father and family, home and homeland. As the place where planets may anticulminate, the fourth governs the end of life and its aftermath. (This is the last stage of the clockwise sequence of the four quadrants, where the Ascendant is birth and youth, the Midheaven is the prime of life, and the Descendant is late middle age or retirement,) Saturn in the Fourth can indicate a wasted inheritance or an early death for the father; Jupiter here can indicate a prestigious and famous father.

Fifth

This is the place of *Good Fortune*. The Fifth is the joy of **Venus.** Paulus uses this place for information about children: benefics in the Fifth signify fruitfulness; malefics in the Fifth signify destruction of children. (Remember that infant mortality rates were higher in these cultures.) Valens tells us that any planet is more beneficial when in the Fifth. Firmicus describes the positive effects of planets when in the Fifth as follows:

- Saturn gives fortune, but over a long period of time.

- Jupiter may signify prosperity and prominence.

- Sun indicates that one is agreeable and successful, getting what one wants.

- Venus has honor and good will here, and also getting what one wants.

Mercury makes great use of the resources of others. The ancient astrological literature does not give the Fifth as an indicator of love affairs. Perhaps this developed later from Venus being in her joy in the Fifth. Nor do they mention creativity as a Fifth place concern. Earlier astrologers might have used the Tenth for what we mean by creativity.

Sixth

This is the place of *Bad Fortune*, since the Sixth is cadent and its zoidion does not aspect the zoidion of the Ascendant. What goes up in the Fifth place of Good Fortune comes down in the Sixth, the following zoidion. This is the joy of the malefic **Mars.** According to our authorities, hardly anything good can be said about planets located here.

Not even having Mars here, in its joy, is particularly lucky. Valens tells us that Mars in the Sixth can indicate a life wasted in public affairs. A person with this placement can become a foot soldier, a beggar, or someone whose life in general goes in the wrong direction. Firmicus adds that Mars may convey illness and evils to a person. Paulus, however, says that Mars - with favorable aspects from other planets - is effective in the Sixth: for example, one could become successful in the military. Because the Sixth, along with the Second, is in trine to the zoidion of the Tenth, this place can also give career indications.

Firmicus gives us some hope for Mercury in the Sixth if there is another planet (presumably a well-favored one) in the Tenth, so that Mercury receives a trine from that planet. Otherwise, Mercury in the Sixth can indicate a fraudulent and malevolent nature, or someone who is mentally sluggish and narrow.

Valens tells us that Venus in the Sixth can signify being unlucky in love, that Mercury can indicate a thief, and that the Moon there can signify being a slave. Sun or Moon in the Sixth can also signify a poor or disreputable parent. Firmicus adds that if Venus is in the Sixth, one's wife may be of low birth or have difficulty in bearing children.

Valens, Firmicus, and Paulus do not include producing illness as an outcome for planets in the Sixth. Ptolemy, however, does mention this in his discussion of the ailments of the body; he specifically cites that malefics in the Sixth and Seventh places can indicate illness. Presumably it was through Ptolemy then that the Sixth received this attribution of illness.

Seventh

Our authorities differ in their descriptions for the *Setting Place*. Planets in the Seventh give indications of marriage, but we also find indications about old age. If the Ascendant, where the Sun rises, describes birth and matters of early life, the Setting Place tells us about matters closer to life's end. Mars may indicate a violent death, Venus a comfortable old age, Mercury a decent income in one's maturity. When discussing Jupiter in the Seventh place, Paulus gives us two possibilities: a happy marriage but few children, or success but in later years. Missing here is any reference to the Seventh being the place of "open enemies." This seems to be a medieval addition.

Eighth

Like the Sixth, the zoidion of the Eighth does not connect with that of the Ascendant, and again our authorities give us a negative picture. This place is called *Idle*, suggesting its effect on planets located here. Valens tells us that benefics in the Eighth can be weak, especially if they govern the zoidia of the Ascendant or the Lot of Fortune. Mercury in the Eighth, governing the Lot of Spirit, can make one stupid, poor in speech, and uneducated. Paulus tells us that Venus in the Eighth makes marriages unworkable. Firmicus adds that Venus in the Eighth means that one's wife is low-class, sterile, or ugly.

According to Paulus, a malefic in the Eighth gives two possibilities: one becomes a wanderer or squanders whatever is acquired. This reminds me of some people who have won a major lottery. Oddly, Valens also tells us that the waxing Moon rejoices in the Eighth place, but this may be a notion peculiar to him. Paulus says that the waning Moon makes one poor and miserable.

The Eighth place signifies the "accomplishment of death," as Paulus says. Benefics here mean that one can make a profit from a death: hence the notion of inheritances that is commonly used in later astrology.

Nowhere is sex mentioned for the Eighth place. Considering how negatively ancient astrologers present this place, this omission might be a good thing.

Ninth

This is the place of the *Sun God* and the joy of the **Sun.** We are on far more pleasant terrain. Planets in the Ninth place, like the Fifth, are in trine to the First. Living abroad, either as an exile or on a journey, is not one of the meanings of the Ninth place. Ancient astrologers, depicting the Ninth, were more concerned with religion, dreams, visions and prophecy.

Valens tells us that a benefic here, especially when governing the Ascendant or Lot of Fortune, increases piety. Even if a person is not the prophet of a great god, they may be regarded as such by others. Firmicus gives us a list of the effects of planets in the Ninth place. In his projected outcomes, Firmicus emphasizes the sect of the planet.

- Saturn by day indicates that one can be a magician, philosopher, or priest. One may be a seer, a diviner, or an astrologer.

- Jupiter produces a person who can use dreams to interpret the gods and tell the future. By night, however, the dreams may be false or be misinterpreted.

- Mars is beneficial if with Jupiter in an evening chart. If placed in the houses of Venus (Taurus, Libra) or Mercury (Gemini, Virgo), Mars can make for a great orator.

- Sun in this place indicates that one can act like a show-off in matters of religious piety and can gain fame and honor that way. It also signifies that one may make holy images - presumably of gold.

- Venus here can give the gift of prophecy. Surprisingly, Firmicus says that Venus in the Ninth can make one sordid and unkempt. We will return to this later.

- Mercury in the Ninth is favorable for becoming an astronomer, astrologer, priest or a magician.

Tenth

The original meanings of this place, *the Midheaven*, have carried forth to the present day. Planets here can indicate reputation and career; this is the place of *praxis* or what one does. The Tenth is a powerful place for any planet that is there. The zoidion of the Tenth always squares the zoidion of the First. As we will discuss in Chapter Eight, this relationship is a *predominating square*.

According to Valens, both benefics and malefics can give positive outcomes in the Tenth, especially when governing the Ascendant or the Lots of Fortune or Spirit. The strength of the lord of the Tenth will say much about overall success in life. Paulus tells us that luminaries in the Tenth can indicate that one has a distinguished father, but that Mars in the Tenth can divide families. Interestingly, Paulus considers marriage and male children a subsidiary significator of the Tenth place.

Eleventh

This is the place of *Good Spirit*, opposite the Fifth place of Good Fortune. **Jupiter** is in its joy in the Eleventh place. Paulus says that good expectations as well as alliances and patronage are connected to the Eleventh. Modern astrologers, relating the Eleventh to friends and "hopes and wishes," are consistent with ancient descriptions. Saturn here by day can achieve its ends; by night Saturn may show laziness and failure.

Valens tells us that the Eleventh place is in the quadrant concerned with matters early in life, i.e.between the Ascendant and Midheaven. A benefic in the Eleventh, if that planet aspects the Ascendant or Lot of Fortune by a sextile or trine, can indicate someone who is successful in youth.

Twelfth

This is the place of *Bad Spirit*, opposite the Sixth - the place of Bad Fortune - and **Saturn** is in its joy here. Later astrologers considered the Twelfth the place of "hidden enemies"; both Paulus and Valens emphasize adversity and treachery as outcomes when planets are located here. The Twelfth is an ineffective place: Valens tells us that the malefics can produce calamities and the benefics achieve nothing. What follows is Paulus' delineation of planets placed in the Twelfth. Do not expect to see much that is pleasant or anything about mysticism here.

- *Saturn* in the Twelfth by day can indicate oppressing one's enemies. (Remember that Saturn is in its joy in the Twelfth. Saturn can always be useful when one is in a difficult situation.)

- *Jupiter* here can indicate a decrease of patronage, can embolden your adversaries, or can result in litigations against you. Jupiter here may be beneficial for those servile to you - for example, servants and four-footed beasts of burden.

- *Sun* in the Twelfth means that your father lives abroad. (For the ancients, being exiled or made to live abroad was a bad outcome.)

- *Mars* here symbolizes treacheries and accusations from those subordinate to us.

- *Venus* here may bring about various miseries ("psychic sufferings") born from love.

- *Mercury* in the twelfth gives us Mercury's least admirable qualities: thievery or hypocrisy.

Planetary Joys

We return to a matter briefly considered in Chapter One: each of the seven planets has one place in which they are particularly comfortable; one could say that these planets "rejoice" when located in one of these places. This was a list that survived well into the medieval astrological tradition.

The Sun rejoices in the Ninth place of the "Sun God." Moon rejoices in the Third place, the "Moon Goddess."

Venus rejoices in the Fifth place of "Good Luck." The other benefic, Jupiter, rejoices in the Eleventh place of "Good Spirit." We will see below that these designations give us added insight into the nature of these two places.

Mars rejoices in the Sixth place of "Bad Fortune." The other malefic, Saturn, rejoices in the Twelfth place of "Bad Spirit." There are two ways of understanding this designation. It is good to have the malefics tucked away in weaker cadent places. The alternate meaning derives from the life difficulties described by these two difficult places: if we are to rise above life's crises and calamities, we may need a dose of the extreme measures of the malefics.

Mercury rejoices in the First. On first inspection, this is not obvious. There are thematic and structural reasons why Mercury rejoices in the first.

I think of Mercury's cleverness, ability to respond to changing situations in life, and many ways of presenting itself. Mercury in the First may promote flexibility in the way we conduct our lives.

Note that the joys of the diurnal planets - Sun, Saturn, and Jupiter - are all above the horizon.

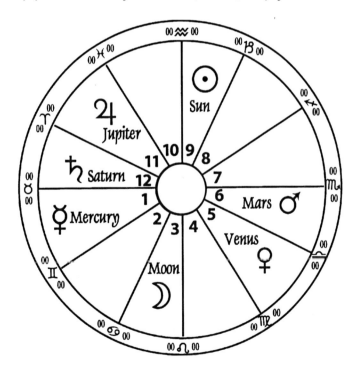

Note that the joys of the nocturnal planets - Moon, Mars, and Venus - are all below the horizon. Mercury's sect affiliation varies, according to whether it is ahead or behind the Sun in the zodiac. Placed in the First, Mercury can be either above or below the horizon, since the Ascendant falls somewhere within the First and Mercury may be above or below that line, inclining either toward being diurnal or nocturnal. Here are the joys of the planets.

We now apply our work to an important area of our lives.

The Third and Ninth Places: Religion and Spirituality

Although ancient astrology may seem worldly by the standards of our modern era, their tradition does lend itself to an astrological consideration of religion and spirituality. For our purposes, I will define "spirituality" broadly as any concern with a transcendent ground of being. "Religion" is a subset of spirituality, where one identifies oneself as belonging to a specific tradition.

In matters of religion and spirituality, the world of late antiquity was not so different from the modern Western world. The ancient world, like our own, had its extremists and religious bigotry, but there was also a diversity of religious expression and some tolerance for different points of view. This was not an era when the government dictated religious loyalty, as was the case in the medieval era, or in some areas of our contemporary world. During the Hellenistic era, as in most of this planet today, people were rarely executed solely for their spiritual inclinations or religious practice. Roman authorities did not persecute Christians because they had different beliefs, but rather because their beliefs forbade their participation in public religious ceremonies; the Christians' crime was not their religion, but their unwillingness to observe social convention. Medieval astrology, on the other hand, was embedded in a culture where alternative forms of religious practice were considered violations of religion itself. The ancient world is a better model for us than the culture of the medieval world or early modern Europe. I suggest that the astrology of the ancient world is also a good model for us for this topic.

There is considerable agreement between Valens and Firmicus - but not as much with Paulus - on the nature of the Third and Ninth places. (Paulus does not mention the Third in the context of religion and spirituality.) Both the Third and the Ninth concern themselves with temples and priests, visions and prophecy. How are these two places different from one another? There is much overlap by Paulus and Firmicus between them.

Within the Hellenistic tradition, it does not appear that the Third and Ninth places mark a contrast between officially sanctioned spiritual expressions (Ninth) and those outside the mainstream (Third). Nor do I see this difference by investigating the charts of conventional and unconventional religious figures for this factor. For example, some eminent and mainstream religious figures have a notable Third.

Although the Third and Ninth places are in opposing zoidia, their topics may be in contrast but are not necessarily opposed. The Third is the place of the "Moon Goddess," and the joy of Moon, and the Ninth is the place of the "Sun God," and the joy of Sun. How do the two luminaries help us understand the roles of the Third and Ninth places?

In spite of the Third being called the place of the "Moon Goddess" and the Ninth being the place of the "Sun God," I don't believe there is a gender issue between the two places. In the ancient world, up to the ascendancy of Christianity, official female deities had their own temples, public rituals, and festivals; conversely, some male deities were worshipped within closed communities using secret ritual. The rites of Demeter from Greece and Isis from Egypt were not restricted because these deities were female. They were simply hidden (Latin: *occult)* arenas for religious expression. Here is another option. The Sun is the luminary of the diurnal sect. Daytime is visible, open, and public. Moon is the luminary of the nocturnal sect. Night is quieter, inward, and personal. The place of the Sun God indicates a public community-oriented expression of spirituality. The place of the Moon Goddess indicates a more private and contemplative expression. Supporting this argument is the simple fact that the Ninth place is above the horizon - visible - and the Third place is below the horizon - invisible.

Sun signifies matters of leadership, fame and steadiness. Moon is more personal and it is moving, adaptable and experiential. When discussing Valens' general depiction of the planets, we noted that he presented Sun as the light of the mind or intellect (*nous*) and Moon as foreknowledge (*pronoia*). A person's outer faith (Sun and Ninth) tends to have a steady and reasonable quality, where the more inner experience (Moon and Third) can be more turbulent and hidden, but ultimately more profound.

Consider one of the people in charge of or guiding a spiritual community, or an officer in such a congregation. Whether the community is conventional or unconventional is not relevant: this person's form of spiritual or religion expression is public. Contrast this to the person who quietly goes to church or temple daily or who has a personal spiritual practice, but does not have an organizational role or social status within a spiritual community. Using the Third and Ninth places in this way, we can see how the same person handles public and private expressions of spirituality.

We now look at some natal charts to see how this might be applied. Happily there are no new techniques for us here. In fact, because we are using the places for topics and the Lots peripherally, our interpretations may have a medieval feel to them.

George W. Bush has stressed his religious connection, and, to a great extent, his political decisions as American President have been strongly influenced by his religious beliefs.

Bush's chart has Leo ascending, therefore his Third place is Libra. In Libra is Moon, in her joy in the Third. Jupiter, who is in sect in Bush's diurnal natal chart and in its own bounds, is also in the Third. To determine whether the affairs of the Third are critical to the individual's life, we look at the planet governing the Third. In this case it Venus, who is in with the Ascendant in the First. These planets convey great aptitude for a private spiritual life, and what we know about Bush confirms this. Jupiter is a planet of confidence and ability; Moon has the personal and adaptable qualities.

Contrast this powerful Third house with the Ninth house, the more public side of the religious life. The ninth zoidion from Bush's Leo Ascendant, is Aries, governed by Mars. Mars is out of sect, occidental, and in the second Place - Mars' condition is mediocre. Governing the public dimension of his spirituality, Mars is significantly weaker than Venus. Mars also governs the Lot of Fortune,

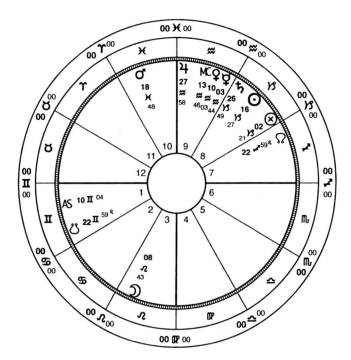

Bernadette of Lourdes

giving rise to displays of religious sentiment that he has used to his political advantage. There are some people who wish Mr. Bush greater success as a contemplative person in private life.

The next few charts are of well-known Catholics. The first is from another century, gender, and manner of living: Bernadette of Lourdes. She is particularly interesting because fame was thrust upon her. Issues of gender also emerge in her spiritual life.

At the age of fourteen, Bernadette, a daughter of a farmer from a small town began to have visions of a "lady". This apparition told her to begin digging in a grotto, and eventually up gushed forth a spring that proved to have healing powers. Many years later, after this spring and its waters had become quite famous, she entered a convent. She died two years afterwards at the age of 35.

Moon is in the Third place, in her joy. From the Ninth place, opposing her Moon, is Venus. (Venus is also the Moon's next application.) Present with Venus are Jupiter and Mercury. These planets in the Ninth all point to gifts of divination and prophecy. The planets governing the Third and the Ninth places, Sun and Saturn, are with each other in Capricorn in the Eighth.

Her discovery became famous for its religious quality, reflecting the strong Ninth place component. The two feminine planets, Moon and Venus in the Third and Ninth places, suggest the importance of the feminine in her spiritual insight and expression.

The planets governing the Third and Ninth places, which are both in the Eighth, bring together the affairs of both places. Although it is tempting to consider her feminist even pagan - on account of the uncertain nature of "the lady" who had told her to dig in the grotto - Bernadette's experience was made to fit conveniently into standard Catholic forms. Bernadette had no particular problem reconciling her personal experience with what was expected of her as a good Catholic. What is the influence of the Eighth, the "Idle" place? One possibility is that she never received any worldly benefit from her experience or example. After she went into the convent, she referred to herself simply as "God's broom," to use or to put away in a closet.

We now turn to another Catholic born in France, but later than Bernadette: Thomas Merton. Thomas Merton, who entered a Cistercian monastery in his late twenties, subsequently wrote the autobiographical classic *The Seven Story Mountain*, as well as many other books on contemplation, spirituality and society. He later became interested in Zen and other religious traditions from Asia. He died in a freak electrical accident in 1968. Merton's natal chart has a strong Saturn in the Third. Saturn is in sect and in its own triplicity, and receives a trine from Jupiter. In the religious life, Saturn has the quality of renunciation. This placement, in a very simple way, points to someone who might lead a strict and humble religious life. Indeed, the order he joined is severe even for monasticism.

Merton has Venus in the Ninth, who is the lord of the Lot of Fortune. This makes Venus very important for Merton. Venus is out of sect and opposes Saturn. Previously we noted Firmicus' rather dim view of Venus, which is out of sect in the Ninth. Here is the text itself:

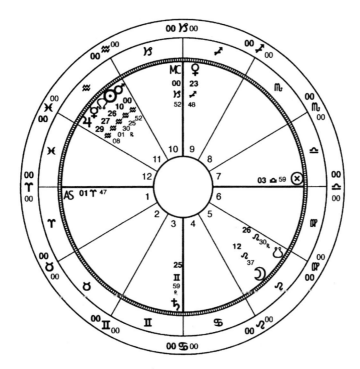

Thomas Merton

"Constant attacks of some demon are indicated by Venus in the Ninth house. The natives go around sordid and unkempt or stay in temples prophesying, claiming that they are announcing the will of the gods. Often they are interpreters of dreams. The effects are stronger if Saturn is in aspect."[6]

Perhaps this may point to a monastic life, since monks are not to be concerned with personal adornment or making themselves attractive. Firmicus would have had no contact with monks as monasticism didn't exist in his era. (Firmicus is much more positive about Venus in the ninth in a night chart, suggesting that holy people and worshippers of the gods could manifest from this placement.)

Noting Saturn in the Third and Venus in the Ninth, we might consider the role of sexuality in Merton's religious life. Like Augustine centuries before, Merton had particular difficulty in this area. His difficulties set the stage for Merton to convert to Catholicism and later to enter the monastic life. Try as he might, Merton was unable to sublimate this longing. He also had the ill fortune to be quite handsome and charismatic and be leading a chaste religious life.[7] Does this not seem like Venus in the Ninth with an aspect from Saturn?

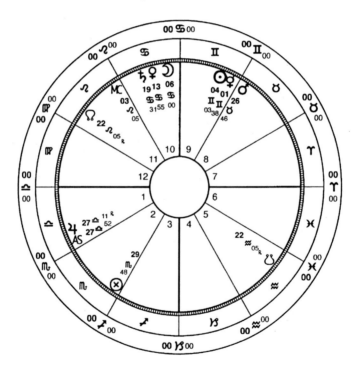

Padre Pio

6. Firmicus Bk. III, p. 96.
7. See Mott, Michael. *The Seven Mountains of Thomas Merton.* (1984) Boston, MA: Houghton Mifflin.

Merton's many Aquarius planets in the Eleventh aspect both Venus and Saturn. In particular, attention should be paid to Jupiter, the lord of the Ninth place. Jupiter is in sect and in its joy in the Eleventh place of the Good Spirit. Jupiter also is with Mercury, which points to Merton's success as a writer on religious and spiritual matters. I also think of how Merton tried, without losing his loyalty to Catholicism, to universalize his religious life by connecting it with different world religions.

Being the author of contemplative books seems a perfect expression of a strong connection between the Third and Ninth places, mediated by Jupiter and Mercury.

Continuing the topic of well-known followers of a monastic life, the next person we will look at is Padre Pio. He was an Italian Franciscan monk who had great healing and clairvoyant abilities. Like Frances of Assisi, Padre Pio was reported to have received the wounds of Christ. Like Bernadette of Lourdes and many other religious figures, Padre Pio was a reluctant celebrity.

His natal chart tells us all about this. His Third place is governed by a strong Jupiter, in sect and at the degree of the Ascendant. We can find his external religious activity symbolized by his Ninth place Sun and Mercury in Gemini, in trine by zoidion to Jupiter without aspects from Mars or Saturn. Here we find someone who will stand out as a religious person.

One sees the reluctant celebrity in his Tenth place from the Ascendant: Moon and Venus have great strength, as Moon is in her own house and Venus in her own triplicity. The presence of Saturn renders his celebrity a mixed blessing at best, and more likely a constriction. The planets in the Tenth, in predominating square to Jupiter, show his contemplative life constrained by his public persona. For all the people who would like to be famous and are not, there are a few like Padre Pio who would rather remain anonymous.

Here's the natal chart of a very public religious man, the late **Pope John Paul II** (Karol Wojtyla), who died in April 2005 after a twenty-five year reign. We will contrast this chart with the chart of his successor, the current (2006) **Pope Benedict XVI**.

John Paul's chart does not have indicators as obvious as the previous ones, and the delineation is more complex. John Paul's Third place, Sagittarius, has no planets in it. However, Jupiter, in its joy in the Eleventh place, governs the Third. This strengthened his private religious life so that it could give sustenance to his long career as a public religious figure.

Moon, out of sect and under the Sun's beams, is in the Ninth place of public spiritual expression. Moon in the Ninth may indicate his ability to use his personal style to convey the authority of the Catholic Church. Moon, a planet of movement, may also indicate his extensive traveling whilst Pope, and perhaps that he would have to come from a country other than Italy in order to become Pope.

Mercury governs the Ninth place. Located in the Eighth and under the Sun's beams, Mercury is not in very good condition. Jupiter and Saturn, both in sect in this diurnal chart, aspect Moon in the Ninth, as well as her dispositor, Mercury. We must take particular note of Jupiter's aspect to Mercury. Both planets are in square and, by degree, of equal power - antiscia - to one another: they have the same distance from the 0 Cancer/0 Capricorn axis. (We will discuss this factor in detail in the next chapter.) This strengthens their connection beyond the aspect of the square.

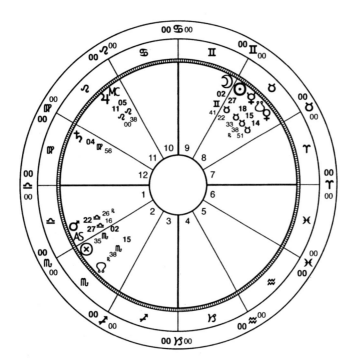

John Paul II

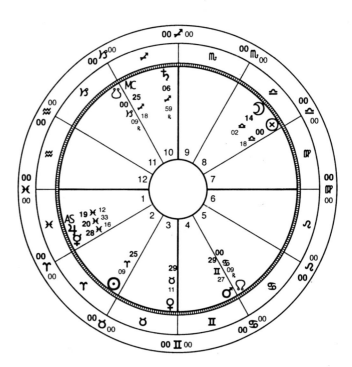

Pope Benedict

Jupiter binds together and strengthens both the Third and Ninth places. John Paul was someone with great confidence in his mission and in his subsequent place in history. As befitting a strong Jupiter, John Paul was completely in his element as a world leader and historical figure. Governing the Third place, Jupiter signifies how much of John Paul's confidence derived from his personal practice of devotion.

Saturn, in his joy in the Twelfth, also has strong influence. Saturn makes no aspect to Jupiter, the lord of the Third. However, Saturn does square Moon in the Ninth and trines Mercury, the lord of the Ninth. John Paul's personal devotion did not involve Saturn. His public role, however, was quite different: in spite of his charisma and personal presence, Saturn subordinated his charisma and personal presence to a very conservative message. (I wonder, as any modern astrologer might, whether the strong square from Saturn to Moon reveals an isolated and lonely person.)

Using his astrological chart, one can easily account for John Paul's personal impact. The Part of Spirit, Mars, and the Ascendant are together in Libra in the First. This configuration brings together an independent spirit, strong energy, and a willingness to fight. For years as bishop of Kracow, he stared down the Communist authorities in Poland. As much as he could, he shaped the modern Catholic Church to conform to his vision. He fought against viewpoints that varied from his sense of truth. The fact that Venus, lord of the First, is with Mercury in the Eighth, helps us understand his role as a communicator.

Now we examine the chart of John Paul's successor, Pope Benedict XVI (Joseph Ratzinger). Perhaps we should begin with what is most striking at first glance about Pope Benedict's chart: Jupiter and Mercury in Pisces with the Ascendant. Both Jupiter and Mercury are oriental to the Sun, and, as we will discuss later, they are "spear bearers" for the Sun. Jupiter is the stronger planet, being in its own house and governing the First. Mercury's position does have some positive qualities: although in fall, Mercury is also in sect and in its joy in the First: This combination in the First points to his life's occupation as a theologian and writer. The strong "predominating" square from Saturn in the Tenth clarifies his long-time role as the church's guardian of orthodoxy. Perhaps it has also kept his personal presence quieter than it otherwise would have been.

What are the religious roots of his activities as a theologian? The Third place of Taurus is strong, with Venus there in her own house. Venus is in sect; neither Mars nor Saturn are in aspect, but instead there is a benevolent sextile from Jupiter in the First. Venus testifies well to Benedict's career indicator, Mercury in the First. This placement emphasizes his strong personal devotion.

The Ninth place of Scorpio is more difficult to interpret. There are no planets in the Ninth; its lord is Mars in the Fourth. Mars is in Gemini, disconnected from the Ninth but angular from the Ascendant. This emphasizes Ratzinger's background from an overwhelmingly Catholic area of Germany. Jupiter in the First receives a predominating square from Mars; Saturn opposes both from the Tenth. Benedict's activity as a conservative theologian is his public contribution to his church. Writing this a year into his papacy, it is difficult to imagine Benedict acting very differently as Pope than he has during his life so far. From him we should not expect world travel but rather a quiet presence who has produced teachings on a diverse group of issues. He is less heroic or flamboyant than his predecessor but he has his own qualities of stability and consistency.

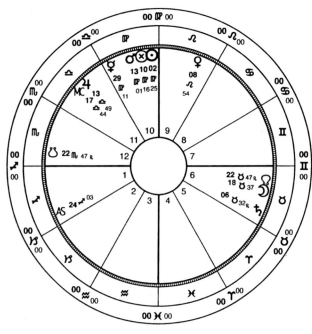

Mother Teresa [8]

We end our survey of famous Catholics with **Mother Teresa**. Although a nun, and indeed the founder of an order of nuns, Mother Teresa seemed the opposite of cloistered. She spent much of her long career in the streets of Calcutta, tending to the poorest and most unfortunate of the people there. Later, after she had achieved world status as a living saint, she became quite influential in her own right. One could not overestimate how revered she had become in the last years of her life. She died in 1997.

As with John Paul, the Third place from Mother Teresa's Ascendant does not stand out. With Sagittarius rising, Aquarius is the Third place. No planet inhabits this place. Saturn, located in the cadent Sixth place, governs the Third. Planets in the Sixth can be ineffective, and malefic planets there can be harmful. Saturn is in sect, but this is small consolation.

In the Ninth we find Venus. Venus is out of sect in Mother Teresa's diurnal chart, but Venus has some dignity in her own bounds. Jupiter inhabits the Eleventh zoidion and is in sextile to Venus in the Ninth, giving strong positive testimony. Saturn, in the Tenth place from Venus and lord of the Third, forms a predominating square to Venus.

Venus did not work itself out for Mother Teresa in the way it did for Thomas Merton or Padre Pio. She founded an international order of women contemplatives, vowed to poverty, whose vocation

---

8.   There are different birth times and dates given for Mother Teresa. For illustrative purposes, I have settled on this one.

is to tend to the most poor and desperate. In this we see a different manifestation of Saturn in strong aspect to Venus.

Sun is lord of the Ninth. Sun has no relationship to the Ninth itself but, along with Lot of Fortune, Mars, and Mercury, Sun is in the very strong Tenth place from the Ascendant. The effectiveness of the planets in the Tenth, particularly Sun as lord of the Ninth, brought Mother Teresa's religious mission into worldwide prominence. Probably this was not something she intended to happen.

In addition to the contrast we have seen between Mother Teresa's Third and Ninth places, we take note of their lords, Saturn and Sun. They are in the Sixth and Tenth places respectively, in an inactive place and a very active place, yet in trine to each other by zoidia. Saturn, governing her Third, strongly influences planets in the Ninth and Tenth.

Mother Teresa did not have a private life, even a private religious life. Her personal contemplative practice *was* her public vocation. We may value a "balanced" life, but it was not for her. With her whole being, she channeled herself into her very austere, public, and hands-on vocation. Personal happiness or privacy was not an issue in her spiritual or personal life.

Notice that Saturn is in the Sixth and governs the Second and Third places. Remember that the Sixth place can assist in determining occupation, since the Sixth is in trine to the Tenth place of *praxis* or "what one does." Convention would dictate that Mercury and Mars in the Tenth are more involved with Mother Teresa's occupation. Saturn, however, governing the Third and in trine to the Tenth, has a strong influence on Mercury and Mars. I remember seeing a movie from the 1980s on Mother Teresa. Her order had become internationally prominent and was attracting ample donations. In one sequence, after a scene where she visits a well-endowed convent in California, workmen are then shown taking out all the soft furniture and tasteful carpeting.

Note that Venus in the Ninth is also with the Lot of Exaltation and is in trine to her Lot of Spirit. This emphasizes the renown given to Mother Teresa for her religious mission and for her independent spirit. Also note Mars in the Tenth, governing the Lot of Spirit: at close range Mother Teresa had considerable ferocity.

We end our discussion with someone who is not Catholic but, like Mother Teresa, has also become a world figure: the **Dalai Lama**. In the late 1950s, this young ruler of Tibet fled from the Chinese into exile and has been outside of Tibet ever since. He has been the public face of the Tibetan people and religion around the globe, and won the Nobel Peace Prize in 1989. He has lectured around the world on many different topics, both spiritual and political, has written many books, and has collaborated with scientific and cultural figures all over the world. His biography is aptly entitled *Freedom in Exile*.

The Third place is inhabited by Moon and the Lot of Spirit, but with Saturn opposing. Oriental Mercury in the Twelfth, dignified in Gemini, governs the Third. These three planets Moon, Saturn, and Mercury give us much information about his spiritual and political life.

Moon, in her joy in the Third, is a planet of personal experience and of adaptability. Moon is made more positive by being in sect, which indicates a rich personal religious life.

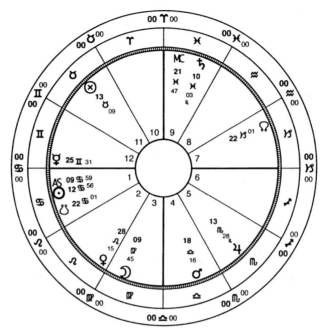

Dalai Lama

An astrologer looking at Mercury might be concerned about its location in the Twelfth, the place of the "Bad Spirit." This could make him a liar, a swindler, or someone who is deceived by others. Mercury is otherwise in very good condition. It is oriental and in its own house, indicating his intellectual and dialectical approach to religious practice. He is fortunate that his personal practice is strongly informed by scholarly debate. Over the years, the Dalai Lama has become an important scholar of his tradition. The fact that Mercury is lord of the Third tells us that it has governed his personal practice. Since Mercury is also lord of his Lot of Spirit, the planet bestows an independent mind that has enabled him to saturate himself with modern ideas from the western world.

Saturn in the Ninth opposes Moon, and Saturn is in a predominating square to Mercury, the lord of the Third. Saturn is out of sect and retrograde. This is a difficult placement, because Saturn can give rise to slander and divisiveness in the public religious life. (The Chinese might agree with this assessment.) At its best, Saturn gives a conservative tendency: this may help his spiritual discipline endure through adversity.

In some ways the Dalai Lama's mental flexibility has allowed his religion to endure. In 1959 the Dalai Lama had fled a Tibet that was closer to a medieval theocracy than a modern nation. As happens to many a politically dominant religion, its spiritual traditions had declined. The Dalai Lama embraced modern political institutions and scientific viewpoints very alien to his native Tibet, and this has helped ensure that his religious tradition would survive in a modern world.

Given the difficulty of Saturn's position, how do we account for its positive impact? Part of the answer is that Jupiter is dispositor of Saturn and lord of the Ninth, located in the Fifth from the Ascendant. (The Great Benefic, governing Sagittarius, is also lord of the Lot of Being Away from Home, the place of exile.)

It is interesting that the Dalai Lama's Lot of Exaltation is present in the Ninth with Saturn. Ordinarily the presence of Saturn would bode ill for the Dalai Lama's positive reputation. Here it seems to be the other way around: the Lot of Exaltation has helped Saturn, as the Dalai Lama has dealt well with his role as the spiritual as well as worldly leader of the exiled Tibetans. Jupiter's position has been useful.

The Dalai Lama is one of a dwindling number of leaders of Tibetan Buddhism who received their education in Tibet but had to pursue their vocations outside of their home country. Deprived of their homeland, they have had to become a "greatest generation" of teachers for the entire world. The fact that the Dalai Lama has experienced grave obstacles is apparent from his chart; that he has overcome them illustrates the most positive features of Moon, Mercury - and especially Saturn.

We have closely examined the twelve places or zoidia from the Ascendant - "the twelve houses." Chapter Eight examines another feature of the astrological birth chart: aspects. Once again, we will find that the ancient tradition solves many of the problems in modern astrology, and provides a model for a consistent approach that we can use successfully.

8

ASPECTS AND OTHER CONNECTIONS

Aspects tell us how planets connect to each other. Although two planets may be far apart from one another in the natal chart and physically far apart in space itself, it is through aspects that they come into contact with one another. One determines aspects by specific distances between two planets in the zodiac. This chapter explores some of the major differences between how ancient and modern astrologers think of and use aspects. Many people learning astrology find that aspects are difficult to learn and use. The astrologer must consider the condition of the different planets involved, their respective signs or *zoidia*, and the nature of the specific aspect, but this need not be so difficult. By examining how ancient astrologers used aspects, we can more skillfully use them in our modern practice. Here are some basic questions about aspects, ancient and modern.

- How is it that planets or other positions influence each other by aspect, when their bodies are nowhere near each other in the natal chart or in space - is this "action at a distance"?

- How do we consider planets that aspect by degree but not are not in signs or zoidia that share the same aspect? For example, one planet in late Aries and another in early Cancer may be just over sixty degrees away from each other. Yet Aries and Cancer, both cardinal zoidia, do not sextile but have a square relationship to one another. Is this then a sextile that is like a square?

- How distant can planets be from "perfection" for the aspect to be considered an aspect?

- Which planet influences which planet by aspect?

- What is the role of minor aspects and multi-planet aspect configurations when interpreting an astrological chart?

- Why have certain aspects been used only in modern times? How are they different from traditional aspects? How might that difference manifest in one's interpretations?

To ascertain how aspects weight in for interpretation, we need to quickly review the steps of natal chart analysis. Where are aspects within that process? We begin by asking a question of the chart, and then we look for chart factors that can respond to that question.

For example, we might look at the lords of Moon and Mercury for information about soul or character, lords of the Lots of Fortune and Spirit for information about luck and initiative, Venus or the lord of one of the many marriage lots for information about love and marriage. We can look at the Ninth or Third places and their lords for religion and spirituality, or the triplicity lords of the Sun or Moon to judge the happiness and fulfillment of the native. You may recall this from Chapter Four.

Once we have determined the significator for an issue, we then analyze the significator's nature and condition, sect and dignity. We also note its position relative to the Ascendant. (Another factor, which we will take up in the next chapter, is the planet's relationship with the Sun: is the significator oriental or occidental or under the Sun's beams?)

Aspect is yet another factor we use to assess the planet or planets signifying an issue. What planet or planets aspect the significator of an issue? The most important is whether the aspecting planets are benefics or malefics. Next in importance is what kind of aspect it makes and the aspecting planet's condition, which also provide information about the positive or negative nature of the aspect. In this way an aspect helps provide essential information about positive or negative influences on the planet that signifies a particular issue.

Thus we may have no need for modern aspect configurations like: T-Squares, Grand Trines, Kites and Yods, as they do not address particular issues nor provide enough specific information about the native: they might not answer the specific question we are asking of the chart. Yet the Hellenistic tradition does have room for configurations of planets, in the form of *doryphoria* or "spear bearers." There are different criteria to identify planets as spear bearers for a luminary or well-placed planet. In this chapter we will work with criteria based on aspect, and in Chapter Nine we will consider the oriental and occidental conditions for doryphoria. Spear bearing may be an ancestor of modern aspect configurations, such as the T-Square, Grand Trine, and so forth. Spear bearing was used to assess whether a chart may portend fame and renown for person, and so it does answer specific questions about the native.

We can simplify aspects without losing sight of their importance or profundity. If you are an experienced astrologer and if aspects are like food for you, I am going to put you on a really good diet. At the beginning you may feel hungry and deprived, but as our discussion proceeds, you will see that the Hellenistic tradition has complexities of its own. After the diet of simplicity we will sample a new ethnic food.

Aspects from Zoidion to Zoidion

Modern astrologers informally use aspects from sign to sign, from zoidion to zoidion, all the time. A planet's placement in a zoidia - regardless of *where* the zoidia is - can make for effective interpretation. Most astrologers work with *synastry*, whereby one interprets a relationship by noting how the planets in two charts connect with one another. This allows one to understand how two people connect in their lives.

Looking at the relationship between someone with Sun in Aries and a partner with Sun in Cancer, the modern astrologer might say that these two people may strongly connect but have

Why the word "aspect"?

What does the word "aspect" mean? The English word "aspect" is interesting and has its roots in ancient understanding; the dictionary gives you three definitions for the noun *aspect*.

1. The action of looking at something, beholding, view, gaze.

2. A way of looking: a position or direction.

3. An appearance

The astrological definition, which is the position of one chart factor in respect to another, seems unrelated to these three. It need not be. The ancient western tradition used several words for our "aspect" and they fall into two main groups:

1. Words that mean perceiving or seeing. There can be a hostile intent, like our word "scrutinizing." We will soon discuss *atkintoboleo* - casting rays - that is an action of perception.

2. Words that mean testifying or witnessing. In a court of law, a *witness* is somebody who sees something and tells about it, positively or negatively. Think of a planet as a person on trial. The aspecting planets enhance or diminish the person by their testimony. You may recall from Chapter Five that the planet ruling character or soul is affected positively by testimony from benefics and negatively by testimony from malefics.

different agendas when it comes to initiative and follow-through, structure and spontaneity. For good or for ill, there is a square by zoidia between their respective Suns. Because both Aries and Cancer are cardinal zoidia, we are looking at two rather decisive people.

If the first person with Sun in Aries also has Moon in Sagittarius and the other with Sun in Cancer has Moon in Aquarius, the astrologer might think better of their prospects, since there is a sextile between their respective Moons in Sagittarius and Aquarius. An astrologer might envision a bond that is intellectual, idealistic, and outgoing, but emotionally reserved. However, the first person with Sun in Aries and Moon in Sagittarius might come across a bit more strongly.

If one person has Mars in Pisces and the other has Mars and Saturn in Sagittarius - two zoidia that square each other - this combination of malefics suggests conflicts of control between the two. If Mars and Saturn in Sagittarius fall in the same zoidion as the other's Moon, that person could feel intimidated. We can get quite a bit of information in this way from the charts of two people. How would this work with an individual chart?

Scorpio rises in someone's chart with Sun in Leo in the Tenth. The planet governing the Ascendant, Mars, is also in Scorpio in the First. You might think, "This is a very stubborn and determined person." However if she also has Moon in Cancer, she now seems far less ruthless. Yet, with the Moon in Cancer and Mars in the First in Scorpio, two zoidia that trine, one would prefer to remain on good terms with her.

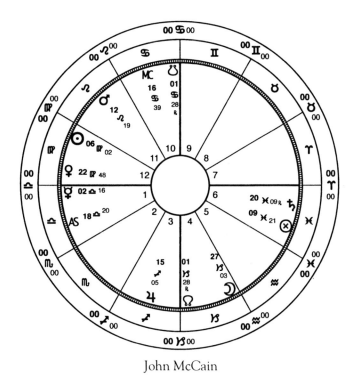

John McCain

It is interesting that modern astrologers often use simple relationships between zoidia without appreciating how much good information they derive in this way. This finding also allows us to address the issue of aspects between planets whose respective zoidia do not share the same aspect as do the planets. To give an example, here is the American politician **John McCain**.

In my view, the closest aspect to Mercury at 2 Libra is Mars, which, at 12 Leo, is 10 degrees away from an exact sextile of 60 degrees. You might notice that Moon, at 27 Capricorn, is aspecting Mercury by trine, since the orb is 115 degrees (5 less than an exact trine). Why would I not consider Moon to be the closer aspect to Mercury than Mars? Mercury in Libra and Moon in Capricorn are not zoidia that trine each other, because they are not in the same triplicity or element. In fact, by zoidia, they are in a square. I would thus consider Mercury in Libra and Moon in Capricorn not to trine but square *because their zoidia square*.

Most astrologers are far more comfortable interpreting Mercury in Libra and Moon in Capricorn as a square rather than as a trine - the facts are clearer. Some astrologers will call a trine between Libra and Capricorn "out-of-sign" - regarding their impact weaker - or say that it is "dissociate." These dissociate aspects would carry some of the meaning of the trine (by degree) and some of the meaning of the square (by zoidion). I find these theories unsatisfying and difficult to use in interpretation. Following these guidelines feels like talking with pebbles in your mouth.

It is always more comfortable for the astrologer to interpret an aspect when the planets are in the zoidia that share the same aspect. Because Libra and Capricorn are cardinal zoidia and one is masculine (Libra) and the other feminine (Capricorn), these two planets *square* each other.

Using aspects that only exist between zoidia means that the relationship between the houses or places is the same as the relationship between the planets in these places. If there is a trine between the Sixth and the Tenth places, all planets in these places are in trine to one another. Using aspects in this way allows the entire natal chart to be more elegant and intelligible. We will now investigate what aspects are and why the "Ptolemaic" aspects are the most appropriate ones to use.

The What's and Why's of Aspects

Is a conjunction strictly an aspect? Modern astrologers would say yes, Hellenistic astrologers would say no. Instead, planets in the same zoidion are *not* in aspect to each other, because they do not see each other and cannot testify to each other. Rather, they are said to be "with" one another. Malefics in the same zoidion may not cause as great a difficulty as malefics that aspect from elsewhere.

Here is an analogy. When you are in a room alone, you fill up that room. If a friend, partner, or mother-in-law comes in, that person also fills up that room: like it or not, you are *with* that person. If one of you then calls a third person from a phone, or another person sees you and your guest through a window, there is a relationship of perception - an aspect - to and from you and the third person.

How Do Planets Connect by Aspect?

What is the medium through which planets that are physically distant from each other - in different zoidia - aspect one another? In Greek (and medieval) physics, there is no such thing as action from a distance. What brings these planets together is also what brings together the sides of a geometrical figure or the notes on a keyboard or from a string to make a harmonious progression of musical tones: *the inherent properties of numbers*. The names we use for the major aspects are either directly or indirectly geometrical. We need to take the whole circle as our frame of reference.

- Planets on opposite sides of the circle - what we would call **opposition** - form the *diameter* of the circle. If there are three hundred sixty degrees of a circle, this is one hundred eighty degrees.

- Planets forming a side of an equilateral *triangle* within the circle are said to be **trine** to each other. These planets will be one hundred twenty degrees from each other.

- Planets forming the side of a *square* within the circle are **square** to one another. A side of a square is ninety degrees.

- Planets forming the side of a *hexagon* are **sextile** to one another. A side of a sextile is sixty degrees.

The Greeks considered the basic equilateral two-dimensional figures of the world to be the line, triangle, square, and hexagon.

Ptolemy also provides us with an explanation for using only these relationships as aspects.[1] His frame of reference is the right angle. The interval of the *diameter*, a line through the circle, gives us 180 degrees. This is, of course, astrology's opposition. Dividing into two gives us the *square* and 90 degrees. If you take the same line of the diameter and divide it into *three*, you get segments of 60 degrees each, which forms the sextile, and two sextiles are the trine. This means that the nature of all these aspects is the nature of one, two, and three - these numbers are building blocks of our intelligible world. Although modern astrologers continuously multiply and divide numbers to get more obscure astrological aspects, our ancient ancestors found all they needed by using one, two, and three.

A Musical Interlude

When discussing the aspects, Ptolemy does something quite revealing. He refers to what he calls the "super-fractions" of one and a third and one and a half:

- One and a third from the right angle (ninety degrees or a *square*) is a *trine* at one hundred twenty degrees.

- One and a half of the sextile (sixty degrees) is the square, the right angle of ninety degrees.

This brings together the numbers of aspects with those of musical intervals in Western music theory. If you play a violin or flute, you might think of what happens to the tone if you place your fingers up or down the string or current of air at places equivalent to these fractions. If you take a string, pluck it, and then put your finger at the halfway point, and pluck it again, you will get another tone one octave higher. This is like the opposition, the diameter of a circle. If you keep your finger at the midpoint and press down halfway between the center and one of the sides, you get a *fifth*, like the astrological square and geometrical right angle. If you divide this same string into thirds, like the sextile and trine, you get a *fourth*. One wonders whether Ptolemy got the logic of these aspects from the musical practice of his day.

The ratio of the musical fifth is 3:2, which is also the relationship between the sextile or side of a hexagon and the square or right angle. The ratio of the musical fourth is 4:3, which is also the relationship between the square or right angle and the trine, the side of a triangle.

The laws of connection between astrology's planets, the medium of their seeing one another, are the same as the relationships between the simple numbers that make up geometry and music. They mirror the structure of our world.

---

1.   Ptolemy. *Tetrabiblos* Book One, Ch.14.

Connections and Disconnections, Harmonies and Disharmonies

In many charts we have seen how important it is whether planets are connected - being with or in aspect to one another - or unconnected: *asundatos* (think of the word "asunder"). Planets without any connection by aspect are also "averse" to one another. They are turned away from one another. A planet who is lord of the Ascendant who is unconnected to the Ascendant is in a more difficult place: the Second, Sixth, Eighth, or Twelfth. A planet that is the lord of a lot but is turned away from the lot provides a weakened outcome unless other factors intervene.

Any aspect from a benefic can be a good thing, and no aspect - no connection - from a malefic can be a very good thing. A trine or a sextile from a malefic that is out of sect can bring bad testimony and hurt the planet being aspected. The consideration of an aspecting planet's benefic or malefic nature outweighs the nature of the aspect itself. This can make for powerful and clear astrological interpretations.

However, the tradition is more complex. Having slimmed down a bit from our diet, here is where we begin to try our new ethnic food.

Zoidia that do not aspect can connect in other ways. There are many pairs of zoidia that do not connect by aspect. There are three factors that can bring together zoidia that are not in aspect to make them sympathetic to each other.

One is being in zoidia that are **like-engirded,** of the "same belt." These pairs constitute the houses of the same planet:

Gemini and Virgo	(governed by Mercury)
Taurus and Libra	(governed by Venus)
Aries and Scorpio	(governed by Mars)
Sagittarius and Pisces	(governed by Jupiter)
Capricorn and Aquarius	(governed by Saturn)

In practice, we tend only to note the pairs of zoidia governed by Venus and Mars. Pairs governed by Mercury and Jupiter are already in a square aspect to one another. Capricorn and Aquarius are more often thought of as being disconnected, as they are next to each other.

How are these zoidia "of the same belt?" Each belt or sphere surrounds the earth and refers to a particular planet governing it, from the Moon to that of Saturn. (This will be familiar to you if you are aware of, for example, the construction of Paradise in Dante's *Commedia*.) Other pairs of unconnected signs or zoidia that have sympathy with one another are those which **equally ascend.**

Aries and Pisces
Taurus and Aquarius
Gemini and Capricorn
Leo and Scorpio
Virgo and Libra
Sagittarius and Cancer

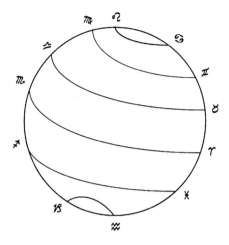

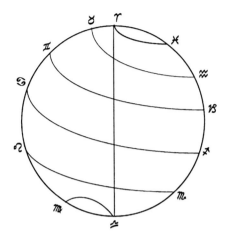

Zoidia of the same belt   Equally ascending zoidia

Note that the fixed pairs of Taurus/Aquarus and Leo/Scorpio are already in square to each other. At the same latitude, it takes these zoidia the same amount of time to ascend (calculated by the same number of degrees passing over the Midheaven). In the northern hemisphere, Aries and Pisces rise in the shortest amount of time, and Virgo and Libra rise in the longest. (This reverses for the southern hemisphere.) We will encounter these pairs again in Chapter Fourteen, as they form the basis of circumambulations or primary directions in prediction.

These zoidia are equally distant from the celestial equator: those in the first six northern zoidia - Aries through Virgo - are called "commanding," and those in the latter six southern zoidia Libra through Pisces are called "obeying." These pairs are placed on either side of the Aries-Libra axis.

The last set is the sympathetic zoidia that connect with each other by being of **equal power**:

Gemini and Cancer
Leo and Taurus
Virgo and Aries
Libra and Pisces
Scorpio and Aquarius
Sagittarius and Capricorn

These zoidia spend the same amount of time above the horizon during the day and the same amount of time below the horizon at night. They also rise and set in the same locations on the horizon. In the northern hemisphere, Gemini and Cancer spend the longest time above the horizon, and Sagittarius and Capricorn spend the shortest time above the horizon. (This reverses in the southern hemisphere.)

Symmetries in Modern Astrology

Here we encounter one of the symmetries that modern astrologers use: "contra-antiscia." These are equal numbers of degrees from the line tracing the opposition from 0° Aries to 0° Libra. Looking at the list above, a planet at 6° Pisces and 24° Aries are both 24° from 0° Aries, and would be the same number of degrees on the other side as 0° Libra. A planet at 28° Leo is equidistant from a planet at 2° Scorpio.

When these symmetries proceed from the line between 0° Cancer and 0° Capricorn, these are antiscia. This is the next condition for sympathetic zoidia, called "equal power." A planet at 6° Sagittarius and 24° Capricorn are both 24° from 0° Capricorn, and would be the same number of degrees on the other side as 0° Cancer. A planet at 28° Scorpio is equidistant from a planet at 2° Aquarius.

It is interesting that these symmetries, so popular among modern astrologers, are based on the effects of the natural features of the tropical zodiac and are based upon ancient practice.

Ptolemy implies that these relationships can bring planets together and save them from being unconnected or averse zoidia. Paulus states that planets that connect in these ways don't have as much familiarity as when they are in zoidia that aspect each other. What remain are the zoidia that are completely disconnected to one another; any two zoidia next to each other that involve one zoidion in the fixed modality:

Taurus and Sagittarius
Gemini and Scorpio
Leo and Capricorn
Leo and Pisces
Virgo and Aquarius

You may notice that *all* these pairs involve one planet in a fixed zoidion.

How can we understand all these various relationships between zoidia? Let us imagine that planets are like people in a work group. Planets that have an aspect can work productively together; planets in aversion can never get their act together. Planets in sympathy but making no aspect to one another can work together *if the need arises*. Perhaps they are like people in different parts of a large organization or like distant relatives whom you see only at weddings and funerals.

Consider again **John Kerry's** Mercury, lord of his Lots of Fortune and Spirit and the *oikodespotes* for his soul or character. Since Kerry's Mercury is in Capricorn, Mercury does not have contact by aspect to Gemini.

It turns out, however, that not only are Mercury and Saturn of equally rising *zoidia* but close to equally rising *degrees*. As we have discussed before, Kerry's Mercury has a clear link to Saturn: Kerry ponders and deliberates and he comes across as more intellectual than inspired. Except when

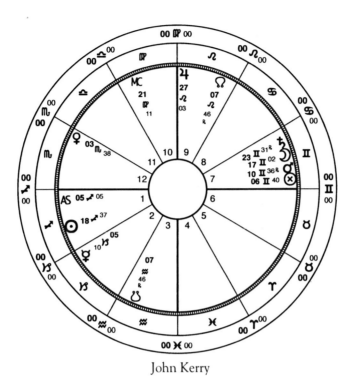

John Kerry

running against George W. Bush, this has been a positive feature for him. The connection to Saturn also manifests in the fact that, throughout his life, he has been at his most articulate and commanding when facing great difficulties.

Harmonious and Disharmonious Aspects

Let's return to planets that connect by aspect. Previously we learned that the nature of the aspect itself - trine, square, sextile - is secondary to whether two positions make any aspect at all. Yet the Hellenistic tradition is also the source of the distinction between "easy" and "difficult" aspects. Some aspects, we have all learned, are more positive than others. We learned that the sextile and trine are flowing or easy and the square and opposition are difficult. This distinction has survived into modern times. Yet the "difficult" aspects are also the more potent. Modern astrologers who do natal or predictive work give priority to square or opposition aspects over trines and sextiles. It is clear from the Hellenistic tradition that squares and oppositions are powerful, in part, because the planets involved are *all angular to one another*. The criteria for whether aspects are harmonious or inharmonious include the gender of the zoidia involved.

Why are the zoidia that connect through trines and sextiles harmonious? These aspects are between zoidia that are both being either masculine or feminine. Paulus adds that the sextiles that cross the tropical signs are *very* harmonious:

Gemini and Leo cross Cancer
Virgo and Scorpio cross Libra
Sagittarius and Aquarius cross Capricorn
Pisces and Taurus cross Aries

Why are squares inharmonious? Because they involve one planet in a masculine zoidion and one in a feminine zoidion, one planet wants to go more quickly but the other wants to slow down. Antiochus introduces us to the concept of "sympathetic squares," which are squares between zoidia that are either equally rising or equally ascending. This means that *all* the squares between planets in fixed zoidia are sympathetic.[2]

• Squares between planets in *Gemini and Virgo* and *Sagittarius and Pisces* are sympathetic since each pair shares the same house lord (Mercury and Jupiter, respectively).

• Squares between planets in *Leo and Scorpio* and *Aquarius and Taurus* are sympathetic because these pairs of zoidia are equally ascending. This is the modern "contra-antiscia," with the Aries/Libra axis at the midpoint.

(Antiochus does not mention zoidia that connect by being of equal power. Others do, however. Using Antiochus' reasoning, I would conjecture that squares between planets in *Scorpio and Aquarius* and between *Taurus and Leo* are sympathetic because these zoidia are equally powerful.)
Why are oppositions inharmonious, since the zoidia are either masculine or feminine? The opposition also places two planets across from one another: when one rises, the other sets.

There is an additional and powerful criterion for harmonious and inharmonious aspects, which we touched upon in Chapter Three when surveying the houses of the planets. These give us aspects based on the natural relationships between governing zoidia. We return to the diagram that we considered earlier.

Aspects from Leo and Cancer (the houses of the Sun and Moon) to the houses of the planets, in the order of the zodiac (from Leo) and in reverse order (from Cancer) carry the nature of the planets onto their aspect relationships.

• *Leo sextiles Libra forward; Cancer sextiles Taurus backward.* Libra and Taurus are the houses of Venus. Sextiles have the nature of Venus, the lesser benefic.

• *Leo squares Scorpio forward; Cancer squares Aries backward.* Scorpio and Aries are the houses of Mars. Squares have the nature of Mars, the lesser malefic.

• *Leo trines Sagittarius forward; Cancer trines Pisces backward.* Sagittarius and Pisces are the houses of Jupiter. Trines have the nature of Jupiter, the greater benefic.

• *Leo opposes Aquarius; Cancer opposes Capricorn.* Oppositions have the nature of Saturn, the greater malefic.

---

2.   Antiochus, Book I, Ch. 16, 17.

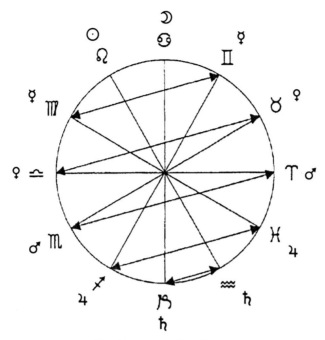

The Houses of the Planets

Modern astrologers think of squares as more dynamic and also more difficult than oppositions; ancient astrologers saw it the other way around. If oppositions are Saturnine, they are more difficult than squares, which have the nature of Mars. This mirrors the difference between the greater malefic (Saturn) and the lesser malefic (Mars).

When Ptolemy discusses interpreting a natal chart for issues of children, he characterizes opposed and disconnected (averse) planets as *equally difficult*. Other authorities in the Hellenistic tradition consider aversion more difficult than opposition (as Ptolemy does elsewhere in the *Tetrabiblos*).

If planets are like people in a workgroup, which relationships are more or less productive? Often those who are chummy with each other may work together less productively, because they question each other less and distract each other more. These are like planets making trines and sextiles to one another. Up to a point, edgier working relationships may be better for getting the job done: people may have better focus and challenge each other more. This resembles planets in square or opposition to one another. The worst relationships are those in which people cannot relate to one another at all. These are like aversions.

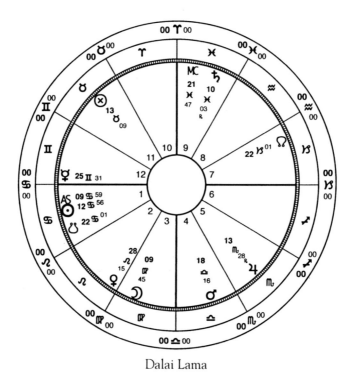

Dalai Lama

Right hand, left hand

We can now train our eyes to notice in which directions the aspects proceed, using the Dalai Lama's chart as an example. Looking at his chart carefully, the direction from Sun in Cancer toward Jupiter is in the direction of the zodiac, or *counterclockwise*. If you visualize the Sun at the top of this natal chart it is easy to see that Jupiter is *to the left* of the Sun.

The direction from the Moon in Virgo to Mercury in Gemini is against the order of the zodiac, or going *clockwise*. If you visualize Moon at the top of the chart, you can easily see that Mercury is *to the right* of the Moon.

•   Counterclockwise = in the direction of the zodiac = to the left (from the top). Elsewhere this is called the "secondary motion", the motion of the planets through the zodiac.

•   Clockwise = against the direction of the zodiac or diurnal direction = to the right (from the top). This is the primary motion, or diurnal motion, and reflects the Sun and the planets as they move during the day and night.

We will encounter this distinction in Chapter Fourteen when we discuss the predictive technique of circumambulations or primary directions. Note the **Dalai Lama's** Saturn in Pisces. Is Jupiter in Scorpio to the right or left of Saturn? In your mind's eye, place Saturn at the top of the chart. Scorpio is backwards in the zodiac from Pisces and is against the order of the signs and so

Jupiter is to the right of Saturn. This also means that Saturn is on Jupiter's left, which you could see by turning the chart so that Jupiter is on top.

From the point of view of Jupiter in Scorpio, Saturn in Pisces is in the direction of the zodiac or counterclockwise in the chart. From the viewpoint of Saturn, Jupiter is in the opposite direction from the zoidia, or clockwise, and to the left of Saturn.

Planets in their Own Faces

A rather obscure category of dignity survived through the medieval era, which we could render as "in one's own face." Note that the Dalai Lama has Sun in Cancer and Jupiter in Scorpio, in trine to one another. Visualize the diagram of the houses of the planets. The relationship between Sun in trine to Jupiter on its left, in this case from Cancer to Scorpio, repeats the direction and distance of the houses of the Sun (Leo) and Jupiter (Sagittarius). In the Dalai Lama's chart, Jupiter would be in its own face.

One could use the relationship on the right for the Moon. A sextile from Moon in Pisces and Venus in Capricorn repeats the direction and distance between the Moon's house (Cancer) and Venus' (Taurus).

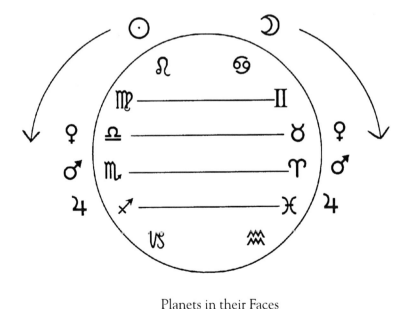

Planets in their Faces

After going through my explanation of right-side and left-side aspects, you may be wondering whether the direction of an aspect is important. Many authorities, ancient and medieval, find significance in the direction of the aspect. William Lilly, for example, values *dexter* aspects - right-sided, against the order of the signs - more than *sinister* aspects - left-sided and in the order of the signs. He mentions this distinction now and again but does not clearly demonstrate how this might be used. How does the Hellenistic tradition consider the directions of aspects?

Looking Ahead, Casting Rays

The meanings of many of the Greek words for aspect involve perceiving and seeing. According to the ancient mind, when we look forward, we send forward a ray from our eyes to the object of sight, which casts its rays back to us. The object's rays are picked up by a medium and transmitted back to our eyes. We synthesize this sequence into a discrete perception. In **Muhammad Ali's** chart, one planet, for example Moon, may *look forward*, i.e. in the direction of the zodiac, to, for example, Mars. Mars would be to the left of Moon, in a counterclockwise direction. Mars, however, *casts its rays* backwards, to the right, as if it was an object of perception. A planet in Capricorn looks ahead to a planet in Aries, because Capricorn is to the left of Aries; but a planet in Aries casts its rays back to the planet in Capricorn, since Aries is to the right of Capricorn.[3]

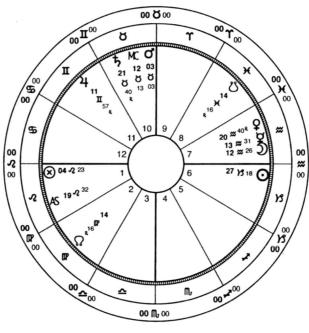

Muhammad Ali

3.   In many translations of the Greek astrologers, Robert Schmidt uses the expression "hurling rays" for the Greek *aktinoboleo*. Since *aktin* and *boleo* tend to refer more to the rays of the Sun, and since this kind of aspect is not considered violent or malevolent. I prefer to translate *aktinoboleo* as "casting rays".

In the Dalai Lama's chart, Saturn in Pisces looks ahead to the Sun in Cancer, and the Sun in Cancer casts rays back to Saturn in Pisces. Also, Sun in Cancer looks ahead to Jupiter in Scorpio, which casts its rays back to the Sun in Cancer. This is a two-way operation. What does the difference in direction signify? The planet looking ahead has superiority over the planet that is casting rays back. A consideration frequently cited is *predomination*, where the planet casting an aspect forward - particularly by square - has dominance over the planet to the left. For any square, the planet in a tenth-place position has dominance over that planet. An example is in the chart of Muhammad Ali.

Although the two malefics are in the Tenth place from the Ascendant, Moon, Mercury, and Venus in the Seventh are related to Mars and Saturn because the Seventh is the Tenth place from the Tenth. For this reason, it would be a safe assumption that the native's tendency to be quirky and charming (Moon, Mercury, and Venus in Aquarius) tames his abrasive or domineering (Mars and Saturn respectively) inclinations.

How do planets *that oppose each other* look ahead or cast rays? One needs to consider the degrees of the planets. We are interested in **Bernadette of Lourdes'** Moon at 8 Leo, which opposes both Mercury at 3 Aquarius and Venus at 9 Aquarius. If you place the Moon at the top of the chart, imagine a line drawn downwards. 8 Leo (Moon) would be at the top and 8 Aquarius would be on the bottom. Mercury, the planet with the lower number of degrees, would thus be at the bottom but

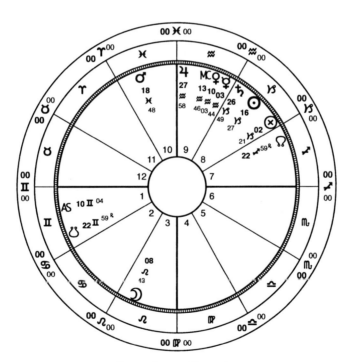

Bernadette of Lourdes

on the left side of the line - just barely - and Venus would be on the right, since it is placed a degree higher than the Moon. Therefore Moon is looking ahead to Mercury, but Venus is looking ahead to Moon. Our next chapter uses this consideration to set the boundary between oriental and occidental.

On Spear Bearing

When discussing planetary sect, Paulus says that Jupiter and Saturn are *spear bearers* for the Sun, and that Venus and Mars are *spear bearers* for the Moon. As co-sectarians of the luminaries, these are the planets that guard them and act as their entourage. Spear bearing is like having people to guard you and act as your entourage. In public, a spear bearer is a good person to have with you (unless you wish to travel inconspicuously). As an entourage, like a motorcade, spear bearers are symbols of prestige and importance. Any planet in the zoidion of its house or in exaltation and in an angular place, especially the First or Tenth, is qualified for having spear bearers. In all cases, the host or principal has to be strongly situated. For Antiochus and Hephaistio, casting rays (backwards in the zodiac) to another planet is a condition for being a spear bearer for the host planet.

Antiochus tells us that spear bearing occurs when a planet, in its house or exaltation, casts its rays onto a second planet that is in its own house or exaltation and also in an angular place. [4] The planet that is casting rays is the subordinate, the spear bearer; the planet looking ahead is the planet in authority, the principal. Here are examples Antiochus uses:

1. Saturn in Capricorn casting its rays onto Venus in Libra. (Venus is the principal; Saturn is the spear bearer.)

2. Mars in Capricorn casting its rays onto Saturn in Libra. (Saturn is the principal; Mars is the spear bearer.)

3. Jupiter in Sagittarius casting its rays onto Venus in Libra. (Venus is the principal; Jupiter is the spear bearer.)

A planet is often a spear bearer to a luminary, but a planet can be a spear bearer for another planet. Even a luminary can be spear bearer for a planet. In any event, the planet that is casting rays is the subordinate; the planet looking ahead is the principal, the planet in authority. You will note that neither the kind of aspect nor the sect conditions of the planets matters here. Using these guidelines, Ali's Mars and Saturn can be, in a limited way, spear bearers for Mercury, Moon, and Venus.

The relationship is stronger when principal and spear bearer are in the same sect: Mars would be a stronger spear bearer for Ali's nocturnal planets in the Seventh than Saturn. Because none of the principals are in their houses or exaltations, spear bearing in Ali's chart is not as potent as it could be. A simple example is that of **Jacqueline Kennedy Onassis**, for whom Saturn is a spear bearer for Sun.

---

4.   Antiochus, Chap. 23.

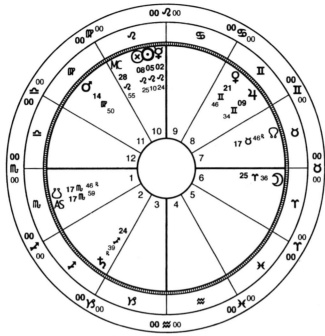

Jacqueline K Onassis

Sun, in the Tenth, in his own house, looks ahead to Saturn in Sagittarius, which casts rays back to Sun. Saturn guards Sun. Saturn is limited, however, by being in the mediocre Second place. Antiochus tells us that when the luminaries are involved in spear bearing relationships, even if the luminary or spear bearer is not in dignity, spear bearing can still occur if the Sun or Moon is in the First or Tenth places. However, the spear-bearing planet must be in the same sect as the luminary. If Moon is in the zoidion of the Ascendant or in the Tenth place, and if Venus casts its rays back at her from Virgo or Libra, Venus is a spear bearer for Moon. (In Libra, Venus would be a stronger spear bearer than if she were in Virgo.) **Woody Allen**'s chart has an example of a planet - Venus - being spear bearer for another planet - Jupiter.

Venus in Libra looks ahead at Jupiter in Sagittarius. Both planets are dignified but neither are in the First or Tenth places. However Venus and Jupiter are not in the same sect and, although Jupiter is angular, Venus is not. This bodyguard, Jupiter, might be a bit too imposing in Venus' entourage. A planet can also be a spear bearer for a luminary, even when that planet is not in the same sect as the luminary. If Sun is in the zoidion of the Ascendant, Venus, who is nocturnal in sect, could be its spear bearer. Perhaps an out-of-sect spear bearer is like hiring a mercenary or contract worker: he or she can do the job but without the same loyalty.

One combination is in the chart of **Marlon Brando**. Here we have an example of *both* luminaries spear bearing for a prominent Jupiter. Jupiter in the First looks ahead at Sun and Moon (and Mercury) who cast rays back to Jupiter. Since the Sun is exalted in Aries and in the same sect

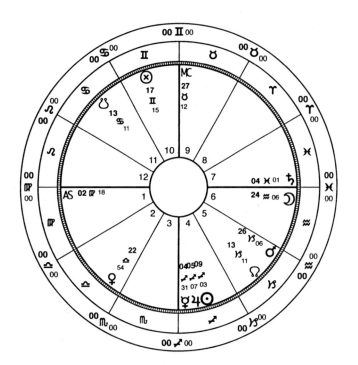

Woody Allen

Marlon Brando

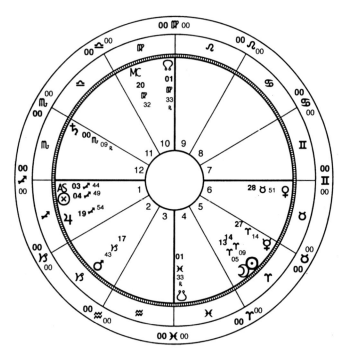

as Jupiter, Sun is an even better spear bearer for Jupiter. Brando pioneered character acting in the 1950s; he made a name for himself (Jupiter in the First) by becoming different people (Sun in the Fifth).

Interestingly, a luminary can act as a spear bearer for a luminary, although there are strict conditions of dignity. The Sun or Moon can only act as a spear bearer for a planet that is in its own sect and in an angular place. A planet must be strong and dignified to have a guard and entourage. In the Dalai Lama's chart, Jupiter in Scorpio casts its rays back to Sun in Cancer in the First. (This is the opposite of Brando's configuration.) Jupiter is a spear bearer for Sun; this is a very positive feature of the Dalai Lama's chart.

Why is the spear bearing planet, the subordinate, one that casts its rays, not one who looks ahead? I am reminded of the old-fashioned protocol for interacting with one's superiors. One does *not* look at a person in authority directly: you are the object of his or her perception; he or she is not the object of yours. Remember the bow and the curtsy. These gestures of respect limit the eye contact of the person who is lower in status.

Now we work through our final factor that impacts the quality of a planet in the astrological chart: its relationship with the Sun.

9

THE PLANETS AND
WHEN YOU SEE THEM

How and when you see planets in the night sky gives us important information about those planets and how to use them in the natal chart. This feature hails from the Babylonian era and was also important in ancient western astrology. Medieval astrology also used criteria based on the planets' visibility, but in modern times these criteria have mostly disappeared from astrological practice. Our astrology would be better if we included them once again.

We need to train our mind's eyes to give us the information we need. I begin with visibility conditions of the Moon.

Seeing the Moon

As part of their early training, I ask my astrology students to pay close attention to the Moon for several months. When and how, in the evening (and sometimes during the day), do you see the Moon? Where in the sky is it? What is the shape of the Moon when you see it? This is important information that puts what we see in the sky into an astrological context.

What determines the visibility and shape of the Moon is its distance from the Sun from the viewpoint of the Earth, so the phases of the Moon are a visible likeness of the movement of the Sun and Moon together as we see them. We can use the zodiacal position of the Sun and Moon to determine what phase the Moon is in, what the shape of the Moon would be.

Beginning with the New Moon, which is invisible to us because Moon is hidden by the Sun's light, one sees a thin crescent above the western horizon just after sunset, after the Sun goes down. As each night passes, the Moon is higher in the sky when the Sun sets and appears larger. Seven days after the New Moon, the Moon is now half full and high in the sky when the Sun goes down. Toward the Full Moon, the Moon has become larger and is seen further east after the Sun sets in the west. During the Moon's waxing half, she is to the *left of the Sun*, ahead in the zodiac, and moving away from the Sun.

At the Full Moon, the Moon rises in the east as the Sun sets in the west. If you go out after the Sun goes down on successive nights you will notice that the Moon rises later and later in the evening and becomes smaller. During the Moon's waning half, she is *to the right of the Sun*, behind in the zodiac and becoming closer to the Sun.

A week after the Full Moon, the Moon rises during the middle of the night. Before the Sun rises in the morning, the Moon can be seen high in the sky, but is now gradually reduced from full to half. When one wakes up in the middle of a clear night, the night is palely lit by moonlight. Then, *each morning*, before sunrise, you can see the Moon further to the east and becoming progressively smaller, until she is a thin crescent that appears just before sunrise and is then no longer seen.

Noticing the Moon for a few months usually gives somebody a fresh appreciation of the natural rhythm of the sky. For astrologers and for everybody else through most of history, the sequence of the Moon's appearances and phases was, alongside the cycle of day and night and the seasons of the year, natural phenomena that set the rhythms of life, and were as ordinary to them as our calendars and clocks are to us.

How did ancient astrologers conceptualize the Moon's phases? I'll present these phases as articulated by Paulus and will add how Ptolemy gives qualities of hot, cold, wet, and dry to the Moon's quarters. This gives us more detail about the Moon's phases and their potential meanings. According to Paulus, the first lunar phase is *concurrence*. The Greek is *sundatos*. (You may remember that when two planets are not connected, they're *a-sundatos*.) A concurrence is a joining, a bringing together. Here the Moon and Sun are in the same degree of the zodiac.

The second phase is *coming forth*. The Greek is *genna*, which is also a word for birth. The Moon now moves ahead of the Sun but the Moon is not yet fifteen degrees from the Sun: Moon is not visible. In an astrological chart, you can see this phase when the Moon is close to the Sun but on its left.

This brings us to the third phase, *emergence*, when the Moon is finally visible as a thin sliver in the west. At this point the Moon will begin to grow as an infant grows into a child.

Emerging Moon

The *crescent* phase begins when the Moon stands at a sextile aspect left of the Sun. At the *first half - Moon*, the Moon is in a left-hand square to the Sun, and looks like half a Moon. At sunset the Moon is close to its culmination in the sky. According to Ptolemy, in first quarter of the cycle, the Moon has become **increasingly wet.** The *gibbous Moon* follows with a left-hand trine to the Sun. During this time, the Moon is fatter and now appears at night in the eastern sky. In Ptolemy's view, the phases from the half Moon to the whole Moon is **increasingly hot.** The *whole Moon* (what we call "Full Moon") is when the luminaries are opposed to each other. The Moon now is at an *acronycal* rising: she rises in the east when the Sun sets in the west. This begins the Moon's waning phase.

Whole Moon

The *second gibbous* phase, now within the waning half of the Moon's cycle, begins when the Moon, approaching the Sun on the right, is in a trine relationship to the Sun. The third phase from whole Moon to waning half Moon is, in Ptolemy's view, is **increasingly dry.**

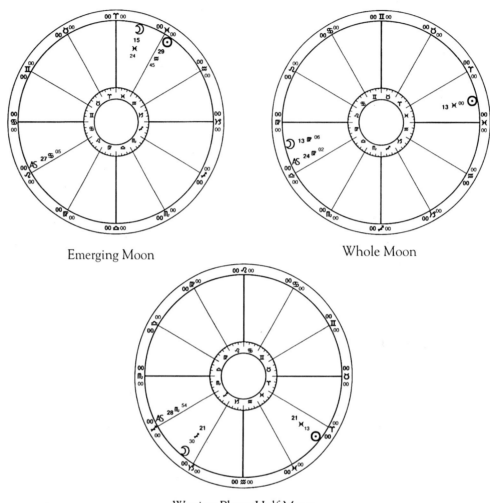

Emerging Moon

Whole Moon

Waning Phase Half Moon

Waning Phase Half Moon

The *second half Moon* occurs when the Moon, approaching the Sun on the right, goes into a square to the Sun. The Moon rises in the east at about midnight, and looks like half a Moon. The *second crescent* occurs when the Moon is in a sextile aspect on the right from the Sun. This ends Paulus' phases. According to Ptolemy, this final phase is **increasingly cold.** From this time, the Moon rises in the east, closer to the Sun as it rises and the Moon becomes smaller and smaller. At the end of the cycle, the Moon is a thin filament barely visible before the Sun's light wipes it out. Soon the Moon reaches the same degree as the Sun and the cycle begins anew. Unfortunately there are no chart interpretations in the ancient literature that utilize these phases, nor do we have guidelines for how to use them in a practical manner. There is precedent, however, in modern astrology.[1]

The starry planets Mercury through Saturn also have phases and conditions of appearing. They are more complicated yet are given interpretive prominence in astrological lore. Perhaps the best introduction is to look at some charts and discuss planetary phases with the Sun and what these phases might mean in the context of those charts.

Planetary Phases

We begin with **John McCain's** chart. McCain was born a few hours after sunrise: his Sun in the Twelfth place had recently crossed the horizon. To the right of the Sun and rising before the Sun that day is Mars, at the time of birth in his Eleventh place. We see that McCain's Mars rises in the morning before the Sun rose, but Mars also does another kind of rising - *from the Sun*. In previous weeks, Mars had been hidden by the Sun's light, but now it has emerged from this light and is now visible to the eye. McCain's Mars is *heliacally rising*.

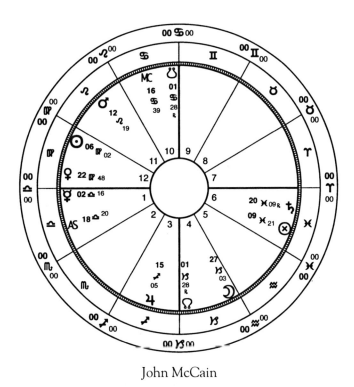

John McCain

---

1.   See Rudhyar, D. *The Lunation Cycle*, Santa Fe, NM. Aurora.

Different planets and stars emerge from the Sun's beams at different distances from the Sun, based upon the different latitudes on earth and from different latitudes to the path of the Sun, the ecliptic. Ancient astrologers wisely kept it simple: when a planet is fifteen degrees or more away from the Sun to the Sun's right, that planet is visible as a *morning riser*.

How do we know that McCain's Mars is moving away from the Sun and is not going into the Sun's beams? Mars, like Jupiter and Saturn, moves more slowly than the Sun. After Mars is conjunct the Sun, the Sun moves further away from Mars at a rate of roughly one half a degree per day. This is because the Sun moves one degree a day and Mars, at its fastest, moves one-half degree a day. Mars will appear to emerge from the Sun roughly a month after its conjunction, since Sun has moved to fifteen degrees ahead of it in the zodiac and Mars will appear on the horizon before the Sun. Mars will continue to move further away from the Sun for many months. When Mars is roughly at a trine from the Sun on the right, it will slow down and soon go retrograde.

How shall we understand McCain's heliacally rising Mars? One possibility is that Mars' nature would manifest early in his life, which was clearly the case. A more general meaning is that, as heliacally rising, Mars is a very powerful planet in McCain's chart.

Looking further at this Mars placement, many interesting features emerge. In his diurnal chart, Mars is out of sect. McCain's detractors have made much about his bad temper, and he is clearly a forceful person who expresses his views and emotions strongly. Mars is in the Eleventh place of Good Spirit. This placement amplifies the potency and positive features of Mars. When Mars is under control, it can work well for McCain, who is known as a tough politician with a blunt style. You may also note that Jupiter in Sagittarius trines Mars in Leo from the left, ahead in the zodiac. Mars looks ahead to Jupiter, Jupiter in turn casts rays back onto Mars. Since Jupiter is in its own house in Sagittarius, this contact is very beneficial to Mars. Perhaps Jupiter invests Mars with a sense of purpose.

Adding the fact that Mars is a morning riser, you have a very powerful Mars. John McCain is clearly at his best when he has a fight on his hands. Considering also that Saturn is the planet signifying his character or soul, McCain presents himself as a definitive and decisive person. (Writing this in mid-2006, I wonder whether these powerful two malefics would allow McCain to become President of the US, except in the case of national emergency.)

Now we look on the other side of McCain's Sun, to Venus in Virgo on the Sun's left. Venus is sixteen degrees away from the Sun and is just outside the Sun's beams. Venus is moving *faster than the Sun* and each day moves further away from the Sun. When McCain was born one could not see Venus rising: after the Sun rises its light prevents Venus - or any other planet following the Sun - from becoming visible. Instead, one sees Venus at dusk as a dim star that appears briefly on the Western horizon at the end of daylight. Each night afterwards, Venus moves further from Sun, becoming brighter and remaining in the sky longer after sunset, just like the waxing Moon. We could say that McCain's Venus also rises from the Sun, but in the evening. Venus and Mercury, when they are to the left of the Sun, and moving from the Sun's rays, rise from the Sun in the evening, and appear as *evening risers*.

How you interpret Venus rising in the evening depends on which authority you follow. According to Paulus, an evening rising planet fulfills its function not in early life, like a morning riser, but in middle age or far later. (This may have to do with McCain's stronger second marriage.) According to Ptolemy, any planet that sets after the Sun, even if has emerged from the Sun's rays, is occidental and less potent. McCain's Venus, in fall and in the Twelfth house, is in difficult condition. At the same time, Venus rising from the Sun increases her stature (according to Paulus), even if this placement might not work well for him - or give its full effects - until middle age or later.

I close this discussion of McCain's chart with his Saturn in Pisces. As noted in Chapter Five, Saturn is the *oikodespotes* for McCain's character or soul. Saturn in Pisces is far away from McCain's Sun in Virgo. (When Mars, Jupiter, and Saturn - the ancient "outer" planets - are on the other side of the chart as the Sun, they are always retrograde.)

If you could turn the chart in your mind's eye so that McCain's Sun is now setting, the Ascendant-Descendant line would be six degrees of Pisces on the Ascendant and six degrees of Virgo on the Descendant. (Fig. 1)

Saturn at that time would be below the horizon and would not be visible until after the Sun has gone down. Within two weeks, when the Sun reaches twenty degrees of Virgo, Saturn rises as the Sun goes down, and earlier in the day Saturn would set just as the Sun was rising. This is like the configuration of a Full Moon. (Fig. 2)

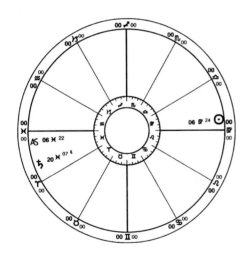

Fig.1
Sunset chart - Saturn is to the *right* of the Sun

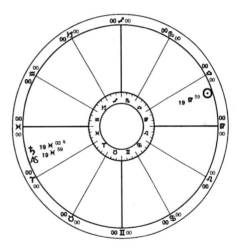

Fig.2
Saturn at opposition

Saturn is having an *acronycal rising*: rising and setting opposite the Sun. (We saw this earlier with the Full or Whole Moon.) From then on, when the Sun disappears from the sky at sunset, Saturn would be seen above the horizon further and further to the west (and thus closer to the Sun), on the left side of the Sun. (Figs. 3 & 4)

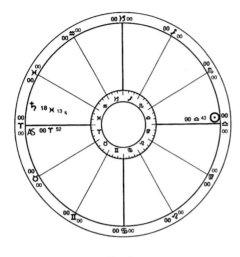

Fig 3
Saturn waning

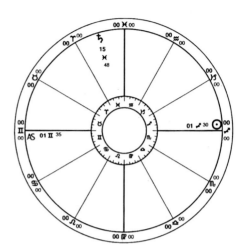

Fig 4
Saturn waning

Several months later, Saturn would be seen only briefly in the west after sunset, and would then go into the Sun's beams. Although Saturn was bright in the sky when McCain was born, and is brightest at acronycal rising when Saturn is at opposition, it is also retrograde. Saturn's situation is not enhanced but diminished by this configuration with the Sun. Since Saturn is *oikodespotes* for his soul, this does not bode well for McCain. This reduces Saturn's effectiveness in providing stability and consistency over the long term. We need to leave McCain behind and call up the chart of somebody completely different from him: Bernadette of Lourdes.

We first look at Bernadette's Saturn. It is ten degrees away from the Sun, behind the Sun in the zodiac, to the Sun's left. As Saturn moves much more slowly than the Sun, the faster Sun will catch up with Saturn. About five days before Bernadette was born, when the Sun had come to fifteen degrees away, Saturn had previously *set to the Sun*, it had "heliacally set." The Greek term for "setting," *dutikos*, has another meaning - sinking. Think of somebody being swallowed up by water in a boating accident, or how the Sun looks when going down into the water at sunset. Think of the feeling that sinking gives us, and you get a sense of what this planet fares, as it goes from visibility to becoming hidden.

Traditional astrologers are familiar with the idea of "combustion": if a planet is within eight degrees of the Sun, it is burnt up by the Sun and is in a weakened condition. Although this concept does not appear in the Hellenistic tradition, its origin may be in the depiction of a planet sunken within the Sun's beams.

Does Bernadette's Saturn, being in a "sunken" condition, imply that Saturn is no good as a planet for her? If so, this might be a particular problem, as Saturn governs her many planets in Capricorn and Aquarius. Indeed, Saturn's placement might have proven more difficult for Bernadette if she pursued the worldly achievements of wealth and fame through the healing waters she uncovered.

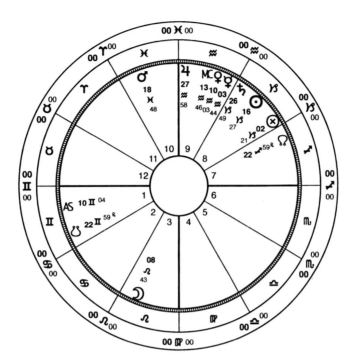

Bernadette of Lourdes

A tell-all autobiography and product line of holy water containers would not have worked well for her. Instead, she lived as self-contained and humble an existence as she could. That she became a cloistered nun indicates one good way for her to use her invisible Saturn. Here invisibility doesn't mean weak: it means invisible.

In Bernadette's chart, Mercury, Venus, Jupiter, and Mars are all "evening risers," as they are seen only after the Sun goes down at sunset. In your mind's eye, move the Sun under its setting position opposite the Ascendant, which happens daily, and all these planets are now visible in the western sky.

Mercury is nineteen degrees away from the Sun and at about a degree and a half a day is therefore travelling more quickly than it. When Mercury was about five degrees closer to the Sun, the planet was visible on the western horizon just after the Sun had set, and could be said to have emerged from the Sun's obscuring presence. Mercury would have evening visibility but soon the planet would slow down and eventually go retrograde.

Venus will continue to move more quickly than the Sun for many months, will later slow down, and, when the Sun catches up to within thirty degrees of Venus, she will go retrograde.

As previously stated, authorities differ on how to assess Mercury and Venus. According to Paulus, Mercury and Venus, emerging from the Sun as evening risers, are in a position of strength. They would be most effective in midlife or later, which would be unfortunate for Bernadette, as she died when she was 35 years old. Ptolemy, however, would call all these planets occidental, setting in the west to the left of the Sun, and see them as diminished in effectiveness.

During the remainder of the winter in which Bernadette was born, the Sun would catch up with Jupiter and then Mars. Like Mercury and Venus, these two planets set to the left of the Sun.

Now we return to the Dalai Lama. Mercury in Gemini rises before Sun in Cancer, on the Sun's right. Venus in Leo, having risen from the Sun in the west, sets after the Sun on the Sun's left. Mercury is a morning star and Venus is an evening star. Moon in Virgo is waxing and moving away from the Sun on its left and, come evening, Moon will be a crescent in the west. Rising before the Sun in a day chart, Mercury is also in strong sect condition as a diurnal planet.

When you see Mercury and the Sun fairly far apart, it's a good idea to find out how quickly Mercury is moving - Mercury may be fast or close to changing direction. Three days before the Dalai Lama was born, Mercury went from retrograde to direct, and is in his natal chart in its direct station. Mercury is the *oikodespotes* of his character and soul, as the Dalai Lama has Moon in Virgo (also governing his Ascendant) and Mercury in Gemini. (See Chapter Five.) According to Ptolemy and as we will discuss later, the direct station for Mercury gives his character a solidness and resoluteness.

Here Venus is close to her maximum distance from the Sun, and would appear very brightly above the western horizon after the Sun goes down. When Venus reaches forty-eight degrees away

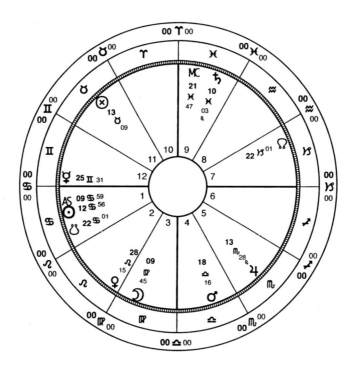

Dalai Lama

from the Sun, she then begins to slow down in her motion and the Sun gradually comes closer. When Venus is thirty degrees away from the Sun, she goes retrograde. (Later, coming out of the Sun as a morning star, Venus will be retrograde until the Sun is thirty degrees away again, and then Venus goes direct.)

Saturn in Pisces is making a right side trine to the Sun. Saturn is no longer a morning riser but is at its retrograde station. (In fact, Saturn went retrograde about two weeks before the Dalai Lama was born.) Jupiter, on the other side making a left-side trine to the Sun, is at its direct station. What happens to Saturn and Jupiter in the weeks after the Dalai Lama's birth? Saturn, now retrograde, will be at opposition to the Sun, and will have its acronycal rising. Saturn then will rise when the Sun goes down, and when the Sun rises Saturn will set. (This is like McCain's Saturn.) Although Jupiter will increase speed and go in the same direction as the Sun, the Sun moves much faster, will eventually catch up, and in a few months Jupiter will go into the Sun's beams as an evening setting planet. From these three charts we now can summarize four phases of planets in relation to the Sun:

- A planet is a **morning riser** when it is to the *right* of the Sun, ahead in the zodiac, and is visible on the eastern horizon before the Sun rises. McCain's Mars and the Dalai Lama's Mercury are both morning risers. All the starry planets can rise in the morning before the Sun: only the Moon cannot. (Closer to the Sun in the morning, the Moon is not rising from the Sun but sinking into her beams.) When Mercury and Venus first rise from invisibility in the morning, they are always retrograde. (Paulus says that Saturn, Jupiter, and Mars are all morning risers from heliacal rising until the planet makes a left-hand trine with the Sun and soon goes retrograde.)

- **Morning planets setting to the Sun** include Moon, Mercury, and Venus, and they are also to the *right of the Sun*, behind in the zodiac. We can see them in the morning just before the Sun rises but soon become invisible under the Sun's beams. They all move more quickly than the Sun in his phase and as they get close to the Sun they sink into invisibility.

- **Evening rising planets** are also Moon, Mercury, and Venus. These are to the *left* of the Sun, ahead in the zodiac. Best seen is the Moon, which first appears as a thin crescent on the western horizon just after the Sun goes down. Because Mercury and Venus at this time move more quickly than the Sun, they come out from under the Sun's beams, appearing in the west after the Sun goes down. They will increase their distance from the Sun each day.

- **Evening planets setting to the Sun:** these include all the five starry planets; they are all left of the Sun and behind in the zodiac but under different conditions:

  Mercury and Venus have gone retrograde and, as the Sun is moving closer, the oncoming Sun's beams swallow them up.

  Mars, Jupiter, and Saturn are farther in the zodiac than the Sun. Because they move more slowly than the Sun, the Sun moves closer and they are last seen as dim stars at sunset and then no more. (Because the Moon always moves more quickly than the Sun, Moon will never set into the Sun's beams in the west.)

Ptolemy's Rising and Setting Planets

Ptolemy gives us a few different depictions of phases of planets with the Sun. The first one is easy to explain. We first saw it in Chapter Two when we discussed the planets and their governance over parts of the human body. Ptolemy uses the words "rising" and "setting" - *oriental* and *occidental* - in a very simple way. It is always in the evening when one can see the planets. Sometime during the evening, do you see a planet *rise*? That planet is rising or *oriental*. Sometime during the evening, do you see a planet *set*? That planet is *occidental*. Being oriental adds to the planet, being occidental subtracts from the planet.

I chose Muhammad Ali's chart to begin with, because he was born not long after sunset. Moon, Mercury, and Venus set soon after Ali's birth, as do Mars, Saturn and Jupiter. All are visible in the sky after the Sun goes down. All these planets are occidental.

Examining Woody Allen's chart gives us different information. At the time of his birth, Mars and Moon had already set and Saturn was setting: these are all occidental planets. Venus, Mercury, and Jupiter will all rise sometime before the Sun rises in the morning; all these are oriental.

All oriental planets are to the right of the Sun up to the degree of the opposition. All occidental planets are to the left of the Sun from the opposition to the conjunction on the other side.

Ptolemy tells us that oriental planets are stronger than occidental planets. (He would call Ali's Mercury and Venus in the Seventh weak because they are occidental; Paulus would call them

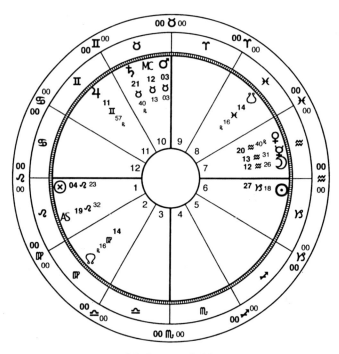

Muhammad Ali

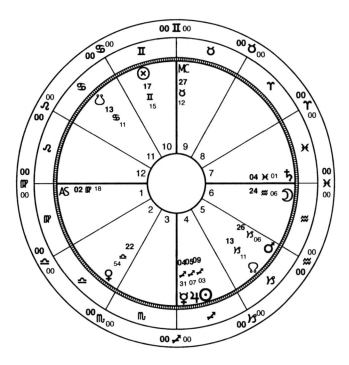

Woody Allen

evening risers and more potent.) There is one difficulty with Ptolemy's simple approach. According to him. Mercury and Venus, when rising out of the Sun's beams as evening risers, would be less powerful than when these planets first appear outside the Sun's beams in the morning. This is paradoxical because, when they are evening risers, Mercury and Venus move faster than the Sun, but when these planets rise from the Sun in the morning, they are retrograde.

    The consensus within the Hellenistic tradition seems to favor Ptolemy's approach, possibly because his criterion is so easy to observe at night. When noting the strength of planets as *chronocrators* or lords of time for purposes of prediction, both Valens and Hephaistio give more positive outcomes when the planet involved is oriental.

Ptolemy's Planetary Phases[2]

Aside from the distinction between oriental and occidental, Ptolemy gives us not one but two other approaches. In the fourth chapter of Book Three of the *Tetrabiblos*, he gives us some interesting ideas about how to assess planets and their effects. When discussing the time of an effect from the natal chart, it is critical whether significant planets are *east and west of the Sun and the horizon*. East is faster than west.

---

2.   In the last chapter of my previous work on this topic (Crane, 1998), I attempted to bring together rising and setting, oriental and occidental, with the phases of the Sun. This was an error. (See Schmidt, 1998, xiii-xxii.)

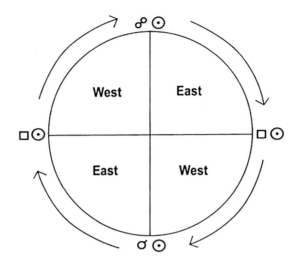

- From the viewpoint of the horizon, a planet is *east* if between the Ascendant and Midheaven degrees or between the Descendant and I.C. These are where planets ascend or descend after being upon the horizon, going above the Ascendant or below the Descendant. This is "east" of the horizon.

- From the viewpoint of the Sun, a planet *east* is when a planet is ahead of the Sun on the right up to a right-hand square with the Sun. East is also when the planet opposes the Sun to making a square to the Sun on the left.

- From the viewpoint of the horizon, a planet is in a *west* when it is from the Midheaven moving to the point of its descent, and when the planet has crossed the I.C. but hasn't yet risen. A planet is west of the Sun, from its square on the right to the opposition, and from the square on the left to the conjunction.

For another sequence, we return to Ptolemy's delineation of soul. Elsewhere in Book Three of the *Tetrabiblos*, he gives us conditions by which to assess the *oikodespotes*. (See Chapter Four for a more extensive presentation of this topic.) Ptolemy distinguishes between four phases of planets with the Sun and likens them to planets at the four angles of the natal chart.

1.   A planet rising from the Sun to its right is like a planet near the Ascendant. Especially if that planet is also in its own face (see last chapter), this person is strong and willful, mentally active and agile.

2.   A planet at its "morning station," (oriental to the right of the Sun) but not yet retrograde, is like a planet at the Midheaven *degree*,(which may or may not be in the Tenth zoidion from the Ascendant). An *oikodespotes* in this situation will make the character of the person more steady and deliberate, vigorous and practical. One's body is strong with good muscle tone.

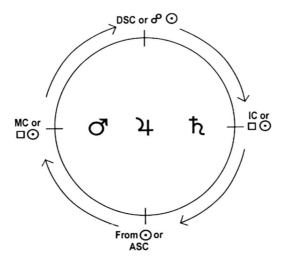

Four Phases of the Planets

3.   In its retrograde motion, the oikodespotes is like a planet at the setting place opposite the Ascendant. The person is unsteady, of low vitality and cleverness, can be vacillating and overly emotional. The body is not well proportioned.

4.   The oikodespotes in its "evening station," going from retrograde to direct, is like a planet at the I.C. This person's condition is mixed: one is not overly active, but is curious and interested in things that are mysterious and occult - perhaps like astrology. One's body is not particularly attractive or strong but holds up well under difficulty.

The sequence for "outer planets" of Mars, Jupiter, and Saturn are:

1.   Rising from the Sun in the East

2.   At its "morning station," soon to go retrograde

3.   Moving retrograde past its opposition to the Sun

4.   At evening station, to go direct

What about Mercury and Venus? In describing the effects of planets at the I.C. or evening station, Ptolemy does mention Mercury and Venus, in their "evening settings by day and morning settings by night." What does that mean? I can only speculate, because Ptolemy gives us no further information. It is possible that he is using two different sequences of phases, depending on whether the chart is diurnal or nocturnal. *For a day birth*, phases of Mercury and Venus can have this arrangement:

1.   Rising from the Sun in the morning, right of the Sun and retrograde

2.   Direct Station

3.   Retrograde station, now as an evening star

4.   Setting to the Sun

For a night birth, we might see a sequence that looks like this:

1.   Rising from the Sun in the evening, on the Sun's left

2.   Retrograde Station

3.   Direct Station, now as a morning star

4.   Setting to the Sun

One difficulty with this arrangement for Mercury and Venus is that these are very uneven phases. The time between the retrograde station and evening setting is much smaller than between the direct station and morning setting. Although I'm not totally comfortable about these sequences, I don't see an alternative to them. I offer a small example of this at work. The Dalai Lama has three planets at station. Of the three, Mercury is the *oikodespotes* of his character or soul. Mercury has great strength in this position already, being in his own house in Gemini and oriental. Mercury is also in sect in this diurnal chart. At its morning station in a nocturnal chart, Mercury would be *as if* near the degree of the IC. This Mercury is not active but steady and is interested in things that are hidden and mysterious - as Western science would be to him. This also favors a more contemplative approach to life. This strong but patient Mercury helps us understand how the Dalai Lama has been able to deal with the Chinese government for the past forty-five years.

Spear Bearers for the Sun and Moon

As we discussed in the last chapter, having a spear bearer is a positive attribute of a luminary or planet in a natal chart. A strong combination of principal and spear bearers can give us the chart of one destined for great fame and honor. Ptolemy also uses spear bearing in a chart to determine whether one's parents are famous and of renown. There are different kinds of spear bearing - in the last chapter we looked at *aspect combinations*; here we use planets in *phases with the Sun and Moon*.

According to Ptolemy and Hephaistio, the Sun's spear bearers are to the Sun's right, rising ahead of the Sun and oriental to it. The Moon's spear bearers are to the left of the Moon, setting after the Moon and occidental to it. Think of this like a parade of planets, similar to an ancient triumphal parade, and the planets as retinue march before the Sun or after the Moon. This is probably the closest that ancient astrology comes to the modern idea of "chart patterns," and this configuration would be visually impressive in the sky.

In his delineation of fame and fortune in the natal chart, Hephaistio has supplied us with an example chart that is evidently that of the **Roman Emperor Hadrian**. Hadrian was emperor at a time of peace and prosperity within the Roman Empire. He was known for a defensive policy at the

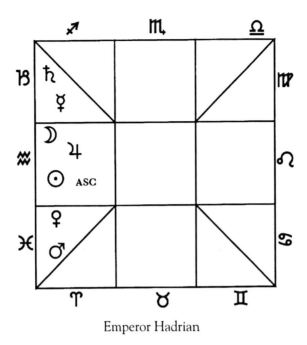

Emperor Hadrian

frontiers of the empire (you might remember Hadrian's Wall to keep the barbarians from the north from entering Roman England). He also brutally put down a Jewish revolt. Domestically, Hadrian reformed taxation, civil service, and law, and was more a competent administrator than an inspirational leader. Americans might call him a "policy wonk". His chart gives us an example of spear bearing for both the Sun and the Moon, and according to Hephastio, these factors in his chart tell us that Hadrian could become emperor.

In this chart, Mercury, and Saturn are spear bearers for the Sun. Jupiter is not out of the Sun's beams yet, but will be after seven days. Mercury is a morning riser, and Saturn is in its own house in Capricorn. Hephaistio does not mention that Mercury and Saturn are in the Twelfth place from the Ascendant; *more important is that they are morning stars rising ahead of the Sun.*

The Moon is the luminary of sect in this nocturnal chart. We look for planets that follow the Moon in the zodiac. The Sun follows the Moon, so Sun could be a spear bearer out of sect. Venus, in its exaltation, and Mars, in its triplicity, follow the Moon.

Although neither the Sun nor the Moon is dignified in Aquarius, both are angular in the First. However, their spear bearers are dignified. (Using Ptolemy's list, Mercury is in its bounds.) This is like being guarded by the front line of an American football team.

Why do the spear bearers for the Moon proceed in the opposite direction as those for the Sun? As the Sun's entourage would precede the Sun before at sunrise, the Moon's entourage would succeed her as she sets in the evening. Remember that the Moon makes its first appearance on escaping the Sun's beams early in the evening. The Sun is the king of the day and the Moon is queen of the night.

How far away from the Sun or Moon can a planet be and still be a spear bearers? Hephastio doesn't tell this to us but others do. Ptolemy's criterion is that a spear bearer right of the Sun, or left of the Moon, can be within ninety degrees. According to Paulus, the Sun's spear bearers rise before the Sun up to a trine. The Moon's spear bearers are following degrees of the zoidion of the Moon or in the following zoidion. There are grades in the potency of spear-bearing configurations of planets. One looks for combinations in which the principal is highly dignified, by being in its own house, exaltation, or on an angle. The spear bearers would be in the same planetary sect as the luminary and are also have dignity or angularity. If one could not predict that an emperor would come of a particular chart (especially these days), one might predict a celebrity or successful politician or friend of powerful people.

In my presentation I have used the chart of many famous people, and only one of them meets this stronger criteria of spear bearing. We return to Jerry Garcia's chart. The Sun's two spear bearers in the diurnal sect are Jupiter and Saturn. Jupiter is in the Tenth and in its exaltation; Saturn is in its triplicity. Who is behind the Moon? In the nocturnal sect is Venus, who is angular and in her triplicity: she is a potent spear bearer. Mars is probably too far away from Moon to qualify as a spear bearer.

Perhaps if Garcia was born earlier in the day and Sun was in the zoidion of the Ascendant, or he was born later and Sun was in the Tenth from the Ascendant, he could have become emperor, or at least president. Nonetheless, any ancient astrologer would have been excited by Garcia's chart.

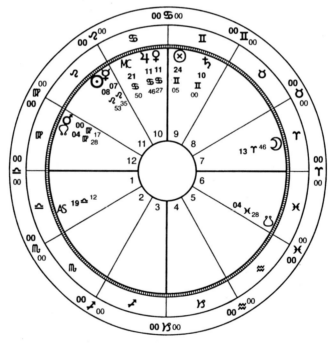

Jerry Garcia

I have found that this method for determining fame and renown does more to thrill the astrologer than to predict fame and renown in a convincing way. However, if you find that your chart has strong spear-bearing planets guarding well-placed luminaries, you should have loftier ambitions, for perhaps the sky is the limit for you!

Over the last two chapters we have worked with technique and now it is time to return to assessing a person's chart for the important issues in life. In Chapter Ten we look once again at marriage and romantic relationships and finding one's family members in the natal chart. Chapter Eleven concludes our study of natal astrology with a presentation of the fixed stars.

10

REPRESENTING LOVE AND PARENTS

We have seen that ancient astrologers used planets, lots, and the twelve places to judge the natal chart for general happiness, fame, renown, wealth, character, and religion. We will add to this the important topic of one's parents. First, however, we will revisit the critical area of love and marriage. In Chapter Four, we began with the discussion of love and marriage by using the triplicity lords for Venus. We will continue by looking at the relevant planets and lots that also shed light on this topic. We will close by examining parental issues in the astrological chart, looking at planets and lots together.

Planets of Love

Although different astrologers used places and lots for specific issues, Ptolemy used planets almost exclusively: his method has been influential over time, and the reader trained in modern astrology will recognize many features. Ptolemy would look at the Sun or Moon for the marriage of a woman or man respectively, as well as Venus and Mars for issues of sexuality in the natal charts of women and men. However, because not all ancient astrologers consistently use these planets, I will not be using Mars to discuss men's "disposition toward love." This doctrine seems too much at odds with the work of other ancient astrologers, who invariably use Venus for issues of relationship and sexuality *for both genders*. We must also factor in Mars's nature as a malefic: using Mars in this fashion symbolically allows sexuality to be a bit too close to violence. This same concern would apply even more to modern astrologers who are inclined to discuss sexuality with the planet Pluto. Ptolemy's use of Mars for sexuality in men and Venus for sexuality in women seems derived from his biological depiction of astrology and seems more theoretical than practical.

The chart of former US President **Bill Clinton** allows us to see how two very different planets account for his rather discordant love life.

Moon, representing his wife Hillary Clinton, is exalted in Taurus. Moon is also lord of the Tenth place in Bill Clinton's chart, and is in the same zoidion as Clinton's Lot of Exaltation (Ptolemy does not use this lot.) All this indicates that Bill Clinton's marriage has increased his stature and standing in life. (This would be especially the case if Hillary became President in 2008 or 2012.)

Not all is so splendid. Moon is in the Eighth place from the Ascendant, which is not a happy place. Moon and its dispositor Venus in Libra have no relationship of aspect but are in "like-engirded" zoidia, both being governed by Venus, in the belt or zone of Venus. This argues that Bill and Hillary are not strongly connected to one another, although there is some connection.

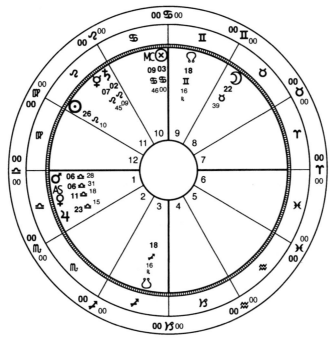

Bill Clinton

What planets aspect Moon? Sun, Mercury, and Saturn in Leo all testify to Moon who is in a Tenth-place relationship of predominance over these three planets. Sun, Mercury, and Saturn are in a strong place in the Eleventh, being connected by sextile with Clinton's planets in the First. The Sun, the luminary of sect in Clinton's day chart, occupies his own house, Leo. Both Mercury and Saturn are oriental and in sect.

What does Saturn signify in his testimony to Moon? According to Ptolemy, this means that the woman is easily fatigued and "austere." What does Mercury signify? That Clinton marries a woman who has a good intellect. What about the Sun? Perhaps that is Bill Clinton himself. That these planets square the Moon means that theirs is a relationship in which there is some conflict.

Note that Moon is in a western quadrant, being in the Eighth place. This would signify that Clinton would marry late, which was not the case. That Moon is in the zoidion of a single body, Taurus, indicates that Clinton would have one marriage. This may be better news for Bill than Hillary. The "double bodied" zoidia are those literally with two bodies: Pisces, Gemini, Sagittarius. These can signify multiple marriages or long-term relationships.

In his presentation on the Sun and Moon in relationships, Ptolemy gives us an early example of *synastry*. This technique, which is common in modern astrology, compares the planets and angles of the charts of two people to discover whether they are compatible or at odds with one another, and in which areas of life. Ptolemy tells us that harmonious aspects between the luminaries of the two charts augurs well for the relationship. If the lights are unconnected or are in square or opposition, this can bring trouble to the two people.

The relationship between the man's Moon and the woman's Sun is especially important to determine compatibility. Since Bill's Moon is in Taurus and Hillary's Sun is in Scorpio, two zoidia that oppose, one cannot say that this is a good omen for enduring happiness, yet, once again, there is an important connection between the two.

Bill and Hillary have stayed together in spite of their difficulties. One notices from Bill's chart that the planets relevant to marriage are in fixed zoidia. The planets of his soul or character, Moon and Mercury, are also in fixed zoidia. This does give him constancy.

Now we consider Venus in Clinton's chart, for other issues of relationship and sexuality. When we look for planets that can signify his associations outside of marriage, one must look at Venus. It is hard to overstate this planet's importance for Clinton's chart, since he has an Ascendant in Libra and Venus inhabits the First in her own house. Venus only weakly connects with the Moon, the planet concerned with the socially contracted marriage. To nobody's surprise, Bill Clinton has been expert at compartmentalizing when it comes to matters of love. Clinton's Venus is with Mars and Jupiter in Libra. Ptolemy says that this configuration makes for a passionate (Mars) but self-controlled (Jupiter) person. Jupiter would bestow self-control, not from Saturnine inhibition, but because Jupiter 's self-restraint is based on social convention.

How, from an astrological point of view, has Clinton's self-control in matters of love left something to be desired? The culprit appears to be Mars, which is out of sect and, in Libra, is opposite his own house. Ptolemy would add that all these planets in the First are occidental to the Sun and are thus not as fortunate for Clinton as they could be. Ptolemy also states that occidental Venus may cause the native to share intimacies with those who are socially inferior. I would add that occidental Jupiter might not have quite enough clout for discretion to govern the native during times of temptation. Anticipating modern doctrine, Ptolemy states that Mars determines a man's disposition toward love, as Venus would in the charts of women. Because Mars is with Venus and Jupiter in Clinton's chart, the analysis would be similar to what we have said before about him. Clinton has a large appetite for attractive women and perhaps thinks of himself as being God's gift to them.

At this point we will examine love more in the style of Dorotheus or Valens, both of whom use the planet Venus (as well as relevant lots) to discuss the vicissitudes of love and marriage. We will leave open the possibility of using the Sun and Moon, following Ptolemy, to discuss the marriage partners of men and women.

I begin with the example of **Marilyn Monroe**, movie actress and Venus icon of the mid-twentieth century. Monroe's Venus is in Aries with the Lot of Fortune. The triplicity lords for Venus are Sun in the Eleventh, Jupiter in the Seventh, and Saturn in the Fourth. These planets are all in strong places, yet declining in positive qualities during her lifetime.

Monroe's Venus is out of sect, opposite her own house in the passionate zoidion Aries, and is a morning riser: this makes Venus quite active and possibly difficult to control. Venus is also in the house of Mars and the bounds of Saturn, and so is governed by two malefics (Sun remains Venus'

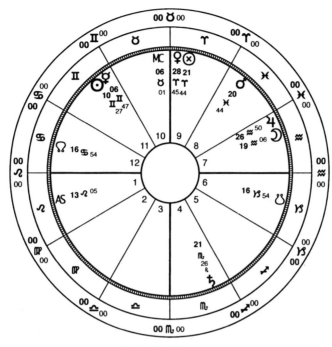

Marilyn Monroe

exaltation and triplicity lord). Venus in Aries is otherwise related to Mars in Pisces, since they are in zoidia that rise equally. A mixture of dignities also relates them: Venus is in the house of Mars and Mars is in the exaltation of Venus. None of this argues for a happy and stable love life - there's entirely too much of the ardent but chaotic influence of Mars impacting her Venus placement.

Note, however, that Jupiter in Aquarius in the Seventh aspects - looks forward - to Venus in Aries. Jupiter, both angular and in sect, has much good testimony to offer to Venus. In the context of love and marriage, Jupiter in aspect to Venus gives an honorable partner and an esteemed marriage. This is just how it happened. Except for a short-lived marriage when she was very young, Marilyn's marriages were to particularly honorable men: the baseball great Joe DiMaggio and the playwright Arthur Miller.

What is the influence of Monroe's Sun and Mercury in Gemini upon her Venus? In sextile to Venus by zoidia, the Sun makes things public. This is especially so as Sun is in the Eleventh, which sextiles the Ascendant. Monroe's marriages were public, as were her marriage break-ups.

The ancient literature tells us that Mercury, which sextiles Venus, can give an intelligent or clever partner, inventive styles of loving, making love with one's servants, homosexuality, or an improper love of children. In Monroe's case, as Mercury is dignified (although under the Sun's beams) and is well placed in the Eleventh, I'll opt for the first choice.

I follow Monroe with another film diva contemporary, **Elizabeth Taylor**. Both have Venus in Aries governed by Mars in Pisces. Taylor was a teenage movie star and a successful and acclaimed star as an adult. She has also dedicated herself to many causes, including preventing and treating AIDS. She has also had problems with weight and substance abuse. However, she is perhaps best known for her many marriages of widely differing length and quality. Can we find evidence in her natal chart for her rather opulent married life?

Taylor's Venus in Aries is in sect and in her joy in the Fifth. Mars in Pisces, governing Venus, is angular and in sect, but is under the Sun's beams. Venus is also an evening riser. Ptolemy may consider this placement of Venus weaker, since it is occidental; others would find Venus as the evening riser more positive than as a morning star. In general, Taylor's Venus has more positive features than we have found with Monroe.

Jupiter gives us further relevant information: Elizabeth Taylor, who was born six years after Monroe, has Jupiter in Leo, halfway across the zodiac from Monroe's Jupiter. Taylor's Jupiter is in its own triplicity in fiery Leo in a nocturnal chart. Jupiter has a strong trine to Venus in Aries, signifying again that she has married distinguished people - at least for the most part. Taylor's Jupiter is the lord of her Sagittarius Ascendant and is also the same degree as her Lot of Spirit. This helps account for Taylor's high degree of personal independence throughout her many marriages. It is the condition of Jupiter, I feel, that helps us understand the difference between Monroe, who had a few turbulent marriages, and Taylor, who had many marriages and has had a much longer and happier life. Although out of sect and in a cadent place, Taylor's Jupiter is more personally creative for her than Monroe's

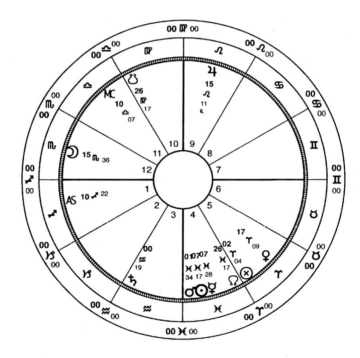

Elizabeth Taylor

Jupiter was for her. Taylor's Saturn is oriental and in its own house, Aquarius, opposing Jupiter. Saturn may indicate her self-destructiveness but also her ability to rebound from difficulties. Monroe's Jupiter has a predominating square from Saturn that is in a more difficult position. Taylor seems in charge of how her Jupiter plays itself out. Monroe's Jupiter in the Seventh may depict more the qualities of her partners than her own.

Lots of Love

In addition to using planets, we can also use lots to describe the vicissitudes of romantic relationships. Three different "Lots of Marriage" reflect different features of love and marriage in our lives. Authorities appear to use them interchangeably, yet the different lots seem to stress different themes of love and marriage. The differences between them are based upon the planets involved in deriving them.

The first lot I present is the most commonly used by ancient astrologers. I will attribute this to Paulus, although it often appears in other sources.

- The Paulus Lot of Marriage proceeds from Saturn to Venus for men, and from Venus to Saturn for women, and then projects from the Ascendant.

  The formula for men is AS + Venus – Saturn

  The formula for women is AS + Saturn – Venus

Since the planet one begins from, the subtrahend, is always the more important planet, this calculation brings together gender and planetary sect: Saturn is diurnal and more masculine and Venus nocturnal and more feminine. The natures of Saturn and Venus reveal that this lot would describe a more formal institutional sense of marriage: a relationship of commitment.

Valens gives us two other lots. The first I will call the "Valens Lot" and the other the "Valens Alternative Lot."

- The Valens Lot of Marriage by day, for both genders, is the arc from Jupiter to Venus, and for a night chart the reverse. Then project the resulting arc from the Ascendant.

  The formula by day is AS + Venus – Jupiter

  The formula by night is AS + Jupiter – Venus

  Marriage, for Valens' Lot of Marriage, seems to have a positive public role and, as it uses the two benefics, it is more likely to describe conditions of marital happiness. Since Jupiter is a planet of abundance and fertility, there is an implication of marrying for wealth or starting a family. Interestingly, Valens calls the opposite position for this Lot of Marriage the "Lot of Adultery."

The second lot that Valens gives us carries another meaning. With this Lot we see love depicted as a *depression or downfall*.

- • The Valens Alternative Lot of Marriage uses the planets Sun and Venus for men, and Moon and Mars for women. Projecting the resulting arc from the Ascendant, one arrives at this Lot of Marriage.

  The formula for men, day and night, is AS + Venus – Sun

  The formula for women, day and night, is AS + Mars – Moon

Valens' rationale makes clear how he considered this Lot: Venus and Mars *compromise* the Sun and Moon, respectively. How? Valens refers to the zoidia of these planets' exaltations and depressions. The Sun is in its depression in Libra, the house of Venus and the Moon is in its depression in Scorpio, the house of Mars. (Note that Valens uses Sun and Moon to denote masculine and feminine respectively.)

For the Alternative Lot of Marriage to have a positive outcome, the man's Lot must agree with the Lot of Spirit (the Lot of the Sun) or the woman's Lot must agree with the Lot of Fortune (the Lot of the Moon.)

Although the Alternative Lot appears to be concerned only with those romantic or sexual relationships that can cause unhappiness or ruin our lives, Valens' interpretations do not appear very different from the Valens Lot involving Jupiter and Venus. Nonetheless, in our chart examples I will consider this lot as describing love as a downfall.

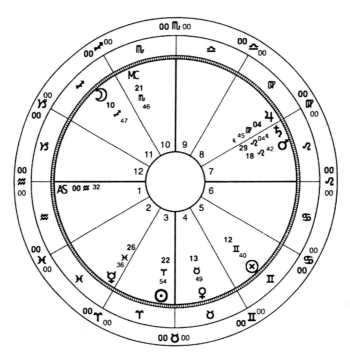

Thomas Jefferson

We first return to the natal chart for **Thomas Jefferson**. The first lot we looked at, involving Saturn and Venus, falls in Libra. Its lord is Venus, who is dignified and placed well in the Fourth from the Ascendant. Venus, however, is in the Eighth place from this Lot of Marriage. We have a suggestion that he had married well but that his wife could have died in an untimely way. Jefferson never remarried after his wife died. This bad outcome is supported by the fact that Mars and Saturn aspect the zoidion of the Paulus Lot of Marriage, with only a weak connection from a weak Jupiter - in the Eighth from the Ascendant.

The Valens Lot, using Venus and Jupiter, falls in Taurus with Venus herself. This would be advantageous except, once again, for the negative testimony from Mars and Saturn in the Seventh.

The Valens Alternative Lot that involves Sun and Venus is in Aquarius, the zoidion of the Ascendant. *Its lord Saturn opposes this lot*. Saturn may indicate the ill-esteemed quality of Jefferson's long-term relationship with Sally Hemmings, who was his slave.

We return to **Bill Clinton's** chart to illustrate further how to use these lots. In Clinton's chart, the Paulus Lot involving Saturn and Venus is in Sagittarius, in the Third place from his Ascendant. The lord of this lot is Jupiter in the First, which is enhanced by the presence of Venus but diminished by the presence of Mars. Venus creates harmony in this marriage, as she is also dispositor over Jupiter in Libra. Mars, out of sect and opposite his own house, destroys harmony.

Clinton's Lot of Marriage involving Jupiter and Venus, is close to the Ascendant, because Jupiter and Venus are close in his birth chart. This does not give us additional information.

The Valens Alternative lot, involving Sun and Venus for men, is 20 Scorpio, exactly opposite the degree of his Moon. The malefics play a powerful role here. Scorpio once again brings us to Mars, which is strongly placed but in a difficult condition there. The Lot itself is also square Saturn in Leo. The Mars influence we have discussed; the Saturn influence points to the high public cost Clinton had to pay for his marital infidelity.

Is there agreement between the Alternative Lot and Clinton's Lot of Spirit? His Lot of Spirit is in Capricorn and is governed by Saturn. There is agreement by sextile of the zoidia of the Lots of Marriage and Spirit themselves, between Scorpio and Capricorn. More importantly, there is agreement by sextile between Mars in Libra and Saturn in Leo, the respective lords of these Lots. In spite of many incidents in Clinton's life, there may be a positive conclusion. Note the position of his Saturn: it is in sect, in the strong Eleventh place from the Ascendant, and is rising from the Sun as a morning star. Although Saturn has brought heavy consequences on Clinton for his extramarital behavior, this planet also has a redemptive quality that may yet play itself out for him. We now take note of the chart of **Monica Lewinsky.**

First we view her chart for its relevant features. Venus is strongly placed in the Eleventh with the Sun in its own house in Leo. Venus is occidental, an evening riser. Of particular interest is the sextile by degree to Venus from Saturn, who looks ahead to Venus. Saturn is also strong: oriental and in its own triplicity in Gemini. All this gives Saturn a strong influence over matters of Venus, which may indicate the ambitious and calculated nature of her relationship with, for example, President Clinton. Lewinsky's Jupiter, Mars, and Saturn all testify to Venus (as they do to her Sun), giving these endeavors a very mixed result. Let's now look at the triplicity lords for Venus in Leo:

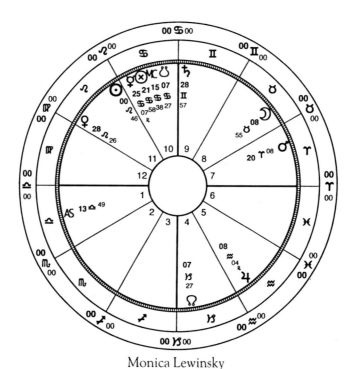

Monica Lewinsky

- We begin with a dignified **Sun**, the diurnal lord for Leo. One does think about the Sun representing a king or leader, or at least someone she would admire. During the first part of her life, Lewinsky would find herself with men who have some honor - at least in her eyes.

- Following is **Jupiter**, Leo's nocturnal triplicity lord. Jupiter is in the Fifth place of "Good Fortune," but opposes Sun and Venus. Jupiter is also in Aquarius, a "human" zoidion. This may indicate a relationship that is less passionate but can give her some personal happiness.

- The long-term forecast for Lewinsky's Venus is positive, as **Saturn** - in sect, oriental, in its triplicity, and exactly sextile Venus - governs the final third of her years of Venus. This may indicate a more settled and creative life than she has experienced to date.

The Paulus Lot of Marriage also falls in Leo, closely sextile to the Ascendant. This lot of the socially contracted marriage indicates, for Lewinsky, marrying somebody who has a public reputation or is greatly esteemed. It is interesting that the Lot that has to do with formal marriage is in strong agreement with what we have discerned from Venus so far.

The Valens Lot of Marriage falls in Taurus, near her exalted Moon. Venus in the Eleventh, lord of the Valens Lot of Marriage, is angular to the Lot. Neither Mars nor Saturn testifies to the Lot itself, creating fewer problems for her. This is another indication of attaining some personal happiness through relationship. Although this lot is in the Eighth from the Ascendant, the condition of Venus gives her a good chance for eventual marital happiness.

The Alternative Valens Lot falls in late degrees of Virgo, in the Twelfth place from the Ascendant. Saturn is in a close predominating square to the Lot, further indicating how intentional (and perhaps tawdry) was her pursuit and maintenance of her relationship with Clinton.

Mercury in late Cancer is dispositor for the Alternative Lot of Marriage. Mercury is in the Tenth place, indicating fame and what one does. The Lot of Fortune is with Mercury, making for much agreement between the Lot of Marriage and the Lot of Fortune, which provides for a positive outcome. I am reminded of Lewinsky's post-scandal interviews, book tour, and handbag line, and now graduate school, subsequent to notoriety.

Now, to review some people we have looked at previously in this chapter. In the natal chart of **Marilyn Monroe**, the Paulus Lot of Marriage is in Pisces with Mars. As lord of Monroe's Venus and Lot of Fortune, Mars is critical for her in all matters of love and marriage. Once again, Mars has the quality of a loose cannon on a ship. Jupiter in Aquarius, the Lot's dispositor, is disconnected from the Lot. The Paulus Lot of Marriage and Mars are in the Eighth place from the Ascendant and the Twelfth place from the Lot of Fortune: this is a difficult placement twice over. Once again Mars is no friend in this matter, and Jupiter is of no help. Instead she needed a positive Saturn - which her chart does not have.

The Valens Lot of Marriage falls in Libra. This gives Monroe's chart more difficulties, as it brings us back to her Venus placement, which is opposite the Lot. You may remember that Valens sees the opposing zoidion from this Lot as the Lot of Adultery, which falls in Aries, governed by Mars where we see Venus. This does not bode well for monogamous matrimony.

Valens' Alternative Lot of Marriage falls in Virgo. Although its lord is Mercury that is happily positioned, the Lot itself opposes Mars in Pisces.

When it involves love and marriage, and using planets or lots, all roads in Monroe's chart lead to Mars, thus all of them lead to turbulent and painful relationships. We now move from Monroe to one of her purported lovers, **John Kennedy.**

This chart, like that of Bill Clinton, is interesting for its contrast between Venus and Moon. At first glance, Venus is not particularly striking in Kennedy's chart. Venus is in Gemini, with some dignity, as she is in her own bound. Venus is within the Sun's beams, but soon rising from the Sun's beams to be an evening rising planet. Looking further, one finds an interesting fact: only the Moon aspects Venus. Saturn, her triplicity lord, is in the zoidion of equal power to Gemini; this leaves Venus relatively unwitnessed by other planets so she may have a tendency to act on her own in this chart.

Contrast Venus with Moon, which Ptolemy would say determines marriages for men. Although Moon is in a difficult place in the Twelfth, other factors are more positive. Moon and her dispositor Mercury have an exchange of dignities: Moon in Virgo is in the house of Mercury, and Mercury is in the exaltation of Moon. Additionally, Mercury looks forward to Moon in a trine relationship. Both malefics and benefics have aspects to the Moon. Additionally, Moon is the lord of Kennedy's Tenth and Lot of Spirit and dispositor for Saturn. This makes for a marriage that can have strength and durability - but not without problems - and is the center of one's life.

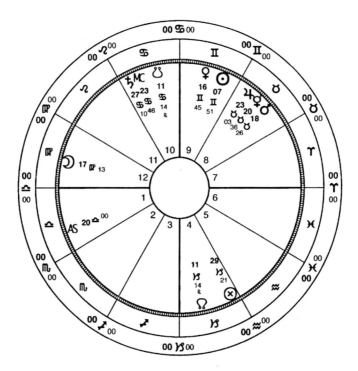

John F. Kennedy

The Moon in Virgo is also important as she is in the same zoidion as Kennedy's Paulus Lot of Marriage that uses Saturn and Venus. Again this argues for the strength of his marriage. As the Lot of Exaltation is also in Virgo, Kennedy's marriage would give him social status. Yet not all is at peace.

Because the Moon is in the Twelfth and the Lot of Spirit is with Saturn, governed by Moon, happiness is not necessarily the outcome for his marriage. This is supported by the synastry between Kennedy and his wife Jacqueline. Kennedy's Moon is in the same zoidion as **Jacqueline's** difficult Mars placement, and Jacqueline's Sun in Leo beholds neither John Kennedy's Sun in Gemini or his Moon in Virgo: there are problems with their connection as people.

Looking further at Kennedy's Moon and Paulus Lot of Marriage in Virgo, one must look more closely at Mercury, that is in the Eighth zoidion from the Ascendant, a difficult place. Mercury is with Jupiter but also with Mars, which is out of sect and, in Taurus, is opposite its own house. Mars is the unwanted guest at this moderately pleasant occasion - it brings contention and instability and the possibility of adultery to a marriage. This is reinforced by the placement of the Valens Lot of Marriage. It falls in Scorpio, governed by Mars. Opposite this lot is the Lot of Adultery - Taurus, inhabited by Jupiter, Mercury, and, once again, Mars.

For the Alternative Valens Lot of Marriage - love and marriage as a downfall - we take the distance from Sun to Venus and project that number from the Ascendant, which, because Sun and

Venus are close to one another, falls in Libra in his First. Of the three Lots of Marriage, this lot is the most favorably placed. Venus in Gemini, governing this lot, is in trine to the lot in Libra.

Mars is not a factor here. Instead we find ourselves dealing with Saturn, in square to the Lot from the Tenth. Saturn is with the Lot of Spirit, which must agree with the Alternative Lot of Marriage in order to have a good outcome for the person. Instead, one can see that Saturn's impact on Kennedy's adventurous love life could lead to guilt and depression if not scandal.

We now work with the Lots of Marriage for **Elizabeth Taylor.** As befits Taylor's married life, there are many complications. Her Paulus Lot of Marriage is happily found in the Tenth in Virgo but with some complexities:

- Mercury, lord for this Lot, is in the Fourth place from the Ascendant and angular, but is opposing the Lot. This sets up prominence and confusion.

- Mercury in Pisces is also in its fall, within the Sun's rays, and also with Mars. The Lot is well placed but its lord is not dignified.

- Mercury is also with the Lot of Fortune. I remember from the 1960s how Taylor was adorned with many diamonds she received during her two marriages to Richard Burton.

- Venus in Aries fails to aspect either this Lot (of Marriage) in Virgo or its lord, Mercury in Pisces. (Venus is with the Lot of Fortune, however, and its hard not to think of all that jewelry from richard Burton and similarly ostentatious men in her life, as well as her jewelry advertisements on television.)

- In no way does Saturn connect with this Lot. A positive connection might give some stability.

- Both Lot and lord are in mutable zoidia, which give further instability.

All this adds up to a great amount of activity, but without resolution or closure. With eight - at the last count - formal marriages, all of which were well publicized, Taylor would find marriage appealing, even to her public image (the Lot being in the Tenth place), but ultimately unsatisfying. The Valens Lot of Marriage is in Aries and in the same zoidion as Venus herself. Now Jupiter makes a favorable trine aspect to the Lot. This seems joyful and high-spirited. What follows is in line with our previous discussion.

Although Jupiter in Leo does not behold Taylor's many Pisces planets, it is in trine to Aries, and thus is favorably involved with Venus, the Lot of Fortune, and the Valens Lot of Marriage. As Jupiter is also lord of the Ascendant and close to the Lot of Spirit, this is a critical planet. It gives promise of great happiness - including marital happiness - yet this strong Jupiter out of sect may promise much more than it can deliver.

The Alternative Lot of Marriage is also in Pisces, along with three planets and the Lot of Fortune. This lot does agree with the Lot of Fortune, but not its lord, Jupiter. On the whole, the Alternative Lot is less favorable than the other two. This may incline Taylor's romantic hopefulness not toward the downfall of extramarital relationships but to formal marriage itself - over and over.

The Paulus and Valens Lots of Marriage signify the possibility of a more public and formal manifestation of love.

Let's continue with a completely different individual. **Jimmy Swaggart** was a prominent televangelist in the 1970s and 1980s in the United States, during a time in which many televangelists captured great public attention. In 1987 Swaggart's hidden life of marital infidelity and sexual excess became public knowledge. Subsequently his ministry was taken from him and he has had to come back slowly. To date he has a small ministry and congregation, and much smaller public presence, but his vocation continues. We will look at his Venus placement closely, beginning with Venus' triplicity lords, then note Swaggart's various Lots of Marriage.

For Swaggart's Venus in Aries - another one - her triplicity lords for the fiery triplicity in a nocturnal chart are Jupiter, then Sun, then Saturn.

Jupiter is in the Twelfth and is out of sect. This is not particularly good news. The Twelfth place brings up the possibility of undercurrents or hidden matters than can become one's undoing. Perhaps Swaggart's secret life began at a relatively early age.

The Sun in Pisces is angular in the Fourth and has a close aspect from Jupiter, its dispositor, in the Twelfth. Unfortunately, a planet in the Twelfth cannot give convincing positive testimony. Sun also has the additional misfortune of being with Saturn. Saturn is oriental but out of sect, and Saturn seems to be the planet responsible for the difficulties that caused his public downfall.

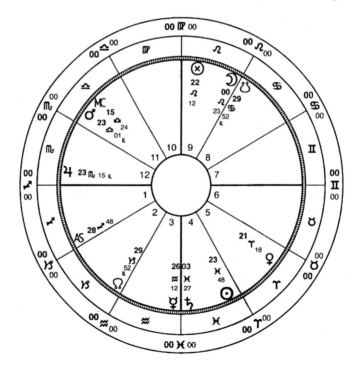

Jimmy Swaggert

Saturn takes over as triplicity lord for Venus for the final third of Swaggart's life. Saturn is angular and Jupiter testifies to it. Jupiter in the Twelfth cannot bring about a positive outcome because it is in the Twelfth. Saturn gives connotations of loyalty and persistence but also corruption or depravity. Being out of sect, Saturn may be inclined toward the latter. Swaggert may manifest many of Saturn's possibilities during a long lifetime. Both Sun and Saturn being angular may argue for some good fortune in his love life. He did have a good marriage, up to a very particular moment in the mid-1980s. As with Clinton, Saturn can also give the possibilities of redemption, of learning from his mistakes and leading a better life. (Clinton's Saturn, however, is far more positively placed than Swaggart's.)

We return to Venus in Swaggart's chart. Venus is in Aries, once again, and, as with Taylor, is in its Fifth place, her joy. Venus is also in sect. This is a favorable placement for Venus. All these factors are positive, even if Venus is opposite her own house. Venus has one other difficulty: the house lord of Swaggert's Venus in Aries is Mars in Libra, opposite Venus. If this configuration seems familiar, we saw it previously in Freud's chart from Chapter Five. Mars testifying to Venus, especially from a difficult aspect, may point to a sexual nature that is difficult to control; that Mars is dispositor for Venus makes these difficulties more urgent. Freud manifested this configuration in a more creative way than did Swaggart. Mercury in Aquarius, aspecting both Swaggart's Venus and Mars, can indicate inventiveness and having liaisons below one's social status. We now look at Swaggart's relevant Lots of Marriage.

The Paulus Lot of Marriage is in Aquarius and is with Mercury. As said before, the presence of Mercury can have a variety of meanings in the context of love, from an intelligent partner, inventiveness in seeking or making love, to an attraction to servants or boys. Mercury is out of sect in Swaggart's nocturnal chart but is in its own triplicity. The Lot and Mercury are testified to from Jupiter in a square, Mars in a trine, and Venus in a sextile. On the whole these are positive. There is one troubling feature, however: the lord of the Paulus Lot of Marriage, Saturn, is out of sect and disconnected to the Lot itself. This points to some of Saturn's less socially redeeming features.

The Valens Lot of Marriage falls in Leo in the Ninth place, on the same degree as his Moon, and in the same zoidion as the Lot of Fortune. The lord of the Lot, Sun in Pisces, is with Saturn and disconnected to the Lot of Marriage. The close proximity of the Moon and this Lot may be favorable, as Moon is in sect in Swaggart's nocturnal chart. Moon also has a variable nature and may lack constancy, even in the fixed zoidion of Leo.

Opposite the Valens Lot of Marriage is the Lot of Adultery. This puts it in Aquarius, opposite Leo, and with Mercury. Here I think of Mercury's inventiveness and that Mercury can also signify relationships with those lower in social status, like prostitutes.

The Alternate Lot of Marriage falls in Capricorn, governed by Saturn. Here Saturn is in sextile to the Lot itself. For a positive outcome, Valens would compare the Lot of Marriage to the Lot of Spirit, which is in Taurus. Although the two Lots are in zoidia in trine to one another, their lords are but weakly connected: these factors combine to give a mixed outcome at best.

Saturn governing the Alternative Lot of Marriage may indicate a longstanding marriage, being married to an older person, or the possibility of sordidness in one's love life. Again we may have all three possibilities for him.

We end this section with a short discussion of **Emily Dickinson's** chart. This allows us to examine the conditions of love and marriage *by their lack*. Can we look at the placement of Venus to understand why Emily Dickinson remained unmarried?

We begin with Venus, which is under Sun's beams; this is not so unusual for Venus. Judging from her life and poetry, Venus under the Sun's beams in a woman's chart does *not* mean that she would have a tendency to hero-worship her male partner. The house and triplicity lord for Venus in Sagittarius is Jupiter, in fall and only connected to Venus by being in a zoidion of equal power. Jupiter cannot be of much help to Venus.

What planets testify to Venus? Mars in Aries is in sect and is in trine to Venus. As Venus "looks ahead" to Mars, Venus is the more dominant planet. This is a relatively positive factor, since both are in sect and Mars is also in dignity.

Saturn in Virgo is out of sect and is in square to Venus. Saturn is also with the Lot of Spirit. Saturn is clearly more important than Mars, and a major source of difficulty for Dickinson's Venus. Noting Saturn in a predominating square over Venus and placed with the Lot of Spirit, part of an answer to why Dickinson remained unmarried is that she preferred a splendid Saturnine isolation. The Paulus Lot of Marriage falls in Leo in the Tenth. This reflects the best attribute of her Saturn-Venus square: the Lot from the two planets would be in a prominent position. The lord of this Lot

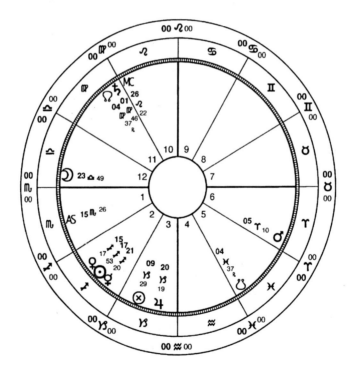

Emily Dickinson

in Leo - Sun in Sagittarius - is in a trine aspect to the Lot. This would bode well for formal marriage, but she chose not to marry.

The Valens Lot of Marriage is in Sagittarius. This Lot is weakened, once again, by the difficult condition of its lord, Jupiter in Capricorn, and the square from Saturn and the Lot of Spirit. Marriage would have worked as a formal relationship - as we define the Paulus Lot of Marriage - but such a marriage would not give her real happiness.

The Alternative Lot of Marriage falls in Aries with Mars. Mars is a strong planet in her chart - in its own house, its place of joy in the Sixth, receiving aspects from both benefics, and in sect. Noting the cadent quality of Mars, one interpretation offers itself: a secret romance is likely but it could end poorly. If Dickinson did have a secret love life, she did a fine job keeping it from modern academics, feminists, and ambitious movie producers.

Parents in the Astrological Chart

Where do we look for information about parents in an astrological chart? As we have seen in Chapter Six, the Fourth place from the Ascendant is the place of one's "father", legal family and ancestry; planets that happen to be in the Fourth place can give indications about them, according to the tradition. For this presentation, however, I will leave the places aside and consider relevant planets and lots.

Modern astrologers, following the ancient tradition, often designate Sun for father and Moon for mother. A variant, suggested by Ptolemy, is to designate the planet by the sect of the natal chart:

> For one born during the day, Sun would represent father; for one born at night, however, Saturn would represent father.

> For one born during the day, Venus would represent mother. For one born at night, Moon would represent mother.

I do not use this variant by sect. Since Venus and Saturn are already laden with so much intrinsic meaning, I would not want to use them in too many ways that overlap. Furthermore, using Venus to signify the mother seems a bit too Oedipal. I use only the Sun to represent father and only the Moon to represent mother, in day or night charts. What follows are the two parental lots:

- The **Lot of Father** takes the arc from the Sun to Saturn in a day birth and from Saturn to Sun in a night birth. Projecting that distance from the Ascendant, you have the Lot of Father.

  The formula for a day chart is AS + Saturn – Sun

  The formula for a night chart is AS + Sun – Saturn

  There is, however, one condition. If Saturn is under the beams of the Sun - within fifteen degrees of the Sun - take the arc from *Mars to Jupiter,* day or night, and add that distance to the Ascendant instead. The formula for this is AS + Jupiter – Mars.

- The **Lot of Mother** takes the arc from Venus to Moon by for a day birth, and from Moon to Venus for a night birth. Projecting that distance from the Ascendant, you arrive at the Lot of Mother.

The formula for a day chart is AS + Moon – Venus

The formula for a night chart is AS + Venus – Moon

We begin to examine these lots by using two charts we have just seen. We look again at **Emily Dickinson.** For Dickinson's night chart, taking the distance from Saturn to Sun and then adding this number to the Ascendant, places the Lot of Father in early Pisces, governed by Jupiter.

The Lot of Father's house lord, Jupiter, and her Lot of Fortune are in the Eleventh zoidion from the Lot. This argues for Dickinson's father's reputation and prosperity. Emily Dickinson's father was well known in his community and had served in the United States House of Representatives. That Jupiter in Capricorn is in fall and cadent to the Ascendant argues that these factors were less positive than they appeared.

The Lot of Father in Pisces also takes an opposition from Saturn and the Lot of Spirit in Virgo. Saturn's opposing this lot does not make for a happy dad. The opposition between the two Lots denotes a difficulty between father and daughter. Who, here, is taking the part of Saturn? It sounds like it is the daughter. With the Lot of Father being opposite the Lot of Spirit, I also wonder whether it was her relationship with father that led to her unmarried and isolated life.

We return to the chart of **Bill Clinton** to interpret parental planets and lots. If we simply use the Sun for Clinton's father, we get a very dignified father. Sun is in his own house, Leo, and also in the Eleventh. The truth is that Bill's biological father died in an automobile accident. After his mother remarried, a stepfather, reputedly alcoholic and abusive, helped raise young Bill. Clinton's Lot of Father gives us a different picture, it falls in Virgo in the Twelfth place from the Ascendant, unconnected to its house lord Mercury in Leo. The problematic status of the Lot of Father represents the paternal person in Bill's life better than his highly dignified Sun. The lot, not the planet, corresponds more closely to a troubled father figure.

Clinton's mother, a stronger figure than his stepfather, could be represented by Moon exalted in the Eighth. I am a bit squeamish about this, as we've already discussed Clinton's Moon as designating Clinton's wife Hillary. Yet Clinton's Lot of Mother also falls in Taurus: there is no escaping the astrological similarity, in Bill's chart, between mother and marital partner. Either position, Moon or the Lot of Mother, is far more powerful and positive than Clinton's Lot of Father.

We now look at the natal charts of some others who have had notable parents. Since we've discussed the Clinton marriage, we could look at **Chelsea Clinton**'s natal chart. She is the only daughter of Bill and Hillary Clinton. Here we again compare parental planets and parental lots. The luminaries seem to work quite well in describing her two parents.

To the best of my knowledge, Chelsea is a young woman who would be a very bright ordinary person and have an ordinary life but for her two distinguished and controversial parents. Looking at

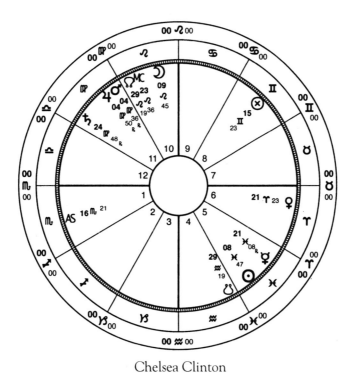

Chelsea Clinton

her parents from her chart will tell us much about who Chelsea Clinton is and who she would rather not be.

If we look to the Sun for issues of the father, we see great complexity. We note that Sun in Pisces is with Mercury but Sun also opposes its house lord Jupiter. The two malefics also oppose Sun. These three planets opposing Sun give us some idea about the strong positive and negative reputation her father has accumulated over time. These oppositions can signify her father's political enemies or even Chelsea herself, as Mars is the house lord of her Ascendant in Scorpio.

Chelsea's Sun placement can indicate her father's inventiveness (Mercury with Sun), that Bill doesn't do a good job covering his tracks or cutting corners (Mercury both in fall and retrograde).

Moon, as representative of Chelsea's mother, is more strongly positioned in Chelsea's natal chart. Moon is in the Tenth with a trine aspect from benefic Venus. Moon also has as spear bearers Mars, Jupiter, and Saturn in Virgo, as they follow the Moon in Leo.

Why are spear bearers important or interesting here? Remember that Ptolemy gave great weight to spear bearers to signify fame, and he uses spear bearers to judge the fame and reputation of a parent. Of Chelsea Clinton's possible spear bearers, Mars is in sect; Jupiter and Saturn are not. Also, Jupiter in Virgo is opposite its own house Pisces and can thus disappoint. Chelsea Clinton's mother - signified by Moon - does have an entourage, although not a strong one. These spear bearers do add some prominence to the Moon in her natal chart.

We now look at Chelsea Clinton's parental lots. The Lot of Father in Chelsea's nocturnal chart falls in Taurus, in the Seventh place from her Ascendant. Its angularity is a sign of a strong father; placed in the Seventh gives Chelsea's relationship with her father some ambiguity.

The lord of the Lot of Father in Taurus is Venus. This makes for a difficult situation, for Venus is in the Sixth house from the Ascendant and the Twelfth from the Lot. Venus is unconnected to the Lot, except that both are in equally rising zoidia. One heartening factor is that Venus is in the same zoidion as Chelsea Clinton's Lot of Spirit. Looking at this psychologically, we see that the daughter would get her own sense of authority and self-reliance from her father. This could happen from her learning not only from his strengths but also his limitations. Using the Lot of Father gives us no information, however, about the fame and reputation of father.

The Lot of Mother falls in the late degrees of Cancer, in the Ninth place from Chelsea's Scorpio Ascendant. *Every planet* casts an aspect to the Lot of Mother - there is abundant testimony but it all conflicts. The Lot is unconnected to the Moon, which is the lady of the house of Cancer. This is unfortunate, as Moon is so well positioned in the Tenth.

In Chelsea Clinton's chart, the indicators for father - Sun and Lot of Father - are somewhat problematic. Oppositions abound with both paternal indicators, possibly indicating some kind of rivalry - perhaps daughter takes on her mother's negativity toward her husband. Indicators for mother, planet and Lot of Mother, are more positive. These maternal indicators are stronger and less fraught with conflict. In Chelsea's chart, the mother is the more dominant and positive figure.

I conclude with the chart of a man with famous and official parents and for whom being their son is an official role: **Prince Charles** of England.

Leaping from the page is Charles' Moon, which, like that of Chelsea Clinton, is exalted, in sect, and in the Tenth place from the Ascendant. In Charles' chart, Saturn casts a trine aspect to the Moon; because Saturn is oriental to the Sun and in sect it is a little less malevolent. There *is* some familiarity between Charles' Moon and Venus, her dispositor, as they are like-engirding zoidia, both governed by Venus. Venus is also in its own house, Libra. One cloud in this sunny sky is that Venus is in a cadent place, although a "good decline."

How does Sun fare as an indicator for father? Sun is angular in the Fourth, the Subterranean Place. Although Sun is fairly strong, the Fourth place cannot compete with the might of the Tenth, the location of the Moon. The Sun in Scorpio is also disconnected with Mars in Sagittarius, its dispositor. This is unfortunate, since Mars is with Jupiter, which is quite happy in Sagittarius. The only planet that testifies to the Sun is Saturn by sextile.

Using the Moon and the Sun as parental indicators, the dominant planet and parent is clearly Moon and Charles' mother, the Queen of England.

What do the parental lots tell us? The Lot of Mother falls in Capricorn in the Sixth, along with the Lot of Spirit. Venus, dignified in Libra, is in the Tenth from the Lot of Mother. Charles' mother certainly has her share of grace and elegance. More important, however, is that the house lord of the Lot of Mother, Saturn in Virgo, is in a trine relationship with the Lot. In spite of being in the Sixth, and Saturn - its lord - being out of sect, the Lot of Mother has some positive characteristics.

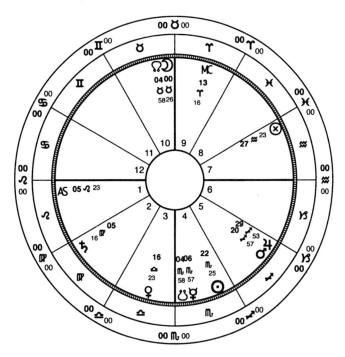

Prince Charles

Both Moon and the Lot of Mother have strong connections to Saturn. Saturn aspects both, and the Lot of Mother is governed by Saturn. In this context, Saturn limits maternal affection and emotional support, but also points to Queen Elizabeth's longevity and endurance. Charles has been Prince of Wales, an understudy monarch, for a long time.

Charles' father is less in the public eye. The Lot of Father falls in Libra and is with Venus.

What planets aspect this Lot in Libra? Saturn is unconnected, which is positive. Mars and Jupiter are in sextile to the Lot, is also positive, as Mars is in sect and Jupiter is a benefic. This Lot of Father seems to indicate a personal strength and close relationship between Charles and his father out of the public eye. Charles' relationship with mother is more complicated, especially as she is a dominant personality and national sovereign.

We have finished our look at natal charts for issues of parents and further information about love and marriage. We go next to a final topic in working with natal charts, the role of the non-wandering or fixed stars. How did astrologers give meaning to these stars? Trickier, however, is determining how we place and measure these stellar bodies across the surrounding sky, so we can integrate them appropriately into the astrological birth chart.

11

THE NON-WANDERING STARS

Although planets are the prime carriers of meaning in a natal chart, astrologers over the centuries have also used the constellations and fixed star positions for natal chart interpretation. In this chapter, we will look at how Hellenistic astrology gave meaning to constellations and stars and what this tradition may teach us. We will then apply important non-wandering stars to sample charts. Before astrologers could include the modern planets Uranus, Neptune, and Pluto in their work, they used non-wandering stars to help account for the extraordinary. The positions of important stars in one's chart could presage great victories or reversals in life.

Constellations and non-wandering stars are not "fixed" as if they *never* move in the sky. Because of *precession*, caused by a small wobble which accompanies the earth spinning on its axis, star positions move slowly over time. Stars near the ecliptic move one degree of the zodiac about every seventy-two years. The Eye of the Bull (Aldeberan), formerly in Taurus, is now in the tropical zoidion Gemini; the Twins of Gemini (Castor, Pollux) are well into Cancer; the Heart of the Scorpion (Antares) is in Sagittarius. Alas, the Heart of the Lion (Regulus) soon moves into tropical Virgo.

The constellations and stars are considered non-wandering, however, because over time they stay in the same spatial relationships with one other. In many thousands of years there are very slight changes of position and some stars will gain or diminish in brightness, yet the stars together (con-stellations) have hardly changed in relationship to one another. How do we measure the positions of these stars to integrate then into a natal chart? All are not tidily along the zodiac, like the planets. Using their closest degrees of the zodiac, as we do for planets, gives us problems and we need to investigate reasonable alternatives.

Symbolic Meanings of Constellations and Stars

Zodiacal Constellations and their Parts as Images
We begin with the zoidia that we have been using all along. We will now look at them through the lens of the images of their background constellations.

The *images* of constellations and stars developed in different cultures over a long period of time. By the time natal astrology had developed in the ancient Western world, ancient culture already had its images and stories of what the constellations and what particular fixed or non-wandering stars were about. These traditions were integrated later into the newer natal astrology. When natal astrology first developed, the constellations in the belt of the zodiac and the twelve tropical zoidia roughly lined up with one another. At that time, the Sun's position at the spring equinox was at the beginning of the constellation and zoidion Aries; the fixed star Regulus, the Heart of the Lion, was mid-way in the constellation Leo. Because of the precession of the equinoxes - its slow backwards movement - and the consequent slow forward movement of the non-wandering stars, the constellations of the zodiac have moved into the following tropical zoidia: the constellation Aries into the tropical Taurus, etc. Medieval astrologers and astrologers up to the modern era continued to use constellational images to identify and describe the tropical zoidia that do not coincide with one another.

Some of these images of the zodiacal constellations may be familiar to you, especially if you work with traditional astrology. The **human** zoidia are those whose figures are shaped like those of human beings: Gemini, Virgo, and Aquarius. (Libra, which does not have the shape of a living being at all, is included as human.) Those that are **terrestrial** (Aries, Taurus, Leo, Sagittarius, and Capricorn) depict creatures that walk on land. Those that are **aquatic** (Cancer, Scorpio, Pisces) live, at least partly, in water. They are also called "mute," because no sounds come from them.

The characteristics of the zoidia can play a prominent role in electional astrology. Here one chooses a time most auspicious for beginning an endeavor by choosing an astrological chart that depicts a fortunate outcome to the enterprise. In traditional electional astrology, one might pick a time based on a chart with a particular zoidion ascending.

Do not choose a time to get a haircut when the Ascendant is in Leo, unless you are a rock musician or fashion model and wish to project a leonine image with your hair. If you were going to begin a meatless diet, the astrological chart would have rising a creature that does not eat meat: the zoidia Taurus, Cancer, Scorpio, Pisces representing the bull, crab, scorpion, and fish respectively. Leo, depicting the carnivorous lion, would be a terrible choice for an Ascendant. Virgo or the other human signs or zoidia would be a fine Ascendant when you either get a haircut or start a vegetarian diet. For many endeavors, choosing a human zoidion - if its governing planet is well situated - is a good idea. Also, some parts of zodiacal constellations have specific features. In discussing those parts that can cause excessive sexual passion and lewdness, Ptolemy and others mention the anterior hind parts of Aries, the area near the Hyades of Taurus (the place of the non-wandering star Aldeberan), the urn of Aquarius, the hind of Leo, the face or hind of Scorpio, and the face of Capricorn.

Ancient astrologers also derive information from particular stars within the constellations. For example, Ptolemy and Antiochus discuss specific fixed stars they associate with blindness and damage to the eyes.

> The sting of Scorpio
> The mane of Leo
> The arrow of Sagittarius
> The Pleiades
> The nebula of Cancer
> The eye of Sagittarius

The spike of Capricorn
The pitcher of Aquarius

Most of these positions depict a vision that is clouded, i.e., the nebulae of Cancer and the Pleiades cluster, or designate objects that can pierce the eye. Particular images of constellations, or parts of constellations, or specific stars, were also used to foretell sickness and death.

Stars and their Planets

Ancient astrologers, particularly Ptolemy and Anonymous of 379, depicted non-wandering stars having familiarity (*oikeiosis*) with specific planets. (*Oikeiosis* is the same word used to describe the kinship between planets and zoidia.) Ancient astrologers did not reduce stars to planets, but rather found correspondences between stars and planets to be convenient for the astrologer's understanding. I have found that exploring the planetary affiliations helps us understand the stars' meanings. Ptolemy simply listed stars and planets together; Anonymous of 379 modified Ptolemy's list in places and gave then more complete interpretations.

Here is a list of stars and planetary correspondences to them, according to Anonymous of 379. Many names of these stars have come to us during the medieval era, mostly from the Arabic. I will retain these names since they are more familiar to us, and they include all the stars we will study in this chapter.

Stars corresponding to *Venus and Mercury* (**Spica, Wega, Cygnus** or **Deneb Adige, Formalhaut, Alphecca**) produce natives who are charming, well spoken, and intelligent. One might, however, be wary of promiscuity and sexual fickleness.

Stars corresponding to *Jupiter and Mars* (**Regulus, Arcturus, Altair, Antares**) are good for generals and leaders, rendering one independently minded and likely to overcome obstacles. If not in a leadership position, one may still enjoy telling others what to do.

Stars corresponding to *Jupiter and Saturn* (**Rigel, Alhilam, Capella, Rukbat, Algol**) may indicate great wealth and many possessions, and one may be fond of husbandry (the farming type) and building construction.

Stars corresponding to *Mars and Saturn* (**Sirius, Castor**) render people who are energetic and adventurous. Expect, however, some rowdiness and coarseness.

Stars corresponding to *Jupiter and Mercury* (**North Scale, Pollux**) indicate people who are articulate and good at public speaking. People with this these stars prominent in their charts have a dignified style and are fond of arts and religion. According to Anonymous of 379, in a nocturnal birth these stars may incline one toward hypocrisy and pretense. It seems that he is likening these stars to a diurnal Jupiter in a nocturnal chart.

Stars corresponding to *Mars and Mercury* (**Betelgeuse, Bellatrix, Procyon, Alpheratz**) allow natives to be clever and versatile but aggressive. They can be tough-minded people who can be successful in their endeavors. In a day birth, with Mars out of sect, one can be daring and coarse to the extreme of being a forger or even a murderer.

Stars corresponding to *Jupiter and Venus* (**Toliman, Achernar**) depict natives with fine qualities, like the benefics associated with them: a love for pleasure but also arts and religion. These stars can also bring wealth from women.

Stars corresponding to *Saturn and Venus* (**Zosma, Denebola, Alphard**) can make the native fortunate but overly desirous. Later in life, they may be more religious or more inclined toward self-discipline.

Stars corresponding to *Mars and Venus* (**Aldeberan, Antares**) may help natives be very good organizers and administrators, if they are given to public life.

Listing Individual Stars

Now we look at these stars one by one. They are the ones that Ptolemy or Anonymous of 379 mention directly. In this list - which is not wholly consistent with some of the attributions above - we see where these stars are within their respective constellations, and some associations from myths and legends that have gathered around them.

First I list the stars in the constellations of the zodiac. For these zodiacal stars I note the closest degree of the ecliptic to that star. These positions are for the year 2000.[1] As you will see below, finding a star's closest position along the ecliptic is far from the end of the matter. Following the stars in the zodiac are twenty additional ones. Their positions appear not in ecliptical longitude on the zodiac but in *declination*, their distance north or south from the celestial equator.

This list provides information about how ancient astrologers described these stars. Where appropriate, I give some updates of the stars' applications, as there are fewer ship builders these days and one hardly finds a charioteer anymore. In some cases I follow Bernadette Brady's updated star meanings (1998). Additionally, this list contains Ptolemy's correspondence of planets with stars, adding those of Anonymous of 379 where these two authorities differ.

Astrology and Greek Mythology

Although modern astrologers frequently use the Olympian myths to depict the natures of the astrological planets, ancient astrologers did not. Astrology was imported into the Greek-speaking world from the east (our Middle East). The pantheon of the Babylonian deities may be more useful to help us understand astrology's planets than those of the Greeks.[2]

Once we come to the non-wandering stars, however, we can use some knowledge of ancient Greek myth. The meanings of the constellations and individual stars were in place in the Greek-speaking world before natal astrology penetrated that culture, and were included in the newer astrological endeavor. Because ancient astrology draws from different cultures of the Hellenistic period, ancient Egyptian star lore is also relevant.

---

1.   Positions for January 1, 2000 from Solar Fire astrology program.
2.   See Baigent, M. (1994.)

Learning the Fixed Stars

These stars given below may seem to be too many to learn at once. I suggest a few approaches:

- Find a good book or software program to learn where the constellations are, and when they bedeck the evening sky. Depending on where you live, you may be able to trace out some constellations or individual stars in the sky above you which will help make them more immediate to your experience and easier to learn about.

- By learning stories of the stars and constellations, you can learn a lot of the background information that contributed to what stars mean in an astrological chart. There are many sources available, and you might want to consult the work of Diana Rosenberg[3] and Bernadette Brady (1998).

- You can begin to work with a manageable number of stars, perhaps ten to fifteen.

- You can find those stars that are most memorable to you. You could first study the Dog Star, the Heart of the Lion and the severed head of Medusa, which we know as Sirius, Regulus, and Algol respectively. You can add more gradually.

- You can study those stars that seem most important in your astrological chart. This time-honored method has helped many an astrologer.

- You can confine yourself to the stars that are in the constellations of the zodiac. I list eleven of them here.

- You can start with those that are brightest in the sky, of "first magnitude." Of the list below, I've designated those that are first magnitude stars.

Star Positions and Descriptions

Stars within the Constellations of the Zodiac
The left eye of the Bull or **the bright star of Hyades (Aldeberan)** is the nature of *Mars* or *Mars and Venus*. 09 Gemini 47. (1st magnitude.) Aldeberan is an aggressive and even a rowdy star. The native is an "enemy to peace and quiet," and can stir up trouble between people. Anonymous of 379 adds that this star can give a wrathful and hot headed temperament but makes one sexually versatile. This star is always opposite Antares in the zodiac. We often see both stars prominent in a natal chart.

---

3.   Rosenberg's web site is http://home.netcom.com/~ye-stars/

The head of the Northern Twin (Castor), is the nature of *Mercury* or *Mercury with Mars and Saturn*. 20 Cancer 15. This twin portends success in racing. Both stars of Gemini relate to an exuberant young athleticism.

The head of the Southern Twin (Pollux), is the nature of *Mars* or *Jupiter and Mercury*. 23 Cancer 13. This is more the boxer than the foot runner.

The heart of Leo (Regulus), from Rex in Latin, is the nature of *Jupiter and Mars*. 29 Leo 50. (1st magnitude.) Although there are brighter stars in the vicinity, Regulus is the kingly star for many different cultures. We think of this as the heart, the center, of the king of the beasts. By anybody's reckoning this is a very fortunate star that can predict fame and glory. Unlike most other stars, Regulus is very close to the ecliptic.

The star upon (Leo's) loins (Zosma) is the nature of *Saturn and Venus*. 11 Virgo 19. It is unclear exactly where this star is in the figure of the Lion. Is it the shoulder, rump, loins, or back? Brady attests that it is the back of the Lion, and particularly where Heracles broke the back of the Nemean Lion.[4] Therefore Zosma corresponds to a victim or somebody abused by the system. One can be secure that this would not be one of the benefic stars.

The tail of Leo (Denebola = "lion's tail") is also *Saturn and Venus*. 21 Virgo 37. (1st magnitude) Denebola, brighter than Regulus, is utterly different to Regulus for its effects on the native. This star is considered a difficult and malefic influence.

The left hand of Virgo (Spica from Latin), is given to *Venus and Mars* or *Venus and Mercury*. (1st magnitude.) 23 Libra 50. This is the ear of wheat from the left hand of the maiden (Virgo) and is a star of the harvest season. Spica's range of meaning includes abundance and innocent virtue. Natives are good at cultivation of the fields and accessing the bounty that comes from a good harvest. According to Aratus, the star represents the maiden who had walked amongst us during times when people were better, during the Age of Gold. According to Anonymous of 379, Spica may show one to have a religious and philosophical side and the native may be involved with religious ritual.

The southern claw of Scorpio (Zuben Elgenubi) is also the **South Scale of Libra. The northern claw of Scorpio (Zuben Eschalami)** is referred to as the **North Scale of Libra**. These are 15 Scorpio 05 and 19 Scorpio 22 respectively. They are the nature of *Jupiter and Mercury*. You will find these mentioned by William Lilly and others as the Chelae, which is the Greek word for "claws." Including these two Claws in the constellation Scorpio would make that constellation the largest in the sky. In the Middle East, however, these stars were considered not claws but scales and a separate constellation. At the time when these stars were near the Sun's position at the autumn equinox, they became part of Libra, the scales. Later authorities considered the South Scale malevolent and the North Scale benevolent. Brady considers both Scales affecting one's position toward the larger

---

4.   Brady (1998), p. 266.

society, but the North Scale is possibly corrupted by one's pursuit of personal gain.[5] Scales carry connotations of weighing and measuring as well as judging. Applying a standard, perhaps of one's society and culture, seems to help us understand the meaning of the two stars, and bestows on them the nature of Jupiter and Mercury. As Ptolemy gives identical planetary correspondences to both stars, I am inclined to give them equal value.

The body (or heart) of the Scorpion, or **Antares,** is the nature of *Mars and Jupiter* or *Mars and Venus.* 09 Sagittarius 45. This is a major star. Thousands of years ago Antares was with the Sun at the autumnal equinox. When the constellation included the Claws and the Scorpio was the largest one in the sky (see above), it was larger than the hunter Orion to the south, who was killed by a scorpion. "Antares" or "anti Mars" refers to the purported red color of this star and its warlike nature. It is important to note that Antares is always opposite Aldeberan in the Zodiac.

The star down from the knee of Sagittarius (Rukbat) is the nature of *Jupiter and Saturn.* 16 Sagittarius 38. This star may carry some of the ferocity of the constellation of the Archer, but with the anchoring that comes from the knee bent in an attacking stance.

Stars outside the constellations of the Zodiac

We proceed from north to south of the equator. I will keep stars in the same constellation together, although the constellation Orion cuts a long path through the sky and some stars are quite far from each other. Positions are derived not from the ecliptic but in declination, going north to south of the equator. We will discuss declination in the following section.

The brightest star in Auriga (Capella), is the nature of *Mars and Mercury.* 46N00. (1st magnitude) The stars of Auriga lead one to be a charioteer. What is the modern equivalent of a charioteer? Would one be a sports car driver, a car racer, a Harley-Davidson devotee, or an airplane pilot? This is a star of competition and adventure.

The bright star of Cygnus or the Swan (Deneb Adige or **Deneb Cygni),** is the nature of *Venus and Mercury.* 45N17. This constellation was originally simply a bird, and later became the swan. In ancient times, the swan was reputed to be a beautiful bird but could be competitive and hostile toward other birds. This star portends elegance and grace but with an edge. Otherwise, authorities write about careers with birds.

The head of Medusa (Algol) is the nature of *Saturn and Mars* or *Jupiter and Mars.* 40N57. This is one of our more memorable stars, likened to the severed head of Medusa. Ptolemy and later astrologers considered it an indicator of death by mutilation and decapitation. Brady, looking at the origins of the myth of Medusa, thinks of this star as pertaining to feminine outrage.[6] The bottom line is that this is an unpleasant star that tends to extremes.

---

5.   Brady (1998) p. 279.
6.   Brady (1998) p. 190.

The bright star of Lyra (Wega) is the nature of *Venus and Mercury*. 38N47 (1ˢᵗ magnitude.) Mercury or Hermes invented the lyre, a stringed musical instrument. He gave it to Apollo, his brother, who later gave it to his son Orpheus. Orpheus charmed not only the birds but also the trees and rocks with his song. (Times became harder for him later.) One could think of this star not just for music and song, but for a strong magnetizing quality. We read in Firmicus that Wega rising can bring about a just and upright person (he also says miserly) who may work in some capacity for courts of law.

The star common to Pegasus and Andromeda (Alpheratz) is given as the nature of *Mars and Mercury* or the nature of *Venus*. 29N05. Alpheratz belongs to two different constellations, the head of Andromeda and part of Pegasus, known as the flying horse. Bringing the two constellations together, we might suppose a combination of femininity and the love of movement.

The bright star of the Northern Crown (Alphecca) is the nature of *Venus and Mercury*. 26N43. This central star of the Northern Crown was affiliated with the crown given to Ariadne. She had fallen in love and eloped with Theseus who then deserted her. She went on to marry Dionysus who gave her a crown and when later she was taken to the sky this became her constellation. Firmicus and Manilius add that Alphecca gives a love of elegance, fashion and graceful living.

The bright and ruddy star in Bootes (Arcturus), is the nature of *Mars and Jupiter*. 19N11. (1ˢᵗ magnitude.) Other Greek names were "Bear Guard" or "Bear Watcher" because of its proximity to the constellation of the Great Bear. This is the star of the warrior, and also one who can be trusted with confidences and with the nation's treasury. Much has been made of this star over the centuries. The constellation itself rises horizontally and sets vertically and would have been a spectacular sight to our ancestors.

The breast of the Eagle, in Latin **Altair**, is the nature of *Mars and Jupiter*. 08N52. The eagle has been a symbol of the empire from Roman times to today. It was the bird of Jupiter and has Jupiter's strong regal quality but also the aggression of a soldier. This strong energy should be applied to some worthy purpose, or one is simply hot headed and a menace in traffic.

The body of the (small) dog (Procyon) is the nature of *Mercury and Mars*. 5N13. (1ˢᵗ magnitude.) Firmicus and Manilius discuss careers with dogs when Procyon is rising. Both say that the native will be more likely to work with the instruments of hunting than with hunting itself. (Firmicus probably used Manilius as his source for the characteristics of stars.)

Now we survey stars south of the equator. We begin with four in the constellation **Orion**. The first two, Betelgeuse and Bellatrix, are north of the equator. I include them in this southern list because most of Orion is south of the equator. Orion is the most spectacular constellation in the night sky. The Greek word for this constellation was "oarion." The initial letter was originally not "o" but "w", which is quite close to our word "warrior."[7] During the winter it is easy for anyone even in urban areas to see the outlines of this fighting man in the sky. All the major stars of Orion indicate a

---

7.   Allen, Richard (1963) p. 304.

strong enterprising nature to the native, especially Betelgeuse and Bellatrix, the stars at the shoulders of the hunter.

The right shoulder of Orion (Betelgeuse) 07N24, (1ˢᵗ magnitude) and **the left shoulder of Orion (Bellatrix)** 06N21 are the nature of *Mars and Mercury*. Firmicus tells us that these people could be great athletes, but their minds are restless and anxious.

The middle of Orion's belt (Alnilam) is the nature *of Jupiter and Saturn*. 01S12. Manilius treats the stars of Orion's belt differently from the stars of his two shoulders. He stresses that Alnilam gives enterprise in hunting and knowledge of the variety of ways to trap and capture one's prey. In modern times hunting can be a metaphor for different activities of pursuit and capture.

The left knee (or the left tip of the toe) of Orion (Rigel) is also the nature of *Jupiter and Saturn*. 08S12. (1ˢᵗ magnitude.) Brady develops the theme that the constellation Orion is the Egyptian god Osiris, who is represented on earth by Egypt's pharaoh. In her view, Rigel gives protection and receptivity to wisdom.[8]

The bright star of Hydra (Alphard) is the nature of *Saturn and Venus*. 08S39. The Hydra is a large and dangerous water snake. You may recall Hercules having to kill the nine-headed Hydra. One thinks of this star as having a dark and sinister influence, perhaps like the Heart of the Scorpion (Antares) but with less machismo.

The mouth of the (large) dog (Sirius), is the nature of *Jupiter and Mars* or *Mars and Saturn*. 16S43. (1ˢᵗ magnitude.) Sirius is the brightest star in the sky. As you may know, the ancient Egyptians began their calendar year when Sirius rose from the Sun during the summer. "Dog Days" refer to those hot days of summer that begin with the rising of Sirius. This star has a strong effect that can magnify anything it touches for good or for ill. We also know of it as the "Scorcher." Firmicus takes a very dim view of Sirius: "whoever is born with this star rising will apply a maddened brain to every kind of monstrous crime."[9] However, attributing the nature of Jupiter and Mars to this star gives it a more benign character.

The mouth of the southern fish (Formalhaut) is the nature of *Venus and Mercury*. 29S38. Based upon these planetary attributions, we get a sense that this is a star of refinement and culture. Manilius, however, is more interested in enterprises that occur on more distant seas, such as diving for booty from shipwreck vessels. (Remember that the southern seas are unknown and dangerous from the ancient Greek and Roman perspective.)

The bright star of Argo (Canopus) is the nature of *Saturn and Jupiter*. 52S42. (1ˢᵗ magnitude.) Argo was the ship Jason took to capture the Golden Fleece and it signifies the adventurous quality of sea faring. Modern careers can involve ships, of course, although in modern times we might emphasize air flight or going into space.

---

8.   Brady (1998), p. 171.
9.   Firmicus, p. 276.

The last star of Eridanus the river (Achernar) is the nature of *Jupiter*. 57S15. (1ˢᵗ magnitude.) Achernar is the end of the mysterious cosmic river that extends from south to north. (Acamar is the origin of this river.) Perhaps this is the star for those who investigate distant ancestry or who search for the first human creature or the first moment of the universe.

The right foot of Centaurus (Rigel Kentaurus or **Toliman**) is the nature of *Venus and Mercury*. 60S50. (1ˢᵗ magnitude.) This star is well-known to modern astronomers as it is physically the closest to us. It is unclear whether the Centaur in this star is the wild "horseman beast" of the mythological Centaurs or the gentler Chiron. (Chiron is also the name of a modern planetary body used by some modern astrologers.) If we go for the gentler Chiron, the motifs for this star are those of teaching, healing, and being a wounded healer.

Now for the more difficult part: how does one locate these stars to integrate them into a natal chart? For this we need a different kind of presentation.

Locating and Using the Stars

When charting the positions of the planets, we usually simply note their ecliptical *longitudes* - where they are on the zodiac, from Aries through Pisces - and ignore their *latitudes* - how far the planet is North or South of the ecliptic. Since planets are usually close to the ecliptic and since the Sun is always on the ecliptic, omitting latitude presents no problem for most astrologers. (The modern planet Pluto, often more than ten degrees in latitude, may be a different matter.)

If we naively use ecliptical longitude for the non-wandering stars, we run into trouble. I give you two short examples that point to the inadequacy of simply using the positions on the zodiac for all stars. These consist of two pairs of stars that are nearby on the ecliptic but far apart in the sky and in their meanings.

- Spica is a star of abundance and fertility; Arcturus is a star of warriorship and protection. The closest positions of these stars to the ecliptic are within one degree - 23 Libra for Spica and 24 Libra for Arcturus - but the stars themselves are in different parts of the sky.

- Both Canopus and Sirius are close to fourteen degrees of Cancer. Tropical Cancer is the most northerly zoidion from the equator, but Canopus and Sirius are far from Cancer, being south of the equator. Sirius and Canopus are also far from one another. Using only ecliptical longitude for these two stars gives us some bizarre results, in light of their positions in the sky. Sirius, the brightest star of all the stars, is sixteen degrees south of the equator and forty degrees south of the ecliptic. Canopus, in the constellation Argo, is thirty-six degrees further south of Sirius, is fifty-two degrees south of the equator, *and seventy six degrees south of the ecliptic*.

The Hellenistic tradition only uses ecliptical positions for stars when they are in the constellations of the zodiac. Ancient tradition gives us two alternatives for the other non-wandering stars: parallels of declination and paranatella. Both have merit and both present us with some difficulties. I now examine all three possibilities.

Ecliptical Positions for Stars of the Zodiac

Anonymous of 379 and others made the distinction between stars that are part of the constellations of the zodiac and those that are north and south of those constellations. For the stars of the zodiac they used the **nearest ecliptical degrees** as we would for planets. Here are the degrees of longitude for these stars for the year 2000.

Aldeberan	09 Gemini 47
Castor	20 Cancer 15
Pollux	23 Cancer 13
Regulus	29 Leo 50
Zosma	11 Virgo 19
Denebola	21 Virgo 37
Spica	23 Libra 50
South Scale	15 Scorpio 05
North Scale	19 Scorpio 22
Antares	09 Sagittarius 45
Rukbat	16 Capricorn 38

(There are two good reasons for dropping Rukbat, near the knees of the Archer, from this list. Rukbat is no longer as bright a star as in ancient times. Secondly, it is eighteen degrees from the ecliptic and over forty degrees south of the equator.)

It seems reasonable to use ecliptical positions for these ten or eleven stars as this is also how we measure the planets - and these stars and the planets are near one another. Using their degrees of longitude on the zodiac is also in line with astrological tradition.

We have seen a few examples of conjunction of fixed stars of the zodiac with planets in a person's birth chart. The presence of a star may enhance a quality that is already there. Both **William Blake** and **Winston Churchill** have Sun conjunct the Mars-like Antares, the Heart of the Scorpion. (Because the fixed star moves about one degree every seventy-two years, both Suns are conjunct the star although Blake's Sun is a few degrees before Churchill's.) To both men this star enhances their combativeness, their enjoyment of the good fight.

In **John F. Kennedy's** chart, Aldeberan, the Eye of the Bull, is conjunct his Gemini Sun. Although Kennedy could be given to fits of temper, he was not a particularly argumentative person; here Aldeberan's rowdiness and sexual versatility may be more at issue.

Clinton's Jupiter in the First is conjunct Spica, a very favorable star. This helps explain his strong personal ambition and his indomitable self-confidence in spite of many obstacles.

Margaret Thatcher and **Jacqueline Kennedy Onassis** have powerful Moons in Leo in the Tenth, both enhanced by the presence of Regulus. In very different ways, both women had both personal popularity and gave off an aura of royalty.

One evening, however, you might look up at the stars and see the brilliance of Sirius, Arcturus, Wega, and the stars of Orion, and want to include them in your astrology. How do we include them? I offer two possibilities.

Parallels of Declination

Hephaistio, in his discussion of fame and rank, mentions that stars in *parallel* to specific planets can be important for this issue.[10] These are parallels of *declination*, which measure locations north and south of the equator.

From our point of view of earth, two planets or stars in parallel would be overhead at the same degree of the earth's latitude. A star at a certain degree of north or south declination would be in parallel with a planet if that planet were within a degree of declination. Using parallels of latitude gives us a coordinate system through which a planet and a star not on the zodiac can coincide.

The Sun ranges from twenty-three and a half degrees north to the same distance south of the equator. Planets are usually within the same range but can be found up to thirty degrees of declination.

These stars within the range of the Tropic of Capricorn and the Tropic of Cancer, in terrestrial terms, might be in parallel with a planet in a natal chart. Less likely is a star whose declination is outside this range being in parallel with a planet. Here are the stars within this range.

Zosma	21 N
Arcturus	19 N
Aldeberan	16 N
Denebola	14 N
Regulus	12 N
Altair	08 N
Betelgeuse	07 N
Bellatrix	06 N
Procyon	05 N
Alniham	01 S
Rigel	08 S
Alphard	08 S
North Scale	09 S
Spica	11 S
South Scale	16 S
Sirius	16 S

Here are the stars that would be parallel with a planet out of range of the Sun's yearly motion but could be in parallel with a planet:

Castor	31 N
Pollux	28 N
Antares	26 N
Alphecca	26 N
Formalhaut	29 S

---

10. Book II, Chapter 18.

If you have a table with the north or south declinations of the planets in a natal chart, you can use the above measurements to see which stars and planets are in parallel. Here are some examples from the charts we have looked at so far.

Thomas Jefferson's Venus in Taurus in the Fourth appears to be a very benign placement, although compromised by Mars and Saturn casting squares from the Seventh. (It is fortunate for Jefferson that Venus is looking ahead at Mars and Saturn; these aspects could be more difficult.) However, Venus is made more unruly by its parallel in declination with both Aldeberan and the malefic Denebola, the Tail of the Lion. This could make one's sexuality more difficult to tame, and further indicates Jefferson's many struggles in this area.

When we return to **Marquis De Sade**, we discover the same two fixed stars, Aldeberan and Denebola, in parallel to his Mars in Aries, and we encounter more information pertaining to his extreme nature. Noting the strength of Mars - in sect, in his own house Aries, angular, and oriental - we see that Mars looks forward to De Sade's Venus and Saturn in Cancer. De Sade's sexual nature becomes very strongly influenced by a Mars that is given to aggressive extremes.

The fixed stars, in parallel of declination, provide for happier outcomes for **Eva Peron**, using her 1908 natal chart. The Ascendant is in parallel to Regulus, the Heart of the Lion. This points to her personal charisma and royal bearing, for one whose childhood was spent in poverty. Venus parallels Alphecca, the Northern Crown. Here we have more evidence of the same. (We may remember the association of Alphecca with the crown given to Ariadne by the god Dionysus, after Theseus left her on an island.) With Jupiter parallel to Arcturus, the warrior-like Bear Guard, we see the populist and visionary quality of her public work.

We can gain information by noting when an important fixed star is close in declination to an important natal position. The advantage is that the stars' declination hardly move over time, and we can learn their locations easily. Since most astrology and astronomy software give declinations for all the planets for a person's time of birth, one can easily find the parallels of declination between planets and stars.

There remains one more way to assimilate natal positions with the fixed stars. This is more subtle but quite powerful and subject to much research in modern astrology: bodily co-risings and paranatella.

Rising and Co-rising

This is a different system, which is not based upon coordinates in space but upon coincidences in time. We move away from measuring a position on the ecliptic or equator to note when stars cross the moving angles from a particular location. When listing stars not on the zodiacal belt, Anonymous of 379 and others do not mark their positions on the ecliptic but instead what degree of the zodiac **co-rises** with that star. When a particular star is *bodily* upon the horizon, anywhere on the horizon, what degree of the zodiac rises at that time?

The Factor of Location in Co-Risings

Since the horizon varies with location, a star's co-rising degrees will vary in the same way. We look at three stars, Wega, Sirius, and Canopus, from cities of three different latitudes: Boston, Hanoi, and Buenos Aires on January 1, 2000.[11] First let's try this from Boston.

- **Wega's** closest position on the zodiac is given as **15 Capricorn 18.** From Boston, however, Wega rises at 2:30 AM when **10 Scorpio** rises.

- Although **Arcturus'** closest position on the zodiac is **25 Libra 14**, when Arcturus rises in Boston **11 Libra** is rising.

- **Canopus**, on the other side of the globe, has **14 Cancer 59** as its closest ecliptical degree. Canopus, further away from the equator south than Boston is north, *does not rise at all that day.*

From Hanoi we get different co-rising times and degrees.

- **Wega** rises later than in Boston, at 4:41 AM, and the degree rising is not is Scorpio but **13 Sagittarius.**

- **Arcturus** rises an hour later than in Boston, at 1:01 AM, and in Hanoi **23 Libra** rises.

- **Canopus** does rise from Hanoi's location. Canopus rises when **11 Leo** is rising in Hanoi. This is twenty-seven degrees from its closest intersection to the zodiac.

Now we compare the co-rising degrees of these cities in the northern hemisphere with Buenos Aires, which is south of the equator.

	Boston	Hanoi	Buenos Aires
Wega	10 Scorpio	13 Sagittarius	*does not rise*
Arcturus	11 Libra	25 Libra	4 Sagittarius
Canopus	*does not rise*	11 Leo	26 Aries

This seems like a sound and sensible approach to locating and using fixed stars in the natal chart. Using this method, one can also arrive at setting, culminating and anti-culminating times for all the stars, planets and all the degrees of the zodiac for a given location. This is now easy to do using modern astrology software programs.[12] One could note co-risings of all the stars even if, like Regulus, they are on the ecliptic or within the constellations of the zodiac. (Their rising times will

11. These positions of Jan. 1, 2000, using the stars data page from *Solar Fire*. Using the rising times from that page, I used *Io Sprite*, distributed by Timecycles, to determine the co-ascending degrees.
12. *Solar Fire*, distributed by Astrolabe, and *Starlight*, distributed by Zyntara, can do this..

coincide with the rising times for that degree of the zodiac.) Bernadette Brady's work on fixed stars uses this approach. This is, however, different from the ancient tradition of using the zodiacal degrees, not co-risings, for the stars of the zodiac. How do we interpret the place of stars that rise *exactly* at the time of one's birth?

Firmicus, when describing the effects of stars, casts stars rising in a positive light, compared to those that are setting. As he often does, Firmicus uses extreme possibilities to illustrate astrological outcomes: if Procyon, the lesser Dog Star, is rising, one may have a fine career taking care of dogs, but if it is setting, one may be mangled by dogs.

According to ancient astrologers, a star at an angle at birth, especially when rising or culminating, is a significant factor for a star in a natal chart. This has not changed over time. The difference here is that we are interested in a star bodily upon an angle, not with its closest zodiacal degree at an angle. For this to be accurate, we need to be very sure - within four minutes - of the time of a person's birth. A few people whose charts we have studied have important fixed stars at angles at their births.

Elizabeth Barrett Browning has a natal chart that does not accent the vigorous or pioneering. That her life became interesting is, in part, an outcome of co-rising Bellatrix, a star on the shoulder of Orion and the nature of Mars and Jupiter. In the natal chart for the **Dalai Lama**, Betelgeuse, the star on Orion's other shoulder, ascends. This star is also the nature of Mars and Jupiter. A self-proclaimed Buddhist monk and the political leader of the Tibetan people, the Dalai Lama has had to pursue a difficult mission for a long time.

Emily Dickinson has Regulus culminating at the time of her birth. Regulus does give her the possibility of great fame. Considering her anonymity during her lifetime, this may surprise us. However, we have also noticed her Lot of Spirit with Saturn and her chart's lack of angularity. Had the Sun, also the lord of her Midheaven, been angular or more strongly aspected, she could have become better recognised within her own lifetime.

Bill Clinton, in addition to Bellatrix culminating, has Deneb Adige setting. The star of Orion helps us understand Clinton's strong political ambition and sense of purpose. The star of the Swan setting is more difficult to interpret. Following Firmicus' attribution of malevolence to stars setting, this star may manifest in the power and endurance of Clinton's political enemies. As far as I know, Clinton has no negative experiences with birds.

We close these examples with **Wolfgang Mozart,** who had two stars at important angles at his time of birth: Denebola rising and Aldeberan culminating. The malefic star of the tail of the Lion did not bestow good looks or personal charisma upon Mozart, but it did give him a fierceness of character - sometimes boorishness. Aldeberan culminating tells us more about the strength of his musical ambition and desire to manifest his genius in the world; Emily Dickinson he was not.

Paranatella

Anonymous of 379 takes co-risings a step further. He relates stars and planets *if they are at the same or at different angles at the same time*. This is called **paranatella** (literally "co-rising") and is a means to bring a planet and a star together. In the modern era Bernadette Brady (1998) has pioneered this approach.

To determine paranatella between a star and a planet, we examine the four angles during the day of a birth or event. A star's influence arises from being with the planet that is at the same time at the same angle or at another angle sometime during that day of birth. (For this purpose I use the traditional day that begins at sunrise and ends at sunrise the next day.) One blends in the meaning of star with the planet involved. According to Anonymous of 379, there are effects specific to the angle upon which a star is found.

- When the star is **rising**, this star has an influence throughout life and its influence occurs from the beginning of one's days.

- The star **culminating** will also be influential throughout life but its effects will be seen in the prime of life.

- The star **setting** will manifest in midlife or older or if one now resides in a different place from where one has been before.

- The star **anti-culminating** describes ones last years and what one may leave behind for others.[13]

There are different ways to incorporate the many possible paranatella of stars with planets into the natal technique we have seen so far. One can look for basic themes that manifest in among different stars, planets, and angles. A military theme stands out strongly in the fixed stars of **Winston Churchill**. Altair, the Breast of the Eagle and the nature of Mars and Jupiter, ascends as Mars culminates. Altair also culminates as Mercury sets, adding bellicosity to his rhetoric. We have discussed Antares and its zodiacal conjunction with Sun: by paranatella, Sun culminates and anti-culminates with Antares. Sun rises as Betelgeuse, the star of the right shoulder of Orion, sets: this may have given success over Hitler. Bellatrix, the star on the other shoulder of Orion, anti-culminates when Churchill's Moon sets. Even the Moon also cooperates with the warrior-like nature of Winston Churchill.

We can trace one or two planets in an individual's chart and see how different stars influence them. When we look at Mercury in the chart of **Elizabeth Barrett Browning**, we see a planet in its fall, opposite its own house, and within the Sun's beams. This planet is critical as it governs her Virgo Ascendant, and hardly seems like the Mercury of a major poet. However, Mercury is configured with the two stars on the shoulders of Orion - when Mercury rises on her day of birth, Bellatrix culminates and Betelgeuse anti-culminates. Both stars give an adventurous and enterprising character to her words and the energy of her life.

---

13.   Brady uses Paulus' sequence of the four angles, which is specific to definite eras of life. A star on the Ascendant gives information about early life, on the Midheaven about the prime of life, at the Descendant more toward retirement, and at the IC later in life and one's foundations. This is slightly different from what is described above.

George W. Bush has Sun in the Twelfth place from the Ascendant in a zoidion also occupied by Saturn. Yet when the Sun rose, Arcturus culminated and Alnilam, the star in the middle of Orion's belt, also rose. This lends many more dynamic possibilities to his difficult Sun position. If one adds to this that Mercury, which is more favorably placed in his chart, rose at the same time as Sirius. This gives Mercury a very intense character that can manifest both in his interpersonal agility and tendency toward verbal blunders. "The Scorcher" tends to magnify the good or bad effects of whatever planet with which it comes into contact.

Bush's former opponent **John McCain** offers other possibilities entirely. When his Mercury ascended, Vega, the nature of Venus and Mercury, culminated: this is a more benign and agile combination - and a more naïve one - than what displays itself in Bush's chart. At the same time McCain's Saturnian character is given a more aggressive nature by the influences of Bellatrix, which culminated when Saturn set, and set when Saturn anti-culminated.

When we return to the chart of **William Blake**, we become interested in the paranatella that involve Venus and Mars. These planets are important to his career and character respectively. When Venus set, Betelgeuse rose. We see here more astrological support for the polemical style of Blake's art. *Procyon*, the minor Dog Star, culminates as Venus is on the IC: although some of Blake's best-known poetry depicts tigers and lambs, I know of none that depict dogs.

Mars rose with *Sirius* the day Blake was born. Sirius is an intense star that can make one driven to greatness or to have a cruel and tyrannical temperament. As Mars is in sect in his nocturnal chart, I would assume the former interpretation. (As tough-minded as much of his work is, Blake did write sweet poetry about lambs). On his IC, representing his last days and his legacy, we have *Arcturus* the Bear Guard and *Rigel* of Orion together. They have a protective and visionary quality, which indeed have been part of Blake's legacy.

I conclude with the former pope **John Paul II.** Mercury does not stand out in his chart, as it is in the Eighth in Taurus and rescued from greater difficulty being along side a dignified Venus. Paranatella with Mercury, however, give this planet a much greater scope. Mercury rose with Formalhaut, the benefic mouth of the Southern Fish, which is associated with refinement. (I think of his youthful occupations as poet and actor.) When Mercury ascended Altair culminated, giving a fiery and driving quality. Mercury, however, is intertwined with the malefic star Algol, who co-culminated with Mercury. In addition to Mars rising in his chart, Algol would render Kracow's bishop Karol Wojtyla a strong and unyielding adversary to the Communist authorities in Poland.

According to Anonymous of 379, paranatella that involve setting stars signify conditions in midlife or in another home. This would apply well to John Paul, who moved to Rome to become pope. We meet the star Rigel, the nature of Jupiter and Mars. Rigel set as Saturn culminates, and co-sets with Mercury. This star at the left knee of Orion is associated with protection, strength, and wisdom, and fits well with his responsibilities as keeper of order in the Catholic Church and as major promoter of its teachings. Additionally, Antares co-set with Sun: John Paul would not hesitate to engage all potential opponents, inside and outside the church.

Paranatella involving stars anti-culminating can describe conditions after one's death and his or her eventual legacy. Two configurations stand out. The fortunate star Spica anti-culminates with Mars and at the same time Jupiter rises: this presages eventual success in his battles throughout his life. We have already seen this with the success of his ministry facing Poland's Communist authorities. He has also succeeded in placing his conservative stamp upon the church, even if he antagonized many of the Catholic faithful in Europe and North America. Sirius anti-culminates as Mars sets: perhaps his policy of confrontation, while successful on its own terms, may bear out to have been more strident than was appropriate.

This concludes our discussion of natal astrology. Now we go further into the waters of Hellenistic astrology, taking on the matter of astrological prediction

12

TRANSITS AND PROFECTIONS

Finally we arrive at a critical matter in astrology: how to understand the past, present circumstances, and more especially, what the future holds. This is the topic of prediction. Almost all my clients come to me with questions like, "What is going on in my life now?" "How did I get into this mess?" "When will this be over?", and "Will things be better or worse for me later?" Self-understanding always takes place within the context of present conditions and decisions.

I have no intention of giving a complete rendition of astrological prediction within the Hellenistic tradition but rather a beginning. Nor am I interested in proving that any specific techniques always work, although I do provide examples of them working. I want to depict some of the predictive techniques in Hellenistic astrology and to demonstrate their use. I encourage the reader to apply them to their own charts and those of their friends. In this way Hellenistic predictive techniques can begin to reclaim their rightful place at the table of astrological innovation.

Some astrologers don't like the word "prediction," but I will stay with it. Literally, a prediction is a foretelling, even a *fortune* telling. I feel that astrologers should not be afraid to make predictions. Predictions occur with regularity in many areas of inquiry. On a daily basis we encounter weather predictions, population and economic predictions, predictions from pundits and politicians, predictions from medical personnel on the course of an illness or the efficacy of a treatment. None of these predictions are infallible, and all are based on past practice and the conceptual underpinnings of their disciplines. In this respect, astrology is no different from meteorology, economics, political science, or medicine.

When we encounter the ancient western tradition of prediction, modern astrologers are in some unfamiliar territory. As we'll see, modern astrological predictive techniques fit nicely with modern conceptions of time and how events occur in our lives, but to understand how Hellenistic astrology used prediction, we have to challenge some of our assumptions about time and the times of a person's life.

Except for solar and lunar returns, modern astrological prediction conceives of time as a continuously moving point that extends from the past through the present toward the future, infinitely in both directions. To the modern mind, there is nothing structurally different between past and future: the future is only less available to us than the past. The present moment is simply another point on the continuum. When events occur, there is a coincidence of causes that intersect at one of these places on the continuum.

Ancient astrologers were concerned rather with events that occur within discrete and divisible units of time. Ordinarily we think of events happening within years and months of our lives, without reference to its place on a calendar, and our ancient ancestors did likewise. As we'll see in the next chapter, different planets have specific numbers that can become years, months, or days in our lives. This is very different from our modern concepts of "objective" time.

We all have times of joy and sorrow, expansion and contraction, of summer and of winter. Yet within larger eras times are smaller units that may contrast with the general times: we have January thaws during cold New England winters, we can have a snap that chills August evenings. This is the same as with our lives. Before you are given notice that your job is to be eliminated - a job you have wanted to leave for a long time - you have an interesting assignment that inspires you or stimulates your next job possibility. You may have just had a romance with person of your dreams, but right now that person's former partner has arrived in town, your prospective significant other is distracted, and you are beside yourself. And your relationship continues, as this turns out to be only a temporary bump.

Often our times have a mixed quality: the good and bad happen at the same time. At your exit interview after having to leave the company you have worked for, the interviewer asks you out, and this becomes a great romance. Your husband is leaving you but your son just signed a multimillion-dollar baseball contract and wants to buy you your dream home.

Ancient prediction depends upon an understanding of the natal chart. The prerequisite for this and the following two chapters is a solid understanding of the previous eleven chapters on natal delineation. From the natal chart, a factor such as the bellicose combination of Mars and Jupiter in Churchill's First, or Onassis' difficult Mars placements, doesn't tell us when in life such a factor will manifest. This is what ancient predictive techniques attempt to do. One would not predict an event or condition that the natal chart could not account for.

In this chapter we look at transits in the ancient world. I begin with transits not because they were the most important to ancient astrologers, but because they are so important to modern astrologers. This topic allows us to examine the contrast between ancient and modern uses of prediction and of transits. Then we will look at yearly and monthly profections, which shed light on conditions within specific years and months of a person's life.

The following chapter is about ancient planetary period of *chronocrator* systems. Modern western astrologers do not use these techniques and perhaps they should. Planetary period systems can shed light on the general tone of a certain time and specific occasions that punctuate those times.

The concluding chapter on prediction is about ancient primary directions or circumambulations. Modern astrologers who use secondary progressions or solar arc directions will find here the source of their technique. Primary directions and their brethren were used to calculate major calamities - death in particular - and also to establish a set of planetary rulers for different areas of life. We will look at directions as setting up a set of planetary lords or *chronocrators* over areas of life for specific periods of time.

Over the course of our previous chapters our discussions have become increasingly complex, and this extends through these final chapters. I promise, once again, that your labors will be richly rewarded. Bon voyage!

Transits, Modern and Ancient

Why are transits so popular among modern astrologers? Transits imply a sense of time and action that is familiar to the modern mind. Transits track planets as they continually move, and imply a notion of time as one continuous motion, like a line extending from past through present to the future. Transits also show one factor - the transiting planet - being the active agent, and the natal position the passive recipient. Transits, along with solar arc directions, reveal how the conventional mechanistic model has influenced astrology.

Transits and the Modern World

According to the modern view, a transit occurs when a moving planet in the sky is near the degree, or aspecting the degree, of a position in the natal chart. Jupiter in my birth chart is at twenty-seven Cancer; Saturn was in tropical Cancer in the autumn of 2004, at the same degree as my natal Jupiter. One would say that transiting Saturn was conjunct Jupiter in my birth chart. In fact, Saturn was at *station* to turn retrograde. In the middle of the following year, Saturn moved again to late Cancer on its way to Leo.

Jupiter in the sky in autumn 2004 had just entered Libra, bringing it into a square with my natal Sun in early Capricorn, and later Jupiter crossed the degree of my Ascendant at 7 Libra. In 2005 Jupiter moved to the final degrees of Libra and was in a square aspect to my natal Jupiter in late Cancer.

If Mars goes through Scorpio, Mars impresses himself upon planets that are in Scorpio, but also those in Taurus by opposition and Leo and Aquarius by square. Depending on the planets contacted by transiting Mars, an invigorating or aggressive turn could take place upon one's sense of integrity or worldly position (Sun), emotional life (Moon), mind and interaction (Mercury) or love life (Venus). Less clear are transits to planets outside the orbit of Mars.

A transiting planet operates upon a natal position as energy does to matter, as the active does to the passive: the transiting planet is the acting force and the natal position is being acted upon. The transiting planet modifies the natal planet's functioning - and the life of the person - according to the nature of the transiting planet. Saturn, acting on Jupiter, may put a wet blanket on Jupiter's optimism and sense of abundance. Jupiter transiting Sun might increase confidence and a desire to participate in cultural or community activities with others; crossing the Ascendant, one might renovate the old wardrobe or begin a health regimen.

The modern planets Uranus, Neptune, and Pluto move more slowly and their transits, going back and forth, occur for a longer time. Modern astrologers, using transits from these planets, can depict conditions lasting up to two years. Transits involving faster-moving planets take place for a few days or even a few hours. For that reason, modern astrologers are less interested in transits from the faster-moving planets. The strongest transits take place under two conditions:

- A transiting planet conjuncts or aspects faster moving natal positions, such as the Ascendant or Midheaven and the planets up through Mars. These faster moving factors are more personal to the native.

- The transiting planet aspects the natal position by conjunction, opposition, or square. Although some modern astrologers use transiting trines or sextiles, it is the "hard" aspects that receive the most attention. Transiting planets therefore most strongly impact natal positions in the same mode. When Saturn was in cardinal Cancer and Jupiter in cardinal Libra, planets in Cancer and Libra, as well as Capricorn and Aries, would be strongly affected. (Ancient astrologers were more comfortable including transits that involve trines and sextiles.)

When does a transit occur? Most astrologers think of transits in terms of application, separation, and exactness. In 2003, Jupiter, transiting through Virgo opposed my natal Mars, located at thirteen degrees of Pisces. The transit gathers force as Jupiter approaches thirteen Virgo, exactly opposite my Mars. Afterwards, the energy is released as Jupiter moves on from the position of Mars. If Jupiter goes retrograde, it can then approach Mars from behind and make another exact opposition. Later Jupiter goes direct and again opposes my Mars position exactly. Afterwards Jupiter moves further from Virgo to Libra, to transit other natal positions.

Following is a Graphic Ephemeris from late 2004 that will help illustrate applications and separations.[1] This table contains the modern as well as the visible planets, and one can see, through their very flat moving lines, how slowly the modern planets move. At the beginning of 2004, Jupiter began the year finishing its transit to Mars.

All the moving lines are the transiting planets and all the straight lines measure out the natal positions from Cardinal (OC) to Fixed (OF) to Mutable (OM) zoidia. All contacts between moving and straight lines denote a transit by conjunction, square, or opposition. One can see Jupiter finishing its transit to Mars at the very beginning of the year. Here are some more examples:

- In late September Jupiter went into Libra and is at the place of my natal Ascendant in late October. Moving from the top down, Jupiter is direct in motion.

- Note the moving Saturn line that flattens out in contact with Jupiter and Neptune and then moves up. This is the station of Saturn and its motion.

To work with transits, we need know only the modes of the transiting planets and natal positions, how quickly or slowly the transiting planets move, and a general sense of how transiting planets impact with natal positions. Here are some difficulties with our modern practice of transits.

- Because they last longer and are more dramatic, modern astrologers emphasize transits of the modern planets Uranus, Neptune, and Pluto. These are planets of extremes, and we rely upon them too much, we tend to stress extreme possibilities in our clients' lives. Most events in our lives, however, take place within a trajectory of what is expectable.

- We tend to over-emphasize when a transit is exact to the degree, stipulating that something specific will happen to the native exactly at that time. Instead, an entire period of time seems

---

1.   From Io Edition, by TimeCycles Inc. Drummond, Ct. See www.timecycles.com

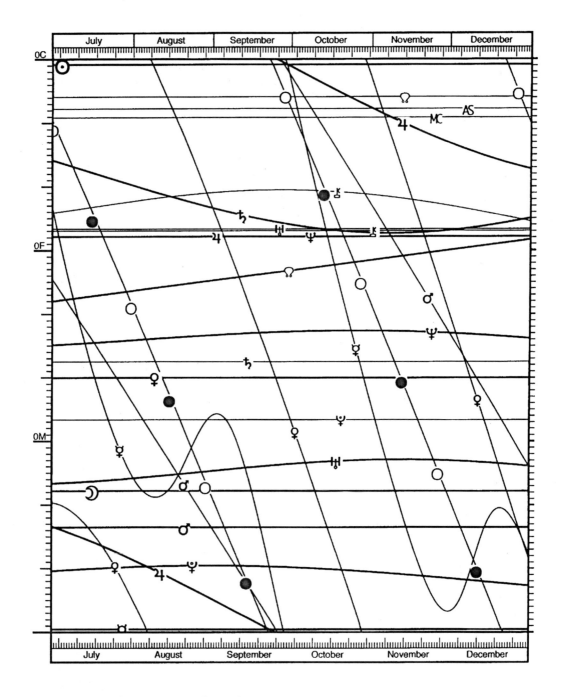

Joseph Crane - Graphic Ephemeris 2004 showing transits to natal chart

to show the influence of the transiting planet. These times may be punctuated by specific events, but these events do not necessarily conform to the exactness of the transit.

- Astrologers are unclear when a transit begins to take effect. Is it when the transiting planet is ten, or five, or two degrees approaching the natal position? What if a planet moves close to transiting a natal position and then goes retrograde before it arrives at the exact degree of aspect?

As with other issues, a review of the ancient doctrine of transits may clear up some of these thorny matters.

Transits and Hellenistic Astrology

Ancient astrologers used transits *only* as an added factor within the context of other indicators - profections, planetary period systems, or directions. Therefore not all transits will manifest in a person's life. They looked at a planet's movement *through an entire zoidion* as the duration of the transit. A transit begins when the planet enters the new zoidion and is in effect for the duration of the planet's course in the zoidion. I have not seen ancient writings that correspond to our modern ideas of transiting applications and separations. When we talk about Saturn transiting Jupiter, this means that Saturn is in a zoidion that is the same or in aspect to the zoidion that natal Jupiter inhabits. I will follow the modern practice of simply referring to the transiting and the natal planets.

Emphasizing a transit's relationship to a zoidion gives transits a structure similar to other features of ancient astrology. As we have seen, astrologers used the twelve zoidia to make up the twelve places from the Ascendant. We also have seen aspects cast from zoidia to zoidia, not from point to point. Transits are an extension of this pattern into the area of prediction. We will see that this is the same as with profections. Because we are not concerned here with the modern planets Uranus, Neptune, and Pluto, the events signified by transits are, generally speaking, more episodic occasions than is the case for modern astrologers. How long do transits last?

- **Saturn** is in a *zoidion* for about two and a half years.

- **Jupiter** is there for close to a year.

- **Mars'** speed varies considerably. When it is close to the Sun, Mars moves quickly - close to half a degree a day - and it can be in a *zoidion* for two months. If it slows down and goes retrograde within a zoidon, as it did in Taurus for most of 2005, it can be there for half a year.

- **Sun** moves through one zoidion per month.

- **Venus** can spend less than a month in a zoidion. If Venus goes retrograde during its transit, it can occupy a zoidion for a few months.

- **Mercury** is similar to Venus, except it moves more quickly. Mercury, like the Sun, can spend only a month or a couple of weeks in a zoidion. If Mercury goes retrograde, which happens four times a year, it can be in one zoidion for six weeks.

- **Moon** spends just two and a half days in a zoidion.

It is not unusual for a planet to go retrograde into a previous zoidion. For example, a planet can go from Sagittarius into Capricorn, turn retrograde, and return to Sagittarius. I imagine that this would be rather disconcerting to ancient astrologers. All planets except the Sun and Moon have retrograde phases.

Interpreting Transits

On the whole, the original interpretations of transits follow our expectations. Transits from the malefics Saturn and Mars are more difficult than those from the benefics Jupiter and Venus. Transits from the malefic out of sect (Saturn in a night chart, Mars in a day chart) will be more difficult; transits from a benefic that is in sect (Jupiter in a day chart, Venus in a night chart) would be more favorable. Transits from Saturn can hinder one's projects and bring difficulties to a person. Transits from Jupiter can lighten one's heavy loads and increase opportunities for activity and wealth. There are some surprises, however.

- Transiting Jupiter onto natal Saturn can destabilize one's career or behavior. Differently from our modern understanding, Jupiter transiting Saturn is a difficult transit.

- Although Saturn transiting Mars is difficult and Mars transits cause conflicts and losses, Mars in transit to Saturn is positive.

"Ingress" and "Transit"

The Greek word we translate as "transit," *epembasis*, is a stepping upon or an approach.[2] This word was translated into Latin as the familiar astrological word "ingress." From the word *ingredior*, an ingress is an entering, a stepping upon, embarking on an activity, and an advance. It is a walking upon but also a walking through.[3]

This secondary meaning, a walking *through*, does not survive in the word "ingress" that astrologers use. Modern astrologers think of an ingress not as a planet passing through a zoidion, as is meant by an ancient transit, but as the *entering* of a planet into a zoidion. To predict political events, mundane astrologers cast ingress charts for the moment the Sun enters 0 Aries and other cardinal points.

The English "transit" is a crossing or a passage, and contains much of the meaning of *epembasis*. Because astrologers use "ingress" simply to mean an entering, I'll use our modern word "transit" to denote a planet's passage through a sign or *zoidion* so that natal positions are effected.

---

2.   See Schmidt, General Note, to *Teachings of Transits* (1995.)
3.   *Oxford Latin Dictionary*, p. 908. (1983) Oxford: Oxford University Press.

- Venus in transit to Saturn and other planets is mostly good for one's relationships. Transits of Venus to Mars contribute to conflicts and jealousies can ensue. In transit to Jupiter, however, Venus causes disturbance and harm: this is not what we expect.

What is the reasoning behind these delineations? They may indicate concepts that are different from modern practice. Here are some speculations.

- Saturn is cold and dry, hard and obdurate. Almost any other influence can bring it greater flexibility and profit the native. Jupiter, transiting Saturn, can compromise Saturn's solidity too much, making too loose what was naturally hard. This is like a nervous job applicant having a stiff drink on his or her way to an interview and then becoming over-talkative.

- Transiting Saturn may thwart Mars' momentum, but Mars gives Saturn ability to focus and act.

- Venus transiting to Jupiter appears to dissipate Jupiter's positive qualities. Jupiter, the great benefic, needs only steadiness and an agenda to accomplishes its purposes: Venus may trivialize Jupiter's good qualities and reduce sociability to gossip.

Additionally, transits involving the Sun tend not to work out well. Robert Hand feels this may be related to the scorching Sun being considered a malefic in Indian Astrology and sometimes in ancient astrology.[4]

Here's a theoretical perspective on transits. In their writings on transits, Valens mentions a transit's *intensity*, while Ptolemy discusses transits as the activity of *intensification* and *relaxation*. This raises some interesting possibilities.[5] Modern astrologers, when emphasizing application and separation, also use a form of intensification and relaxation: an applying transit increases in intensity, as the separation from exactness is a downshifting of the transit. This would be the case either when the transiting planet is direct or retrograde. Ancient astrologers seemed to think of intensification and relaxation as the activity of the transiting and the natal planets together. One might think of planets not on a single scale of intensity or relaxation but each having *its own way* of being intense or relaxed, in conformity with the nature of the planet.

One could think of Saturn having its own manner of tensing the planet it contacts - perhaps a dull and heavy manner. Different planets would respond to this differently. Transiting Mars may pick up the pace for natal Saturn and produce benefit. If Mars focuses Saturn, Jupiter confuses it. Transiting Mars may pick up the pace in a harsher more extreme manner for Jupiter and make for problems. Venus, on the other hand, may relax Jupiter into becoming too slack and therefore ineffective.

The notion of intensification and relaxation gives us new and interesting possibilities for understanding transits. One consideration, again, is that transits accompanied other predictive techniques and were not used in isolation. I will include examples of transits in the next section to accompany a more widely used predictive technique: profections.

4.   Hand, Introduction to *Teachings on Transits* (1995.)
5.   Schmidt, General Note to *Teachings on Transits* (1995.)

Advancing Profections

A profection, which means an "advance," is a form of astrological *direction*. A direction moves a natal position, like the Sun, Moon, or Ascendant, according to a predetermined rate and ignores the natural movement of a position during a day or year. Faster Mercury and slower Saturn both move at the same rate. As we have seen with transits, time divides into units bounded by a planet's transit through a zoidion. Profections advance whole zoidia to progress time into segments of years, months, and units of two and a half days, corresponding to yearly, monthly, and daily profections. (Twelve segments of two and a half days each give us a thirty-day month.)

Yearly profections go from zoidion to zoidion, year after year, regardless of where in the zoidion the natal position may be. Whether, for example, your Ascendant or Sun is two or twenty-nine degrees Aquarius, the profected zoidion of Ascendant or Sun in your second year is Pisces, your third Aries, and so on. At age twelve (beginning your thirteenth year), the profection returns to the natal zoidion, and the process continues.

Monthly profections, which we will encounter below, advances a position one zoidion per month of thirty or twenty-eight days. Stay tuned. (In this presentation I will not consider daily profections.)

Later Profections

Medieval and modern traditional astrologers have used yearly profections differently from the ancient tradition. These astrologers advance profections not one zoidion per year but thirty degrees per year, moving continuously. This means than an Ascendant at fifteen degrees would change zoidia halfway through each year, not at the birthday. Only when one has a position at 0 degrees would that position change on the birthday itself. A position in early degrees would change zoidia just before one's birthday, and one of late degrees would change by profection shortly after one's birthday. Some also profect according to one quadrant house per year, regardless of how many or few zodiacal degrees are in that house.

A modern predictive technique similar to medieval profections is the Huber age-point progression. Beginning with the Ascendant at the time of birth, one point moves counterclockwise from house to house, using the Koch system, at the rate of six years per house. This moving point will aspect planets and change signs within its six-year journey through a modern house.[6]

How would one calculate yearly profections using the Hellenistic model? This is quite elegant in its simplicity, using the arithmetic most of us mastered when we were about ten years old. We start with a simple question of how old one is: which year of life are you currently going through?

---

6.   Huber, Bruno. *Astrology and the Spiritual Path: The Spiritual Significance of the Age Progression*. (1990) York Beach, Me. Samuel Weiser.

If somebody has Gemini rising, Cancer is the zoidion of the yearly profection at one year old (the second year), Leo at the age of two (the third year), and so on. When one turns twelve (the thirteenth year), the profected Ascendant is Gemini again, and so on. Here is a yearly profection for somebody who is thirty-two years old:

> This is the person's thirty-third year.
>
> For the thirty-third year, *what is the next lowest multiple of twelve?* That would be twenty-four.
>
> What's the *difference* between the number of this year (33) and the next lowest multiple of twelve (24)? The answer is 9.
>
> ...g on the person's birthday, the yearly profection for this year is *nine* zoidia. With ...sing, the profected Ascendant falls in Aquarius. If Sun is in Pisces, the Sun's zoidion moves by profection to Scorpio. The profection will change each birthday. It was eight zoidia last year and it will be ten next year.

What positions do you move by profection?

Valens emphasized the Sun, Moon, and Ascendant but would also profect *any planet and some lots*. Ptolemy casts the profection only for Ascendant, Midheaven, Sun, Moon, and Lot of Fortune. When a profected position lands on a particular zoidion, what planet or planets govern this profection?

Ptolemy, anticipating later tradition, used the lord of the profected zoidion as the planetary ruler of the profected position. The profected lord of the Ascendant, later called "The Lord of the Year," is the planet who is the house lord of the profected Ascendant. Continuing with the example above, the yearly profection being nine zoidia, Saturn is the yearly profection lord of a Gemini Ascendant that has Aquarius as the profection; even if the person has other planets in Aquarius in the natal chart. For a Pisces Sun advancing into Scorpio within a ninth year, Mars becomes the profected lord of the Scorpio Sun for that year.

Valens gives us another approach that I have found useful and will use in this chapter. The planetary lord of a profected zoidion is the planet or planets *inhabiting* that zoidion. If Sun in Pisces advances to Scorpio and Saturn is in Scorpio, it is Saturn, not Mars, who is the lord of the profected Sun. Valens' designation of any planet in the profected zoidion governing the profection has a major problem. If somebody has many planets in Aquarius, which planet would you use for the profection that has moved into Aquarius?

The astrologer can look at the planets in zodiacal order and one will follow another over the course of the year. If one has only Moon in Aquarius, the ruler of the profected Ascendant would be Moon, not Saturn who governs Aquarius. If, however, one has Moon, Sun, Venus, Mercury, and Saturn all in Aquarius, the year could be mixed in quality or changeable - changing according to the sequence of the planets in Aquarius.

I will opt for Valens' second option: one can also bring the planets together to interpret the profection. In natal interpretation we would mix the natures of co-inhabitants of a zoidion, and this should be able to extend to predictive work. Additionally, it is not clear how to measure the time belonging to each planet in sequence in a zoidion. Valens says that if *no planets* inhabit the zoidion of a profection, the house lord of the profection is its lord. If a planet *transits* the zoidion of the profection, the transiting planet also becomes important in predicting an outcome of a profection. We will see these occurring in the examples below.

Interpreting Profections

Ancient astrologers used yearly and monthly profections to predict situations and circumstances one would encounter within a given year, month, or day. One interprets profections within the context of the life situation of the client and of the more general indicators given by the planetary lords or *chronocrators*. (Determining these is the topic of the next two chapters.)

What is the relationship between a natal position and its profected lord? The natal position "hands over" to the profected lord, who "takes up" the charge. I think of a relay race, where the baton passes from one runner to another. A better analogy may be that each position represents a project that the boss delegates to one subordinate now and a different one later. The handing-over position is the boss; lord of the profection is the subordinate. For yearly profections, each year a new subordinate takes over the job. How well the year's project goes depends greatly on the effectiveness of this year's "go-to" person and the prospects for the project itself (the natal position). In our work lives, some of us surely have had assignments from above that proved impossible to accomplish successfully: much depends on the competence and resources of the boss and his or her project. What are the tasks that each boss gives? They are different with each natal position. Ptolemy lists the five positions that one would profect:

- The Ascendant is the most general indicator for the person. The Ascendant is the health and activity of body and soul.

- The Sun is one's reputation and public status, as well as one's father.

- The Moon, according to Ptolemy, include relationships of cohabitation. Valens stresses that Moon is about body and its ailments

- The Midheaven degree is one's action and livelihood.

- The Lot of Fortune is one's fortune in general, but especially material prosperity. The Lot of Fortune is a secondary indicator of career, indicating our sources of income.

Valens used other positions. Here are their projects:

- The Descendant is the matter of death and difficulty. Remember that the seventh zoidion from the Ascendant is the "Setting Place."

- The Imum Coeli or IC is foundations, buildings and matters that are old.

- Saturn takes apart what has been brought together, especially one's prosperity. Saturn also concerns itself with a father's legacy and illnesses that are hidden.

- Jupiter is one's reputation and alliances of friendship or utility.

- Mars is military matters but also those of public action.

- Venus is one's partner, love affairs, or activities specifically related to women.

- Mercury is writings, business accounts, and matters of community.

Having determined the matter of the planet "handing over," we then analyze the condition of the planet of the profection, the one "taking up."[7]

- Is the planet a malefic or benefic?

is it in dignity, aspected by a benefic or malefic, direct or retrograde, within the beams of the Sun or outside the Sun's beams, oriental or occidental?

Valens writes that it is better for a malefic to hand over to a benefic, e.g. Saturn to Jupiter, than for a benefic to hand over to a malefic, e.g. Jupiter to Saturn. Why? In the former case the affairs of the malefic come off better than anticipated; in the latter, the good possibilities given by the benefic are upturned or diminished by the malefic. Now we can apply transits and profections to the lives of people.

Using Transits and Profections Together

To provide examples of transits and profections working together, I look at the lives of two people who have had many ups and downs in life. I start with **Winston Churchill**, in 1915, a terrible year for him.

At the beginning of the First World War, Churchill was England's Lord of the Admiralty. He was a rising star in government and holding an important position, even though his brusque manner tended to alienate opponents and keep potential allies at a distance. At the beginning of 1915 England had hoped to bring the war to a quick and successful conclusion. Churchill and other military leaders thought that if they conducted a naval expedition through the straits of Dardenelles, this could cut off Turkey from Germany and Austria and relieve and strengthen Russia. Thus surrounding Germany and Austria, they would sue for peace. Churchill and others would bring the war to a quick and victorious end.

Due to bad timing, bad weather, and a well-prepared Turkish adversary, this expedition was a disaster. Ships were blasted out of the water by mines, thousands of troops were lost at Gallipoli, and blame for the entire disaster fell on the Lord of the Admiralty's head. Churchill took the fall for this catastrophe and was sacked from his position but allowed to continue attending government meetings. In November 1915, near his birthday, Churchill resigned from the government and went to the front as a VIP soldier. He had no impact on the rest of the war, to his heartbreak, and later returned

---

7.   See Valens *Anthology*, Book IV, Chapters 17-25.

to government to take a domestic position. Here is Churchill's chart and the planets' location at the end of November 1915, when he resigned from the government.

The year before his resignation, in November 1914, Churchill had turned forty. Most of 1915 would be his forty first year. Subtracting forty-one from thirty-six, the fifth zoidia becomes his profection for that year. The Midheaven in Cancer, concerned with what one does, hands off to Scorpio. As Mercury is in Scorpio, it takes up the matter of Churchill's MC Mercury is oriental and in decent condition. Mercury receives aspects from natal Saturn (square) but from no other benefic or malefic. The profection alone does not portend any major difficulties.

By the end of 1915, however, Mars transiting Leo was also in square to Scorpio and Mercury, the planet taking up matters of the MC at that time. When transiting Mars intensified Mercury toward the end of 1915, Churchill gave up trying to stay in government and went directly into the war. Churchill's Sun in Sagittarius, indicating his leadership and public reputation, hands off to Aries and the Seventh zoidion from his Ascendant. Mars, as the lord for the Sun's profection, did keep Churchill involved with matters of war. Mars' natal position, in the First and conjunct Jupiter, is not a drawback at all. However, the Seventh place, the profection of his Sun, is the Setting Place and does point to diminishment of activity. Transiting Mars in Leo was in trine to Sun and Venus in Sagittarius when Churchill left government.

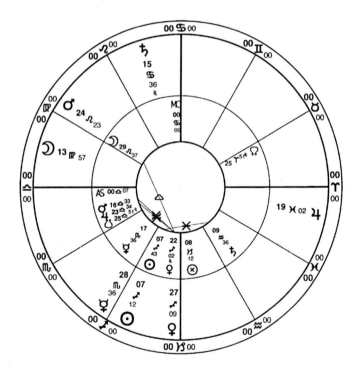

Inner Wheel - Natal Chart Winston Churchill
Outer Wheel - November 30, 1915

From Libra, the Ascendant and his warlike planets Mars and Jupiter hand over to Aquarius. Saturn, inhabiting and governing the Fifth place, takes up these positions. In addition to Ascendant, Mars, and Jupiter advancing to Saturn, *transiting* Saturn was in the tenth zoidion - in square to Mars and Jupiter and the zoidion of the Ascendant. We see too much Saturn impacting Churchill's Mars and Jupiter, which is what helps to make this such a difficult time for him. Because here we're working only with transits and profections, we see not permanent but changing circumstances. In four years, Churchill was back in government again and more adventures awaited him.

Fast-forwarding to the spring of 1940, we have a different time for Churchill. He was back in government and had been ~~~~~~ military and ultimately

defeat them. This was the greatest challenge and completing it was the highlight of his life.

In November 1939, six months before becoming Prime Minister, Churchill turned sixty-five and thus began his sixty-sixth year. As the next lowest multiple of 12 from 66 is 60, Churchill's profections would advance six zoidia.

- Midheaven in Cancer gives over to Sun and Venus in Sagittarius. What he does aligns itself with his reputation as a fierce combatant. (His Sun is conjunct the Mars-like fixed star Antares.)

- Sun in Sagittarius hands over to Taurus. Churchill has no planets in Taurus. We can look at Venus, but more urgently we notice Saturn transiting Taurus at this time. When Churchill took over as Prime Minister, the Sun and Mercury had joined Saturn in its transit of Taurus. These indicate mixed fortune regarding reputation and honor. 1940 was a year that was difficult for him but was also a highlight of his life.

- Mercury in Scorpio hands over to Aries and Mars. Churchill was known then and is known now for the defiant and bellicose rhetoric of this time. Early in the war he was far better known for his stirring speeches than for any strategic decisions he made.

- Again we look at handing over from Ascendant, Mars, and Jupiter in Libra. Six zoidia from Libra advances these positions to Pisces, the domicile of Jupiter. This is positive when we look at natal Jupiter. It becomes even more positive if we look at *transiting* Jupiter beholding Mars and Jupiter from Aries. At this time Churchill exuded a sense of visionary command.

Once again we meet with strong indications from Churchill's Mars and Jupiter in the first. Unlike 1915 that featured Saturn transiting, here we find in the forefront a transiting Jupiter. We could see that this is a difficult year for Churchill, although, with a world to save, he was in his prime. We move forward to 1945, and what a difference five years can make.

The good news was that the allies won the Second World War in Europe and Hitler was defeated. The bad news for Churchill was that, at a time when he was idolized all over the world, he and his party lost in parliamentary elections and he was cast out of government.

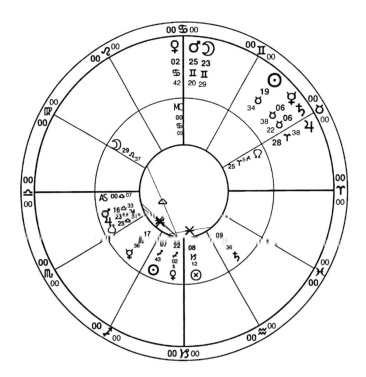

Inner Wheel - Natal Chart
Winston Churchill
Outer wheel - May 10, 1940

Inner Wheel - Natal Chart
Winston Churchill
Outer Wheel - July 26, 1945

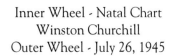

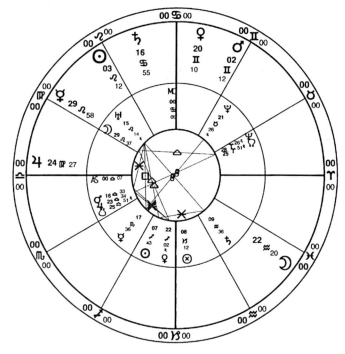

In November of the previous year Churchill had turned seventy. The next lower multiple of twelve • sixty • from his seventy-first year puts profections to eleven zoidia. At this time Churchill would resume his private life. We see this in the handing over of Ascendant, Mars, and Jupiter in Libra to his natal Moon in Leo.

Sun and Venus in Sagittarius hands over eleven zoidia to Mars and Jupiter, Libra being eleven zoidia from Sagittarius. This should be quite positive. Transiting Saturn, thirty years after his terrible year 1915, was once again in Cancer in his Tenth and in a predominating square to his natal Mars, Jupiter, and Ascendant.

Just before the election, Mars had entered Gemini and into an opposition to Sun and Venus in Sagittarius. Increasing its potency was that Mars, along with Jupiter, was also the profected lord of Sun and Venus. This combination would have been more appropriate to fighting another world enemy than attempting to be a popular politician.

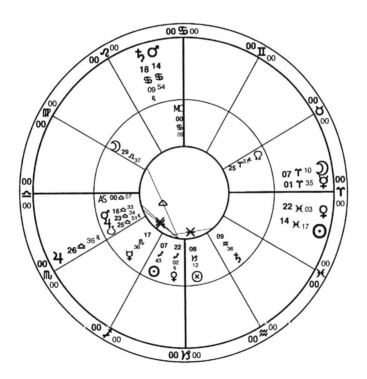

Inner Wheel - Natal Chart Winston Churchill
Outer wheel - March 5, 1946

As a private citizen, Churchill spent time painting and writing, recovering his energy, and trying not to give in to depression. Like many other former politicians, he toured and gave set speeches. Although politically defeated at home, he was received elsewhere as a hero of the victory over Nazism. In March 1946 - the following year - Churchill gave the famous "Iron Curtain" speech in Fulton, Missouri. At that time he predicted the coming of the Cold War between Communist and Western nations: this became his new warning to the world. His profections were now twelve zoidia. In this year, *Mercury* was strongly involved both as a planet handing over and taking up.

- The Sun and Venus hand over to Mercury.

- Mercury hands over to Ascendant, Mars, and Jupiter.

- Midheaven hands over to Mercury, lord of Gemini.

- Ascendant, Mars, and Jupiter hand over to Mercury, lord of Virgo.

During this prophetic time, Saturn continues to be in his Tenth and in square to his planets in the First. Complicating things in late winter 1946 was that transiting Mars joined transiting Saturn midway through Cancer.

Churchill's "Iron Curtain" speech, as historically important as it was, did not find a world audience eager for its message. Recovering from a devastating war and eager to recover and rebuild, nobody wanted to hear about any more major conflicts. As with his warnings about Hitler and the Axis in the 1930s, Churchill was correct.

With Churchill we've seen how profections aided by transits can help us understand the differing qualities of certain years of a person's life. I continue by highlighting a signal event in **Jacqueline Kennedy Onassis'** life, and here we will work with profections by the month.

The First Lady and November 22, 1963

It is difficult to us now to imagine what Jacqueline Kennedy went through in the late days of 1963. She had become a popular first lady, a model of personal style and class, and the mother of two young children. She was sitting next to her husband when he was shot and killed. After the assassination, she became a national icon and the most sought-after celebrity in the world. Her subsequent life events and marriage to billionaire Aristotle Onassis virtually launched the supermarket tabloid press in the United States. By the late 1970s, after Aristotle Onassis had died and after a bitter court fight, Jacqueline Kennedy Onassis finally received some of the privacy she sought. She died of cancer in 1994. We look at the profections and transits for November 22, 1963.

In the summer of 1963 Jacqueline turned thirty-four, beginning her thirty-fifth year. From thirty-five, the next lowest multiple of twelve (24) would bring her profections to eleven zoidia.

- Since Moon is the planet of cohabiting relationships, we should first see if there is an indication of the death of her husband. Moon is in Aries and eleven zoidia away is Aquarius, governed by Saturn. Note also that transiting Saturn is also in Aquarius at this time. Transiting

Moon was in Aquarius on November 22. This astrological pile-up of Saturn onto Moon, profected and transiting, gives us some indication of her husband's death.

- Saturn in Sagittarius hands over to Libra, governed by Venus in the Eighth. Again, natal Venus in the place of death. The transits to Saturn for November included Mercury and Venus but also Mars. Remember that a Saturn transit to Mars is favorable but a Mars transit to Saturn is not favorable.

- Eleven zoidia from Venus and Jupiter in the Eighth is the Moon in Aries. During this year

Jacqueline's public apotheosis is evident from the handing over of Part of Fortune, Sun, Mercury, and Midheaven to the planets Venus and Jupiter.

- Ascendant has handed over to Mars, which is an indication of misfortune, since Mars is out of sect in her diurnal chart. At the same time, Mars itself has handed over to the Moon, which could signify her marriage as the area of difficulty.

At this time it is appropriate that we turn to monthly profections. There are two ways of determining monthly profections, from Valens and from Ptolemy. I will leave it to the reader to try both procedures and make a preference between them.

According to Valens, one subtracts the zodiacal position of the Sun of the date in question from the Sun of the natal chart. This would yield the number of *zoidia* to profect for the month.

Jacqueline Kennedy Onassis' husband was assassinated when the Sun was at twenty-nine Scorpio and twenty-seven minutes. Her natal Sun is 05 Leo 09. The distance between the two Suns is a little over 114 degrees. Between 90 and 120 degrees, her monthly profection would be *four* zoidia from the places of her yearly profections.

The yearly handing over for the Ascendant was to Mars in the Eleventh place. Four places from the Eleventh - the eleventh being "number one" - is the Second, which Saturn inhabits. In November 1963, Mars was the yearly and Saturn the monthly profection for her Ascendant.

The yearly handing over for the Moon in Aries is to Saturn, ruling and transiting Aquarius. Her monthly profection, four zoidia from Aquarius is Gemini, where one finds Venus and Jupiter in the place of death.

The Sun, Midheaven, Mercury, and the Lot of Fortune hand over to Venus and Jupiter in the Eighth for the year. Four zoidia from the Eighth is the Eleventh, inhabited by Mars. Here we see interplay between both malefics and her Venus and Jupiter in the Eighth.

Now we examine the procedure Ptolemy uses for monthly profections. Ptolemy uses "months" that are twenty-eight days long. This at first seems odd to the modern reader but there is an interesting rationale. Twenty-eight days correspond to the time of the Moon's passage through the zodiac, but that does not seem to be Ptolemy's reasoning.

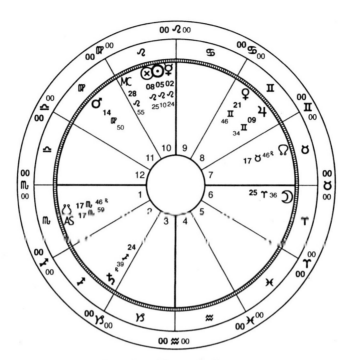

Jaqueline Kennedy Onassis

Divide the days in a year by twenty-eight and you get thirteen. Put another way, thirteen twenty-eight day months is 364 days, a day and a quarter short of a year. At first this doesn't seem to help matters much, yet it leads to an interesting and elegant system.

For the *first* twenty-eight day month, the zoidion of the monthly profection is the same as the yearly profection, and each month one advances one zoidion. At the *last* twenty-eight-day month of the year, the monthly profected zoidion returns to the first one. This means that at the time of one's birthday, the yearly and monthly profected zoidion will both be one zoidion ahead of the yearly and monthly profection of the previous year. In this way, without any discontinuity, yearly and monthly profections coincide at the beginning of each year. This requires that each year be divided into thirteen units of twenty-eight days each.

We have seen the same logic in the dodekatamoria, or "twelfth-parts" or thirteenth harmonic, which we discussed at the end of Chapter Three. In this system, the first and last segments of each zoidion are the zoidion itself.

This device, as counterintuitive as it may seem, had an intellectual attractiveness, but one that needs to be borne out in practice.

For Jacqueline Kennedy Onassis, her twenty-eight day months are as follows. They would be the case for every year of her life.

1. July 28 (her birthday)
2. August 25
3. September 22
4. October 20
5. November 17 (before November 22)
6. December 15
7. January 12
8. February 9

13. June 29

November 22 is within the *fifth month*, not the fourth. These two systems will frequently give different results.

In this monthly division, the Moon, handing off to Saturn in its yearly profection, hands over to Venus and Jupiter in the Eighth. This gives us a simple picture of the death of her husband. Twenty-eight-day monthly profections also help explain Jacqueline's social apotheosis following her husband's assassination. For the yearly profection, Venus and Jupiter hand off to the Moon in the Sixth. Five zoidia from the Sixth gives us the Tenth, where we find Sun, Moon, Mercury, and the Lot of Fortune.

In this example, one derives good information from both systems of months. I request that the reader use one of them and stay with it long enough to know whether it works for you or not.

Now we fast-forward to Jacqueline's marriage to Aristotle Onassis, which occurred on October 20, 1968. If losing her husband made Jacqueline Kennedy an international icon, marrying the older shipping tycoon brought her heightened criticism and negative scrutiny.

Marrying Aristotle Onassis, regardless of how long he would live, would also make Jacqueline Kennedy wealthy for the rest of her life. By 1968, when the United States was experiencing difficult times, she also wanted to get out of the country.

Mrs. Onassis-to-be was in her fortieth year and her profections for the year would be four zoidia. Mercury, Sun, Midheaven, and Lot of Fortune advances to Scorpio, governed by Mars. Importantly, while the marriage was first made official, Venus had been transiting Scorpio. Here we see the content of her fame and personal notoriety - matters of love and marriage.

The Moon in Aries handed over to the Moon, lady of Cancer. Moon represents partnerships. Importantly, Saturn was also transiting her natal Moon in Aries. This could imply marrying somebody who was older, or indicate a difficult and restrictive marriage. The universe seemed to have chosen both possibilities.

Venus and Jupiter hand over to Mars in the Eleventh. Mars could indicate that the marriage would be a stormy one. It also suggests that Jacqueline marrying Onassis was as much an act of defiance as agreeing to a real relationship of marriage. This preponderance of malefics would make any astrologer advise Jacqueline Kennedy to be careful.

Both thirty-day and twenty-eight-day monthly profections give us the same result. October 20 is the first day of her fourth twenty-eight day month.

The clearest indicator that this marriage was an unwise move is from the yearly handing over of Venus and Jupiter in Gemini to Mars in Virgo. Mars, the lord of yearly profection, hands over to Saturn in Sagittarius for the monthly profection. Again we see the two malefics in control.

We see Saturn again with the monthly profections of Sun, Mercury, Midheaven, and Lot of Fortune in the Tenth. The yearly profection is to the Ascendant in Scorpio, governed by Mars. For the monthly profection, four zoidia from Scorpio brings us to Aquarius, governed by Saturn and opposite her positions in the Tenth. Onassis' fall in public acclaim brought down the meteoric rise that had accompanied her first husband's assassination.

We now note Churchill's monthly profections for his election defeat and for his Iron Curtain speech less than a year later. Valens' method of thirty-day months would give monthly profections of eight zoidia for Churchill's election defeat. The fourth degree of Leo - the Sun's position in July 1945 - is eight zoidia from his natal Sun at eighth degree Sagittarius.

Here are Ptolemy's months for Churchill, and July 26 would be nine zoidia away from the yearly profection for the monthly profection.

1. November 30
2. December 28
3. January 25
4. February 22
5. March 22
6. April 19
7. May 17
8. June 14
9. July 12
10. August 9
11. September 6
12. October 4
13. November 1

I will confine myself to these monthly profections of nine zoidia. Churchill's yearly profection for 1945 is eleven zoidia. Ascendant, Jupiter, and Mars hand off to Moon in Leo for the year. Nine zoidia from Leo gives us Aries, governed by Mars. The Midheaven hands off to Venus, the lady of Taurus. Nine zoidia from Taurus give us Capricorn, the house of Saturn.

In Churchill's monthly profections for a difficult moment in his life, the malefics are strongly involved. Another signal event in Churchill's life was his "Iron Curtain" speech. Because he was born in late November, most of 1946 would contain profections of twelve zoidia. Valens' and Ptolemy's

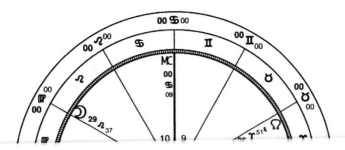

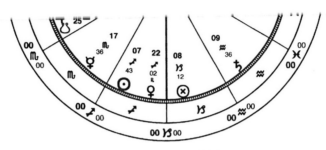

Winston Churchill

techniques of monthly profections coincide here and give monthly profections of four zoidia for early March 1946.

Monthly profections show Saturn and Mercury dominating, ably assisted by Jupiter. We know that Churchill was far more popular abroad than at home, and that he had continued to be controversial. We also know that speaking and writing was his occupation as a wartime politician out of office, and no words he penned or spoke at that time were more important than his "Iron Curtain" speech.

- Mercury's yearly profections go to Ascendant, Mars, and Jupiter in Libra, which is helped by *transiting* Jupiter. Monthly profections from Libra go to Capricorn, domicile of Saturn and inhabited by the Lot of Fortune.

- The Sun and Venus in Sagittarius hand off to Mercury in Scorpio for yearly profections. Four zoidia from Scorpio gives us Aquarius again and more Saturn. This adds a sobering and melancholy tone.

- The Midheaven in Cancer hands off to Mercury, lord of Gemini. Four zoidia from Gemini is Virgo, the domicile of Mercury. This suits a person whose public contribution was to be a speaker and writer.

- The Moon in Leo hands off to Cancer. Four zoidia from Cancer brings us again to Libra, inhabited by Ascendant, Mars, and Jupiter, and transited to by Jupiter.

- The Ascendant, Mars, and Jupiter hand off to Mercury for the year, as Mercury is the lord of Virgo. Four zoidia away from Virgo is Sagittarius, happily inhabited by Sun and Venus. This is positive for Churchill maintaining his stature as a post-war leader.

Afterword:
George W. Bush's Terrible Year (from mid-2005)

In 2005, a year being re-elected for another four-term as President, George W. Bush and his administration encountered one difficulty after another. Any astrologer's curiosity would be aroused by such a turn of events for him.

I sense that his problems began soon after his birthday in July 2005, and the remainder of 2005 was just terrible for him.

August 2005 featured a camp-in by Cindy Sheehan, who had lost a son in Iraq, nearby Bush's ranch in Texas. Instead of being a minor nuisance, Ms. Sheehan's activity received international attention.

At the end of August, Hurricane Katrina arrived in Mississippi and Louisiana, flooding New Orleans. His administration's non-response illuminated issues of cronyism, incompetence, as well as policy and personal indifference to poor people. For Bush and his administration, Katrina was an administrative and public relations disaster.

Following this were criminal charges made against Vice President Chaney's Chief of Staff, "Scooter" Libby. In November 2005, the first members of Congress began to advocate a speedy withdrawal of American forces from Iraq. Toward the end of the year came the disclosure of a warrant-less wiretapping program. We begin with transits occurring at the beginning of his difficulties.

Saturn entered Leo on July 16, 2005, soon after his birthday. If we include the fact that Mars entered Taurus and his Tenth place, on July 28 - just before Bush returned to Texas for a dismal summer vacation - transits of the malefics give us some timing for his current difficulties. His profections would set up these transits to be so difficult for him.

Bush turned fifty-nine in July 2005; for our purposes we think of the year being his sixtieth. Subtract from sixty the next lowest multiple of twelve (48) and the number of his profection for this year is twelve. His Leo Ascendant advances into Cancer, Sun and Saturn in Cancer advance to Gemini, and so on. The Lots of Spirit and Exaltation are in Taurus. Here we will advance the two major lots:

Bush's Lot of Fortune in Scorpio advances by profection twelve zoidia to his Moon and Jupiter in Libra. Jupiter also had been transiting through this zoidion. The Lot of Fortune signifies money and health and also the ingredient of luck in one's life. This is a positive development for him; it does not explain his current difficulties.

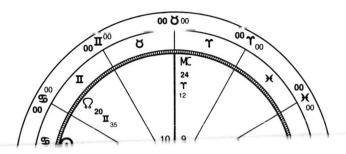

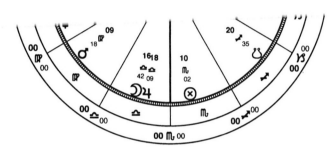

George W. Bush

Moon and Jupiter themselves have moved by profection to Virgo wherein lies Mars. If Moon and Jupiter present themselves in Bush's life as emotional confidence and a positive outlook, the profection to Mars is more like landing on a land mine. This gives us our first indication of difficulties.

Advancing Mars in Virgo twelve zoidia, we find ourselves with the Ascendant, Mercury, and Venus in Leo. These two planets with his Ascendant point to Bush's interpersonal savvy and persuasiveness. Advancing Mars - the malefic out of sect in his diurnal natal chart - to this position brings increased conflict and hostility. Venus and Mercury take up the matters of Mars, which can be quite forceful and directed. During this time, however, Saturn has been transiting through Leo. Mars by profection combines with Saturn by transit to make a rather nasty storm on his usually beneficial Ascendant-Mercury-Venus configuration. Mars may present itself as Bush taking up a fighting stance to force Congress and public opinion to go along with his agenda. Transiting Saturn, however, puts a leaden weight on this activity. As a result, Bush loses his credibility with the American people. In Bush's public appearances of that time we have seen the action of two malefics on the place of his Ascendant.

If we advance Bush's Ascendant-Mercury-Venus combination in Leo we are with the Sun and Saturn in Cancer in the Twelfth. This has the feel of stepping onto a bear trap.

In Taurus, the Tenth place from Bush's Ascendant, is his Lot of Spirit and his Lot of Exaltation. Ordinarily these are very strong and positive influences in Bush's chart. Venus, governing these

Lots and the Midheaven, is angular to the Ascendant and also to the Lots of Fortune and Spirit..

By profection the Lot of Spirit moves to Aries. Mars governs Aries, so that by profection Mars also influences the zoidion of his Midheaven and Lot of Spirit and Exaltation.

It is here that we must consider Mars transiting through Taurus - Bush's Tenth. Mars crossed into Taurus at the end of July 2005, at the beginning of Bush's many difficulties. Mars then went retrograde on the first day of October, went direct on December 10, and finally left Taurus in February 2006.

By transit and by profection, Mars has much influence on critical positions in Bush's natal chart:

- *Mars* profects to Ascendant, Mercury, and Venus.

- The Lot of Spirit advances to Aries, which is governed by *Mars*.

- Transiting *Mars* moves through the zoidion of both the Lot of Spirit and Exaltation.

- Venus in the First governs these Lots, and Venus receives the profection of *Mars*.

Mars signifies not only oppositions and conflict but, as Mars is involved with both the Ascendant and the Lot of Spirit, by profection and by transit, one must consider the manner in which Mr. Bush would address his situation. Transiting Mars over his Tenth brings Mars out more prominently and publicly. This tempts one into a fighting response even when such a response is counterproductive.

Since Bush's Lot of Spirit pertains to what he does on his own, his response, influenced by Mars, has been one of stubborn defiance. Mars transiting the zoidion of his Lot of Exaltation symbolizes that he was fighting to rescue his diminishing standing with just about everybody.

One might have predicted difficulties in the previous year, from his birthday in 2004 until his birthday in 2005. That year his profections were eleven zoidia.

Eleven zoidia from Bush's Mars in Virgo is Cancer, where we find Bush's Sun and Saturn and, during that year, Saturn also transiting Cancer. Based on this feature alone, one would expect that year to be difficult. Not only did political disaster elude Bush but he was re-elected President. There are many positive conditions to account for this.

Moon and Jupiter in Libra advanced to his Ascendant-Mercury-Venus combination. This is wholly positive.

Sun and Saturn in Cancer profected to Taurus, inhabited by the Lots of Spirit and Exaltation. This is a mixed blessing, as it does show limitation due to the profection of Saturn. Venus in the First, governing Taurus, does come to the rescue. Even with the presence of Saturn on his profected Tenth and transiting through the zoidion of his Sun and Saturn in Cancer, Bush overcame his many detractors where it counted: he did well enough with the public to be re-elected.

Nor was there the duration of Mars' negative influence during the year. It is indeed the Mars transit in Taurus that rendered the second half of 2005 so utterly difficult for President Bush.

Having toured transits and profections, we go further into foreign territory in the next chapter, where we discuss predictive systems based upon planetary lords or *chronocrators*.

13

PLANETARY TIME LORD SYSTEMS

...... feature or ancient predictive systems that is most foreign to modern astrology: systems of planetary periods. Ancient astrologers used sequences of planetary time lords or *chronocrators* to predict events and trends within a person's life. Although an important feature in Indian astrology, or Jyotish, these systems have not been in use in western astrology since the medieval era.

In this chapter we focus on one system called "decennials," a version of which survived into the medieval era. We will practice calculating decennials and interpreting them. This ancient predictive system uses the planets to denote both larger spans of time and the smaller periods nested within them. An examination of decennials will give you the means by which to examine the other planetary period systems that will conclude this chapter.

In this chapter we will do some of the basic calculations that are required for planetary time lord systems. These techniques are currently under-represented in today's astrology computer programs, so this chapter provides the interested reader with the tools required for working independently with these important predictive techniques. [1]

Why would modern astrologers want to investigate and possibly to adopt predictive systems based upon planetary lords?

- They allow us to see more clearly how modern astrologers use time and number differently from our ancient ancestors. Temporarily side-stepping our habitual prejudices of mind, we can open ourselves to possibilities that other astrological traditions can offer us.

- They may enable us to see more clearly the connection between a planet's functioning in a natal chart and its use in prediction. Time lords no longer seem like planetary energies intruding upon a person's life as if from the outside. Indeed, one function of planetary period systems is to determine *when* a feature in the natal chart will actualize itself in a person's life.

---

1. A notable exception is *Delphic Oracle*, developed by Curt Manwaring. I have used this program for the information through this and the next chapter. See http://www.astrology-x-files.com/news/. As of of 2008, Kepler Astrology Software includes Hellenistic material.. See http://www.patterns.com/

- The astrologer may find that one of these systems, or one in combination with others, provides good information about one's life and those of others. This has certainly happened in my practice.

Ptolemy's Planetary Ages of a Person and the Numbers of the Planets

Earlier we discussed Ptolemy's seven stages of human development that correspond to the seven visible planets. You may remember that a specific number was used for each planet that would correspond to years of life.

Ptolemy's system of planetary ages is a rudimentary system of planetary periods, based on the general qualities of the seven planets: only one planet is used for an era of life, and there is no variation from person to person regarding the lengths of planetary periods or when they change.

- **Moon** governs the first age of life, corresponding to infancy and toddler-hood. The Moon's period is **four years**.

- **Mercury** governs the next **ten** years, to age fourteen. This corresponds to one's school years.

- **Venus** governs the adolescent years, **eight** years in all, bringing the person to twenty-two years.

- **Sun** is in charge of the following **nineteen** years, the prime of life, that brings us to age forty-one.

- **Mars** governs the following **fifteen** years, which is a time of greater strain and strife. This carries one to age fifty-six.

- **Jupiter,** governing the **twelve** years following Mars, brings some of the wisdom that comes with experience. At the end, one is sixty-eight.

- **Saturn** governs the **final years** of one's life. Saturn is old age and the withering of life up to the time of death.

All the planets have numbers assigned to them. In fact, these numbers are part of the natures of the different planets. That a planet can have the nature of a number is a notion that does not appear in modern astrology.

I now add another set of numbers for the seven planets that we will use throughout this chapter. These numbers can represent years, months, or days and can manifest as whole numbers or as fractions. They give proportions to designate for how long the individual planets share time within a larger span of time. Robert Hand states that the ancients derived these numbers from the repetitions of planetary conjunctions with the Sun (or synods) that occur within whole numbers of years.[2] The numbers of years that correspond to these conjunctions become the years of the planets.

---

2.   Editor's Introduction: Valens, *Anthology: Book II* (conclusion.) & *Book III* (1994).

- **Saturn's number is thirty.** Every thirty years there are twenty-nine conjunctions of Sun and Saturn.

- **Jupiter's number is twelve.** This is not because it takes twelve years for Jupiter to go through the zodiac - the sidereal cycle - but that there are eleven conjunctions with the Sun every twelve years.

- **Mars' number is fifteen.** During fifteen years of 365 days each, there are seven conjunctions of Mars and the Sun.

- **Venus' number is eight.** In exactly every eight years, there are five Venus-Sun conjunctions, if you note direct and retrograde conjunctions separately. If you plotted these successive positions on a circle and traced lines between them, you would have a five-pointed star. Plotting the longitudes of Venus' direct or retrograde stations separately give a five-pointed star in an eight-year span.

- **Mercury's number is twenty.** In twenty 365-day years there are sixty-three Sun-Mercury conjunctions.

- **Moon's number is twenty-five.** In twenty-five 365-day years, there are 309 conjunctions of Sun and Moon.

(Perhaps it is a reflection of life's unfairness that the malefic Saturn has the longest time allotted and the benefics Jupiter and Venus have the shortest. There is an additional set of numbers that reverses this trend: unfortunately this set is used to help determine the length of a person's life!) These numbers, added together, yield 129. The total number will be important in a moment.

Decennials as as Example of a Time Lord System

Decennials are mentioned in the writings of Valens, Hephaistio, and Firmicus. Because they appear in Firmicus, who wrote in Latin, decennials survived into the medieval era of Europe. At first glance the system of decennials seems almost as simple as Ptolemy's seven planetary ages, except that it uses sub-periods and thus two planets instead of one.

Although the name "decennials" refers to the number ten, the larger span of time is not exactly ten. Each person has a general planetary period of ten years and nine months, each governed by a *general time lord*. Ten years and nine months add up to 129 months, the total number of the seven planets. One usually begins with the Sun or Moon. At the end of the span of the ten years and nine months, the following planet in the zodiac takes over as general time lord.

At the beginning of a general time period, a second planet, a *specific time lord*, is the same as the general time lord. That specific planet's period will last until the *months* corresponding to the planet's number have elapsed. If one has just begun a general period of 10 years 9 months governed by Jupiter, the first 12 months - corresponding to the number of Jupiter - belongs to the planet as the specific time lord. Then the following planet in the chart, in the order of the zodiac, takes over as specific time lord, which will last as many months as that planet's number. This continues until all seven planets have taken their turns as specific time lords. Then one begins a new general period. Here is an expanded example:

> If one enters a Moon period, Moon is the general time lord for ten years and nine months. For the first twenty-five months of that time (corresponding to the Moon's number), Moon is also the specific time lord: this is a Moon/Moon period.

> If the planet following Moon in Aries is Jupiter in Gemini, the Moon's period as specific time lord changes after 25 months to Jupiter for 12 months: this becomes a Moon/Jupiter period.

> After these twelve months, the next planet in the zodiac, perhaps Venus in Libra, takes over as specific time lord for eight months: this is now a Moon/Venus period.

> This continues for the remaining planets until 129 months have elapsed. Then one begins with the next ten year nine month period, during which time Jupiter in Gemini is general time lord.

> An older person could complete all seven general periods of seven segments of ten years and nine months each. One then returns to the beginning planet and continues.

We now entertain our first factor of complexity: *from which planet do you begin at the time of birth?* Firmicus writes that for a night birth one begins with the Moon and for a day birth one begins with the Sun. However, both Hephaistio and Valens say that the beginning place, the releaser or *aphesis*, must be effectively placed in the natal chart.

Hephaistio writes that if the luminary of sect is unconnected to the Ascendant, instead use a planet that is in an angular place. (He does not tell us what to do if we have two angular planets or no angular planet.)

Valens says that if the Sun in a day chart or the Moon is not favorably placed relative to the Ascendant - in a cadent or place unconnected to the Ascendant - one should use the other luminary. If neither luminary is in an effective place, use the first planet that rises after the time of birth.

In all cases, once we have determined the beginning planet, we proceed through the other planets in their zodiacal order from that planet.

George W. Bush has a day chart with Sun in Cancer in the Twelfth. Bush's Moon is in the cadent Third. To begin Bush's decennials, Hephaistio and Valens would use Mercury in the First, then proceed to Venus, and so on. For our purposes here, I will follow Valens: if the luminary of sect is not well placed, we first look to the other luminary. If this is not well placed either, one begins with the planet that rose first after the time of birth.

Our second complexity is this: *what is the length of a year and a month?* As we know, our standard months are uneven and arranged according to convention. "Thirty days have September..." As months relate to the Moon, one could justify using months of either twenty-eight or thirty days. Twenty-eight days is the return of the Moon from one degree of the zodiac to the same degree. Each thirty days there is one complete cycle of the Moon and Sun together: this justifies a thirty-day month. These cycles also vary from month to month - twelve "months" of thirty-days is a year of *360 days*, five and one quarter days shorter than the solar year. Interestingly, the Egyptians, who may have originated some ancient predictive systems, did use a "year" of 360 days and added five intercalary days to keep the cycles right.

Firmicus does not mention years of either 365.25 or 360 days for decennials. *Both Hephaistio and Valens are clear that for decennials a "year" is 360 days.* As strange as this seems, this is how one

time and change, human time may be more appropriately the Moon's domain, not that of the Sun. One also finds the Moon used as a marker for timekeeping and prediction within Indian and Tibetan astrological systems.

I have seen again and again that planetary period systems using 360-day years give good results, even better than when using a conventional year. The argument against using a 360-day system is that it makes our calculations more complicated. Doubtless a skilled ancient astrologer could have performed these calculations flawlessly, but fortunately we can resort to calculators and astrological software.[3]

To convert my conventional age into 360-day years I have to do some simple arithmetic. If I am about to turn 50 in solar years, I have to multiply 50 by 5.25, the difference between the solar year and the 360-day year. I get 262.5. My conventional fiftieth birthday was therefore 263 days *after* I would have been "50" by means of years. My birthday in 360-day years would be 263 days *before* my conventional fiftieth.

Using the 360-day year for decennials, here is the age at which everybody changes general time lords.[4]

10 years	218 days:	ends the first planet
21 years	70 days:	ends the second planet
31 years	287 days:	ends the third planet
42 years	140 days:	ends the fourth planet
52 years	357 days:	ends the fifth planet
63 years	209 days:	ends the sixth planet

---

3.   *Delphic Oracle*, designed by Curt Manwaring, calculates decennials and other planetary period systems using either conventional years or 360-day years, so one can compare results. See http://www.astrology-x-files.com/news/

4.   Here is the procedure. The total days of a general period are 3870. (30-day months times 129 months) Divide 3870 by 365.25 days in a solar year. For the first period the result is 10.595. To find out how many days correspond to .525, multiply that number by 365.25. The days come to 217.32 days. I round *up* to make 218 days. For subsequent general periods, multiply 3870 by the number of the period and continue as above.

74 years   62 days: ends the seventh planet and we return to the first planet
84 years   279 days: ends the first planet, and so on.

Using a 360-day year instead of the solar year is similar to learning how to drive using a car with a standard transmission, with a clutch and stick shift, as opposed to the more common automatic transmissions. Initially the standard transmission is more difficult but in time one becomes accustomed to it and it becomes natural - even preferable.

At the end of this chapter I provide an illustration of calculating decennials, using Martha Stewart's chart. I also supply a chart to convert days of the years to numbers for finding the appropriate day in a person's life.

Interpreting Planetary Periods

In order to interpret planetary periods, we need to bring together both general and specific time lords. How do they influence each other; how do they together carry responsibility for the times?

In explaining the distinction between general and specific time lords, one could use ideas like "form" and "matter" or "background" and "foreground." I prefer an analogy from how modern sports teams are managed. At the top of a sport team's organizational chart we find the *owner*, the CEO, and the chief executive officers of a team. This is the person ultimately responsible for the team. The executive level is the overall life of the native. Below the top of the organization is the *general manager*, whose decisions give the team its general outlook and strategy and who sets the roster of players. However, the general manager does not manage the team directly. Hired and fired by the general manager is the *field manager* or *head coach*, who prepares the team and makes the immediate decisions on the field.

The general manager is like the *general time lord*, the planet who, for decennials, reigns for 129 thirty-day months. The field manager or head coach is the second or *specific time lord*, who, in the case of decennials, reigns for as many months as is the number of that planet. The general time lord sets the tone and the specific lord makes the game decisions. (The system of decennials gives us not only sub-periods governed by second-order particular planetary lords but smaller sub-periods within, governed by third-order and even fourth-order planetary lords. These *particular time lords* would be like the coaches who assist the field manager to work with particular situations. We will look at these time lords below.)

It is clear from both Firmicus and Hephaistio that the *specific* planetary lord - the field manager - carries more responsibility for the quality of a time in a person's life. In decennials, the general planetary lord governs for a long time. The specific lord governs the shorter-term changes that are more obvious to us.

Both Firmicus and Hephaistio give delineations for combinations of general and specific planetary time lords[5]. Some but not all the important criteria should be familiar to you from previous

---

5.   See Hephaistio, Book II, Chapters 29-36 and Firmicus, Book VI, Chapters 34-39.

sections. How do we assess a planetary lord and whether that planet will bring the native advantage or disadvantage? Here are some important factors:

- Whether the *sect* of the time lord is the same as the chart as a whole. This is especially the case with the malefics Mars and Saturn, whose sect condition may dramatically alter their virtue for the native.

- If the planet is in a *fortunate or unfortunate place* with regard to the Ascendant,

.... presages a better outcome for the native. This is also true for Mercury and Venus.

- Whether the Moon in the natal chart is *waxing or waning*. Simply put, waxing is better.

- Both authors deem *Sun* periods difficult, as if there's too much energy or activity.

Our first example is that of America's "domestic diva," **Martha Stewart**. We are interested in Ms. Stewart's fall from grace in 2004, when she was convicted and later jailed and put under home

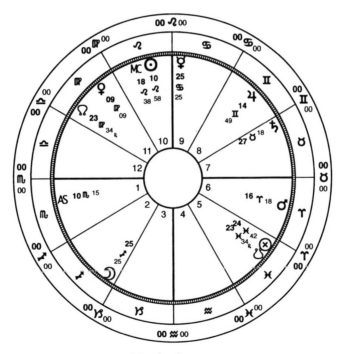

Martha Stewart

confinement for obstruction of justice. We are also interested in the events that lead up to this change of circumstance for her. What do decennials tell us about this turn of events? The first order of business is to list the planets in the order in which they would change for yearly and monthly decennials. For Martha Stewart they are as follows:

Sun-Venus-Moon-Mars-Saturn-Jupiter-Mercury

What are the general chronocrators for her at different ages? We return to the list of general time lord changes for everybody. This is where we would begin:

10 years	218 days:	ends the first planet
21 years	70 days:	ends the second planet
31 years	207 days:	ends the third planet
42 years	140 days:	ends the fourth planet
52 years	357 days:	ends the fifth planet
63 years	209 days:	ends the sixth planet
74 years	62 days:	ends the seventh planet and back to the first planet
84 years	279 days:	ends the first planet

During the 1980s, Stewart's years of greatest corporate growth, when *Martha Stewart Living* and her product line became public, the general time lord - the general manager - was Saturn. This might be a surprise until one looks at this planet in her chart: Saturn is in sect and oriental to the Sun. Saturn is angular but in the more ambiguous Seventh place, opposing the zoidion of the Ascendant. In Taurus, Saturn is in a trine position with the lord of Taurus, Venus in Virgo in the Eleventh. This can denote a relatively positive time for her. Specific planetary lords will indicate the ups and downs within that larger time.

During much of the time of her expanding prosperity, her specific time lords were Venus and Moon. Venus is in fall in Virgo but in the prestigious Eleventh zoidion from the Ascendant, and has an aspect from Jupiter in Gemini. Venus is also angular to Stewart's Lot of Fortune in Pisces and also her Lot of Spirit in Gemini. Moon is out of sect like Venus but is waxing, which is more positive than a waning Moon. Within the general times governed by Saturn, these times are favorable for her.

The general period of Jupiter began in July 1994. Like Saturn, Jupiter is in sect in Stewart's day chart. Although Jupiter is oriental, its position in the Eighth zoidion from the Ascendant and in Gemini - opposite its own zoidion - renders a Jupiter period productive but with some problems. That Jupiter is in the same zoidion as the Lot of Spirit strengthens Jupiter's importance and reinforces Stewart's tendency to take the initiative - perhaps to be dictatorial - in all matters.

Stewart's problems began in the late autumn of 2001 when, after some discussions with her stockbroker, she began to sell remaining shares of stock, allegedly benefiting from illegal insider trading. (She was later convicted of lying about these transactions to federal authorities.) At that time, the general time lord Jupiter had *Mars* as specific lord, its "field manager." Stewart's Mars is in his own house in Aries but is out of sect. Mars is the lord of Stewart's Scorpio Ascendant but it is in the cadent Sixth. Mars, carrying the water for Jupiter, has the tendency to be excessive or rash, especially when out of sect. Hephaistio likens a Jupiter-Mars period with Mars out of sect to "random rumors about oneself, suspense and fear and unemployment." I find this fitting in the context of events in Stewart's life during this time.

The transits of the time supply us with further indication of difficulty. Transiting Saturn was in Gemini, the zoidion of Stewart's general time lord Jupiter. When Stewart was interviewed by federal authorities and was apparently deceiving them, transiting Mars was in Aries, in the same

judge dismissed the most serious charges against her for lack of evidence. Although Jupiter/Saturn would promote reputation and alliance (says Hephaistio), Saturn can be confining. Stewart had made such grievous errors previously that Saturn's role was to manifest their repercussions. She even rejected a plea bargain that would have only given her probation. Instead Stewart chose to go to trial, was found guilty and was sentenced to prison.

As Stewart's Saturn specific period continued, she went to jail to serve a six-month sentence. By the time of her release in 2005, Mercury was the general and specific time lord. Mercury in Cancer is oriental and in sect in Stewart's chart, and this general time would be better for her. However, transiting Saturn continues in Cancer, pressing down upon Mercury. Since her prison sentence was followed by six months of home confinement, the Saturn influence would continue to be felt. After transiting Saturn went into Leo, she was released from home confinement.

We next look at the decennials for **George W. Bush**. As mentioned above, we cannot use the Sun as the beginning general time lord - the "releaser" - since his Sun is in the Twelfth zoidion from the Ascendant. Moon is also cadent but in a "good decline" and in the Moon's joy. Nonetheless, following Valens, cadent Moon is excluded. This brings us to Mercury, the first planet to rise after Bush was born. It is a strong planet in the First, although occidental and out of sect.

I begin in the mid-1980s. Bush had been in a Moon period for most of that decade. During a Moon/Mercury period, Bush stopped drinking, joined a Bible study group, and turned his life around. It is interesting that his religious conversion took place during the time when the lords of the Third and First places were general and specific planetary lords.[6]

The general period of Jupiter began in late 1988, after his father was elected President. This period brought Bush the son into a national stage. George W. Bush was elected governor of Texas in the mid 1990's, during a Jupiter/Mercury period.

His run for presidency and his two terms as President all took place within a general period governed by Sun. Although Sun is a proper planet to be general time lord when one is a national leader, his Sun in the Twelfth with Saturn is not particularly well placed. His disputed election

6.   See Chapter 7 for a discussion of Bush and his significators of religious practice.

occurred in the last months of Sun/Sun. Two weeks before his inauguration, Sun now had Saturn as specific planetary lord. Sun/Saturn continued until a few months after the invasion of Iraq, when Mercury took over from Saturn. Specific periods of Mercury seem to work out well for Bush, for during this time he was re-elected.

Bush began his second term with Sun/Venus. Since Venus, the specific lord, is in the First with a fine aspect from Jupiter and none from Mars or Saturn, this could have been a high water mark as President. Problems accumulated afterwards when Mars took over as specific planetary lord; Mars is a difficult planet in Bush's chart. Sun/Mars continued to mid-January, 2007. Moon then became his specific time lord for the rest of his term. The Sun/Moon period will take him well past his Presidency; depending on other factors, things may improve for him.

Having mentioned George Bush, I cannot resist bringing in **John Kerry**, Bush's 2004 presidential opponent. Kerry had Mercury as his general time lord from 1996 past the 2004 Presidential election. Mercury is occidental and in sect in his nocturnal chart, but in the mediocre Second. It is also strongly connected to his many planets and the Lots of Fortune and Spirit in Gemini.

Before the spring of 2004, however, his specific time lord was Saturn, making Mercury/Saturn. This brings him some problems, mitigated by the close relationship between Mercury and Saturn in his natal chart. It may also signal Kerry's early campaign and the perception of him as dry, tedious, and boring. Aided by Saturn's perseverance (and a great deal of his own money,) Kerry was able to win important primaries.

In April 2004, Jupiter took over from Saturn as his specific time lord, making Mercury/Jupiter. Hephaistio tells us that this combination, by day or night, can indicate a fine time. Firmicus tells us it's a "quiet time, free from all disturbances." Somebody clearly forgot to tell that to Mr. Kerry.

Being his specific time lord, Kerry's Jupiter in Leo in the Ninth was of greater advantage to him than was Saturn. Being nominated to run for President and running a national campaign is of the nature of Jupiter. That Jupiter is out of sect, and that Bush's indicators were better, contributed to his losing cause.

I continue with **Jacqueline Kennedy Onassis**. A general period of Moon began shortly after she moved into the White House in 1961. This does not portend happy times for her, as Moon is in the Sixth, out of sect, and is waning. Oddly, the specific time lord was Jupiter at the time of her husband's assassination in 1963, making for Moon/Jupiter. This should have indicated better times for her; Jupiter, however, is in the Eighth place from the Ascendant, squared by Mars and opposed by Saturn, and could not deliver personal happiness to her. She achieved prominence and public stature - conforming to the nature of the great benefic - during a personally catastrophic time.

Five years later she married Aristotle Onassis. Moon continued as the general planetary lord, but now Mars was the specific time lord. Out of sect in her diurnal chart, the fiery planet is also occidental. Moon/Mars repeats much of the same symbolism as provided by Mars in her profections and transits at this time: her decision to marry Onassis was defiant and impulsive.

Now we examine the decennials for **Winston Churchill**. I begin with his terrible year of 1915. By the beginning of the First World War, oriental Mercury was Churchill's general planetary time lord and Moon was his specific lord, making for Mercury/Moon. This pairing does not seem terribly significant for him.

In February 1915, however, during the ill-fated Dardenelles campaign, Mars took over as specific time lord from the Moon. Mercury/Mars governed until April of the following year. Mars gives us a sense of his mission in wartime but not its outcome. Hephaistio says that there could be difficulties, losses and accusations during this time but, in a nocturnal chart, the native would probably escape the worst. Churchill's public standing did slide precipitously but h~ ~~~~~~~ ~ ~~~~~ ~ ~

~~~~ ~ ~~~~~~~~~~~ ~ ~ ~~~~~~ ~~~~~~~~~~~ without that, Saturn would defeat what may have been otherwise an inspired military strategy.

We return to Churchill's becoming Prime Minister during the Second World War. From 1938 Churchill's general time lord had been Saturn, taking over from Venus. Because Saturn's number of thirty is quite large, this planet was also the specific one - for thirty "months" - into 1941.

Saturn/Saturn was in place when Churchill took over as England's Prime Minister. Saturn seems not to describe becoming a nations' leader; it well describes the difficulty of his task. Saturn is out of sect but is in its own house in Aquarius and is in the positive Fifth place from the Ascendant. Saturn was also prominent in his profection. The reader may also remember that Saturn was also Churchill's third triplicity lord, corresponding to the last third of his life.

From early 1943 until the spring of 1945, Churchill's specific time lords were Mars and then Jupiter, both of which are in his First. During this reversal of the allies' fortunes, Jupiter, not Saturn, was transiting Churchill's Tenth. This is an appropriate sequence for a successful war leader: Mars can help the native when undertaking an activity - like being at war - consonant with its nature. By the end of Jupiter being a specific planetary lord (although transiting Jupiter had moved on,) victory was all but assured. These years toward the end of the war conformed to the period when Churchill held greatest stature as a war hero and world statesman.

Churchill's removal from office occurred as the time for Mars and Jupiter as specific time lords ended. The conclusion of the European Second World War in 1945 was signaled by Mercury taking over from Jupiter as specific time lord, making Saturn/Mercury. Mercury is oriental but afflicted by a square from Saturn. Firmicus describes Saturn/Mercury as reviving old quarrels. You may recall that during the Second World War Churchill governed a basically unified nation. With the prospect of victory looming, earlier political divisions were revived.

Saturn/Mercury continued through the time of Churchill's "Iron Curtain" speech and his ascension to the status of elder world statesman. It would be a few more years before he assumed governmental leadership again.

I continue with **Muhammad Ali**. On February 25, 1964, at the age of twenty-two, Muhammad Ali - then Cassius Clay - beat Sonny Liston and became world heavyweight champion. Venus had begun as his general planetary lord the year before. Usually one would not associate becoming

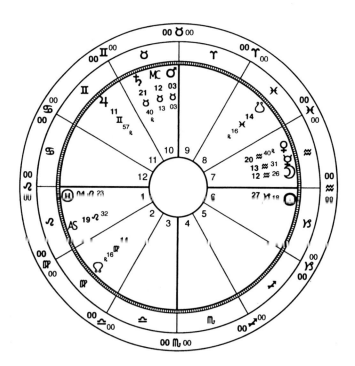

Muhammad Ali

boxing champion with a Venus general period - yet, when we consider that in the winter of 1964 the specific time lord was Mars, making for Venus/Mars, we may feel we're getting closer.

Venus, the general time lord, is in sect and angular but occidental. Venus is the lord of his Tenth place and is significant for matters of career. Venus is also in a dominating square to his planets in the Tenth, as the Seventh is the Tenth place from the Tenth.

Mars, the specific planetary lord during this time, is in the Tenth and is also in sect. You may remember Mars' prominence for determining career in Ali's chart. Yet this time is also conditioned by the presence of Saturn with his natal Mars.

He first angered the sports establishment by beating the reigning world champion and publicly gloating over it. He further angered the sports world - and many white fans - by acknowledging that he had converted to Islam. His name was changed to Muhammad Ali and he began to speak out on social and political issues. A few years later, after refusing to enter the Vietnam draft, Ali was stripped of his heavyweight title: this came at the end of a long Venus/Saturn period. As his is an evening chart, Saturn is out of sect and, with Saturn the specific planetary lord, Ali saw a diminishing of the fortunes that he had established during the Venus/Mars period.

Later still during the general Venus period, Ali returned to the ring. He had to start his boxing career over again, and when Mars took over from Venus as general time lord and was also the specific planetary lord, Ali's career resumed where he had left off. Ali first beat Joe Frazier and then George Foreman to regain his heavyweight title. Several years later, at the end of the general period of Mars, Ali retired, returned to the ring to fight a few times more, and then ended his boxing career.

It was during the next general period, governed by Saturn, that Ali was afflicted with Parkinson's disease and lost his speech. In 1995, however, Jupiter took over for Saturn as general time lord. Jupiter is in its joy in Ali's Eleventh zoidion. This period, which lasted until August 2005, enshrined Ali as a universally revered sports icon

manager and the specific time lord is like the field manager, *particular* lords constitute the coaching staff that work for the specific lord, the field manager.

One can subdivide specific planetary periods in two ways: for the particular time lords, Hephaistio and Valens give us one option and Valens mentions another. Both methods of time division have their attractions and their difficulties.

The 129-day alternative
The first method for the third-order particular time lords, mentioned only by Valens, divides each specific period into equal segments of 129 days each. Within these 129-day segments, each planet distributes days according to its number, e.g. Venus has eight days and Saturn thirty. This gives us a fourth order or *daily* time lord. This method has the disadvantage of giving unequal distributions of 129-day segments, depending on the length of the second-order or specific period. For example, at the end of a specific period for Venus (240 days or 8 months) or Mars (450 days or 15 months), the third and fourth levels, the particular and daily lords end without finishing the distribution of all seven planets.

To illustrate 129-day periods for particular and daily time lords, let us bring back **Muhammad Ali** for a rematch.

As stated above, when Clay became boxing champion and changed his name to Muhammad Ali, the general time lord was Venus and the specific (second-order) time lord was Mars. The championship fight was on February 25, 1964, and, soon afterwards, on March 6, Clay adopted the name given to him by Elijah Muhammad. The 129-day rotations began on November 24, 1963 and the first segment of 129 days brings us to April 2, 1964. Mars governs the third or "particular" division of Ali's decennials, making for this time Venus/Mars/Mars.

For that 129-day period of time, Mars itself was the fourth level or daily time lord from November 24 for 15 days, corresponding to Mars' number. This brings us to December 9.

- *Saturn* took over as daily time lord for the next thirty days, corresponding to Saturn's number. This brings us to January 8, 1964.

- *Jupiter* was the daily time lord for the following twelve days, taking us to January 20.

- *Sun* took over for the following nineteen days, up to February 8.

- Cassius Clay won the heavyweight championship when *Moon* was his daily time lord. During this important time his time lords were, in order of general/specific/particular/daily: Venus/Mars/Mars/Moon. All four planets are in sect in angular houses, all configured with one another: Venus and Moon are in square to Mars from the Seventh to the Tenth.

- On March 4, Mercury took over as daily time lord. Mercury, like Venus, is angular, and Mercury is the Moon's next application. Appropriately, during this period the name change was made public.

Beginning on April 1, the next 129-day segment has Saturn taking over from Mars as the third-order or particular time lord. On August 8, Jupiter took over from Saturn as the particular time lord. These cycles of 129 days (and within them the days of the planets) continue and abruptly stopped at the end of the Venus/Mars period. Then Ali's decennials became Venus-Saturn. The first 129-day period belonged to Saturn, and the first 30 days of that time also belonged to Saturn as the daily planetary lord.

The Proportional Alternative

Both Valens and Hephaistio give us the option of deriving proportions and using them for third and fourth order divisions. Although somewhat unwieldy, this method may give better results than the 129-day method described above. The idea is simple: if Saturn has a relatively large number compared with Mars or Venus, a particular Saturn period should reflect that larger number, and the particular periods of Mars and Venus should be smaller. In contrast, the 129-day method makes all the particular period the same length. How do we go about figuring this out? The steps are straightforward and very easy to reckon on a calculator:

1.   We begin with the numbers of each planet and add them up.
      [Saturn 30 + Jupiter 12 + Mars 15 + Sun 19 + Venus 8 + Mercury 20+ Moon 25 = 129]

2.   We then divide each planet's number into the total of 129 to get each planet's share of any length of time.
      [Saturn 23.26% + Jupiter 9.3% + Mars 11.63% + Sun 14.73 % + Venus 6.2% + Mercury 15.5%+ Moon 19.38% = 100%][7]

3.   Because each specific time lord is as many months as the planet's number, we multiply the planet's days of year by its percentage above to get how many days that planet is the third-

---

7.   (Another way is to divide the planets into which portions they each get of 360-day years. The percentages of the numbers of the planets to the total of 129 do not divide into whole days. Rounded off, the reckoning is as follows: [Saturn 84 + Jupiter 33 + Mars 42 + Sun 53 + Venus 22 + Mercury 56 + Moon 70 = 360].)

level of *particular* time lord. Here again, the proportions do not add up to whole days, and for practical purposes we may want to round the numbers off into whole days.

    a.   Saturn is specific lord for 900 days, which multiplies Saturn's number (30) by thirty-day months.

        i.   Of these 900 days, Saturn gets the first 209 days and six hours as particular lord. We get this number by multiplying the 900 days for Saturn by Saturn's

                                                                                      ... (30) by thirty

day months.

        i.   Of these 450 days, Saturn gets 104 days and about eight hours. This multiplies Mars' 450 days by the percentage that is Saturn.

        ii.   Mars gets 52 days and about twelve hours.

From these examples, we see the result of the proportional result of the greater malefic Saturn (30) is always exactly twice that of the lesser malefic Mars (15). The raw numbers for both planets will change, based upon the amount of time for a specific planet's period.

The table below breaks down the particular periods of the planets into days and parts of days. The horizontal row signifies the general periods of the planets and the vertical row their specific periods. For example, a Saturn specific period within a Sun general period is just over 132 and one half days.

	Saturn 900	Jupiter 360	Mars 450	Sun 570	Venus 240	Mercury 600	Moon 750
Saturn	209.34	83.7	104.67	132.57	55.8	139.5	174.6
Jupiter	83.7	33.48	41.87	53.03	22.32	55.8	69.84
Mars	104.67	41.85	52.34	66.29	29.9	69.75	87.3
Sun	132.57	53.01	66.29	83.96	35.34	88.35	110.58
Venus	55.8	22.32	27.91	35.35	14.88	37.2	46.56
Mercury	139.5	55.8	69.78	88.38	37.2	93	116.4
Moon	174.42	69.75	87.23	110.48	46.5	116.26	145.5

As you study this list, its beauty should be obvious. One can simply bring these numbers to a specific time lord to yield a *particular* planetary lord for an amount of time proportionate to that planet's number within all seven. The beauty, however, is only skin-deep. The system necessitates dividing the day into odd fractions that will render hours and minutes. This would seem daunting to all astrologers, modern or ancient.

Here I encounter my own resistance to the tradition, as I am reluctant to break up days. For it is the day that is the most indivisible unit in our life experiences as human beings. On the other hand, the ancients, without our calculators and software programs, used - or at least wrote about - systems that employed such fractions. Another planetary period system, Quarters, also uses proportions in determining specific time lords. We will discuss the Quarters system later in this chapter.

For an example of proportionate decennials, I return to **Jacqueline Kennedy Onassis**. Her particular and daily planetary lords are of considerable interest. Mrs. Kennedy had Moon/Jupiter from May 31, 1963 to May 24, 1964. During this time, Jupiter was also the third or particular time lord, then Venus, Mercury, and the Sun. On November 12, 1963, Mars took over as particular time lord. And, for the week of the assassination and the funeral of John Kennedy, her daily planet was - you guessed it - Saturn.

When Jacqueline Kennedy married Onassis four years later, she was in a Moon/Mars period that lasted from April 1968 until the middle of 1969 (when Saturn took over.) During October of that year, when her marriage was announced and made official, Moon was the particular lord and Mercury the daily lord. The repetition of the Moon, as specific and particular planetary lord, gives us the content of the event: a marriage, since Moon signifies cohabiting relationships. Mercury, fittingly the daily lord when her marriage was announced, is not prominent in her chart although Mercury is the lord of Venus and Jupiter in the Eighth.

When we look at **John Kerry's** 2004 presidential campaign, the particular time lords add to our information about the course and outcome of that campaign. He was in a Mercury/Jupiter period during that time.

- When *Sun* was his third-level or particular planetary lord, Kerry won his party's nomination. Sun is also in the First in his natal chart, with a trine from its dispositor, Jupiter. During the convention, however, the daily lord was *Saturn*. This corresponds to the cautious approach he and his party took during and immediately after the convention.

- August and September featured *Mercury* as the particular planet. Mercury is in the second house and, in Capricorn, is governed by Saturn and exchanges dignities with Saturn. Kerry's penchant for subtle distinctions and nuanced responses did not serve him well. Interestingly, *Sun* was his daily planet at the time of his first debate with Bush, which he won handily.

- During October and into mid-November, *Mars* was his particular time lord. Mars is in sect and is angular in his natal chart. Kerry became more aggressive and made it a closer race. As Mars is in his natal Seventh place, it did not work out as positively for him as it would if Mars was in his First or Tenth.

- When the election happened and Kerry lost, Venus was his daily time lord. In Kerry's natal chart Venus is in Scorpio and is in the Twelfth zoidion from the Ascendant. This would not make for a happy outcome for that day or the next.

Other Time Lord Systems

Decennials are but one time lord system of several that appear in Vettius Valens' *Anthology*. The next two systems only appear in Valens. Does this mean that the other time lord systems are peculiar to him? No. *The Anthology* discusses many natal and predictive techniques Valens had become familiar with during his career. It is quite likely that other notable astrologers also used the systems he wrote about, but their presentations are now lost. Many astrologers, of course, did not write and

but divides all the numbers by four. These numbers below become the lengths of the general times. Both general and specific times vary in months according to the number of the time lord that has governance.

Saturn has the number thirty: if these were years in a general period, this time is seven years and six months.

Jupiter has twelve as his number: this converts to three years.

Mars has fifteen: this gives three years and nine months.

Sun, with nineteen, gives four years and nine months.

Venus, with eight, gives two years.

Mercury, with twenty, gives five years.

Moon, with twenty-five, gives six years three months.

Valens appears to use a solar year of 365.25 days when working with Quarters. After our discussion of decennials with its years of 360 days, this may comfort the reader.

The beginning planet, or releaser, is not the luminary of sect but can be any of the seven planets. The beginning planet is the one that follows the Moon's position at the New or Full Moon before a person was born. Both Martha Stewart and Muhammad Ali were born with waxing Moons, so New Moons proceeded their times of birth. Stewart and Ali both have Sun as the planet appearing next to both New Moons: both begin life with a Sun period of four years and nine months.

Because Winston Churchill was born during a waning Moon, one begins with the planet following the Moon's position at the prenatal Full Moon. In his case it is the Moon who is the first planetary lord for the first six years and three months of his life.

Very often the first planet is not the Sun or Moon, especially if the birth time is well within the waxing or waning Moon phases. For somebody with a Moon that is waning, one would begin with the next planet in the zodiac from the Moon's position. This might be on the other side of the chart from the Sun's position.

As with decennials, the planets follow the beginning planet in the order in which they appear in the zodiac. All seven planets take turns as a general time lord; at the end of all seven, a person is thirty-two years and three months old (129 divided by 4 is 33.25, which corresponds to 33 years and 3 months.) At this age everybody begins a new rotation of planetary lords.

However, the next rotation begins not with the original beginning planet but the *fourth* one in order. And no, I do not have a compelling explanation for this. After Martha Stewart's first rotation of planetary lords, her next rotation would start not with Sun but Mars. Ali would begin a second rotation with Venus, his fourth planet from his Sun.

For everyone, at the age of sixty-four years and six months, after the completion of the second rotation of planetary lords, one goes forward *another four planets* for the third rotation. Because the general periods are shorter than those of decennials, they will show more frequent major changes in life than we find with decennials.

Having determined the general time lords for Quarters, we move to the specific time lords. To determine the specific planetary lords, we use proportions of the (one-quarter) numbers of the planets. Below are the specific proportionate periods for the seven planets. To arrive at particular time lordships, one would continue to divide by proportion. How would we do that? One way is to take the percentages of each planet as part of the entire seven planets and subdivide those within each division of each of the seven planets. The percentages given above for proportionate decennials become the <constant> function on your calculator.

Valens gives us another possibility in Book IV of *The Anthology*.[8] Within a solar year, how many days are allotted to each planet? One simply multiplies that number of days - fractions and all - by the numbers (divided into four) of the seven planets. For a solar year, the days of the planets are as follows:

Saturn:	85
Jupiter:	34
Mars:	42.5
Sun:	53.83
Venus:	22.67
Mercury:	56.67
Moon:	70.83

All these days add up to a solar year of 365.25 days. Here is the list of *specific* times converted into days.[9]

---

8.   Chapters 1, 3.
9.   This and following tables are inspired by Dave Stricker, 1996.

	Saturn 7.5 yrs	Jupiter 3 yrs.	Mars 3.72 yrs.	Sun 4.75 yrs.	Venus 2 yrs.	Mercury 5 yrs.	Moon 6.25 yrs.
Saturn	635.5	255	318.75	403.75	170	425	531.25
Jupiter	255	102	127.5	161.5	68	170	212.5
Mars	318.75	127.5	159.39	201.97	8.5		

For further divisions into particular periods, you would continue to subdivide the specific periods for all the planets within that general period. If you dare. Here are a few examples of Quarters at work.

At the beginning of the First World War, **Winston Churchill** was in the middle of a Sun period that began in 1912. In 1914, when war broke out, Moon in Leo in his Eleventh zoidion was the specific lord, giving Sun/Moon. In February 1915 Mars took up the specific lordship from Moon. (We have seen this before.) Mars is strongly placed in Churchill's chart, being in the first zoidion and conjunct Jupiter and in sect. We previously noted its pervasive influence during the time of Saturn on Churchill's Mars-Jupiter conjunction by profection and by transit. Mars, without proper measure, can backfire. Churchill was sacked as Lord of the Admiralty when Saturn was particular or daily time lord. When Moon was particular time lord, Churchill resigned his government posts for his version of private life, and became VIP soldier on the front lines in Europe for the remainder of the war.

Fast-forwarding several decades, Saturn was Churchill's general time lord from 1939 until late 1946, spanning the entire war and its immediate aftermath. We see Saturn everywhere at this time in his life. We have seen Saturn's strong role in decennials, being Churchill's third triplicity lord for the final third of this life, and being the general time lord for his Quarters during the Second World War. In Quarters, Saturn was also the specific lord for the time when Churchill took over as Prime Minister.

It was during a Sun period that the allies were victorious in the Second World War. Shortly afterwards, Churchill's party came in second in the parliamentary elections and he had to leave office. Sun was also general time lord at the time of his Iron Curtain speech in early 1946.

When Sun was also the specific time lord, Germany surrendered. When Saturn was the specific time lord, he lost the election. When Jupiter was the specific lord, he gave the Iron Curtain speech.

Martha Stewart had Moon as her general time lord from 1999 until early 2006. From September 2001, however, when her troubles began, Saturn was her specific lord. When Stewart learned that a company she had invested in was going to be in some trouble, Saturn was also the particular lord. When she had lied to federal investigators about selling off stock in the company, the charge for which she was later found guilty, Jupiter had taken over from Saturn as particular lord. We also saw from decennials that Jupiter, a benefic in sect and oriental in her chart, can cause her to overreach. This might doubly be the case within a Saturn specific period.

Stewart's trial and conviction occurred with Moon continuing as her general time lord but Mercury as her specific time lord. Mercury is oriental, in sect, and in the Ninth place from the Ascendant. This does not seem so difficult except that Saturn was also transiting Cancer, the place of Mercury, at the time. Stewart went to jail as Sun took over as specific lord: she had become the most famous prisoner in the United States.

For Jacqueline Kennedy Onassis, from autumn 1961 to autumn 1966, Mercury was her general time lord. In her natal chart, Mercury is in the Tenth, along with the Sun and Lot of Fortune. In 1962, Sun was the specific planetary period lord, giving Mercury/Sun. This was the peak of her fame as First Lady: being married to the US President. After a specific period of Mars, Saturn took over as her specific planetary lord: *one day before John Kennedy was assassinated.* Because Saturn had just taken over at this time, it was also the particular or daily time lord. Saturn is in sect in her diurnal chart but is opposed to her Venus and Jupiter in the Eighth.

By the time Jacqueline Kennedy married Aristotle Onassis, Sun had become the general time lord. During this time she was a worldwide celebrity. When her marriage to Onassis was announced, the *specific* time lord was - maybe you guessed it - Saturn. At this time, the particular time lord was Mercury, perhaps denoting the announcing itself.

Zodiacal Releasing from the Lots of Fortune and Spirit

Valens was drawn to zodiacal releasing and gave us quite a bit of detail about how to use it. He felt that this was a very powerful predictive technique - we should therefore take it seriously.

Here we are back to 360-day years. All levels of periods of time are given by the zoidia and their governing planets. The planetary numbers give us time lords for the general times and all its subdivisions. For general time lords, we take the numbers to conform to years in a person's life. These numbers are the same as in decennials, except for Saturn governing Capricorn, which has twenty-seven years rather than thirty. (Valens explains that this is because the greater years of the Sun and Moon, 120 and 108 respectively, dividing from these numbers yields thirty for the masculine zoidion Aquarius and twenty seven years for the feminine zoidion Capricorn.[10]) This means that if you have one of these Lots in Capricorn, you will be fifty-seven years old (twenty-seven for Capricorn plus thirty for Aquarius) when Saturn finally gives over to Jupiter, when Pisces becomes the zoidion of the releasing.

For issues of health, finances, and the general quality of one's life, one begins from the zoidion of the natal Lot of Fortune; one begins from the zoidion of the natal Lot of Spirit for psychological health and for career. (According to some of Valens' example charts, the line between Fortune and Spirit is not always clear.) If you are born at a new or full Moon, when the two lots would be in the same zoidion, releasing for the Lot of Spirit begins with the zoidion *following* the Lot of Fortune.

---

10.   Valens *Anthology.* Book IV, Chapter 6

For the specific times, take thirty-day months that correspond to the numbers of the planets governing the respective zoidia. This is the same as in decennials discussed above. Zodiacal releasing is a non-proportional system, so that when time runs out in a general period, the time runs out for all subdivisions, even if some planets haven't appeared as specific or particular time lords.

If one is in the middle of a lengthy general period governed by Sun, Moon, Mercury, or Saturn, one will go through all the zoidia and their lords. Instead of repeating the original zoidion,

of nineteen. The first nineteen months - of thirty days each, totaling 570 days - belong to the Sun. Dividing 570 days by twelve gives 47.5 days. Dividing those numbers of days by twelve gives a shade under 4 days. Here's the breakdown of planets into *four* divisions of times.

	General	Specific	Particular	More Particular
Saturn	30 years	900 days (30 months)	75 days	6 days 6 hours
	27 years	810 days (27 months)	67 days 12 hours	5 days 15 hours
Jupiter	12 years	360 days (12 months)	30 days	2 days 12 hours
Mars	15 years	450 days (15 months)	37 days 2 hours	3 days 1 hour
Sun	19 years	570 days (19 months)	47 days 12 hours	3 days 23 hours
Venus	8 years	240 days (8 months)	20 days	1 day 18 hours
Mercury	20 years	600 days (20 months)	50 days	4 days 2 hours
Moon	25 years	750 days (25 months)	62 days 2 hours	5 days 2 hours

Although we use the zoidia to list the general, specific, and particular times, we primarily use the planets that are their house lords for interpretation and analysis. Here are some examples of zodiacal releasing.

Muhammad Ali's quest for his first championship and victory over Sonny Liston took place during a Virgo general time and a Scorpio specific time, ruled by Mercury and Mars respectively. We saw both planets featured in Ali's decennials. At that time Ali was becoming known not only for his ferocity in the boxing ring but his outspoken verbally combative quality. That the planets were angular and Mars was also the significator of his profession tells us about his success and subsequent fame and notoriety.

Beginning with the zoidion of Lot of Spirit, Ali was in a Libra/Sagittarius period. Venus and Jupiter, governing both zoidia, are in trine to one another in his natal chart. Jupiter, the specific lord, is out of sect, retrograde, and opposite its own house, but is quite happily placed in its joy in the Eleventh. During this time Ali became a national figure, and would triumph over adversity in the ring and become internationally known. At this time Ali was buoyant and inspired by his own sense of purpose. Later, when his specific time lord moved from Jupiter to Saturn, as the releasing moved from Sagittarius to Capricorn and then to Aquarius, the negative publicity and controversy from his refusal to be drafted began to take its toll.

Martha Stewart's situation is more dramatic. Beginning from the zoidion of her Lot of Fortune, the general period was Cancer and governed by the Moon for twenty-five years, from 1995 until 2020. Her legal problems began during a Scorpio specific period: its lord, Mars, is out of sect and cadent in her chart. She was indicted during a Sagittarius period, governed by Jupiter. Capricorn and Aquarius, and thus Saturn, took over from late 2003, just before her trial, until early 2008. Judging from this alone, it would take some time for her to rebuild her business and financial empire to the condition it was before her problems began.

Releasing from the Lot of Spirit, from December 1985 until September 1, 2004, Leo, whose lord is the Sun, signified the general times. Since Sun in her natal chart is in Leo in the Tenth, much accomplishment came during this time. Her legal problems began shortly after the last zoidion before Leo, Cancer, took over for the specific time and Moon became her specific time lord for twenty-five thirty-day months.

Here comes the compelling surprise. You may remember that, having gone completely around the zodiac, one does not return to original zoidion - in this case, Leo - but the zoidion opposite. One month before Stewart was indicted, Aquarius took over and therefore *Saturn* became her specific time lord! This commences a Saturn period of hard times.

Interestingly, Martha Stewart went into jail only a few days before *Virgo* took over from Leo, so the general planetary lord changed from Sun to Mercury. This would begin a completely new era in Martha Stewart's life that will continue, with its ups and downs, for twenty years.

Saturn times need not always be difficult, especially if Saturn is prominent in the natal chart. **Margaret Thatcher** became Prime Minister of England in 1979. At the end of that year a Sagittarius period ended and Capricorn took over for her Lot of Fortune, yielding Saturn as time lord. Saturn would be general time lord for the next fifty-seven years of her life as the releasing proceeds through Capricorn and Aquarius. How is it that Saturn would signify the attainment of power? You may remember that Thatcher's chart features an exalted Saturn in sect conjunct the Ascendant.

Saturn was the specific time lord during the first several years of the Thatcher government, which included her renovating all areas of domestic policy and the Falklands campaign, during which England attained a military victory over Argentina concerning disputed territory. In fact, Thatcher was Prime Minister until Leo indicated the general times: Sun also became her specific time lord. Seeing the poor condition of her natal Sun - in fall and in the Twelfth - it is no surprise that her good fortune left her during this time.

Sometimes, as with Margaret Thatcher becoming Prime Minister and Martha Stewart's general time lord changing as she enters prison, there's a strong correlation between an event in a person's life and a change of general planetary time lord. I illustrate with a person whose chart we have not encountered here before: **Arnold Schwarzennegger**. For the Lot of Spirit, Schwarzennegger became governor of California at the end of a Mars period (Mars is in the Twelfth) and the beginning of a Venus period (Venus is in the First.) At that time he changed from a character in action movies to a politician. This seems to follow the symbolism quite nicely.

This concludes our introduction to some Hellenistic planetary time lord systems. I hope you have enough information and inspiration to continue the work with these powerful techniques. I

days in a 365-day year. If you want to see how many days are eighty-five from today - March 19 - you would find this is 78 days of the year. Adding 85 to 78 yields 263, which is September 20. The next step is to list when *for everybody* the 129-month general time lords or chronocrators would change. Again our reference is not a calendar date but the age of a person.

10 years	218 days:	ends the first planet
21 years	70 days:	ends the second planet
31 years	287 days:	ends the third planet
42 years	140 days:	ends the fourth planet
52 years	357 days:	ends the fifth planet
63 years	209 days:	ends the sixth planet
74 years	62 days:	ends the seventh planet and back to the first planet
84 years	279 days:	ends the first planet

We first see that Ms. Stewart would have turned sixty in August 2001. She was within a Jupiter period that would have started many years previously. This gives us a chance to go through the divisions of the general time lords. When did her Jupiter period begin?

Using the table above, we convert August 3 to numbers of days:
Converting August 3 to days, year of 1941   215 days
The fifth planet Saturn ended at 52 yrs. <u>357 days</u>

$$572$$
$$- \underline{365.25}$$
equals 1994   207 days

This brings us to July 26 1994, which would begin Jupiter as the general and specific time lord.

Jupiter's period is 360 days, which is Jupiter's number 12 x 30 days in a month.

1994   207 days
+   <u>360 (Jupiter period)</u>

Table to convert calendar dates to the number of days in a 365-day year

Day	Jan	Feb	Mar	Apr	May	Jun	Jul	Aug	Sep	Oct	Nov	Dec
1	1	32	60	91	121	152	182	213	244	274	305	335
2	2	33	61	92	122	153	183	214	245	275	306	336
3	3	34	62	93	123	154	184	215	246	276	307	337
4	4	35	63	94	124	155	185	216	247	277	308	338
5	5	36	64	95	125	156	186	217	248	278	309	339
6	6	37	65	96	126	157	187	218	249	279	310	340
7	7	38	66	97	127	158	188	219	250	280	311	341
8	8	39	67	98	128	158	189	220	251	281	312	342
9	9	40	68	99	129	160	190	221	252	282	313	343
10	10	41	69	100	130	161	191	222	253	283	314	344
11	11	42	70	101	131	162	192	223	254	284	315	345
12	12	43	71	102	132	163	193	224	255	285	316	346
13	13	44	72	103	133	1 64	194	225	256	286	317	347
14	14	45	73	104	134	165	195	226	257	287	318	348
15	15	46	74	105	135	166	196	227	258	288	319	349
16	16	47	75	106	136	167	197	228	259	289	320	350
17	17	48	76	107	137	168	198	229	260	290	321	351
18	18	49	77	108	138	169	199	230	261	291	322	352
19	19	50	78	109	139	170	200	231	262	292	323	353
20	20	51	79	110	140	171	201	232	263	293	324	354
21	21	52	80	111	141	172	202	233	264	294	325	355
22	22	53	81	112	142	173	203	234	265	295	326	356
23	23	54	82	113	143	174	204	235	266	296	327	357
24	24	55	83	114	144	175	205	236	267	297	328	358
25	25	56	84	115	145	176	206	237	268	298	329	359
26	26	57	85	116	146	177	207	238	269	299	330	360
27	27	58	86	117	147	178	208	239	270	300	331	361
28	28	59	87	118	148	179	209	240	271	301	332	362
29	29	(60)	88	119	149	180	210	241	272	302	333	363
30	30		89	120	150	181	211	242	273	303	334	364
31	31		90		151		212	243		304		365

567 days
- 365.25
202 days of next year.

Jupiter's specific period lasts until July 21, **1995**.

Mercury is next specific time lord. Mercury's period is 600 days, which is Mercury's number

73

Mercury's specific period lasts until 2 years and 73 days into that year - until March 14, **1997**.

Next is Sun. The Sun's period is 570 days, which is 19 x 30.

1997	73
+	570 (Sun Period)
	643
-	365.25
	277

Sun's specific period lasts until October 3, **1998.**

Next is Venus. Venus period is but 240 days, 8 x 30

1998	277
+	240 (Venus Period)
	517
-	365.25
	152

Venus's specific period lasts until June 1, **1999.**

Next is Moon. Moon's period is 750 days, 25 x 30

1999	152
+	750 (Moon's Period)
	902
-	730 (2 yrs)
	172 (- leap yr is 171)

Moon's specific period lasts until June 20, **2001**

Now we're close. Next is Mars. Mars period is 450 days.

```
2001     171
+        450 (Mars Period)
         621
-        365
         256
```

The Mars period, where her problems began and accumulated, lasted until Sept. 13, **2002**.

There's but one planet left, Saturn. Saturn's period is the largest of them all, 900 days.

```
2002     256
+        900 (Saturn's Period)
         1156
-        1095 (3 yrs)
         61
```

Martha Stewart is released from Saturn, and would begin a new general period governed by Mercury at the end of **February 2005**.

14

The material in this chapter is different from the techniques discussed in Chapters Twelve and Thirteen, but is closer in some ways to modern astrological prediction. As with the previous discussion on transits, we will begin with modern practice and then discuss its ancient roots.

We will first look at the modern methods of secondary progressions, solar arc directions, and ascendant directions. My aim is not to cast any one as better than any other, but to illustrate a range of techniques that relate to one another and are rooted in ancient predictive methods.

Modern Progressions and Directions

Secondary Progressions

Secondary progressions advance all planets so that each day of planetary movement corresponds to each-year of life. This month I am fifty-one years and five months old. To find my secondary progressed positions, one would find the planets' locations fifty-one days and ten hours after their positions at my birth. (If, in secondary progressions, 12 months of the year is 24 hours, then 1 month is 2 hours.)

To illustrate: I was born on December 23, 1954. Counting forward in the ephemeris fifty-one days on from then, we get to February 12, 1955. During this time natal Moon in Sagittarius had circled the zodiac once and was now Libra. Sun had moved from 0 Capricorn to 22 Aquarius. During that time, Mercury progressed from 29 Sagittarius to 24 Aquarius, having gone retrograde nine days earlier (conforming to nine years ago in my life.) Venus, on the other hand, had just turned direct when I was born and had been going very slowly; by 51 days, corresponding to 51 years of life; she had moved from 20 Scorpio to 7 Capricorn. Mars moved from mid-Pisces to mid-Aries. The planets outside the orbit of Mars had moved hardly a degree, direct or retrograde.

Some people are uncomfortable with secondary progressions when learning about them for the first time. This is understandable, since we tend to think of time as *one* continuum. According to the modern astrological view of time, however, all cycles have the same structure, so one period of time can illuminate another that is larger or smaller. In this spirit, astrologers use *the days* after one's birth to consider *the years* in that person's life.

Why are these progressions called "secondary"? This brings us back to the primary and secondary motions that we discussed in Chapter One and elsewhere. Secondary motion is the motion counterclockwise, west to east, in the direction of the zodiac. This motion contains the movements of the planets at their own rates of speed through the zodiac. By secondary motion, the Moon travels through the zodiac in twenty-eight days, Saturn in twenty-nine years, and Pluto in about 260 years. This is contrasted with the primary movement, which is clockwise, from east to west, marking the rising, culminating, setting, and anti-culminating of planetary bodies and the degrees of the zodiac. (This is the diurnal cycle.)

We now return to the chart of **Winston Churchill** for his secondary progressions during his terrible year of 1915. (We will use his chart and his life to illustrate many other methosds of prediction, modern and Hellenistic.) At that time he was the Minister of the Admiralty and was blamed for a botched attempt by England to end the First World War by a naval expedition through the Dardenelles. Eventually Churchill had to leave the government and he spent the rest of the war outside of a policy position. He was forty years old during this year; his secondary progressions therefore move all his planets forty days from the day of his birth, corresponding to forty years of his life. Since his birthday was at the end of November the previous year, if we add three hours to forty years we arrive by progression to the middle of January 1915.

Since secondary progressions are a modern technique commonly used by modern astrologers, I feel at liberty to use modern planets within this predictive system.

If you compare this chart with his natal chart, you will notice that the planets from Jupiter on out move hardly at all: if in forty days in real time these planets move little, they will move very little by progression. The Sun moved roughly one degree a year, from 7 Sagittarius to 18 Capricorn, about forty one degrees, from November 1874 to January 15, 1915. Mercury moved more quickly, coming close to a conjunction with Sun. Venus, having turned retrograde and is now direct, 11 degrees *behind* its original position in the natal chart. The Moon, moving about a degree a month, conforming to its movement of about thirteen degrees a day, had gone around the zodiac once and was now at the opposite zoidion from its natal position.

Of these progressed positions, which are the most interesting to us? During this year, Churchill's progressed Moon was moving toward a square to Mars. After a sextile to Venus, Moon becomes conjunct to Saturn, and then Moon opposes Uranus. The progressed Moon can give us the timing of occasions during the year. Note the hard aspects to malefics, slightly mitigated by Venus. The application to Uranus hardly helps in the matter.

Also important are (1) that the Moon is in opposition to the progressed Midheaven and (2) that the progressed Ascendant, conjunct Jupiter, opposes Neptune. Moon opposing Midheaven shows a division between Churchill and authority, which is ironic because he was the authority at that time - except that he lost his job *being* the authority. Progressed Ascendant conjunct Jupiter opposite Neptune portrays one whose lofty stature and grand plans (Jupiter and Ascendant) are undermined by illusion and wrong thinking (Neptune opposite Ascendant).

Having just mentioned the progressed Ascendant, how would we calculate this? I must hold off on this for now, pending a lengthier discussion.

Next we look at Churchill's secondary progressions for May 1940, when he became Prime Minister and declared war on Hitler. There are many changes in Churchill's life and by progression

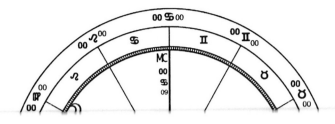

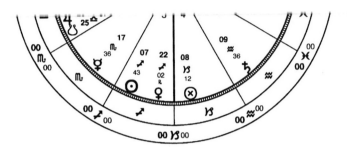

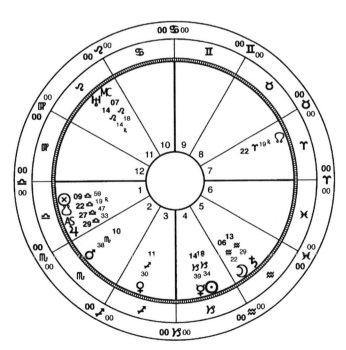

Winston Churchill -
Secondary progressed chart
to January 15, 1915

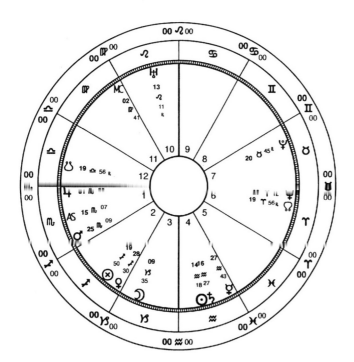

Winston Churchill -
Progressed to May 1940

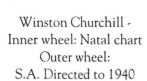

Winston Churchill -
Inner wheel: Natal chart
Outer wheel:
S.A. Directed to 1940

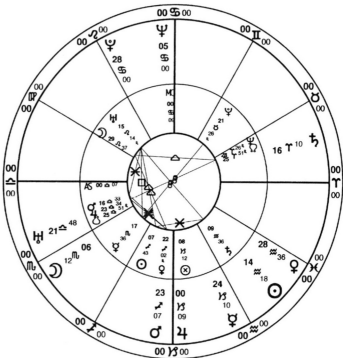

during the twenty-five years between 1915 and 1940. In 1915, he was at the beginning of a progressed Sun-Moon cycle - Sun was in Capricorn and Moon moving away from the Sun in Aquarius. 1940, as you can see, is toward the end of this Sun-Moon cycle, as Moon in Capricorn closes in on Sun in Aquarius. (Churchill would have a progressed new Moon in mid-war.) The timing of the progressed lunation cycle correlates with *transiting Saturn*, which had returned to Churchill's Tenth place, where it also was during his terrible year 1915.

Solar Arc Directions

In general, directions are not about cycles of time - at least not directly. By solar arc directions, we advance *all planets and Ascendant and Midheaven* the same distance as the Sun has moved by progression. When I turned fifty, the Sun by progression had moved about the same number of degrees. By solar arc, *everything*, from Ascendant to Saturn to Pluto, would move fifty degrees.

Because all positions will move at the same rate as the progressing Sun, directed planets and angles are always in the same positions relative to one another. As with transits, solar arc directions are concerned with aspects to natal positions. For Churchill's solar arc directions in 1940, everything has moved 66.5 degrees, matching the movement of the progressing Sun. You see that this is properly presented as a bi-wheel with the natal chart inside and the directed positions outside. In this way one can see the contacts between directed positions and natal positions. We also see that the Sun by direction is in the same position as in his secondary progression, but everything else is different.

What is interesting here? The directed Ascendant has moved to a conjunction with Sun, and the directed Midheaven forms a square to the Sun. The Ascendant and Midheaven are the two most important personal points in the chart, depicting the presence of the native (Ascendant) and his or her activity (Midheaven). Both positions contact Churchill's Sun, which is the planet of leadership. Noting that Churchill's natal Sun is also conjunct the fixed star Antares, this is a good indication that, for example, he would become leader during wartime. Here we see a major event in his life triggered by the arcing Ascendant and Midheaven. Jupiter has come into a square with his Ascendant degree. Mars had been conjunct Venus - ruler of the Ascendant - a year before. His enthusiasm and grandiosity will be on vivid display.

Astrologers use secondary progressions and solar arc directions differently. Secondary progressions can highlight turning points or climate changes in a person's life. For example if a person's Sun moves by progression from Aries to Taurus, gradually one will see this person's Sun taking on some Taurus qualities. These changes also occur when a planet changes from one zoidion to another or is at a direct or retrograde station, or when an aspect becomes exact. Solar arc directions are more often used to predict discrete events. When one is unsure of a person's birth time, astrologers often use solar arc directions to "rectify" the chart by looking at the timing of important events in a person's life. When we look at the legacy of ancient astrology we see that they used their form of directions in both of these ways.

I now offer another predictive possibility: *Ascendant arc directions*. This yields different results from solar arc directions, since the arc of the progressed Ascendant will be different from the progressed Sun, as the two move at different rates by progression.

If you look back at Winston Churchill's solar arc directions for 1940, you would note all positions, including the Ascendant and Midheaven, advanced by that of the progressed Sun: 66.5 degrees - about his age. By progression, however, Churchill's Ascendant has moved only 47 degrees! With an Ascendant at 00 Libra, the degrees of the zodiac that follow Churchill's Ascendant will rise slowly. If he was born instead with a 0 Aries Ascendant, this progression would move far more

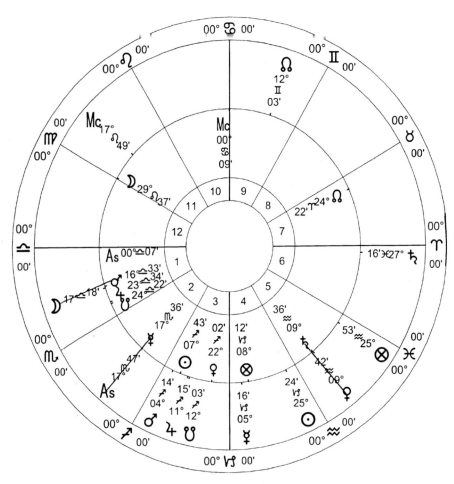

Winston Churchill -
Ascendant Arc Directed to May 5, 1940

quickly: sixty degrees into Gemini *by the time he was twenty*. This large disparity is due to the position of the Ascendant in the zodiac and the latitude of birth.

Ascendant arc directions are available in the Solar Fire computer program. They are not as popular as solar arc directions but they have an interesting rationale: the primacy of the Ascendant itself in the natal chart.

In May 1940, the progressed Ascendant, 47 degrees past the natal Ascendant, was just past

the beginnings of different phases of life. This would strongly interest ancient astrologers.

Progressed Angles and Ascensions

When I was first studying secondary progressions, a point of bewilderment arose for me: under the year-for-a-day formula, if the entire chart moves around during an entire day, why, then, don't the angles go all around the zodiac each year? Instead, the Midheaven progresses only a degree a year and the Ascendant progresses an average of only a degree a year.

Later I found out that the progressed angles move not according to the secondary motion through the zodiac but actually according to the primary - diurnal - motion. (The exception to this is Quotidian Secondary Progressions, which move the angles full circle during a year and whose ever-changing angles can time specific events within a day or two.) As previously mentioned, within the diurnal cycle all planets rise, culminate, descend, and anti-culminate. The twelve zoidia culminate for periods of roughly two hours each per day, yet the zoidia ascend for varying amounts of time during the day.

To progress the angles, our reference is the Midheaven. Here, one degree over the Midheaven is equivalent to one year of life. We recall that one degree a year is the same rate as the movement of the progressed Sun. Ancient astrologers were far more interested in the movement of the Ascendant than the Midheaven, since the Ascendant is far more important in a natal chart. Because the Midheaven yields a consistent measure of a day's time and because movement through the Midheaven corresponds to the time of day for a given location, progressing the Midheaven is the basis for progressing the Ascendant, in ancient and modern astrology

Before discussing the rate of the progressing Ascendant, there in one point to consider: When we say, "one degree over the Midheaven", we need to specify how we are measuring this. Some astrologers have used as their measurement one degree of longitude on the ecliptic, from, say, 12 to 13 Sagittarius. Many modern astrologers who use ecliptical longitude use its *average* movement over the Midheaven, which is the Naibod system. Most modern astrologers, however, use an average not of ecliptical longitude but of degrees on the celestial equator, which are degrees of right ascension. Using right ascension gives us more uniform and accurate measurements of time. By right ascension, the moving degrees of the Midheaven conform to our time of day and how time changes according to the movement of the sky. For example, a planet to the left of the Midheaven in square by RA to the Midheaven's RA will take 6 hours to culminate. Here is the arithmetic: if 1 hour of time is 15 degrees of right ascension (24 hours = 360 degrees), then 90 degrees of RA divided by 15 degrees an hour gives us 6 hours. If 15 degrees equals 1 hour of 60 minutes, 1 degree of right ascension equals 4 minutes.

Compared to the steady movement of degrees over the Midheaven, the degrees of the Ascendant vary widely. We have seen how Churchill's progressed Ascendant moves, based upon its location in the zodiac: more slowly in Libra, very quickly in Aries.

What is the ascension of a zoidion? Ascensions tell us how many degrees pass the Midheaven during the time it takes a particular zoidion to fully ascend. If you want to know the time a particular zoidion rises during the day, multiply the number of degrees over the Midheaven for that zoidion by 4 and that will give you the number of minutes for the full zoidion to rise. If you wish, for example, to measure the distance of 15 degrees by ascensions, take the number of ascensions in the zoidion and divide that by 2. If the distance of 15 degrees goes from one zoidion to the next, find the proportions corresponding to the number of degrees of the two zoidia and add them together. We will illustrate these below.

For my latitude of birth, Libra's ascent lasted almost two and three quarter hours. During that time, the Midheaven moved from 0 Cancer to 6 Leo: 36 degrees. However, it took less that an hour and a quarter for Aries to rise and the Midheaven only moved 15 degrees during that time.

In the Northern Hemisphere, an Ascendant in Pisces or Aries takes the shortest time to rise. Leo/Scorpio and Virgo/Libra take the longest time to rise. This is reversed in the Southern Hemisphere.

These pairs of zoidia rise in equal amounts of time: Aries/Pisces, Taurus/Aquarius, Gemini/Capricorn, Cancer/Sagittarius, Leo/Scorpio, and Virgo/Libra. Recalling our previous discussion on aspects and pairs of sympathetic zoidia, ancient astrologers called these pairs "equally ascending." Modern astrologers note these same symmetries but by degrees, from the 0 Aries- 0 Libra axis, as "contra-antiscia."

As we have seen, ascensions also depend on the latitude of the place of birth. The closer one is to the earth's equator, the closer are the ascensions to one another; the further north or south of the equator, the further apart will be the the six pairs of zoidia from each other. What are the ascendions of all the zoidia for a given degree of latitude? The table below will provide this information. For a person's exact latitude of birth, one might have to interpolate between whole numbers of latitude. Hellenistic astrologers may have simply rounded up.

The degrees of latitude for a place of birth go in an upward and downward direction, while the six pairs of equally ascending zoidia go across. In each cell is the number of degrees that go over the Midheaven as these zoidia fully rise.[1] Refer to table overleaf. For southern latitudes, invert the six pairs of zoidia, so that: instead of Aries/Pisces to the far left, substitute Virgo/Libra, and instead of Taurus/Aquarius, one would read the second column as Leo/Scorpio, and the third column Gemini/Capricorn as Cancer/Sagittarius, and so on to the right.

Degrees of Latitude	Equally Rising Zoidia					
	Ar/Pi	Ta/Aq	Ge/Cp	Ca/Sa	Le/Sc	Vi/Li
00	27.91	29.91	32.18	32.18	29.91	27.91
05	26.89	29.09	31.85	32.52	30.73	28.93
20	22.23	23.28	30.28	34.08	34.94	33.39
28	21.72	24.85	30.10	34.26	34.91	34.11
30	21.18	24.41	29.92	34.45	35.41	34.64
31	20.91	24.17	29.82	34.54	35.64	34.91
32	20.62	23.94	29.72	34.65	35.88	35.20
33	20.34	23.69	29.61	34.75	36.12	35.48
34	20.04	23.45	29.51	34.86	36.37	35.78
35	19.74	23.19	29.40	34.97	36.63	36.08
36	19.43	22.92	29.28	35.08	36.89	36.39
37	19.11	22.65	29.16	35.20	37.16	36.71
38	18.79	22.37	29.04	35.32	37.45	37.03
39	18.45	22.08	28.91	35.45	37.74	37.37
40	18.10	21.78	28.78	35.58	38.04	37.72
41	17.75	21.47	28.64	35.72	38.35	38.07
42	17.38	21.14	28.50	35.87	38.67	38.44
43	17.00	20.81	28.34	36.02	39.01	38.82
44	16.61	20.46	28.18	36.18	39.36	39.21
45	16.20	20.09	28.02	36.35	39.73	39.62
46	15.78	19.71	28.84	36.53	40.11	40.04
47	15.34	19.30	27.65	36.72	40.51	40.48
48	14.88	18.88	27.45	36.92	40.93	40.94
49	14.41	18.44	27.23	37.13	41.38	41.41
50	13.91	17.97	27.00	37.36	41.85	41.91
51	13.40	17.48	26.76	37.61	42.34	42.43
52	12.85	16.95	26.49	37.87	42.87	42.97
53	12.29	16.39	26.20	38.17	43.43	43.53

Table of Ascensions for the Twelve Zoidia

To find the Ascensions for Churchill, one would have to go between the horizontal lines for 51 and 52 degrees of latitude. His latitude of birth was 51N52. Interpolating between whole numbers of latitude, the results are as follows:

Aries and Pisces:	12.91 years
Taurus and Aquarius:	17.01 years
Gemini and Capricorn:	26.52 years
Cancer and Sagittarius:	37.85 years
Leo and Scorpio:	42.81 years
Virgo and Libra:	42.90 years

Then we convert the numbers of degrees of ascension to years of his life. Here we see large variations in the ascensional times for the different zoidia, reflecting the difference in the rates of the progressed Ascendant and the latitude of Churchill's birth.

The differences in the zoidion's ascensions are even more extreme for the British Prime Minister Tony Blair, born further north in Scotland: Aries/Pisces is a small 10.43 and Virgo/Libra an enormous 45.39. Muhammad Ali, born in Kentucky, has ascensions for Aries/Pisces of 18.70 and Virgo/Libra at 37.12 - the differences are narrower for him, as he was born farther to the south than either Prime Minister.

When we look at the Ascendant directed to, for example, Saturn below the Ascendant, we are noting not the travel of the Ascendant through the zodiac - for that would be the secondary motion - *but of Saturn rising*. This technique of ascension is the root of the Hellenistic "circumambulations", which have come down to us as "primary directions."

Having designated ascensions, circumambulations, or, if you wish, primary directions, how would we use this information? Ancient astrologers used these methods to help predict the length of one's life, anticipate times of crises, and to determine planetary lords for different areas and periods of life. We will examine all three possibilities.

The Diurnal Motion and the Length of Life

Using astrology to calculate the length of someone's life may strike the modern reader as offensively fatalistic. I would, however, misrepresent the Hellenistic tradition if I didn't present a sample from the many techniques used by astrologers during the ancient era. In the example below, the techniques do *not* work. I do not propose a way to calculate the length of somebody's life but to show how one would calculate the use of circumambulations for predictive purposes. Later in this chapter we will examine part of Ptolemy's doctrine used to predict length of life, but is also part of his predictive method.

To look at the astrology of Princess Diana's untimely death in 1997, I will be using techniques depicted by Vettius Valens in *The Anthology*, Book III. The modern reader may take comfort in the

---

1.   Data for this table and other Ascensional times in this chapter is from the *Delphic Oracle* computer program. Inspired by a similar table designed by Robert Hand.

fact that the techniques I offer do *not* accurately predict her untimely death, I offer this for the purposes of illustration.

The first thing to do is to find the "predominator": the position in the chart that we can use to tell us how long a person may live. Ideally this is a planet in strong position. The Ascendant or Midheaven is used as a backup when no planet qualifies.

One first looks at the luminary of sect: the Sun in a day chart, the Moon in a night chart [text obscured]

[text obscured] by measuring the degrees of the zodiac between the angles. When determining the length of life, ancient astrologers tended to use modern-looking quadrant houses. Why?

The pivotal moments in the day cycle for a planet are that planet's rising, culminating, setting, and anti-culminating. The references for these events in an astrological chart are the degrees of the Ascendant, Midheaven, Descendant, and Immum Coeli. It is logically consistent, therefore, that techniques based on the diurnal cycle refer not to zoidia but to quadrants. Ancient astrologers did not use quadrant systems for natal issues but to locate planets to determine major crises in someone's life and when that life may end. We move on.

We need to determine the predominator in Diana's chart. In his text, Book III of the *Anthology*, Valens gives a rather unsystematic rendering of choosing the predominator. In Diana's chart, the Moon is the luminary of sect but is in the mediocre Second place. The Sun is angular in the Seventh; because it opposes the Ascendant, the Seventh is not as strong as other angular places. We will first go to the default place for all these questions, the degree of the Ascendant, and then we will look at the Sun and Moon.

I will take the degree of the Ascendant to the degree of Saturn; this affliction could terminate the life. When we do that we are actually determining the Saturn rising for this chart. By using the ascensions of the zoidia, using a portion of Sagittarius and a portion of Capricorn, we are actually turning the chart clockwise. Diana's ascensions for the twelve zoidia are as follows:

Aries and Pisces:	12.38
Taurus and Aquarius:	16.48
Gemini and Capricorn:	26.25
Cancer and Sagittarius:	38.12
Leo and Scorpio:	43.33
Virgo and Libra:	43.44

The Ascendant position is 18 degrees of Sagittarius and 24 minutes, which is 18.4 degrees. Saturn is 27 degrees of Capricorn and 48 minutes, which is 27.8 degrees. (If you wish to use a calculator, it is easier to decimalize the minutes in a degree. Simply divide the number of minutes by

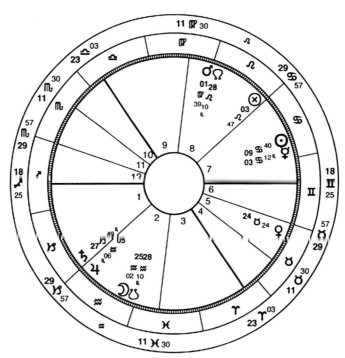

Princess Diana

60. For example, 30 minutes becomes .5 of a degree.)

We now take the proportion of Sagittarius remaining. 18.4 degrees of 30 degrees of Sagittarius leaves 11.6 degrees. Divide 11.6 by 30 to get the proportion of the zoidion Sagittarius remaining. This comes to 0.3866. Multiply that number by the ascensions of Sagittarius for her latitude, 38.12, and the result is 14.74 years for the remainder of Sagittarius.

Now we take the proportion of Capricorn. Diana's Saturn is 27.8 into the 30 degrees of its zoidion, which is 0.9267 of the entire zoidion. Multiply this by the ascensions for Capricorn, 26.25, and we arrive at 24.325.

14.74 plus 24.325 gives us 39 years and a little bit. Taking this number to represent years after Diana's birth, we arrive at just after her birthday in 2000.

At this point you may wish for greater accuracy, since her death occured in 1997. It would be a pretty bad astrologer who would caution Diana about her mortality two years after its usefulness had expired. (Perhaps one would want to "rectify" her time of birth to reflect this direction for 2000, not 1997.)

We now try the luminaries to see if either works as a predominator. We could use her Sun and see how many ascensions occur before the Sun reaches the Descendant - before it sets. How many ascensions are there between her Sun at 09.65 Cancer and Descendant at 18.4 Gemini, that would correspond to the years of her life?

Again, using what remains of Gemini, which is 11.6, multiplying that proportion of the

Primary Motion and Grim Necessity

Why were ascensions or primary directions used to depict how long a person will live? Predicting length of life was one forecast that ancient astrologers had to get right and they had to find a tool that had an aura of inevitability to it. Consider that the diurnal cycle used by circumambulations is very regular. This is the main ~~~~~~~~~~~~

knew well. God or the Demiurge is creating the soul of the universe. After doing some interesting things with fractions and proportions (which relate to musical scales), the Demiurge divides the resulting compound into two parts, which he joined in the center in the shape of a Greek *Chi*, a large X, and around on its other side. This gives us two bands that cross on one side and also on the opposite side, as would two circles cross if you put them at angles from one another. Here one circle is outside the other.

The outer circle depicts the *motion of the same*, the inner circle depicts *the motion of the other*. The outside circle of the same he left undivided and single, and the circle for the other he divided into six parts and made seven unequal circles upon which the planets move in their natural motions. *The circle of the same is the celestial equator, and measures diurnal motion. The circle of the other is the ecliptic and our familiar zodiacal coordinates, upon which the planets move at their own speeds.*

The celestial equator, the circle of the same, represents order and relative changelessness in nature. The ecliptic, the circle of the other, represents the changing nature of our lives and of the physical world. To arrive at a hard determination of the end of life, and not just noting life's ever-changing circumstances, one must reckon from the diurnal motion, from the sphere of the unchanging.

entire zoidion (.3867) by the ascensions for Gemini (26.25) gives us 10.15 years. We add to that the zoidion Cancer up to her natal Sun's position (9.65 degrees). We take that as a proportion of the entire zoidion - .32167 - and multiply that by the ascensions for Cancer, 38.12. This gives 12.261 years. Adding these two numbers together we get just under 22 and a half years. This is far too early in her life.

Or one could also use the distance between the Sun and Saturn - how many ascensions are there to move Saturn in Capricorn until it reaches the degree opposing Sun's position? There are 16.15 degrees between the Sun and the opposition to Saturn, which is .53833 of the entire zoidion Cancer. Multiplying this by the total ascensions of Cancer, 38.12, one arrives at twenty and a half years old.

Instead, we could use the Moon as predominator. Diana's Moon is 25 degrees of Aquarius. If we directed the Moon up to the opposition to Mars in early Virgo - which is Mars *descending* into an opposition to Moon - we would have a date in Diana's childhood. If we directed Moon to Saturn we arrive at a different number. The remainder of Capricorn corresponds to 1.925 years, and the portion of Aquarius corresponds to 13.75 years. Adding the numbers together, Diana is a teenager when, in the diurnal cycle, Moon arrived at the place of Saturn.

To be fair to the ancient tradition, the techniques to determine length of life are more complex than this example indicates. Added to what we have already done, Valens would include the bound lord of the predominator and various ways of determining the numbers of relevant planets, based upon their conditions in the natal chart. He also did some interesting things with the Lot of Fortune. Ptolemy has a few of his own innovations, to say the least.

Using ascensions to direct one position to another is used for other purposes than what we have discussed so far. What follows is a curious technique by Vettius Valens, so curious that modern astrologers might want to give it special study.

Using Ascensions of the Zoidia and Numbers of the Planets Together

You may find this next predictive technique unfathomable, yet it appears to be quite powerful. The goal is not determining the length of one's life but the times of life's crises. Its source is Valens, once again, mostly from Book VII of his *Anthology*.

This technique attempts to determine *when* a particular feature or configuration in a person's natal chart will manifest. Ancient astrologers, like Valens, and also those of today, think of the birth chart as a potential that will become active in different ways during someone's life.

His general technique can be stated very simply: we add the ascensional times described above to the numbers of the planets. As we discussed in Chapter Thirteen, the numbers of the planets are Saturn 30, Jupiter 12, Mars 15, Sun 19, Venus 8, Mercury 20, and Moon 25.

Although we may try to be exact when taking ascensions of a particular degree and minute of latitude, Valens actually used idealized approximations for ascensions and rounded them up. In that spirit we will round up to give not precise dates but specific years in which personal crises could take place.

We return to Winston Churchill for a quick example. The ascension of Sagittarius corresponds to Churchill' s 38th year. Churchill has Sun and Venus in Sagittarius: this adds 19 and 8 years for these two planets. This places the maturation of Sun and Venus and Sagittarius when he was 65, close to his becoming Prime Minister.

What follows may shock the modern reader: *we can take major fractions of these numbers*. To the ancient astrologer, this would seem more natural and less arbitrary than it would to us. According to the understanding of the ancient era, the intelligible world is made up not of matter but of number. Certain numbers - one, two and three - were found to be the building blocks constituting the world we can know. These numbers become proportions and can be expressed as fractions. In Chapter Eight, the astrological aspects connect planets through those aspects dividing the line by halves and thirds. Valens does this here.

I now supply an example from my own files. A client of mine, at the end of her nineteenth year, has Venus in Gemini opposed by Saturn in Sagittarius. As both planets are angular, this is a potent feature in her chart. This configuration may manifest as a permanent relationship, a relationship with an older person, or a marriage of convenience. As she is studying theatre and would like to be an actress or director, and Venus is in her Tenth, this opposition, when it manifests, may bring about a crisis of some sort in a dramatic career. From the context of her life as a whole, we

Cancer/Sagittarius	34.07
Leo/Scorpio	34.52
Virgo/Libra	33.57

(One can tell she was born far closer to the equator than our two Prime Ministers, the ascensions of the zodia are far closer to one another.)

We also take major fractions of relevant numbers and/or the numbers of the planets.

We can look at Venus (8), Gemini (31), and Mercury, Lord of Gemini, (20). This would total 59. Looking at simply Venus and Gemini we find ourselves at 39 years old. Halving 39 gives us *nineteen years*, when she had found herself in her first real romantic relationship. Venus had clearly spoken.

Yet Saturn opposes Venus in her chart, so this fine time is hardly the end of the matter. Saturn can intrude from a transit, profection, or as a planetary time lord. Although Saturn is a diurnal planet in her diurnal chart, activating this opposition from a malefic can cause difficulties in matters that pertain to Venus. Depending on the predictive indicators and the changing circumstances of her life over time, these difficulties can manifest in many ways.

I would like now to submit an example from Valens himself. Here is Chart Eighteen from Book VII of his *Anthology*. This example also gives us a sense of the precariousness of someone's life in the late Hellenistic era. Indeed his times of crisis and ours may be different. It also appears that Valens knew this individual personally and tracked his changing situations over time.

When Valens' client was thirty-three years old - in his thirty-fourth year - he was about to get the big promotion, but opposition from others resulted in his being sentenced to a mine. In the Roman world, this was the most abject and dangerous form of slavery. There is a trine from Mars in Leo to the Sun in Sagittarius, which Valens considers an affliction to the Sun. The years of Sun are nineteen and the years of Mars are fifteen. (Mars in the Twelfth is also in the Sun's house.) This adds up to thirty-four, and he was in his thirty-fourth year when defeat overcame apparent triumph. Here Valens does not use ascensions for the relevant zodia but simply numbers of the relevant planets.

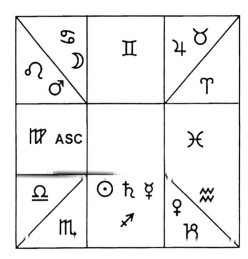

In our person's thirty-sixth year he was released from the mine, thanks to the intervention of highly placed people. He was wounded at the time, due to the activation of Mars' zoidion Leo by ascension. Note that Valens used not Mars but the zoidion in which Mars was placed. However, also add together the numbers of Jupiter (12) and Valens' ascension for Taurus (24) and one also arrives at 36. Jupiter's role is important because the great benefic is in a dominating tenth-place square to Mars, which is in the difficult Twelfth place from the Ascendant. This was also the year in which the other benefic Venus becomes active. Add together the number for Venus (8) and Valens' ascension for Capricorn (28) and you also get 36. In this year, many features of this man's natal chart became active.

The vicissitudes of life being what they were, in his thirty-ninth year (age 38) Valens' client was exiled to an island. Again this was due to persistent animosity from others. In this person's natal chart, Sun and Mercury are with Saturn in Sagittarius and all take a trine from Mars in Leo. Add together the numbers for the Sun (19) and Mercury (20) and you arrive at 39. Take these numbers together and add the Sun again, as Sun is the house lord of Mars and you get 58. Take two-thirds of that and you get 38 years and 8 months. Valens uses a major fraction of the total number 58 to arrive at the smaller relevant year in his life.

Finally Valens' client gets his big break. During his fortieth year he had been having financial difficulties, but his wife came to the rescue by settling some of his debts and making him joint owner of her possessions. Jupiter in Taurus in Capricorn is in trine to Venus and Venus is the dispositor for Jupiter. Add together the numbers of Jupiter (12) and Valens' ascensions for Capricorn (28) and you get forty.

Valens gives us another element of this technique. Elsewhere in Book Seven, he discusses the importance of the Moon joining a planet if that planet is within a day's motion of the Moon - thirteen degrees - even if the joined planet is in the next zoidion. We see this in the previous chart as Moon in Cancer joins Mars. Add together the numbers of Moon (25) and Mars (15) and you also get forty.

Now we apply Valens' technique to some of the notable nativities we have worked with in previous chapters. Combining numbers of planets and ascensions of zoidia is not a skill that modern astrologers, including this one, have needed to use. This is potentially a powerful technique that needs to be practiced a great deal to yield its fruits.

I begin with **Muhammad Ali**. He has Mars strongly placed in his Tenth in Taurus governed by an angular Venus. Adding the numbers for Mars (15) and Venus (8) together, I arrive at 23. Ali's

and 30 together gives us 50, and one half of that is 25. When Ali was twenty-four, his fame was eclipsed by his difficulties with the US government and boxing agencies over his refusal to be drafted for the Vietnam War. Saturn was activated during that period in another way: add together Saturn's number 30 and the ascensions of Taurus (23) and we get 53, one half of which is 26 years. Ali's difficulties would continue for some time.

Perhaps Ali's best-known and best-documented fight was the "Rumble in the Jungle" in 1974. He and George Foreman fought in Zaire and Ali regained the heavyweight boxing title as a result of that fight. By this time Ali's fame was worldwide and almost exclusively positive. Here his Sun in Capricorn became active: add together 19 for the Sun and 30 for Capricorn and you get 49. Two thirds of that is 32, the year Ali fought Foreman in Zaire.

Looking at the **Dalai Lama**'s chart, I was curious if his Sun-Jupiter trine became active when he won the Nobel Prize in 1989, but I could not find any indication for that. Instead I discovered that by adding the number for Sun (19) and the ascensions of his Sun's zoidion Cancer for his latitude (36), you get his 55th year. He won the Nobel Prize when he was fifty-four years old. Interestingly, at that time his Moon-Mercury square was also active: add together the numbers for the ascensions of Gemini, where his Mercury is located, (30) and add the number for the Moon (25) and you also get 55. Winning the Nobel Prize gave the Dalai Lama an internationally prominent voice.

We return to **Jacqueline Kennedy Onassis**. Adding the numbers of Venus and Jupiter together (20) with the ascensions of Gemini (29), we get 49 and half of that is in her twenty-fourth year. This was the time of her engagement to Senator John Kennedy. Adding twenty for Venus and Jupiter and fifteen for Mars, which squares both planets, we get 35. When she was thirty-four years old, President Kennedy was killed.

Matters changed by the time of her engagement to Aristotle Onassis. Add together 8 for Venus and 30 for Saturn, activating the opposition between these two planets, and we're in her thirty-eighth year. Interestingly, the numbers for Sun (19) and Leo's ascensions (39) - her Sun's placement - gives us 58. Two-thirds of this returns us to 38. Her engagement to Onassis was at once a marriage of convenience to an older man (Saturn-Venus) and an international news story (Sun in Leo).

I end here this display of bringing together numbers of planets and ascensions of zodia. This technique becomes more powerful and predictive as the astrologer grows in the experience of using it, and I encourage you to try this out for yourself. It has yielded some interesting results in my chart and you could begin this with your own.

Circumambulations and Planetary Lords

Another use for the ascensions is for "circumambulations." This is from the Greek *peripatos*, which means 'a walk around'. This technique yields planetary lords as directed positions successively come into aspect to planets. If, for the example, the Midheaven circumambulates to the degree of Venus, she would be the planetary lord for the matters relevant to the Midheaven. This would continue until the Midheaven would conjoin or aspect another planet, who would take up as planetary lord.

Using this method, there is a great variety in the lengths of time to circumambulate different parts of the zodiac - this is especially so at high northern or southern latitudes.

Once again, we are directing planets as if they were the Ascendant in the astrological chart, regardless of their position in the natal chart. This is different from the Ascendant arc directions we explored previously. That technique moved all positions *the same rate* as the progressing Ascendant. Circumambulations, on the other hand, take the ascensions of relevant zoidia, *as if that position were ascending*.

Because we are calculating from the Midheaven using ascensions and not right ascension, calculations for the Midheaven between circumambulations and progressions, which use right ascension, can yield very different results. **Tony Blair**, who was born in Scotland has an Aries Midheaven. This gives us an extreme example of the difference between using ascensions and the usual procedure of using right ascension. Here is his chart, using our standard system of twelve places.

For Blair's far northern latitude of birth, the ascensional times for Aries or Pisces are a mere 10.43 years. Therefore the Midheaven circumambulates much more quickly than the approximately one degree per year by Right Ascension.

By ascensions, Mercury was conjunct the Midheaven in 1989 when Blair was a mere 36 years old. In Blair's chart Mercury squares the Midheaven: by progression, using one degree of right ascension per year, this conjunction wouldn't occur until Blair was close to ninety years old. By ascensions, Blair's Sun was conjunct the Midheaven in 1997, when Blair was only 43; by progression, however, he would be over 110 years old when Midheaven would conjoin the Sun!

The important positions directed in circumambulations are the Ascendant, Midheaven, Sun, Moon, and Part of Fortune. These are the five places of releasing or *significators*. (We discussed them in Chapter Twelve as the five positions Ptolemy would advance by profection.) The Ascendant is about the body and the viability of the life as a whole. The Midheaven is about profession, what one does. Sun also considers matters of career along with leadership and reputation. Moon is about personal relationships. The Lot of Fortune can be about health but is mostly about money.

Looking again at **Winston Churchill**, his Ascendant did not cross Mercury - or Mercury rise - until the end of 1941. As Churchill has Libra rising, these ascensions will take longer in his life

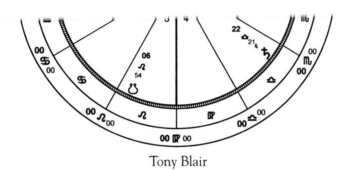

Tony Blair

than his Midheaven walking through Cancer and Leo. It was five years previously, in 1936 that his Midheaven moved to a contact with Mercury by square. In 1939, the Sun by circumambulation was also aspecting Mercury, by square from the other direction. In that way, the planetary lords for AS, MC, and Sun were all Mercury during the Second World War. This is befitting a person whose wartime speeches are considered historical and literary achievements.

Another example of circumambulations and planetary lords is with **George W. Bush**. One year before his father was elected U.S. President, the directed Midheaven - signifying what one does - formed a trine to Jupiter. During the first year of his father's Presidency, Jupiter was *planetary lord* for his Sun. During the time his father was President, Bush made many of the personal contacts and political alliances that allowed him to launch his own political career.

In 1994, when Bush became governor of Texas, Venus had replaced Jupiter as planetary lord for Sun, since Sun and Venus were now conjunct. (Venus rose to the same location as his Sun.) Six months previously, the Ascendant had also circumambulated to a sextile to his Sun. Being elected governor brought Bush into national prominence and became the background from which he would later run for U.S. President.

Bush's Sun circumambulated to a conjunction with Mars in late 2006. Mars has a difficult placement in his chart, and appears in extreme fashion in his life. This does not presage a happy time for Bush.

I now introduce another planetary lord that impacts circumambulations. Although I have stressed the importance of the diurnal cycle in understanding ascensions and circumambulations, one also directs significators *through the bounds*, so that the bound lord becomes an additional planetary lord. (We discussed the bounds or terms in Chapter Three.) Most Hellenistic astrologers considered the bound lord to be secondary in importance to the lord formed by aspect to a significator, although one later astrologer using the Hellenistic tradition, Abu Mashar[2], give primacy to the bound lords.

Here is an example of using both lords. When we look at the circumambulations of **Martha Stewart**, we notice Sun - indicating fame and reputation - directed to a *trine to Saturn* in June 2000. Additionally, *Saturn* had been bound lord for Sun during her times of troubles: Sun walked through the final bounds of Virgo in mid-2001 and the early bounds of Libra beginning in late 2003. Saturn governs both segments.

Wolfgang Amadeus Mozart, 1781

What follows is an example that uses the different predictive techniques that we have discussed in the last several chapters. We will include circumambulations to see what information they can add.

We look for the astrological indicators for early 1781, a time that was pivotal in Mozart's life. Except for some short-term work in other cities, Mozart had been employed as court musician by the archbishop of Salzburg. Mozart was very unhappy with this position, as he could not compose operas in Salzburg, its orchestra was mediocre, and he felt treated like one of the servants and not as the artist that he was. What happened next was important for the subsequent history of music.

In the winter of 1781, Mozart and the archbishop were both in Vienna, which was one of the great centers of culture in Europe. In May, the two men had a confrontation. On the next day Mozart gave his resignation, which the archbishop eventually accepted. This freed Mozart to live and work in Vienna. This event made Mozart's life less certain but gave him the inspiration and support of a great musical community. Most of the music that Mozart is remembered for was composed in Vienna, where he lived until his death.

We begin with some of the predictive techniques we have explored in previous chapters. Mozart's transits in early 1781 included Saturn in Sagittarius, in the zoidion of his Moon in the Fourth. The Fourth is the place of home and father, this did point to the family dimension of his decision to break with the Archbishop. Mozart's mother had died not too long beforehand. For financial as well as personal reasons, Mozart's father greatly disapproved of Mozart's decision. This also meant that Mozart had to find his own home.

Mars by transit was in Capricorn. Transiting Mars was opposing natal Mars in the Eleventh place with his Lot of Spirit. This points to the resentment and outright angry indignation that Mozart displayed at this time. We also see much of Mars as a planetary lord, and the transit would accentuate Mozart's personal rebellion.

Mozart's profections for 1781 give us a more positive picture of this time. He turned twenty-five at the end of January. Subtracting his twenty-sixth year from the next lowest multiple of twelve

---

2.   *On Solar Revolutions*. (1999) Cumberland, Md. Golden Hind Press.

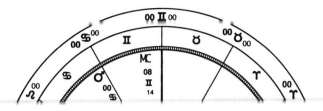

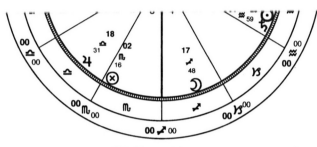

Wolfgang Mozart

- 24 - all positions profect (advance) 2 zoidia. This brings his Ascendant from Virgo to Libra, wherein lies Jupiter, the great benefic. The year's profection also brings Jupiter to zoidion of his Lot of Fortune. The Lot of Fortune profects to Sagittarius, where one finds the Moon - governed by Jupiter but still transited to by Saturn. During this time Mozart made his home in Vienna, became engaged, and began composing the music that would bring him recognition and connections within the musical community in Vienna. He became successful almost immediately.

In Chapter Thirteen we explored "decennials." In this planetary period system, one has a major planetary time ruler - or *chronocrator* - for each ten years and nine months of 360-day years. Mozart's first time lord was Moon in the Fourth, the second was Saturn, and the third was the Sun, which took over is 1766. In 1781 the specific planetary lord, the more important of the two, was Mars. Because Mars is with the Lot of Spirit and can cause difficulties for him, this time was full of conflict. Making matters more difficult is that in his natal chart, Sun and Mars, the general and specific time lords, have no aspectual relationship to each other.

Other planetary lord techniques from the Hellenistic tradition support the Mars-like quality of this time of his life. The zodiacal releasing from the Lot of Fortune had been a long (12-year) period governed by Sagittarius, giving Jupiter as the general time lord. Cancer, where Mars resides along with the Lot of Spirit, took over as the specific lord four months before the confrontation with the archbishop. For our discussion of Mozart's circumambulations during this time, we need to look again at his natal chart. Here are the ascensions for Mozart:

Aries/Pisces	14.96
Taurus/Aquarius	18.95
Gemini/Capricorn	27.48
Cancer/Sagittarius	36.89
Leo/Scorpio	40.86
Virgo/Libra	40.85

The circumambulations from Sun was governed - again - by Mars, in aspect by trine, for the previous twelve years; this wouldn't change until 1784. The bound lord from mid-1779 was also Mars, corresponding to the fourth segment of Pisces. Saturn, corresponding to the final degrees of Pisces, would take over in 1783.

Forming a square to the Ascendant, Mars was also the planetary lord from early 1780. Saturn was the bound lord from 1779, corresponding to the Ascendant circumambulating to the fourth segment of Virgo. Saturn would take over in 1782. Ascendant is the most general indicator of the nature of the individual, and any planetary lord over this position would have great influence in all the affairs of the person. Saturn here indicates the fact of his professional and artistic confinement.

For the Midheaven, governing what one does, Venus was planetary lord briefly from Jupiter before *Mars* took over by conjunction from 1777 for the rest of his life. We see a restless spirit informing his career.

Circumambulations from the Lot of Spirit yield Mercury as the governing planet, forming an opposition from 1776. The bound lord from 1779, however, was Saturn. We can see again Mozart's sensitivity to any restriction of his creativity.

Because Mozart's natal Mars is with his Lot of Spirit, he was naturally an independent person, unable to docilely follow the path given to most composers. In many of the predictive systems we have looked at, Mars was the planet prevailing when he broke with the archbishop of Salzburg, which resulted in his new life in Vienna. This would not last forever, however. A decade later, after many ups and downs, his musical style had reached new heights of inventiveness and Mozart was becoming commercially successful once again. During this time *Mercury* had taken over as planetary lord by aspect or bound for many of his circumambulations. Mercury is not a planet that could account for his early death. It may however point to Mozart dying att he height of his creative genius.

Ptolemy's Reform

Circumambulations based upon ascensions were prevalent throughout the Hellenistic tradition of astrology, yet not everybody was comfortable directing all significators as if they were the Ascendant. Some astrologers, Ptolemy in particular, felt that the different positions in the natal chart should have different timing due to where they were in the chart. Consistent with his naturalistic style of astrology, he felt that a position at the Midheaven should move at the rate of the one degree per year, which its natural diurnal motion. A position culminating should be timed according to how long in a day this position actually culminates. This may seem obvious, but this was not to most ancient astrologers, who used ascensions regardless of where a position appears in the chart.

Churchill's Moon is 29 degrees of Leo, 58 degrees from his Midheaven at 01 Cancer, almost the entire two zoidia of Cancer and Leo. How much time that day would it take his Moon to reach

culminate. Using ascensions for all positions anywhere in the chart may be fine symbolism but nature gives us different numbers. This quandary is the source of Ptolemy's reform of circumambulations. His reform is the basis for the systems of primary directions that developed in the centuries after him, and from that would develop our modern system of secondary progressions. Ptolemy's system of circumambulations, or primary directions, is also the basis of today's most popular quadrant systems of house division.

Ptolemy's explanation is in *Tetrabiblos III*, Chapter 11, in his discussion of finding the length of life from the natal chart. All of his examples concern directing a significator to a position that would end the life of the native. In the final book of *Tetrabiblos IV*, Ptolemy does mention this technique in the context of an overall system of prediction that also uses bound lords of directions, different profections, and finally transits.

After much of the technical material we have gone though in previous chapters and in this one, it is my hope that the reader, like me, will find in Ptolemy's explanation the intellectual tour de force that it is. Giving full attention to the following material will pay off handsomely for the modern astrologer.

Here is Ptolemy's problem: if a planet is on the Ascendant we can use ascensions and if on the Descendant we can use *descensions* - the times it takes the zoidion to completely set in the West - to move a planet along the diurnal motion. This is as we saw with circumambulations. If a planet is on the Midheaven or Immum Coeli, we can use equatorial measurements - the degrees of right ascension - to move that planet along diurnal motion. This is what we do in modern secondary progressions.

What happens, then, most of the time, if the significator you wish to direct is not conjunct or opposite the Ascendant or Midheaven but lies in between?

We are at the difficult task of bringing together both horizon and meridian axes to divide the quadrants. These two lines have different frames of measurement and are almost always oblique to one another. What these two lines have in common, however, is that these four angles highlight a planet's movement through the day and night, and the entire zodiac passes through the four angles in one day. All planets rise, culminate, set, and anti-culminate. Ptolemy's solution was to note *corresponding proportions* between these positions relative to the previous angle and the next one. When two planets have the same proportionate distance between one angle and another, those planets are brought together by primary direction.[3]

We begin with a common experience: the changing lengths of our day. As we discussed in Chapter One, when the Sun is in the most northernmost zoidia Gemini and Cancer, the Sun is above the horizon for the longest amount of time and the day has the most hours of sunlight. When the Sun is in the southernmost zoidia Sagittarius and Capricorn, the Sun is below the horizon for the shortest amount of time and the nights are the longest. These conditions reverse in the southern hemisphere.

In astrology we sometimes look at time using traditional *planetary hours*. This system of hours, frequently used by traditional horary and electional astrologers, divides the daylight into equal hours of daylight, and night also consists of twelve equal hours. This means that depending on the season of the year and the latitude of the location, daylight hours are shorter and change very quickly (winter in the northern hemisphere) or take much longer (during the summer).

Several years ago a photographer friend of mine spent a summer at a centuries-old Greek Orthodox monastery on an island in the Aegean. Several months later I went to an exhibition of photographs he took during this time. As we were discussing his visit to the island, he told me he could not make sense of how they told the time of day: the hours they were using had nothing to do with what his watch was telling him. I asked, "Did you find that their hours took longer than yours?" The hours seemed longer than what his watch told him: they were using planetary hours, not clock hours. Here, briefly, is how planetary hours work.

Each day begins at sunrise and the planet whose day it is governs the first hour - that is, one twelfth of the time the Sun is above the horizon. If today is Tuesday, the planetary lord for the first hour of daylight is Mars; if today is Sunday, it is the Sun. The planetary hours go from the first hour's planet to the next one in the descending order from Saturn to Moon and then around again. At the beginning of the next day the following day's planet and first hour's planet are the same. If the first hour of Monday is the day and hour of the Moon, Saturn governs the second hour, and then Jupiter, going in order so that the following hours yield the planetary hour and day of Mars at sunrise on Tuesday.

Now we take an important step. As we discussed in Chapter One, each degree of the zodiac rises, culminates, sets, and anti-culminates each day. This means that once daily each degree of the zodiac is conjunct to the Ascendant, Midheaven, Descendant, and Imum Coeli. This occurs so that the northernmost zoidia (in the northern hemisphere) are above the horizon the longest time and the southernmost zoidia the shortest. This is just as we have seen for the Sun's position during the seasons of the year.

I bring back the "European" chart of English poet William Blake to illustrate this. This chart is not pretty but is very useful to us right now. As Blake was born well north of the equator, and

---

3.   For this articulation I am indebted to Robert Hand's presentation on this topic, in his lectures in the 1990s and in his commentary on Montulmo, *On the Judgment of Nativities* (1995). Also valuable is Robert Schmidt's commentary on Ptolemy's *Tetrabiblos III* Chapter 11.

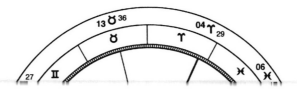

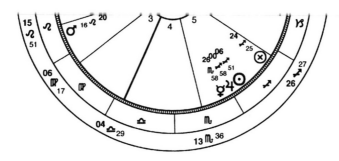

William Blake

since Cancer is a northernmost zoidion, it takes a long time for his ascending degree to culminate: the thirtieth degree of Cancer has a very large *diurnal semi-arc*. You can be sure than on the day Blake was born - as with any other day for that latitude, or anywhere in the Northern hemisphere - Sagittarius and Capricorn had a much smaller diurnal semi-arc. When we look at proportionate distances we judge the amount a planet has gone from one angle or pivot to another, although the size of the quadrants - as with this chart - can be very uneven.

Consider that *each degree* of the 360 degrees of the zodiac has a diurnal semi-arc. Each degree also has a nocturnal semi-arc, the distance between setting and anti-culminating. We can use a computer program to measure the varying amounts of time for different places on the zodiac for their diurnal and nocturnal semi-arcs. Indeed the Placidus house system, featured above with Blake's chart, does just that. Here we are interested in the diurnal and nocturnal semi-arcs expressed in *hourly times*, which is the number of degrees of right ascension that pass in one seasonal - "planetary" - hour. A *seasonal hour* is one-twelfth of the total time that a planet is above or below the horizon. Our *standard hour*, on the other hand, always corresponds to 15 degrees of right ascension.

From one angle to the next one, from rising to culminating to setting to anti-culminating and back to rising, there are always six seasonal hours. How many degrees of right ascension pass the Midheaven in one seasonal hour for each degree? This is called the *hour portion*.

We factor these in with the *meridian distance* - how many degrees of right ascension there are between the positions in question (or its opposite for a planet under the horizon) and the Midheaven.

At this time you might be getting a little dizzy. For the sake of the faint-hearted I have shown Ptolemy's four example calculations in a separate Appendix. Happily the first three involve the same two points, yet he places them at different angles in the birth chart.

APPENDIX
PTOLEMY'S FOUR EXAMPLES

Consider an Ascendant at the first degree of Aries, which always means that the first degree of Capricorn is on the MC. The significator is the Ascendant, and we direct to the first degree of Gemini. Because Ptolemy presented this to calculate the length of life, 0 Gemini represents what he would call the "destructive degree", which would signify the ending of a life. For ordinary predictive purposes, we would call this place the *promittor*, a place that promises an outcome of some kind.

How much time will occur until the "destructive degree" of 0 Gemini rises? We already know that there are by definition six seasonal hours between the Ascendant and MC. At this degree of latitude, the hourly times (the right ascension for one hour) for 0 Gemini is given as 17. This corresponds to how many degrees of Right Ascension go over the Midheaven each hour when this degree is on the horizon. When 0 Gemini is rising, the total distance to the Midheaven is 102. How did we get that? We simply multiply the 17 for 0 Gemini and the six hours between the Ascendant and Midheaven together and we get 122. This corresponds to the diurnal semi-arc of 0 Gemini.

There are 148 degrees from 0 Gemini to the Midheaven in Capricorn in right ascension, reflecting that it would take just under ten of our hours for 0 Gemini to culminate. But here we are

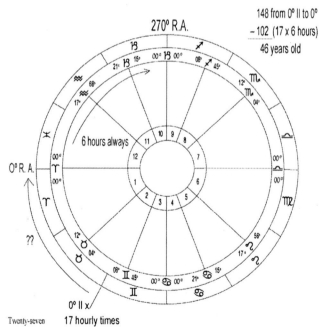

Example 1 - Directing from 0 Gemini to Midheaven at 0 Capricorn.

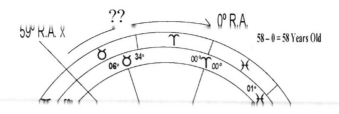

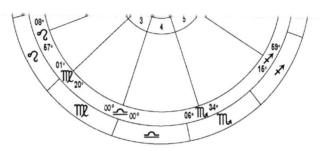

Example 2 - Directing from 0 Gemini to Midheaven at 0 Aries

trying to get 0 Gemini to rise, to come to the Ascendant. If we subtract the 102 times from the Ascendant to Midheaven (17 times 6 hours) from the total of 148 from 0 Gemini to the Midheaven, we see that 46 times remain. This becomes the proportion of the quadrant remaining that proceeds from 0 Gemini to the rising degree, which is just above three hours of our time. (Remember that 15 degrees is one hour of standard time.) Ptolemy writes that the native would live until is 46th year.

In the second example, the Midheaven is 0 Aries, and the destructive place remains at 0 Gemini. The matter then becomes how long it will take until 0 Gemini culminates if currently 0 Aries is the Midheaven. The Right Ascension of 0 Gemini is 58 and the Right Ascension of 0 Aries is always 0. Here we can simply subtract the two numbers and the native will live until his 58th year. This reflects that in just under four of our conventional hours, 0 Gemini in this chart would culminate.

Ptolemy's third example makes us work once again. 0 Libra is rising and therefore 0 Aries is at the Descendant. The destructive degree remains at 0 Gemini. The Midheaven degree is 0 Cancer. Once again we're going to move between 0 Aries and 0 Gemini but now to the place of setting.

0 Aries, now the setting place, is 0 degrees of right ascension, as that is the starting point of the circle. 0 Gemini is 58 degrees. The right ascension of Cancer is always 90. The *meridian distance* from the point at 0 Gemini to the 0 Cancer Midheaven is 90 minus 58, which is 32.

There are, as given in the first example, for the hourly times for 0 Gemini is 17. Again we have six hours within a quadrant, but now between the Midheaven and the Descendant. These six hours times seventeen is once again 102.

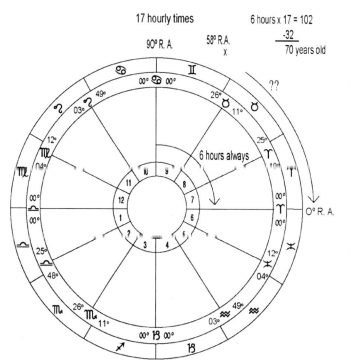

Example 3 -
Directing from 0 Gemini
to Descendant at 0 Aries

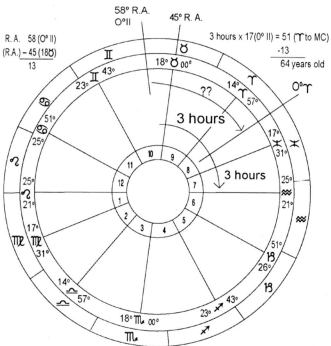

Example 4 -
Directing 0 Gemini
through Midheaven to
Position Occupied by 0
Aries

Simply subtract 32, the meridian distance between 0 Gemini and the 0 Cancer Midheaven, from 102, the semi-arc of the quadrant. (This corresponds to almost seven conventional hours for Gemini to go from rising to culminating.)

Taking 32 from 102, you arrive at 70, a new number entirely, yet based on another difference between 0 Aries and 0 Gemini in the zodiac. If fifteen degrees is one hour of time, by conventional

Midway along this quadrant, between culminating and setting to a point at 0 degrees of Right Ascension, because this is always the value of 0 Aries. This being so, 18 Taurus at the Midheaven corresponds to 45 degrees (half of 90 degrees) of right ascension and three hours earlier than 0 Aries culminating in this chart.

The right ascension of 0 Gemini, once again, is 58. From that number take 45, the distance between 0 Aries and 18 Taurus Midheaven in right ascension, and you get 13. This becomes the distance in right ascension left of the Midheaven, between the Midheaven at 18 Taurus and 0 Gemini. Remember also that the hourly times for 0 Gemini is 17. And we also know that there are three seasonal hours between 0 Aries and the Midheaven. Multiplying 17 by 3 hours, we get 51. This gives the distance to the right of the Midheaven.

Add the 13 degrees from the MC to 0 Gemini to the 51 degrees and you get 64. That's the "arc of direction," which gives the length of life.

Depending on where they are located diurnally, with respect to the angles, the same sixty degrees of ecliptical longitude between 0 Aries and 0 Gemini yield 46, 58, 70, and 64 years. These differences are based on the time it takes in the diurnal cycle for different degrees of the zodiac to move and contact other positions in the chart.

Most of us, myself included, have to study these calculations attentively to arrive at an understanding of using proportionate time within the quadrants to determine the temporal distance between two points in the zodiac. At this time these calculations have not returned to the modern astrologer's predictive toolbox, but have survived as the basis of many quadrant house systems used by modern astrologers.

Much research and development needs to be invested over many years for this to become useful for prediction, – prompted maybe by the curiosity and inspiration of using an important predictive technique that has fallen into obscurity. Hopefully our current discussion is a step in the right direction.

CONCLUSION

Hellenistic astrology, the original formulation of Western astrology, has much to say about all these topics. Because there is so much richness here, and because so little of the Hellenistic tradition is available to the modern student of astrology, this presentation has had to be thorough but it cannot be complete. Others, I hope, will proceed further than I have.

Like practitioners of any organized discipline, astrologers can be conservative in their approach to their craft. Most astrologers have worked hard to attain the level of proficiency that they now have. The price of this confidence can be that we become too intellectually secure; we stop examining our ideas and their applications. Perhaps we stop asking questions entirely. When we cease to inquire, however, our work begins to become stale. It is my desire that other astrologers, like me, will find the Hellenistic legacy provocative and challenging, and, through their work with this tradition, their astrology will become better - for themselves, their students, and their clients.

I would also like to see the Hellenistic contribution better represented by today's astrologers. I would like to go to astrology conferences and see more people presenting on Hellenistic astrology and books on Hellenistic and modern astrology alongside those of other divisions of our discipline. As a result of greater explication and application by a community of interested people, different ideas and applications from the Hellenistic tradition could come into contact with one another. This material deserves a wider community of practitioners, for much remains to be done.

The Hellenistic tradition can also inform the philosophical implications of astrology. Over the past fifty years and more, many lines of thinking have influenced astrologers to greater creativity: the theosophical movement, the psychology of Carl Jung and many others, "New Age" ideas, and the emergence of post-modern thinking in our culture. Part of the strength of astrology is that it adapts well to many evolving viewpoints within a culture.

I would like to add to this the richness of the philosophical ideas of astrology that informed the Hellenistic tradition. Astrologers can benefit greatly from becoming better acquainted with the natural philosophy of Aristotle and the Stoics, and the cosmic spirituality of Platonism and Neo-Platonism. The ideas of Aristotle and Plutarch, among many others, can help astrologers better understand their roles and help guide people toward living a happier life. Throughout Western intellectual history, great thinkers have greatly progressed through a reassessment of relevant ancient wisdom; astrologers can also benefit in the same way.

BIBLIOGRAPHY

Aristotle, *Nicomachean Ethics*. Tr. H. Rackham, (1994). Cambridge, MA. Loeb Classical Library, Harvard University Press

Augustine, *The Confessions of Saint Augustine*. Tr. Ryan, (1960). New York, Image Books, Doubleday

Dorotheus of Sidon, *Carmen Astrologicum*. Ed. Pingree, (1993). Mansfield, Ascella

Epictetus, *Discourses, Books I-II*. Tr. Oldfather, (2000). Cambridge, MA. Loeb Classical Library, Harvard University Press

Firmicus Maternus, *Mathesis*. Tr. Bram, J. R., under the title *Ancient Astrology, Theory and Practice* (1975). Park Ridge, NJ. Noyes Press

Hephaistio of Thebes, *Apotelesmatics, Book I*. Tr. Schmidt, ed. Hand, (1994). Cumberland, MD. Golden Hind Press

Hephaistio of Thebes. *Apotelesmatics, Book II*. Tr. Schmidt, (1998). Cumberland, MD. Golden Hind Press

Lilly, William, *Christian Astrology*. (1985). Exeter, Regulus Publications

Manilius, *Astronomica*. Tr. G. Goold, (1997). Cambridge, MA. Loeb Classical Library, Harvard University Press

Montulmo, Antonius De, *On the Judgment of Nativities Part 1*. Tr. R. Hand, (1995). Cumberland, MD. Golden Hind Press

Montulmo, Antonius De, *On the Judgment of Nativities Part II*. Tr. R. Hand, (1995). Cumberland, MD. Golden Hind Press

Paulus Alexandrinus, *Introductory Matters*, Olympiodorus, *Commentary on Paulus Alexandrinus*. Published as *Late Classical Astrology: Paulus Alexandrinus and Olympiodorus*. Tr. D. Greenbaum, (2001). Reston, VA. ARHAT

Plato, *Timaeus*. Tr. B. Jowett in *The Collected Dialogues of Plato*. Ed. E. Hamilton & H. Cairns, (1989). Princeton, NJ. Princeton University Press

Ptolemy, *Tetrabiblos*. Tr. F. E. Robbins, (1994). Cambridge, MA. Loeb Classical Library, Harvard University Press

Ptolemy, *Tetrabiblos, Book I*. Tr. Schmidt, ed. Hand, (1994). Cumberland, MD. Golden Hind Press

Ptolemy, *Tetrrabiblos, Book III*. Tr. Schmidt, ed. Hand, (1996). Cumberland, MD. Golden Hind Press

Ptolemy, *Tetrabiblos, Book IV*. Tr. Schmidt, (1998). Cumberland, MD. Golden Hind Press

Vettius Valens, *The Anthology Book I*. Tr. Schmidt, (1993). Cumberland, MD. Golden Hind Press

Vettius Valens,.*The Anthology Book II Part 1*. Tr. Schmidt, (1994). Cumberland, MD. Golden Hind Press

Vettius Valens, *The Anthology Book II, III*. Tr. Schmidt, (1994). Cumberland, MD. Golden Hind Press

Vettius Valens, *The Anthology Book IV*. Tr. Schmidt, (1996). Cumberland, MD. Golden Hind Press

Vettius Valens, *The Anthology Book V, VI*. Tr. Schmidt, (1997). Cumberland, MD. Golden Hind Press

Vettius Valens, *The Anthology Book VII*. Tr. Schmidt, (2001). Cumberland, MD. Golden Hind Press

Secondary Sources and Modern Astrology

Allen, Richard Hinckley, *Star Names: Their Lore and Meaning*. (1963). New York, Dover

Baigent, Michael, *From the Omens of Babylon*. (1994). London, Arkana (Penguin Books)

Barton, Tamsyn, *Ancient Astrology*. (1994). London and New York, Routledge

Brady, Bernadette, *Brady's Book of Fixed Stars*. (1998). York Beach, ME. Samuel Weiser

Braha, James, *Ancient Hindu Astrology for the Modern Astrologer*. (1986). Hollywood, FL, Hermetician Press.

Brummond, R. & Rudolf, V, *Handbook of Techniques for the Hamburg School*. (1991). Plantation, FL. Penelope Publications

Cornelius, G, *The Moment of Astrology*. (Revised edition 2003). Bournemouth, The Wessex Astrologer.

Crane, Joseph, *A Practical Guide to Traditional Astrology*. (1997). Reston, VA. ARHAT

Peters, F.E, *The Harvest of Hellenism*. (1996). New York, Barnes and Noble

Rudhyar, Dane, *The Lunation Cycle*. (1967). Santa Fe, NM. Aurora Press

Zoller, Robert, *The Arabic Parts in Astrology*. (1989). Rochester, VT. Inner Traditions

INDEX OF NAMES

INDEX OF TOPICS

Printed in the United States
113781LV00005B/62/A

9 781902 405247